安徽省高等学校"十三五"省级规划教材

英语跨文化交际教程

主　编　夏蓓洁
副主编　黄　莹　崔斯佳　李　洁
参　编　卢　杨　张千梅　岳俊辉
　　　　胡　萍

中国科学技术大学出版社

内容简介

本书以跨文化交际基础理论为框架,以日常生活、学习和工作为场景,通过实例使学习者了解中、英语言在言语交际和非言语交际方面的差异和特点,展现因受文化观影响在日常交际、教育方式、沟通模式和方式等方面的差别,旨在帮助学习者了解英语文化的同时,进一步理解中国文化及其沟通方式,并客观公正地对待其他文化,在跨文化交际中促进中国文化传播,提高跨文化交际效率。本书体现"以学生为中心"的原则,以案例教学为主,辅以相应的网络资源和电子资源,注重提高学习者的自主学习能力、合作学习能力、发现问题和解决问题的能力以及跨文化交际能力。

图书在版编目(CIP)数据

英语跨文化交际教程/夏蓓洁主编. —合肥:中国科学技术大学出版社,2023.9
ISBN 978-7-312-05711-3

Ⅰ. 英… Ⅱ. 夏… Ⅲ. 文化交流—英语—高等学校—教材 Ⅳ. G115

中国国家版本馆 CIP 数据核字(2023)第 119211 号

英语跨文化交际教程
YINGYU KUA WENHUA JIAOJI JIAOCHENG

出版	中国科学技术大学出版社
	安徽省合肥市金寨路96号,230026
	http://www.press.ustc.edu.cn
	https://zgkxjsdxcbs.tmall.com
印刷	合肥市宏基印刷有限公司
发行	中国科学技术大学出版社
开本	710 mm×1000 mm 1/16
印张	26.5
字数	693千
版次	2023年9月第1版
印次	2023年9月第1次印刷
定价	49.00元

Preface
前　言

全球化、信息技术革命和便捷的交通方式带来了人员的频繁流动,不同文化群体在外交、商务沟通、教育医疗和社会生活领域的交往互动更加频繁。不同的文化价值观、行为方式的差异显而易见,语言、非语言和社会习俗的差异影响着跨文化交际的有效性和得体性,文化的借鉴、交融与冲突在交际中相伴相生。

《外国语言文学类本科教学质量国家标准》(2018)(以下简称《国标》)确立了"培养适应我国对外交流、国家与地方经济社会发展、各类涉外行业、外语教育与学术研究需要的各种外语语种专业人才和复合型外语人才"的培养目标。2020年颁布的《普通高等学校本科外国语言文学类专业教学指南》(以下简称《指南》)中将"跨文化交际能力"概括为"态度、知识和能力",即"尊重世界文化多样性,具有跨文化包容性和批判性意识;掌握基本的跨文化研究理论知识和分析方法,理解中外文化的基本特点和异同;能够对不同文化现象、文本和制品进行阐释和评价;能有效和恰当地进行跨文化沟通;能帮助不同文化背景的人士进行有效的跨文化沟通"等等。同年颁布的《大学英语教学指南》针对基础级、提高级和发展级教学目标,提出了跨文化交际能力的明确教学要求。以上文件为外语教材和课程建设提供了依据和指导,有助于培养国际化人才,提高中国的国际传播能力。

一、编写依据与教材特点

《英语跨文化交际教程》是安徽省高等学校"十三五"规划教材(2017ghjc190)。本书以《国标》和《指南》中"跨文化交际"专业核心课程的要求为指导,面向地方院校学生,以立德树人为根本,以学生为中心,以提高跨文化交际意识和能力为目标。本教材适用于地方本科院校、高职高专英语类专业二、三级,也可供大学英语四级以上水平的非英语专业学生及其他自学者使用。

本书以广为接受的"情感态度、知识认知、行为技能"ABC模型为理论基础,参考最新的文献和研究成果,结合中国对外交流实例,旨在帮助学习者掌握基本的跨文化研究理论知识和分析方法,理解中外文化的基本特点和异同、尊重世界文化多样性、有效和恰当地进行跨文化沟通。

本书坚持"价值引领、知识传授、能力培养"的宗旨,编写体系适应信息化教学形势和个性化发展需求,调动学习者自主学习能力,促进讨论式、探究式教与学,助力教师的个性化课堂设计,主要特点如下:

1. 以立德树人为根本,思政要素贯穿始终。根据习近平总书记"讲好中国故事,传播好中国声音,展示真实、立体、全面的中国"的指示,书中内容立足中国文化语境,根据中国学习者特点,介绍跨文化基本知识;对比多元文化,感悟中国文化,发挥专业课的协同育人作用,培养"有家国情怀、有全球视野、有专业本领"的"三有"人才。

2. 以能力培养为目标,体现学习者主体地位。本书以学习者为中心,以任务驱动为手段,以能力输出为导向,将文本阅读、小组活动和交际实践相结合,注重学习者的参与和互动,将语言应用、文化认知和交际实践相结合,促进跨文化能力培养。

3. 采用模块化编排和辅教助学资源,利于个性化教学。本书以跨文化能力培养要素为依据,采用模块化设计。"跨文化交际基本理论""文化差异与冲突""跨文化交际实践"三个模块既相互独立,又彼此联系和支撑,便于教师根据校情、学时和学情选择内容和安排自学任务,适应多样化教学目标;自学者也可根据个性化发展需求灵活选择。电子教学资源包中的"教学建议"围绕教学目标,体现以"学"为本的理念,有助于个性化教学设计,提高教学效率。

4. 平面教材与线上教学资源相结合,适应混合式教学模式。本书依托安徽省精品线下开放课程"英语跨文化交际"(2018kfk122)编写,除了纸质平面教材,还可以进入超星"学习通",在"示范课程包"内搜索"英语跨文化交际",使用其中的教学课件、知识点微课视频、章节测试等辅助学习资料,拓展学习空间和内容。

二、内容编排与使用建议

本书以实用为原则,分为三大模块,即"跨文化交际基本理论""文化差异与冲突""跨文化交际实践",分别对应《指南》中的跨文化能力三要素,即"培养多元文化意识、掌握跨文化基本知识、提高跨文化交际能力"。本书共 10 章,包含"跨文化交际中的文化身份""交际与文化""文化价值观""言语交际""非言语交际""英中文学鉴赏""跨文化礼仪""跨文化学习与教学""多元文化职场沟通""做跨文化交际者"等内容。每章围绕 Learning Objectives(学习目标)设计,包括 Pre-class Tasks(课前任务)、Lead-in Tasks(导入任务)、Case Studies/Activities(案例分析与活动)、Test Your Reading(阅读测试)、Extended Reading(拓展阅读)和 Post-class Tasks(课后任务)等,各章均包括理论和实践,但各有侧重。

以上内容针对学习目标,从易到难,旨在鼓励师生以及学习者之间的互动和创新,教师可根据校情和学情,灵活选择模块和各章的面授、自学和讨论的内容,培养文化共情意识,掌握规避和处理冲突的技能,提高交际有效性和得体性。建议课堂教学32学时,可结合配套的电子资源酌情增加课前课后自主学习内容。

1. 落实课程育人理念,讲好"中国故事"

本书以育人为本,每章的Teaching Tips(教学建议)中均列出Focus of the Chinese Core Values(思政要点),并辅以Extended Reading(拓展阅读)和Telling China's Stories(讲中国故事)的学习任务,旨在引导学习者辩证客观地认识中外文化差异,提高文化思辨能力,从而既"会外语、通文化、懂世界",又"知中国、爱中国、讲中国",强化中国文化认同,提高中国国际传播力。

2. 根据专业特点和需求,设定个性化学习目标。Learning Objectives(学习目标)以学习者为中心,明确相关章节的知识、能力和素质目标,便于实施有目的阅读和教学;Pre-class Tasks(课前任务)依托网络和智慧学习工具,针对学习目标,实施课外学习,旨在提高自主学习能力,掌握基本知识要点,为课堂学习和任务做准备;Lead-in Tasks(导入任务)便于检测课前学习效果,促进思考,衔接正文。教师可根据课程目标、学习者水平和就业方向选择、补充案例分析和活动,实施个性化教学。

3. 根据学习者水平,可重组模块、章节和任务。正文内容基于学习者的前知识,围绕学习目标,遵循语言规范,控制词汇难度和语句复杂度,以便于理解为原则,具有适度高阶性。正文中穿插Case Studies/Activities(案例分析与活动)和Test Your Reading(阅读测试)。Case Studies/Activities(案例分析与活动)以文化认知为基础,以交际能力培养为导向,培养发现、分析和解决问题的能力;Activities(活动)分为个人、同伴或小组任务,以观察、对比和分析为手段,提高跨文化交际意识和能力;Test Your Reading(阅读测试)旨在培养学习者阅读、归纳和思考的习惯,提高跨语言学习能力。Extended Reading(拓展阅读)选自《中国日报》和《人民日报》(海外版),兼有外籍人士撰文和外国文化介绍,旨在提高学习者的文化自信和文化包容性,培养多元文化观。Post-class Tasks(课后任务)分为Self-test Tasks(自测)、Group Work(小组任务)、Telling China's Stories(讲中国故事)和My Learning Reflection(学习反思)等,分别为基础、较高和较难三个层级,评估知识水平和技能的掌握情况,以适应差异化的个体需求,有一定挑战性,可参考其设计目的和要求,选择采用。Telling China's Stories(讲中国故事)的话题贴近学习者的生活、学习经历,建议结合地方文化,提高语言应用能力,传播中国文化。My Learning Reflection(学习反思)鼓励学习者思考、分析和归纳所学与所思,提高英语应用能力,体现创新性。

线上教学资源包中的Teaching Tips(教学建议)列出教学重难点、思政要点,提供教学活动的设计目的、要求和解释,便于教师组织教学;Reference Keys(参考答案）提供书中练习的参考答案以及任务设计目的和要求，供使用者参考。征订教材的高校如需获取本书配套的电子教学资源，请发送邮件至 yaoshuo@ustc.edu.cn。

    本书编写人员均来自教学一线，确保了教材的实践性与应用性。夏蓓洁教授多年来致力于跨文化交际课程教学，主持安徽省精品线下课程"英语跨文化交际"，负责本教材的统筹规划、整体设计和编审，并编写"跨文化交际中的文化身份""文化价值观"和"多元文化职场沟通"等章节。其他章节的分工如下："交际与文化"由黄莹编写，"言语交际"由卢杨编写；"非言语交际"和"做跨文化交际者"由李洁编写；"跨文化学习与教学"由张千梅编写，"英中文学鉴赏"由岳俊辉编写，"跨文化礼仪"由崔斯佳编写。黄莹、崔斯佳和李洁还承担了电子资源的收集和编排以及平面教材的校对等工作。在此，衷心感谢各位编者的辛勤付出和贡献。

    本书在立体化教材的编写理念和实践中，得到上海外国语大学陈坚林教授的悉心指导和帮助，在此深表谢意。同时，感谢安徽大学朱跃教授、詹全旺教授和戚涛教授的建议和指导。编写过程中，参考了大量文献资料（详见参考文献），对于因来源难以查询而未能一一列出的资源，在此向作者和出版机构深表感谢。在此，特别感谢中国科学技术大学出版社的大力支持及帮助。

    《英语跨文化交际教程》为外语教育的跨文化能力培养做了一些尝试，希望能够"抛砖引玉"。虽然竭尽全力、力求完美，但是疏漏之处在所难免，恳请专家、同行和广大读者不吝赐教，以便不断完善。请将您的宝贵意见和建议发至：xiapeijie@hfuu.edu.cn。

夏蓓洁
2022 年 10 月

Contents

Preface ··· (i)

Module One Basics of Intercultural Communication

Chapter 1 Cultural Identities in Intercultural Communication ········ (3)
   I . Lead-in Tasks ··· (3)
   II . Understanding Intercultural Communication ······················· (4)
   III . Intercultural Communication Competence (ICC) ················ (14)
   IV . Cultural Identities in Globalization ·································· (25)
   V . Extended Reading ··· (42)
   Post-class Tasks ·· (43)

Chapter 2 Communication and Culture ································· (46)
   I . Lead-in Tasks ··· (46)
   II . Understanding Communication ······································ (47)
   III . Understanding Culture ·· (55)
   IV . High-context and Low-context Cultures ··························· (75)
   V . Extended Reading ··· (82)
   Post-class Tasks ·· (83)

Chapter 3 Cultural Patterns ·· (86)
   I . Lead-in Tasks ··· (86)
   II . Understanding Values as Core of Culture ·························· (87)
   III . Value Orientations to Compare Cultures ·························· (91)
   IV . Case Studies of Specific Cultures ··································· (123)
   V . Extended Reading ··· (129)
   Post-class Tasks ·· (131)

Module Two Cultural Differences in Intercultural Communication

Chapter 4　Verbal Communication (137)
　Ⅰ. Lead-in Tasks (137)
　Ⅱ. Understanding Language (139)
　Ⅲ. Relationship between Language and Culture (148)
　Ⅳ. Language Use in Intercultural Communication (158)
　Ⅴ. Working as Interpreters (175)
　Ⅵ. Extended Reading (181)
　Post-class Tasks (182)

Chapter 5　Nonverbal Communication (185)
　Ⅰ. Lead-in Tasks (185)
　Ⅱ. Understanding Nonverbal Communication (186)
　Ⅲ. Nonverbal Messages in Intercultural Communication (195)
　Ⅳ. Extended Reading (225)
　Post-class Tasks (227)

Chapter 6　English and Chinese Literature (232)
　Ⅰ. Lead-in Tasks (232)
　Ⅱ. English and Chinese Poetry (234)
　Ⅲ. English and Chinese Novels (247)
　Ⅳ. Literature Helps Cultural Fusion (258)
　Ⅴ. Extended Reading (262)
　Post-class Tasks (264)

Module Three Intercultural Communication Practice

Chapter 7　Intercultural Etiquette (269)
　Ⅰ. Lead-in Tasks (269)
　Ⅱ. Understanding Etiquette (270)
　Ⅲ. Social Etiquette across Cultures (271)
　Ⅳ. Extended Reading (295)
　Post-class Tasks (298)

Chapter 8　Intercultural Learning and Teaching ·············· (301)
　Ⅰ. Lead-in Tasks ·············· (301)
　Ⅱ. Culture in Education ·············· (305)
　Ⅲ. Teaching Chinese across Cultures ·············· (316)
　Ⅳ. Some Considerations ·············· (326)
　Ⅴ. Extended Reading ·············· (328)
　Post-class Tasks ·············· (329)

Chapter 9　Working in Multicultural Business Context ·············· (332)
　Ⅰ. Lead-in Tasks ·············· (332)
　Ⅱ. Communication Factors in Multicultural Workplace ·············· (333)
　Ⅲ. Communication Barriers in Multicultural Working Context ·············· (340)
　Ⅳ. Extended Reading ·············· (363)
　Post-class Tasks ·············· (367)

Chapter 10　Leaning to Become Intercultural Communicators ·············· (370)
　Ⅰ. Lead-in Tasks ·············· (370)
　Ⅱ. Understanding Barriers in Intercultural Communication ·············· (373)
　Ⅲ. Developing Intercultural Competence ·············· (391)
　Ⅳ. Extended Reading ·············· (399)
　Post-class Tasks ·············· (400)

References ·············· (404)

Module One

Basics of Intercultural Communication

Chapter 1 Cultural Identities in Intercultural Communication

Learning Objectives

- To summarize the basic concepts and principles of intercultural communication as practice, a discipline and a course;
- To identify oneself appropriately in communication with the basic concepts of identities;
- To enhance Chinese cultural identity and multicultural inclusiveness for a community with a shared future for mankind.

Pre-class Tasks

- Read the textbook and watch the concerned clips in *xuexitong* (学习通).

I. Lead-in Tasks

Activity 1

Take a pre-test with the help of the Intercultural Communication Sensitivity (ICS). Refer to: Chen G M, Starosta W J. The development and validation of the intercultural communication sensitivity scale [J]. Human Communication, 2000, 3(1): 20.

Activity 2

Read the following to find out the features of intercultural communication.

(1) A male student from the northwest China bargained in stores when he traveled to Guangzhou.

(2) The president of a Chinese university received the visiting group of a German university.

(3) The Chinese engineers guided the Tanzanian workers in the construction site of the local railroads under the "Belt and Road" Initiatives.

(4) Students have bed-time chats in university dormitories with members from several provinces in China.

(5) A Chinese teacher instructs students in making Chinese Knots at a Chinese Confucian Institution in France.

(6) President Xi Jinping had a phone talk with President Putin.

(7) How do you think of such events as Monk Jianzhen's Mission to Japan, Marco Polo's stay in China, Zheng He's Voyages to the Western Seas, the business on the Silk Road?

Activity 3

Work in groups to answer the questions.

(1) Is there intercultural communication in China among Chinese people?

(2) How do you define intercultural communication?

II. Understanding Intercultural Communication

Intercultural communication is frequently mentioned with increased globalization and intense interactions between individuals from other countries or cultures by means of telecommunication and tourism, and foreign languages have thus become vital in communication. As shown in the examples of Activity 2 in Lead-in Tasks, intercultural communication is more than exchange of information in foreign languages, involving people with such cultural background as nationalities, races or ethnicities, it also concerns with people in the same country or cultures with different regions, educations, occupations, ages and so forth. In other words, intercultural communication takes places among ordinary beings on the daily basis or at workplace, sometimes in the same language.

A. What Is Intercultural Communication?

Intercultural communication, also known as IC in its initials, refers to communication between or among people **with different cultural backgrounds**. When IC is mentioned, it may refer to one of the following, IC as human practice, IC as one of academic disciplines or IC as one of courses in educational institutions.

Intercultural communication **as human practice** has existed as long as the human history when people from one tribe encountered members of another, or when people travelled from one place to another interacting with local people along the way. Spices, silk, tea, and coffee made their way to Europe from China, Southeast Asia, and the Middle East via trade routes along the Silk Road as a result of intercultural communication. Other examples are those traders who sailed from the Western Europe to the Far East on the voyage of discovery with guns, modern medicines and even bread. Not only commodities but also ideas were exchanged between different cultures by intercultural communication. For example, Zheng He in the Ming Dynasty pioneered many countries with his fleets and promoted Chinese culture by doing business with the local merchants. The Reform and Opening-up Policy in the 1980s of the 20th century and the entry to World Trade Organization (WTO) at the turn of the 21st century have provided China with more opportunities for intercultural communication by means of cooperation with international businesses, and increasing tourists from other countries to China have made it common for average people to be exposed to intercultural communication in English or other foreign languages.

People engaged in intercultural communication have noticed that there are some problems preventing them from effective communication even though they speak the same language in most of cases.

Case Study 1

What is the problem of the American in England?

An American who travelled to England was having a talk with his English friend about something that was bothering him.

American: I feel uncomfortable with many of the people here, but I'm not sure why. I speak the same language, so there shouldn't be any problem. Back home, I usually get along with people. You know that I am very friendly.

Englishman: Yes, that is true, but you are friendly in the way that Americans are friendly.

American: I am not sure I understand.

Englishman: Well, for example, at the meeting the other night, you immediately called people by their first names. We do that here, but not when we first meet someone.

American: That's how we make people feel comfortable. People feel friendlier toward each other when they use first names.

Englishman: It's different here. For example, when you met my boss you should have used his last name. Also there's something else that you do that English people don't often do.

American: What's that?

Englishman: You touch people on the shoulder quite a bit, especially when you compliment them.

American: I guess I've never thought about that before, I suppose that is what I do at home.

Do you have similar experience when you communicate with people from other parts of China? Or have you ever felt puzzled when you speak fluent English but you sensed something wrong in communication with foreigners?

Intercultural communication **as one of academic disciplines** started in the United States, where it's known for its multicultural citizens from almost every corner of the world. In the 40s to the 60s of the 20th century, increasing Americans went abroad for various purposes, and the Institute of Foreign

Services was thus set up to train its diplomats, soldiers and business people to work outside of the US with knowledge of other target cultures, which later became a discipline as a result.

Edward T. Hall, an American anthropologist, who was then involved in the training, is believed to be one of the founders of study of intercultural communication. He has published such works as *Silent Language* (1959), *Beyond Culture* (1976), *the Hidden Dimension* (1966) and *the Dance of Life* (1983) which are regarded as the founding of this discipline (Figure 1.1).

Figure 1.1 Books by Edward T. Hall

Hall found that the ways that people communicate is greatly but unconsciously influenced by its corresponding culture, i.e. communication is culture and communication is culture. And that is why in IC courses, some efforts are exerted in understanding culture and communication in order to understand the relationship between them, i.e. how culture affects the ways of communication.

As a discipline, intercultural communication studies how communication is influenced by culture. To make it simple, IC study tries to find out **what is proper for who in specific culture says what to whom at what time in what way by understanding the elements and characteristics of culture and communication respectively.** In terms of communication, the experts of intercultural communication are interested in the communication in words and/or without word, known as verbal communication and nonverbal communication accordingly. People communicate in different ways not only because they speak different languages but also because they see and perceive the world in different ways, which are referred to as cultural values, one of the crucial focuses of intercultural communication. In other words, intercultural communication focuses on how culture affects communication between/among social groups or individuals across different cultures in social contexts with varied religious, social, ethnic, and educational backgrounds.

Then in the 90s, studies of intercultural communication accelerated as a result of speedy transportation and extensive use of advanced technologies in communication such as the Internet and smart phones. People speaking different languages with diverse convictions were convinced that it had become more difficult to live one's own life without being affected by others' opinions or actions. This "interconnectedness" as the theme of globalization, has made people come to realize that they must learn to live and work together despite of the likelihood of conflicts.

The 21st century has seen a great progress in the study of intercultural communication to a mature stage with more people involved in and more topics explored in more diverse fields. And it is believed that each individual is a compound of cultures with more identities, and communication as a process involves many factors that influence the efficiency and results. Therefore more academic achievements are expected to contribute to the well-being of individuals, cooperation among nations and regions, and the peace of the world.

Intercultural communication **as one of courses** appeared in schools, colleges or universities first in the US in the 70s to 80s of the 20th century and then in more other countries. Knowledge of other cuntries in addition to mastery of a foreign languages turned out vital in communicating with people from other cultural background because they have to coincide with the international trend for cooperation and development as the world becomes smaller as a village. And these courses helped result in more studies on communication between individuals, institutions and countries.

The study of intercultural communication is of multidisciplinary nature and it involvessuch disciplines as anthropology, psychology, physiology, sociology, history, religion, linguistics, geography and etc. In other words, for a better intercultural communicator, one has to be equipped with the general knowledge of culture and communication together with knowledge of specific cultures, especially of one's own and that of the counter-communicators in addition to foreign languages and knowledge of human beings. Besides, each human being is unique and different and one has to take personal traits together with the cultural and physical context into consideration in communication to avoid stereotyping.

Therefore, intercultural communication as a course mainly concerns how to communicate between people with various cultural backgrounds, such as different countries or regions who speaks English as lingua franca due to the fact that the English language has now become one of the frequently used languages worldwide. As far as learners of the English language in China, intercultural communication refers to effective and adequate interactions in English with those from other cultures.

Test Your Reading 1

Decide whether the statements are True (T) or False (F).

(1) Intercultural communication is part of daily practice as long as human history. (   )

(2) Globalization and technology have made intercultural communication necessary and inevitable. (   )

(3) Intercultural communication was first employed as training programs for people going abroad for fun in the United States. (   )

(4) Schools, colleges and universities began to offer IC courses because they would like their students to be equipped with knowledge of communication with people around the world. (   )

(5) People do not need to know about intercultural communication if they are not engaged in translation, international business, foreign language teaching or foreign affairs. (   )

(6) A good mastery of English language alone will ensure effective intercultural communication. (   )

B. Where Does Intercultural Communication Take Place?

In general, intercultural communication refers to interactions between or among people with different cultural backgrounds. It may occur within a geographic boundary of a country where people speak the same language, for example, a Cantonese travels to Mudanjiang, the northeast part of China for timber purchase, or a new-married couple from Shanghai enjoyed their honeymoon in the Xishuangbanna Dai Autonomous Prefecture (西双版纳傣族自治州). Intercultural communication may extend beyond national territories due to convenient transportation. For example, growing numbers of Chinese people travel around the world in these decades for various reasons, including sightseeing, business potentials, further education, academic exchanges, governmental visits and etc. Intercultural communication may also take place anywhere when people speak a lingua franca, for example English at international institutions such as the United Nations, the World Health Organization, the Group 20 (G20) summits or the World Economic Forums to discuss on the shared issues concerning human interests in the more globalized world.

Intercultural communication comes up at different levels and the word "communication" is translated into "交流""传播" or "交际" in Chinese respectively according to the context. When communication takes places between nations, it is referred to as "交流". For example, at the Boao Forum when the President of China communicates with any of the heads of the states present, it is international communication even though they greet and talk in person. When media takes the role of communication to its own people or people abroad for information, entertainment and education, it plays an important role to communicate between cultures as well. For example, *China Daily*, *The 21 Century*, *People's Daily* in English and China Media Group (CMG, 中国中央广播电视总台) are engaged in the construction of the national image of China and Chinese cultural transmission for the international role of China, and they are referred to as "传播" in Chinese.

As far as individuals are concerned, communication is translated into "交际" in Chinese. For example, it is regarded as inter-regional communication if someone from Harbin (哈尔滨) in Heilongjiang Province talked to a Cantonese on the train as each of them has his/her own regional cultures, or when one travels to Xishuangbanna Dai Autonomous Prefecture in the Guangxi Zhuang Autonomous Region, he/she will have inter-ethnic communication with the local people. That's why there are more intercultural communications in the United States than any other countries as a result of its multicultural nature in terms of races, ethnics, religions and beliefs. Therefore intercultural communication is not something new or rare but pervasive in the daily life, which deserves more attention in the dynamic world.

Intercultural communication is sometimes used synonymously with cross-cultural communication. In this sense it seeks to understand how people from different countries and cultures act, communicate and perceive the world around them. Cross-cultural communication usually refers to comparisons of the differences of any two or more cultures while intercultural communication focuses on what exactly happens when people from different cultures communicate. Therefore, cross-cultural communication emphasizes comparison between cultures while the later for the dynamic process which involves cultural factors, which is applied in this textbook.

Test Your Reading 2

Decide whether the statements are True (T) or False (F).
(1) Intercultural communication takes place only when people speak different languages. (　)
(2) Communication between a Chinese university and a Japanese one is an example of intercultural communication. (　)
(3) Communication between people from different regions is the practice of intercultural communication. (　)
(4) The discipline of intercultural communication concerns how culture influences communication in various contexts. (　)
(5) It helps language learning by knowing more about intercultural communication as we are in the same world for the same goal of a community of shared future for mankind. (　)

C. Intercultural Communication in China

Intercultural communication **as practice** has existed in China as long as Chinese history. China interacted with neighboring countries and regions with goods and migrants for the purpose of harmonious relationships. For example, the four great inventions by Chinese together with medicine, arts and Confucianism have been transmitted beyond the Asian countries to Europe.

Examples of Chinese going out for voluntary communication are Zhang Qian's travel to the West, Monk Jianzhen's mission to Japan and Zheng He's voyages to the Western Seas. Meanwhile, Marco Polo's stay in China, the Japanese diplomats to the Tang Dynasty brought foreign languages and cultures to China as amicable intercultural communication within China. However, it has to be noted that Chinese people also experienced compulsive and humiliating intercultural communication from invasions of other nations before the New China was founded in 1949.

Intercultural communication once again became popular and intense for Chinese people with many foreign firms coming to China and a lot more Chinese people going abroad since the 1980s with the Open-door Policy. The Belt and Road Initiative since 2013 has prompted China more perspectives for international cooperation both at home and abroad, and the growing economic power of China in the recent decades magnify the Chinese saying in the international organizations, where more Chinese are employed with fluent foreign languages and multicultural competence as international talents.

Studies of Intercultural communication **as a discipline** were introduced to China by Hu Wenzhong and many other scholars who studies abroad in the 1980s when China began to open to the world and more people were keen on learning foreign languages, among which English is in particular. Intercultural communication was therefore known first in the field of foreign language teaching and learning as language is a part of culture which influence the ways of communication. As shown in the graph (Figure 1.2), Chinese people learning English are expected to communicate with not only those from the Inner Circle as their native language, but also those from the Outer Circle as their second/third language, and even more of the Expanding Circle, who speak English as lingua franca or as a foreign language together with their own cultural heritages.

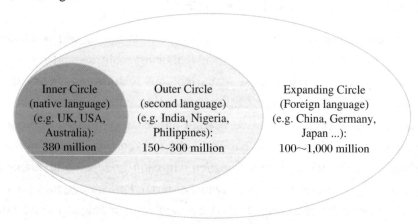

Figure 1.2 Three Circle Theory from Braj Kachur

Intercultural communication has also become prominent in management of international business as people from different countries have to work together for shared goals. Later intercultural communication has gained more attention in media studies for the national image of China and the transmission of Chinese culture. In the recent decades, intercultural communication has become increasingly significant for teachers of the Chinese language who either teach Chinese as a second language to international students in China or as a foreign language in the Chinese Confucius institutes or classrooms in other countries.

Globalization has extended the vision of Chinese people when mutual understanding serves as the basis for a better world. Intercultural communication was therefore included **as a course** for the first time in *the English Teaching Syllabus for English Major's in Colleges and Universities* (《高校英语专业教学大纲》) issued by the Ministry of Education in April, 2000 with an effort to cultivate English majors "awareness and tolerance of cultural differences and flexibility in dealing with cultural conflicts" to meet the requirements of the new era of the 21st century.

The growing economic power and political influence of China in the 21st century has increased the Chinese saying in the international organizations such as the United Nations, and the Belt and Road Initiative has provided China with more perspectives for intensive international cooperation both in China and in other countries. Accodingly international talents are urgently demanded, who are supposed to know well about international rules with Chinese patriotism and global mindset since the world of today is experiencing great changes that have ever experienced in a century. Therefore Intercultural Communication Competence (ICC) had become even more important in dealing with personal, institutional and national relationships than ever before and that is why intercultural communication competence as one of the key qualifications of English majors for international talents is speculated in *the Teaching Guide of Foreign Language and Literature for Undergraduates in Colleges and Universities* (《普通高校外国语言文学类专业教学指南》) issued in 2020. Once again in the history of Chinese culture, there comes the urgency of the voluntary and equal intercultural communication for China to realize its dream of the rejuvenation of the Chinese nation by responding to the national strategies and meeting needs of organizational cooperation and individual development as well.

Test Your Reading 3

Decide whether the statements are True (T) or False (F).

(1) Intercultural communication started again in China when the Open-door Policy was implemented in the 80s' of the 20th century. (   )

(2) Studies of intercultural communication are applied to many fields such as foreign language education, media, management and translation. (   )

(3) Intercultural communication takes place at individual, regional, ethnical or national levels. (   )

(4) English learners in China belong to the Expanding Circle according to the theory by Braj Kachur. (   )

(5) People who are not going to have interactions with foreigners do not need to learn something about intercultural communication. (   )

(6) The New Era of the socialism with Chinese Characteristics led by Xi Jinping calls for patriots with global mindset for the Chinese Dream of the rejuvenation of the Chinese people. (   )

III. Intercultural Communication Competence (ICC)

Intercultural Communication Competence is vital in the communication with people of different cultural backgrounds, and nowadays it has gained more attention in more practical fields as communication aims for survival of human beings.

A. What Is ICC?

ICC stands for Intercultural Communication Competence, referring to competence of predicting and solving problems in intercultural communication, including knowledge of one's own home culture and host cultures, awareness of cultural differences and the abilities of foreign language and culture together with cognitive ability.

ICC has gained increasing attention as communication is the lifeblood in the modern society for survival either for individuals or for families or for institutions. That's why the *Teaching Guide of Foreign Language and Literature for Undergraduates in Colleges and Universities* takes the cultivation of intercultural competence as one of its teaching objectives, so does *National standards for Undergraduates Majoring in Foreign Languages in Colleges and Universities*(《大学英语教学指南》), 2020.

ICC has been widely studied globally for the development of the youth in many countries or regions, such as Europe and the United States. In 2013, the United Nations Education, Science and Culture Organization (UNESCO) issued *the Intercultural Competences: Conceptual an Operational Framework*, in which intercultural competences are demonstrated as a tree (Figure 1.3).

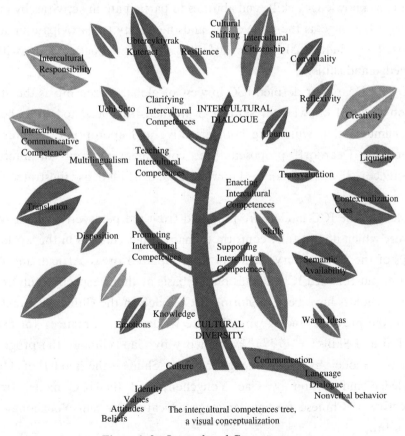

Figure 1.3 Intercultural Competences
(UNESCO, Intercutual Competences: Conceptual and
Operational Framework, Paris.)

As shown in Figure 1.3, knowledge and abilities in culture and communication are rooted as the basis for ICC with many other competencies, such as values, languages, knowledge and emotions, which include competences for individuals to become the global citizen in the world. This "tree" is convincing for English language learners in the way that language alone may not ensure effective communication, and the goal of learning English has shifted to being intercultural communicators instead of speaking English as fluent as native speakers.

There are many models of ICC advocated by scholars in the US or other countries, which stress different aspects of intercultural competence. For example, Michael Byram defined ICC in connection with culture and language learning as knowledge, skills and abilities to participate in activities by means of the target language as the basic code, and the ability to participate in activities organized by individuals from different language backgrounds with such knowledge and skills.

D. K. Deardorff defined ICC in view of global citizenship as the ability to develop targeted knowledge, skills and attitudes that lead to visible behaviors and communication which are both effective and appropriate in intercultural interactions. Deardorff proposed three constituent elements of intercultural competence, i. e. attitudes, knowledge and skills, as illustrated in the Figure 1.4.

Most of the ICC models are proposed from the perspective of the Western cultures, which do not fully conform to many other cultures in the world. Since the 90s of the 20th century, scholars from Japan, Korea, African and Arabian countries put forward ICC models on the basis of their respective cultures. And Chinese scholars have been exploring ICC models in the Chinese context on the basis of the previous studies with Chinese wisdoms and practice, for example, the "Tao and Skills" ("道"与"器") theory by Gao Yihong, the progressively interactive model by Xu Lisheng and Sun Shunv, the model of Unity of Knowledge and Action by Gao Yongchen, and the ICC model from the perspective of Chinese foreign language education by Sun Youzhong, just to name a few.

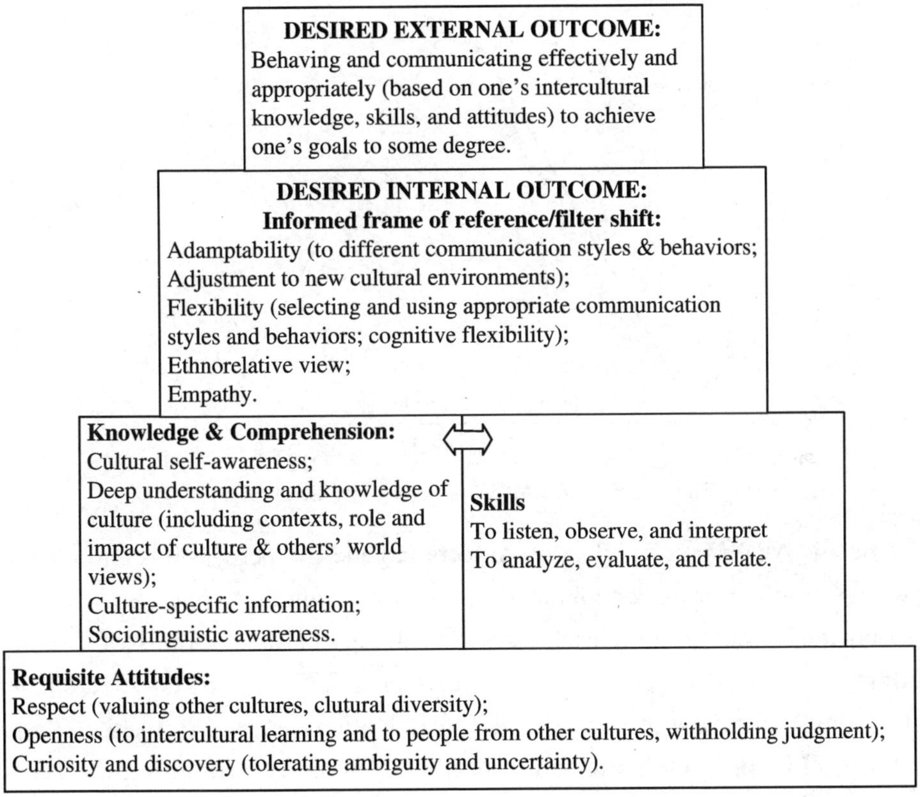

Module One Basics of Intercultural Communication

DESIRED EXTERNAL OUTCOME:
Behaving and communicating effectively and appropriately (based on one's intercultural knowledge, skills, and attitudes) to achieve one's goals to some degree.

DESIRED INTERNAL OUTCOME:
Informed frame of reference/filter shift:
Adamptability (to different communication styles & behaviors;
Adjustment to new cultural environments);
Flexibility (selecting and using appropriate communication styles and behaviors; cognitive flexibility);
Ethnorelative view;
Empathy.

Knowledge & Comprehension:
Cultural self-awareness;
Deep understanding and knowledge of culture (including contexts, role and impact of culture & others' world views);
Culture-specific information;
Sociolinguistic awareness.

Skills
To listen, observe, and interpret
To analyze, evaluate, and relate.

Requisite Attitudes:
Respect (valuing other cultures, clutural diversity);
Openness (to intercultural learning and to people from other cultures, withholding judgment);
Curiosity and discovery (tolerating ambiguity and uncertainty).

Figure 1.4 The Pyramid Model of Intercultural Competence (Deardorff, 2006)

B. What Is the ABC Model?

Though scholars have not agreed on a unified model for what constitutes intercultural communication competence as intercultural communicators are culturally specific, they have reached consensus that ICC is fundamentally composed of such elements as knowledge of culture, motivation and attitude towards intercultural interactions, linguistic abilities and communication skills together with critical cultural awareness, etc. The one that is widely accepted is the ABC model or the Triangular Model by Chen, Starosta and Zhang Hongling, etc (Figure 1.5). The ABC model entails such basic components as affective competence, cognition competence and behavioral competence. It's believed that these three, with each supporting one another, are the basic qualifications in intercultural communication.

Figure 1.5   ABC Model of ICC (Dai, Chen, 2014)

In this ABC Model, **Affection Aspects** include the perceptions and attitudes towards intercultural communication in that whether one is willing to participate in intercultural exchanges, including the assumptions of the alien culture, such as "it is strange and unbelievable" or "it is different and interesting", and how to treat the cultures of others', i.e. "to dislike, despise and neglect it" or "to tolerate and respect it". Therefore, attitudes towards one's own culture as "the only best one", known as ethnocentrism should be avoided, and the relationship with others as "the inferior one to others" as cultural inferiority is unacceptable neither. The preliminary affection in intercultural communication is sensibility of the cultural difference based on the understanding and love of one's own culture in addition to the knowledge of and respect for other cultures with an international mindset in thinking globally and acting locally.

Behavioral Aspects entail the techniques and skills to behave appropriately in specific contexts with particular participants on the basis of cultural equality and respect for cultural diversity, i.e. "Do as Romans do in Rome" as the Golden Rule. It also includes a good mastery of verbal expressions, nonverbal behaviors together with appropriate etiquette in the context of the counterpart communicator as well. In addition, it includes the skills to manage conflicts in workplace or at other events with people across cultures.

Cognitive Aspects refer to the knowledge of cultural general (一般文化) and cultural specific (特定文化) together with communication, language and etiquette of one's own culture and that of others, which requires ongoing learning of culture at all levels and aspects. Additionally, the basic skills are vital in intercultural communication such as listening, observing, evaluating, analyzing, interpreting, relating and critical thinking.

To specify the ABC Model in the Chinese context, Zhang Hongling holds that cognitive aspects include the study of the target culture, knowledge of other cultures in the world and further understanding and reflection of one's own culture. On the basis of extensive contacts and interpretation of differences between cultures, one would enhance recognition of the Chinese culture with more open and inclusive understanding and appreciation of other cultures.

In 2020, the Integrated Model for Chinese Students' Intercultural Competence Development (IMCSICD) was proposed by Zhang Hongling and her team to implement the goal of intercultural competence development in the context of foreign language education in China from primary school pupils to college students with global mindset and Chinese patriotism (Figure 1.6).

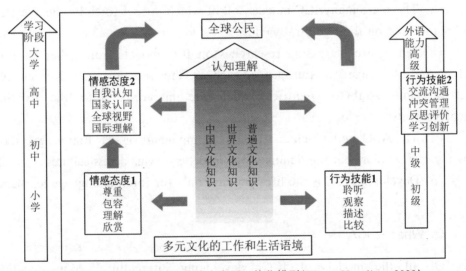

Figure 1.6　中国学生跨文化能力发展一体化模型(Zhang Hongling, 2020)

Based on the needs of Chinese students, a "4 - 3 - 2 - 1" theoretical framework is put forward for cultivation of intercultural competence, from four perspectives in three dimensions within two contexts on one platform. In other words, by learning foreign languages on the platform from the primary school to college, Chinese students are trained to adapt to the contexts of multicultural life and work from perspectives of communication behaviors, personal relationships, cultural conflicts and cultural identities in the dimensions of knowledge of culture-general, Chinese culture and world cultures.

In conclusion, intercultural communication competence is complex in composition which varies from individuals and cultures, and the process to develop ICC is a consistent progress which involves curiosity and interest in learning and practice with reflections.

Test Your Reading 4

Decide whether the statements are True (T) or False (F).

(1) ICC refers to the competence of predicting and solving problems in IC practice on the basis of awareness and tolerance of cultural differences, the knowledge of other cultures and the abilities of the target language and communication skills. (   )

(2) There are many ICC models, all of which are set forth by the Western scholars based on their cultural values. (   )

(3) There are increasing researches on ICC models from other cultures other than Americans or Europeans, such as Chinese, Japanese, Korean and African and Arabian countries which are integrated into the existing achievements. (   )

(4) The ABC model includes the basic components of ICC that is agreed on by most of scholars but the details of the model is varying across cultures. (   )

(5) Developing ICC is the life-long task only for foreign language learners. (   )

C. What Is ICA?

Of all the models of ICC, developing intercultural communication awareness (ICA) is what is considered as the core of ICC, i.e. the knowledge of one's own culture and other cultures and the ability to understand the differences by objective and non-judgmental comparisons. ICA helps interpret what one says and does in terms of culture, thus facilitating effective personal communication either in daily life or at work.

Davis, who has been teaching English for years in China and has experienced different cultural perceptions while in China, identified the levels of ICA in the following table.

Activity 4

Study the table to find out at which level you are now.

Table 1.1 Four Levels of ICA (Davis, 2005)

Level	Information	Way of Knowing	Interpretation
1	Awareness of superficial or very visible cultural traits; stereotypes	Tourism, textbooks, TV and films, popular opinions	Unbelievable, exotic or bizarre and possibly entertaining
2	Awareness of significant and subtle cultural traits quite different from one's own	Cultural conflict situations	Unbelievable in a frustrating way; it seems irrational
3	Awareness of significant and subtle cultural traits quite different from one's own	Study about the culture; formal study in school	Believable but only at a thinking level
4	Awareness of how a culture feels to someone who is a member of it	Getting into and living the culture	Believable at an emotional level as it is lived experience

Test Your Reading 5

Decide whether the statements are True (T) or False (F).

(1) ICA is the kernel part of the development of ICC. (　)

(2) It will be helpful for one's own ICA to know about the cultural difference by means of movies, media or stories of others. (　)

(3) Being nonjudgmental on cultural differences is based on the knowledge of other cultures and continuous learning of more cultures. (　)

(4) It is regarded as a way to learn about the invisible culture by going into another country for a vocation. (　)

(5) It enables to reflect and understand more about one's own culture by learning about other cultures in comparison. (   )

D. What Are the Principles of Developing ICA?

As culture is an instrumental variable in human interaction, problems may arise in communication with people from different cultural backgrounds. Engaging in intercultural communication is a complex activity and five caveats are provided by Samovar and his colleagues for effective intercultural communication as follows (Adapted from *Communication Between Cultures* by Samovar et al.).

Individual Uniqueness

That no two people are alike is what is accepted as common sense since behaviors of people is shaped by a multitude of sources with culture being but one, i.e. **they are more than their culture**. Their worldviews, attitudes and behaviors are influenced by the genetic makeup (known as DNA), social group experience, language, gender, age, individual and family history, political beliefs, education level, perceptions of others, the existing circumstance, economic resources, the region and neighborhood they were brought up and many other aspects that make them who they are and what they do. Even though culture is a powerful force in the shaping of human behaviors, one has to be cautious and prudent when making cultural generalizations as people are more than their culture, and they are individuals.

Generalization

Generalizations are based on limited data and are then applied to a larger population. In intercultural communication, this means ascribing characteristics to a larger group of people based on attributes by a smaller group. For example, "all Asian students make good grades." People would like to generalize other cultures because it is easy. **It is same easy to fall into traps of overgeneralization.** Certain precaution should be taken to minimize the misleading effects of generalizing. First, cultural generalization must be viewed as approximations, not as absolute representations as the English writer Robert Burton indicated "no rule is so general, which admits not some exceptions." Second, generalization should be dealt with the primary values and behaviors of a particular culture because it is these core values and learned behaviors that occur with enough regularity and over a long enough period of time that tend to correctly identify the members of a particular culture. For example, in Mexico, friends usually embrace; in Japan and India, people bow; in German and the United States, people typically shake hands and in China, people would nod to each other on the casual basis. Third, generalizations should be supported by a variety of sources. Finally, conclusions and statements about cultures should be qualified so that they are not absolute but only as cautious generalizations. Words such as "usually" "often" "on an average" "more likely" "tend to" are used to imply that not everyone in the culture is exactly alike so that over-generalization is avoided.

Objectivity

According to *Random House Dictionary of the English Dictionary*, being objective means "not influenced by personal feelings, interpretations, or prejudice; based on facts; unbiased: an objective opinion". In intercultural communication, it is difficult to be objective because one will approach and respond to other cultures from the perspectives of his/her own culture consciously or unconsciously. The habit of overemphasizing one's own culture is known as ethnocentrism, as Ferraro and Andreatta defined "the belief that one's culture is superior to all others." For example, direct declines of an invitation or an offer by an American would be regarded rude by Northeastern cultures where indirect approach is regarded as appropriate in expressing disagreement.

Objectivity requires an open mind and avoiding being judgmental when approaching each new situation. To reject someone simply for having a different skin color, living in a different country, exposing different worldviews, or speaking English with an accent diminishes the person and keeps one from having new cultural experience. Objectivity promotes learning to interact and value distinct groups of people regardless of their culture, race, ethnicity, religion, country or gender.

Compromise

Intercultural knowledge and skills will not eliminate cultural conflicts, and encountering disagreement is a natural characteristic of intercultural communication with individuals who have different perceptions of what is right or wrong, good or bad, acceptable or unacceptable, etc. What is important is whether or not conflicts will occur, because it will, but rather how to successfully manage the situation. Normally the best resolution to external conflict is one where both parties are satisfied. The internal conflicts usually more problematic as it involves values. For example, how would an international student in Madrid, Spain handle the invitation to bullfight from the host family is an internal conflict as the student has a strong feeling for animal rights and animal cruelty. Even though there are no standard procedures for this situation, **one has to handle it with an open mind rather than a win-lose perspective, and finding a middle ground or even accepting the situation may be the best way.** In some cases where personal feelings, attitudes, beliefs or values are hurt in an uncompromising position, one may make his/her position clearly in a sincere and concise manner.

Communication Is Not the Universal Solution

Although communication is taken as the valuable tool for resolving numerous interpersonal difficulties, **it has to be noted that communication cannot solve all problems.** In fact, there are occasions when communication may worsen the situation with bruised emotions or hurt feelings as a result of irreconcilable differences between the participants, which occur not only at the interpersonal level but also through all strata of society, including relations between nations. In spite of this, it is worthy improving interactions with people of varied cultures.

Test Your Reading 6

Decide whether the statements are True (T) or False (F).

(1) Since conflicts in intercultural communication are inevitable, it is suggested that one takes part in as few intercultural interactions as possible. ( )

(2) Each individual is a representation of his/her culture as human beings are cultural animals with the general characteristics of one's own culture. ( )

(3) It is more acceptable to compromise with an open mind and sincere attitude in dealing with conflicts. ( )

(4) Conflicts will be finally resolved as long as one applies various approaches of communication with efforts. ( )

(5) Generalizations help in understanding cultures but they may bring about stereotypes if overused in regardless of context and individuals. (   )

IV. Cultural Identities in Globalization

When various cultures share similarities in general, a specific culture diverges among others. In each society there usually is a mainstream culture (also known as a dominant culture or an umbrella culture), which seems "normal" to most of the members thus being held and widely accepted by a large number of people residing in it. And at the same time each individual in the culture belongs to different subcultures (also known as co-cultures), which is shared by some portion of the total population under the same mainstream culture, such as ethnicities, religions, geographical regions, genders, ages, occupations or education levels in the society, who sometimes behave differently from those in mainstream cultures.

Activity 5

Write 10 sentences beginning with "I am + noun phrases/ adjective phrases" to answer the question of "who I am." The more you will write, the better.

I am _____.
I am _____.
I am _____.
I am _____.
I am _____.
I am _____.
I am _____.
I am _____.
I am _____.
I am _____.

When one tells about who he/she is or what he/she is like, for example, "I am a Chinese" "I'm female" or "I'm Han Meimei", he/she is identifying what he/she thinks of himself/ herself as a member of a group to which he/she indicates the sense of belonging as part of his/her culture or subcultures.

Each of the co-cultures or subcultures represents some of cultural traits which identify themselves from others. For example, most ethnical groups in the Southwest China dress differently from Han people in general and they have their New Year celebrations other than the Spring Festival. Subcultures can be rebellious or non-conforming to the umbrella culture with no vital harm to the mainstream culture, for example DINK families or queers. And in most cases, they own different identities in religions, regions, professions, ages, genders or a sum of a few, which make an individual the unique one known as one's cultural identities. For example, a Chinese male college student from Tibet belongs to several subcultures as a male, a college student, maybe a Tibetan or a Han or any other ethnics, or a Buddhist, a Taoist or an atheist, and at the same time he is at the age of 18~22. Above all, he is a Chinese.

As a result, nobody will necessarily reflect the total aspects of the mainstream culture but in some ways bears aspects of some of the subcultures he/she belongs to, and it is difficult and complex to reply to the question of "what a Chinese is like" because Qu Yuan, Li Bai, Jackie Chen, Yao Ming, Yuan Longping or any Chinese are Chinese but none of them is a model or template of Chinese as each of them bears some characteristics of Chinese in various aspects.

In any country the mainstream cultures co-exist with many subcultures or co-cultures with various cultural images, and each individual shares the dominant one with corresponding co-cultures to his/her ages and gender with regional, educational or professional traits. That is why it is vital to have clear understanding of culture identities of oneself and others in communication.

Activity 6

Identify yourself and two others (Table 1.2), either your friends in life or characters in movies, in terms of the mainstream culture and sub-cultures in beliefs, regions, ages, genders, education, hobbies or occupation, etc. to find out which makes you different from others and what you share as commonalities.

Table 1.2 Identify Yourself and Others

	Mainstream culture	Sub-cultures	Overlapping cultures
A (yourself)			
B			
C			

A. What Are Cultural Identities?

"Who you are" is determined by your past; and who you will become is a product of your future which indicates the importance of identity acquisition and development. As identity is pervasive in social interactions and particularly a critical factor in intercultural communication, it deserves a thorough understanding of what it entails.

Identity is an abstract, complex and dynamic concept, which is hard to define. But "who I am" and "who and what help to define me" will provide insights into some of identities and sources of these identities. Samovar holds that "Identity is a multifaceted, dynamic, abstract concept that plays an integral role in daily communicative interactions and particularly in intercultural communication." Cardiner and Kosmitzki see identity as "a person's self-definition as a separate and distinct individual including behaviors, beliefs and attitudes." Simply speaking, identity is the answer to the question "who I am" to oneself, or in some ways, identity is what Ting-Toomy defined as the reflective self-conception or self-image that we derive from our family, gender, cultural, ethnic and individual socialization process.

According to B. J. Hall, there are three levels of identity depending on the context, which are termed as personal identities, relational identities and communal identities, which may or may not be salient in the interactions with others. Personal identities are those that make one different and unique from others, such as the biological features of DNA. For example, on the first day of school, a girl will answer this question of "who you are" in her full name as Han Meimei, but at a family party, she will automatically reply in her first name, i.e Meimei.

Relational identities are those in relations with others, for example, children/parents, a husband/ a wife, teachers/students, doctors/ patients, employers/employees, etc. Relational identity is prominent in communication as it determines the ways that one interacts with others. For example, the language and communication style between a male teacher and his students is different from that of father and his children.

Communal identities are related to large-scale communities, such as nationalities, ethnicities, races and genders, and religious or political affiliations. Personal and relational identities are usually noticeable but communal identities are culture bond, which is referred to as cultural identity.

As shown in the list of Activity 2, there are many answers to "who you are" as one has multiple identities in terms of the mainstream culture and subcultures he/she belongs to, such as the nationality, race, ethnicity, region, occupation, education, gender, social class, and familial background, but the ones that go first to one's mind is apparently the identity that he agrees on and accepts in the specific context. For example, in the hospital, the patient will reply in his/her full name to "who you are." But at the China International Import Expo (CIIE), the answer to the same question will turn out to be "I am the Sales Manager of ACS Company of Turkey." As to "where you are from", an international traveler would reply in "I'm from Canada", but in a Chinese university dormitory of freshmen, the answer would turn out to be "I'm from Hunan" or " I'm from Sichuan". Then what are the possible replies to the same question in one of Anhui local universities?

Test Your Reading 7

Decide whether the statements are True (T) or False (F).

(1) Identity is the answer to the question of" who I am", which implies what one agrees and accepts as who he/she is in a context. (   )

(2) One's identity is determined by relationship to others in all respects. (   )

(3) Identities are generally classified into personal identity, relational identity and communal identity, all of which are corresponding to culture. (   )

(4) "I am a student of ×××University" indicates the communal identity. ( )

(5) Identity influences the ways of communication and is determined by the context. ( )

Activity 7

Classify the list of "who you are" you've written in Activity 5 into the three categories for personal, relational and communal identities.

Personal _____
Relational _____
Communal _____

It's difficult to construct a single, concise definition of **cultural identity** agreed on by everyone and that's why Ting-Toomy and Chung defined cultural identity as " the emotional significance that we attach to our sense of belonging or affiliation with the larger culture", which makes one feel the membership in a group in which all people share the same symbolic meanings, for example, filial piety to parents and ancestors as Chinese or independence and freedom as Americans.

Cultural identity or identity is related to one's nationality, geographic region, ethnicity, race or profession, which affect the communication styles, i.e. the ways to interact with people, such as Swiss-Germans and Americans tend to be more direct in communication as they are in low-context cultures while Chinese, Japanese and Koreans prefer indirect communication styles in most of cases. Within a particular culture, there are also varied communication preferences, for example, people from the northeast China tend to be more humorous with distinctive linguistic features as part of their identity.

Cultural identity represents one's entity and sense of belonging in cultural heritages and behaviors. For example, male Muslims wear beard and females have veils and long black dresses. Global celebrations of the Spring Festival in other countries in the recent decades indicate the increased acceptance of identity of Chinese culture beyond the geographic boundaries of the People's Republic of China.

Cultural identities entail varied aspects of life. **Racial identities** are associated with one's external physical traits such as skin colors, hair texture and eye shapes. As modern science has discovered very little generic variations among humans, it erodes the belief that people can be categorized by races, and "ethnic group" is recommended to describe any social group with more cultural traits, for example, African Americans, Chinese Americans, Anglo Americans or Hispanics. Collier holds that **ethnic identity** or **ethnicity** is derived from a sense of shared heritage, history, tradition, values, similar behaviors, geographical area of origin, and language. For example, many Americans usually view their ethnicities as a product of their ancestor's home of origin before immigrating to the U.S. Another example is that more than 98% of the Chinese population is Han people with the other 55 ethnicities taking the rest of 2%, who all share the same national identity as Chinese.

The majority of people associate their **national identities** with their countries where they were born, and national identity is normally become more apparent when people are away from their home country. When asked where they are from in the international context, response with the national identity is more often than not. For example, at the Olympic Games, the athletes are referred to in national identities. Samovar noticed that identity is changing over time, younger Europeans are adopting "transnational identities". For example, Anne (Ana) Hidalgo, the first woman to be elected Mayor of Paris, France was born in Spain, immigrated to France with her parents, and took French citizenship accordingly. When asked in an interview in 2014 if she felt Spanish or French, Ms. Hidalgo responded, " I feel European."

Some nations are a home of more than one cultural group, and one of the groups may exercises most power, whose culture is thus referred as the dominant culture as its members are more influential in economic, political and institutional organizations. This dominance leads to the construction of a "national character", as Allport held that "members of a nation, despite ethnic, racial, religious, or individual differences among them, do resemble one another in certain fundamental matters of belief and conduct, more than they resemble members of other nations." For example, the ethnicity of the Western European origins and the corresponding cultural heritages are regarded as the national character of the United States. The same is true of Singapore with Chinese culture as the national character. National identity therefore often plays a prominent role in overcoming divisions within a nation, for example, both the residents of the Korea feel like Koreans in international contexts and they jointly ran the Winter Olympics Games in 2018.

Most countries are divided in geographical regions with various cultural traits in ethnicity, language, accent, dialect, customs, food, dress, or historical or political legacies. For example, in Belgium, there are three official languages, i.e. Dutch, French and German spoken by Flemish, Walloon and German ethnic groups resembling the corresponding **regional identities**. Other examples of languages as regional identities are in the United States, Japan and China. Cuisines as well can be the signs of regional identities, for example, there are Eight Major Cuisines in China, each of which represents the corresponding regional cultures, of which the local people are proud.

Gender identity is a socially constructed concept that refers to how a particular culture differentiates masculine and feminine social roles, which is different from biological sex or sexual identity derived from birth. Gender identity influences one's appearance, such as hair or mustache, family roles and social expectations in career, for example, females as school teachers or nurses in some cultures. Language is influenced by gender identity as well. For example, in the Japanese language there are different words used by males and females for the same meaning.

Organizational identity is another source of identity in collectivist cultures more than in individual ones. For example, both in China and Japan, the group orientation is more than that of one's own interest, which one takes great pride as a member of the company. And the collective culture emphasizes identity through group membership with much hierarchy while individual culture orientates the individual identity with more egalitarianism.

Personal identities are those qualities that set one apart from other in his group, i.e. things that make one unique and influence how he/she sees himself or herself. Self-construal is used to denote how individuals view themselves in relation to others. People from individualistic cultures, such as in the US and the Western Europe, who are of high level of independent self-construal, tend to employ direct communication. Conversely people from collectivistic cultures, for example the Northeast Asians, are more likely to emphasize their group membership with indirect communication for harmonious relationships. With the development of the Internet and communication technologies, people have gained cyber and virtue identities with nicknames in QQ groups, Wechat, Meta (previously known as Facebook) and Twitter as well.

Test Your Reading 8

Decide whether the statements are True (T) or False (F).

(1) Cultural identity represents one's acceptance and belonging to a specific culture. (   )

(2) Regional identity can be demonstrated in terms of language and food but not clothes. (   )

(3) Gender identity determines one's language and communication styles in one's own cultural context. (   )

(4) An individual from the Democratic People's Republic of Korea and the one from the Republic of Korea share the same ethicality but different nationality. (   )

(5) Racial identities entail varied apparent physical traits as well as generic variations in humans. (   )

(6) A global citizen refers to someone who has the nationalities of all countries. (   )

(7) Expressions such as "our company" "our city" and "our class" let out more group identities than personal ones. (   )

(8) One owns many identities which functions together in a specific context. (   )

Activity 8

Recognize the culture identities in the following statement for someone in intercultural communication.

> "I am Chinese, and I am a teacher of the English language in a university. Most of my students are from Anhui Province."

B. What Are the Features of Identities?

One has more than one identity with the process of socialization through lifetime as **identity is dynamic and multiple**. For example, one is born as a loved baby of parents, a grandchild or a younger brother or sister of someone else. In this way, the newborn is related to people around him/her by biological or familial relationships. With socialization he/she gets more identities by dropping off some old ones and keeping some permanent ones unchanged. For example, he is a student when he goes to school, and at the same time he retains his identities as a son, a grandchild, a cousin. As one grows up, his/her identities change and he/she then has to adjust relationship to new identity in communication which is different from the previous ones. For example, a baby-girl will grow up into a student, and a wife and a mother, and she also learns to be a citizen socially at the same time. Professionally she might get employed as a teacher, or a manager, or a doctor, or a Prime Minister. One gets more identities as one grows up, having more contacts with others and learning more communication models.

In terms of communication, **identity is contextualized**, i.e. one's identity changes as contexts change because individuals have learned the desired way of communication in regard with the context and constantly adjust identities in relationship with others. For example, a male Chinese at home would be a son, a husband and a father. The same individual also is an employee, a Managing Director or an ambassador to the Great Britain. In different context one of his identities stands out with some others hidden while still others remain unchanged. For example, when a general manager of a Chinese motor company is negotiating with a British counterpart, his identity as a Chinese general manager is salient with the hidden identities as a husband and a father, and the identities of gender, nationality, ethnicity and race, etc. remain unchanged.

Activity 9

> Work with your peers and discuss "my life stories" that helped form your relational and cultural identities.

C. How Are Cultural Identities Acquired and Developed?

Identity development plays a critical role in the individual's psychological being, and it's one of responsibilities of any culture to assist its members in forming identities to ensure effective communication since identities help one know who he/she is, what his/her roles are and what expectations of him/her in communication. For example, Chinese children at home are trained to obey parents without arguing or speaking back. The role of students and teachers in Chinese classrooms are traditionally defined and followed, i. e. students are expected to listen to the teacher attentively without asking questions. Same in classrooms in the United States, American students are encouraged to interrupt lectures by asking questions at any time as culturally established norms.

Communication establishes Identities. Communication allows one to have human interactions and collect information about others. As wood said, "self is not innate but is acquired in the process of communication with others." The process of communication helps define who one is, where he/she belongs, and where his/her loyalty rests. For example, personal identities are established when one interacts with people who take care of him. Relational identities with parents, teachers, friends and colleagues are developed in family, at school or at work by daily life, school learning or cooperating for teamwork. Communal identities are constructed and reinforced as a family member, a member of class and school, an employee of a company, one of ethnical groups, a region and a country. For example the identity as a Tibetan or a Northeasterner in China and a Chinese, are evoked from the sense of cultural belonging by doing something specific at certain occasions, for example, dress, food or recreations or holiday celebrations.

Identity acquisition is one of functions that family entails. It's in the family that one gains its personal identity as a human being together with relational identities as a son or daughter of the parents, brothers or sisters, grandchild or cousins. It's also in the family that one reinforces his/her identities in communicating with others and develops the communication styles to his identities. Family is the first place that one develops communal identity with the sense of belonging, practicing treatment of in-groups and out-groups. For example, the Chinese saying that "follow the man you marry, be he a fool or a crook" indicates the inferior status of the wife in the family and identifies her as a follower.

Together with family, socialization helps construct one's identities, which is the process of internalizing the social and cultural norms of a society in relationship with others, which prepares oneself to be a socialized member of a specific culture. Socialization begins at home, continues in schools, spreading over life for one to learn what is accepted, or what is "normal" and "moral" so that one will live and survive. For example, the sayings that "have ears but no mouth" and "parents are always right" requires respects and obedience in relationship with elders.

Identities can also be ascribed or avowed based on whether they are obtained involuntarily or voluntarily. Identities such as racial identity, ethnical identity and sexual identity are ascribed as they were assigned at birth with no choice. But other identities such as a university student or a lawyer are avowed because they are what one chooses to have and work hard for. Some identities are both ascribed and avowed. For example, one is born with the Chinese nationality as ascribed but later has changed to another nationality by immigration as avowed.

Cultural identity is a social construction with the influence of culture, such as mainstream culture and the co-cultures. Each individual is affected by the mainstream culture at the same time belonging to other subcultures in terms of gender, age, education, profession or political affiliations, which defines his/her identities accordingly.

Case Study 2

What are the cultural identities of Li Yunkai?

> "My name is Li Yunkai from Guangzhou and I am a male student of English language in Beijing University. I am fluent in both Cantonese and Putonghua, and English will make me a better intercultural communicator."

This discourse displays identities of Li Yunkai in his name of his national identity, regional identity, gender identity, educational identity and his age identity as well. After all, his cultural identities can be a Chinese learner of English language from Guangdong, and his identities are established in the process of communicating with others.

As identities are established, maintained and modified through social interactions, they influence interactions through sharing expectations and motivating behaviors for what is appropriate or inappropriate in specific settings. A lack of clarity of "who I am" will lead to identity confusion and confused roles in one's life because individual identities influence and guide expectations about oneself and others, and help understand one's social roles and provide guidelines for interactions with others.

Test Your Reading 9

Decide whether the statements are True (T) or False (F).

(1) One's identities change as one grows, some remain fixed, some are lost and some are gained. (   )

(2) One's identity in relationship with others depends on the context in communication. (   )

(3) A university student speaks to his/her parents in the same way as he/she interacts with teachers. (   )

(4) An ABC, the American born Chinese, may be confused as being an American or a Chinese in socialization, especially as a teenager. (   )

(5) With ascribed identities, one would like to gain more avowed identities as result of self-realization. (   )

(6) Education and learning about foreign cultures help one reinforce his/her cultural identities for cultural confidence. (   )

D. How Do Cultural Identities Function in Intercultural Communication?

Cultural identity is created and recreated through communication. Aware of it or not, individuals display their cultural identities in interactions, and at the same time they collect information of identities of others, who are usually "strangers" in most intercultural cases. Identities are used to identify similarities and differences in behaviors, interpretations and norms. In order to communicate effectively, one has to know how to present himself on the basis of the information sent by others. And in the course of interactions, both parties observe and recognize cultural identities of others, adjusting one's own to the context, relationship and language for the best of communication. For example, Donald and Tony in the American movie *Green Book* are from different races, classes and professions with individual cultural identities. Their piano tour began with stereotypes and prejudice towards each other but ended up as intimate friends because they had learned, during the trip, to manage their relationship on similarities as human beings and respect the differences across races and classes. In other words, they had negotiated their individual identities to create the shared identities for the common goal.

Personal cultural identities help create the national image in globalization. Identities concerns how an individual accepts who he/she is while images refer to how an individual looks like in others' eyes. For example, an American born Chinese may feel like an American as a US citizen or a Chinese in the United States with Chinese cultural identity but he/she is seen as an Asian or Chinese by some Americans for images of Chinese people because of the Chinese cultural traits. Consequently personal identities are related to both individual images and collective cultural identities and images.

Same as identities, images are constructed in communication with others as well, and individual images help build up the cultural image of a group of people, for example, the national image, the ethical image or a regional image. In the process of socialization, there are moments or incidents at some point that one's sense of belonging moves from identities based on "I" to those based on "we", the shared identities, i.e. the cultural groups and main institutions of the culture, for example, religions, regions, genders, occupations and nations, etc. A good example is the national image of China constructed by the two Olympic Games in 2008 and 2022, in which individual Chinese athletes and the Chinese government and people exerted efforts to create a national image of progressive economy, prosperous society and friendly people.

Contrary to the belief and dire predictions made by some, globalization does not appear to be producing a cultural homogenized global society. Technologies and increased globalization have made understanding of identity an essential aspect in the study and practice of intercultural communication since globalization and multiculturalism have given rise to a revival of local cultural identities in different part of the world. It becomes common for people to acknowledge multiple identities due to globalized economy, immigration, ease of foreign travel and communication technologies, and intercultural marriage has brought about increased mixing of cultural identities, and recognition of "dual citizenships" in some countries have increased the community of intercultural transients, as Onwumechili refers to, "frequently move back and forth across cultural borders and must manage both cultural changes and identity renegotiations." How do you think of the cultural identities of Aileen Gu?

Intercultural communication has made identity and the corresponding behaviors more complex since what is taken appropriate in one culture may be regarded as impolite or even rude behaviors in another culture. For example, Japanese people greet each other with bows while most Westerners shake hands as greetings. Realizing diversities in communication behaviors, individuals have learned to adjust to context so as to respect cultural identities of others and keep one's own identities. For example, nowadays at business meetings for Americans with Japanese, both have adapted to slight bows with handshakings to show respect to others and keep one's own cultural identities.

Identities are developed in communication because differences from others in communication styles and norms from other cultures makes individuals be aware of his/her cultural traits for identities. Hall claims that culture hides much more than it reveals, and strangely enough, what it hides, it hides more effectively from its own participants. And it is in communication that one finds that the same intention or feeling, such as appreciation, gratitude or disagreements, can be expressed in varied words or by nonverbal behaviors, making one be aware of his own cultural identities. For example, when a Chinese is engaged in business overseas, the foreign language, exotic food, distinctive city layout or social customs etc. will facilitate him to be more conscious of his national identity as a Chinese and he is more likely to display the Chinese identity.

Cultural identity will be reinforced with motivation to learn more about one's own culture while knowing about others. With adequate knowledge of other cultures to communicate effectively across cultures, it is by comparison of the communication norms, styles and behaviors with others in intercultural communication that one not only learns more about cultures of others but also enables him/her to reflect more on his/her culture, which are usually taken for granted, thus cultural awareness is strengthened for ones' cultural identities as Hall believes that "the ultimate purpose of the study of culture is not so much the understanding of foreign culture as much as the light that study shed on one's own."

As identity is established through communication, a set of communicative behaviors appropriate for the identity are employed to each communication context, and communicating with others from other cultures may carry considerable potentials for creating anxiety, misunderstanding and conflicts across cultures as the communicators involved have varying expectations for identity display and communication styles. For example, the use of silence and eye contacts as nonverbal behaviors may imply contradictory interpretation across cultures, i. e. in most Asian, Latin American and African cultures, silence displays respect or agreement while for most European cultures, silence is a sign of refusal, dislike or no interest; and direct and frequent eye contacts indicate honesty and friendliness in conversations in the English-speaking cultures while avoidance of eye contact exhibits respect to power and authority in Asian, Africa and most of Latin American cultures.

Sense of cultural identity serves as the basis for cultural confidence for cultural interpretation and exchange. Knowledge about one's own culture together with the in-depth understanding on heritages of cultural values fosters confidence of one's own culture with the increased sense of cultural identity in communication across cultures. With the profound changes unseen in a century, it is the due obligations to interpret the history, values and worldviews, etc. in order to erase misunderstandings, stereotypes and prejudice between cultures.

In order to communicate effectively in intercultural interactions, one's avowed identity and communication style is expected to match the identity and communication style ascribed to him or her by the other party so that the potential tension and misunderstanding will be lessened. In other words, individuals have to consequently negotiate between what you call yourself and what other people are willing to call you. Therefore, effective intercultural communication is achieved when the participants find commonalities in ascribed and avowed identities. That is to say individuals have to know about the cultural norms of communication of others in addition to one's own for the middle ground, which requires flexibility and adaptation.

Activity 10

Answer the question by watching the video clip of the 8th Chinese Bridge

Chinese Proficiency Competition for Foreign Students at the link of http://bridge.chinese.cn/c18//214/214_9546_1.html.

> (1) What are the shared identities of the contestants at this competition?
> (2) What is ascribed and avowed identities of Shi Yu from Egypt at this competition?
> (3) Are there the individual cultural identities for each contestant in addition to the shared identity at the competition? What are they in general?

Figure 1.7　The Logo of the 8th Chinese Bridge Chinese Proficiency Competition for Foreign Students

As far as China is concerned, it has become popular for individuals and institutions to go abroad for development, which increases contacts across cultures. The Belt and Road Initiative and the successful control of Covid-19 in China have constructed the bright new image of China, which enhances the personal identity as Chinese in intercultural contacts. Nowadays China is more confident in initiating encounters with more nations in economy, education and culture, which makes it necessary for each individual to learn about the host cultures and more about Chinese culture, improving the Chinese identity and cultural confidence for a community of shared future of mankind.

Gone is the Chinese cultural image as "Sick Man of the East Asia" since the founding of the New China. And the People's Republic of China has now become the second economic entity in the world. With the splendid cultural heritages and development and innovations since the Open-door Policy, the

Chinese cultural image as a strong, prosperous, responsible nation has been forged in the international community. However there are still stereotypes and prejudice against China or some bias about Chinese culture, the government and its people for various reasons, among which is the traditional image of China due to lack of understanding of China.

As a Chinese in the 21st century with global mindset, it is one of the priorities to determine one's cultural identity both as a Chinese and an intercultural communicator. Each individual from China is more referred to as "the Chinese scholar" "the Chinese athlete" or "the Chinese student" and so forth, and personal aptitudes and competence will be associated with China as well. In this way, each Chinese is presenting the image of China, and the national identity as a Chinese is the most salient one regardless of the other personal identities such as ethnicities, regions, ages or genders.

The Chinese identity is also exhibited with the confidence in beliefs of the path, theory, system and culture of socialism with Chinese characteristics by fully understanding the Chinese history, cultural traditions in addition to love of China and the Communist Party of China (the CPC). In other words, the competence to tell the stories of China to the world in foreign languages in the intercultural context on the basis of world culture helps improve cooperation and development of the world with the Chinese wisdoms and strategies. Thus the Chinese identity functions with motivation, knowledge and skills in increasing intercultural interactions at interpersonal, institutional and international levels and an open and inclusive Chinese image striving for cooperation and progress of the world is constructed and maintained by each Chinese with his/her Chinese identity and by behaving appropriately and effectively in the corresponding contexts.

Test Your Reading 10

Decide whether the statements are True (T) or False (F).

(1) The image of Shandong people is that people from Shandong Province are straightforward, helpful and generous. (   )

(2) China has presented itself at the Opening Ceremony of Beijing Winter Olympic to the world with an image of a sunny, prosperous, open and hopeful

country with Chinese cultural confidence. (　　)

(3) What are considered appropriate conducts in one's own culture may be applied in intercultural communication as shared cultural similarities. (　　)

(4) New identities are negotiated with flexibility and adaptation in intercultural communication on the basis of one's confidence on his culture. (　　)

(5) For any Chinese in intercultural communication, being Chinese goes first both as national identity or image before others as cultural recognition. (　　)

V. Extended Reading

President Xi Jinping on a Community of Shared Future for Mankind
(Excerpted from his speech at the UN headquarters on 18th January, 2017)

Mankind is in an era of major development as well as profound transformation and changes. The trend toward multi-polarity and economic globalization is surging. IT application in social development and cultural diversity are making continued progress. A new round of scientific and industrial revolution is in the making. Interconnection and interdependence between countries are crucial for human survival. The forces for peace far outweigh factors causing war, and the trend of our times toward peace, development, cooperation and win-win outcomes has gained stronger momentum.

On the other hand, mankind is also in an era of numerous challenges and increasing risks. Global growth is sluggish, the impact of the financial crisis lingers on and the development gap is widening. Armed conflicts occur from time to time, Cold War mentality and power politics still exist and non-conventional security threats, particularly terrorism, refugee crisis, major communicable diseases and climate change, are spreading.

Pass on the torch of peace from generation to generation, sustain development and make civilization flourish: this is what people of all countries long for; it is also the responsibility statesmen of our generation ought to shoulder. And China's proposition is: build a community of shared future for mankind and achieve shared and win-win development.

We should build an open and inclusive world through exchanges and mutual learning. Delicious soup is made by combining different ingredients. Diversity of human civilizations not only defines our world, but also drives progress of mankind. There are more than 200 countries and regions, over 2,500 ethnic groups and multiple religions in our world. Different histories, national conditions, ethnic groups and customs give birth to different civilizations and make the world a colorful one. There is no such thing as a superior or inferior civilization, and civilizations are different only in identity and location. Diversity of civilizations should not be a source of global conflict; rather, it should be an engine driving the advance of human civilizations.

Every civilization, with its own appeal and root, is a human treasure. Diverse civilizations should draw on each other to achieve common progress. We should make exchanges among civilizations a source of inspiration for advancing human society and a bond that keeps the world in peace.

The ancient Chinese believed that "one should be good at finding the laws of things and solving problems". Building a community of shared future is an exciting goal, and it requires efforts from generation after generation. China is ready to work with all the other UN member states as well as international organizations and agencies to advance the great cause of building a community of shared future for mankind.

Post-class Tasks

Self-test Tasks

1. Answer the questions in your own words.

(1) What is intercultural communication? What are the key points involved in it?

(2) How does one benefit by taking the course of intercultural

communication?

(3) How do you put the suggestions by Samovar in your life to improve intercultural communication awareness?

2. Decide whether the statements are True (T) or False (F).

(1) Identity is the self-conception or self-image derived from one's family, nationality, ethnicity, gender or cultural group. In short, it is the answer to "who I am". (   )

(2) All the identities that one owns are ascribed at birth without choice by oneself. (   )

(3) Cultural identity is the sense of belongings with shared beliefs, values, social norms and specific actions or behaviors, such as celebrating festivals with common practice. (   ).

(4) One acquires his/her identity first at home, carrying them all of the old ones when gaining new ones. (   )

(5) Identities are classified into personal, relational and communal ones. (   )

(6) Identities are multiple, dynamic and contextualized. (   )

3. Give your opinions on the following questions.

(1) When you communicate with someone from a Swiss University, what are the identities of yours that stand out, what are the hidden ones and what remain unchanged?

(2) How do you identify yourself in English language learning in China? What is your cultural identity in intercultural communication?

Group Work

1. Share in the group what you found **different** in life when you came to university as freshmen.

2. As a Chinese student, tell about one of your intercultural communication experiences.

3. Interview at least 3 international students on campus by asking "who are

you?" and make notes of the answers to see how the identities are displayed by negotiating "what you call yourself and what other people are willing to call you."

Telling China's Stories

Heroes are regarded as part of culture that influences its people in behaviors and values and there have been many heroes in the history of China either in life or in legends. Draft an email telling one of your cyber friends about a Chinese hero that you think will impress him/her.

My Learning Reflection

1. What have I learned about Chinese cultures/ myself?

2. What have I learned about other cultures?

3. What impressed me most in this chapter?

4. What still confuses me?

Chapter 2　Communication and Culture

> **Learning Objectives**
>
> - To identify definitions, elements, functions and characteristics of communication and culture respectively;
> - To analyze cultural conflicts with concepts of culture and communication on the basis of the characteristics of high/low-context communication by E. T. Hall;
> - To recognize communication styles on the basis of cultural diversities.
>
> **Pre-class Tasks**
>
> - Read the textbook and watch the concerned clips in *xuexitong* (学习通).

I. Lead-in Tasks

Activity 1

Work in groups to answer the questions.

(1) Do you have to communicate with others to survive? If yes, why? If not, why?

(2) What is the most important factor when you communicate?

(3) What are the general features of your communication? For example, are you more active or passive? Do you prefer direct or indirect communication?

II. Understanding Communication

Before going to anything about communication, there is one question that one has to think about, i.e. why do humans need to communicate every day? Or can anyone survive without communication?

A. Why Do People Have to Communicate with Each Other?

The hierarchy of needs proposed by Abraham H. Maslow, an American psychologist (1908—1970), states that human beings are motivated by a series of needs, which is categorized into physiological needs, safety, love and belonging, esteem, self-actualization, as shown in the pyramid, which may be helpful in understanding functions of communication (Figure 2.1).

Figure 2.1 Theory of Hierarchical Needs by Maslow

Activity 2

Table 2.1 is an example of communication events by a student. Read it carefully to find out the components involved in communication, and make a list of your communication events of yesterday to find out what is most influential in communication (Table 2.2).

Table 2.1 Examples of Communication of a College Student

Participants	Locations	Means	Purposes	Feedback
Shop attendants	Shops near the dormitory	Oral, face to face	Purchasing	Effective
Classmates	On campus/in the classroom or dormitories	Wechat, QQ, phones, Face to face	Asking for help	No response
The Counselor	On campus/in the office, classroom	Wechat, QQ, phones, Face to face	Being asked to attend a meeting	Unwillingly obeyed
Parents	Anywhere	Phone/Wechat	Persuading your parents	Agreement/ disagreement
Strangers	At the English Competition Contest	Face to face	Collecting information	Friendly or unfriendly
Students in other countries	Facebook, Virtual exchanges	Computers, Smart phones	Knowledge about others or cultures	More curious, Interested and tolerable

Table 2.2 Your Communication Events of Yesterday

With whom	Where	How	Why	Results
			purchasing	Effective
Classmates		Wechat		No response
The Counselor	Office	Wechat		
Parents			Persuading yourparents	
Strangers		Face to face	Collecting information	

The tables above show that people communicate with purposes. People are basically social creatures and are motivated to communicate, therefore communication is the basic approach that satisfies a great deal of needs in life. In *Communication between Cultures*, Samovar sums up the functions of communication as follow:

Communication helps fulfill interpersonal needs;
Communication assists with personal perception;
Communication establishes cultural and personal identities;

Communication has persuasive qualities.

The tables also indicate that communication involves others with purposes and means of communication, and most impressively, communication brings about feedback in whatever form, i.e. positive, negative or silence.

Maslow's hierarchy of needs indicates that when lower needs are satisfied, more needs are to be copied with, and all the needs in the pyramid have to be fulfilled with help of communication. In other words, people need to communicate same as they need air, water and food to live by listening and speaking, and they also have to communicate in order to have a better life when they want to share their ideas, feelings or their control over others by writing and speaking. They also communicate for self-realization by learning and researching. And at the same time, they benefit from human cultural resources and personal advice by reading books, watching videos and films, and talking with others. In one word, people cannot live without communication, and communication is the basic need of humans in whatever forms.

B. How Does Communication Function as a Process?

In view of what is discussed above, human communication is defined by Samovar as a dynamic process in which people attempt to share their thoughts with other people by use of symbols in particular settings. In other words, communication is **the act or process** of conveying intended meanings from one entity or group to another through the use of the mutually understood signs and semiotic rules. As this act goes on, it involves changes at any moment as participants are cultural animals. Figure 2.2 illustrates the elements of communication.

To understand communication better, one has to know about **the elements of communication** and the process involved in it. The models of communication show that communication apparently starts when a message is sent through a channel to another end with a response going back to the initial point as a process, in which the message is encoded and decoded then by the receiver who will encode another message in turn as a feedback to the Sender, as shown in the following:

The Sender (a speaker or a writer) encodes a message, which he sends to the Receiver (a listener or a reader) via a channel (face to face, by phone, mails, videos, signs, gestures, dressing, space, etc.).

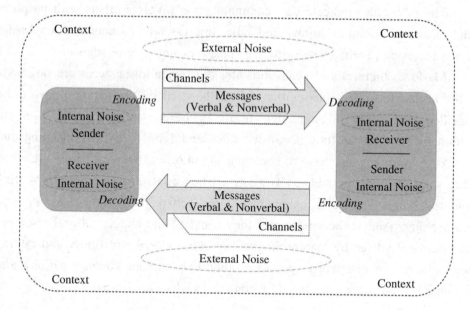

Figure 2.2 Elements of an Interactive Communication

The Receiver, when getting the message, will immediately decode the message and encode the reply to respond, which is also known as "feedback", thus becoming the Sender in the communication.

This process may go on for many "rounds" as the communication goes on, and the Sender and Receiver exchange their roles respectively. In addition to the roles of Sender and Receiver, there are also invisible influential elements in the process which consist of an effective communication, such as the context, participants, messages, channels, noise and feedback.

Context is the interrelated conditions of communication, including physical settings, such as locations, time, light, temperature, distance, and seating arrangements. In other words, the location is where the communication takes place, such as in the classrooms, at shops, or at home, etc. It also contains the historical episode, the background of communication, which is referred to as the cultural context. The psychological states of the participants are part of the context which is relevant to culture in the forms of shared beliefs, values, symbols and behaviors.

Participants are those who are involved in the communication, i.e. the

Sender and Receiver of the message communicated. The Sender forms the messages and attempts to communicate them through verbal and/or non-verbal symbols and the Receiver processes the message received and reacts to them both verbally and/or nonverbally.

Each individual is a product of his/her experience, feelings, ideas, moods, occupation, religion and so forth. As a result, the meaning sent and the meaning received in communication may not be exactly the same. Three variables affecting the participants are relationship, gender and culture, which determine the "meaning of the message". To detect the meaning of what is said, questions are to be asked: what is the relationship of the communicators? What is the cultural background of the interaction? What is the cultural identity of people involved, such as genders, ages or status?

Messages are the words transmitted from one to another, and the meaning is the pure idea and feelings that exist in a person's mind representing meanings. **Symbols** are the words, sounds, and actions that communicate meanings. Both the route travelled by the message and the means of transportation are referred to as **Channels** of communication, for example, face to face, in digital, by phone, or in writing, etc. **Encoding** is the process of transforming ideas and feelings into symbols and organizing them, and **decoding** is the process of transforming messages back into ideas and feelings. It has to be noted that conflicting meanings are created when the verbal symbols are contradicted by the nonverbal cues.

Noise is any stimulus that interferes the communication. Either external noise or internal ones to the participants will interfere with the sharing of meaning. External noise is related to the physical surroundings, i. e. the temperature, light, space, settings or seating of the venue that draws the attention of the participants away from the intended meaning while internal noise is concerned with the psychological and emotional sphere of the participants containing thoughts and feelings that interfere with the communication process. For example, one of them is pleased while the other is upset, or they are in a crowded clinic. In addition, there are semantic noises as well, which are unintended meanings aroused by certain verbal symbols that can inhibit the accuracy of decoding, e. g. different words for the same thing to both or different meaning by the same word to one of them.

Feedback is the verbal and/or nonverbal responses, which serve as messages in the next round of communication. Suppose how the communication ends up if there is no reply from the Receiver at the first round. Will it go on as the Sender expects? Or does it mean there is no "feedback"? Or is there "response" even though the receiver does not reply the Sender with a message?

Test Your Reading 1

Decide whether the statements are True (T) or False (F).

(1) Communication is a product rather than a process for exchanging ideas. (　)

(2) The context partly decides the meaning of the message exchanged as it is closely related to the relationship of the communicators. (　)

(3) The roles of the Sender and Receiver are fixed in a specific round of communication but keep exchanging during the on-going rounds. (　)

(4) Being sick is one of examples of exterior noise in communication. (　)

(5) No response to a message is usually taken as a negative feedback in communication which will end the communication. (　)

Activity 3

Observe a conversation in a movie or a natural conversation in life to identify the roles of communicators, the elements of communication and signal of ending by drawing the process of the conversation and counting the rounds (Table 2.3).

Table 2.3　The Observation List of Conversations

Participants	Location	Topics	Roles	Channels	Feedback	Noise
Communicator 1						
Communicator 2						
Communicator 3						
Communicator 4						

C. What Are the Characteristics of Communication?

Since communication is a series of on-going activities which are in continuous interactions with one another in the cultural, physical and emotional context, it bears the features in that it is dynamic, contextual, irreversible, systematic, meaning-loaded, symbolic, self-reflective, and most importantly, it has a consequence.

Human communication is a **dynamic** process because it involves a host of variables like seeing, listening, speaking, smiling, touching, guessing the meanings of what is said and anticipating what will happen next. Understandably, it's much more easier for people with more similarities of the same culture to communicate than those from different countries as culture sets the background of the context of the communication, therefore communication is also **contextualized**. The context concerning the number of people involved, the location and occasion, time, etc. helps determine the words and actions that people generate and the meanings given to the symbols received. For example, "Good morning!" in different tones or stress signifies relationship to a friend, a stranger, one's boss or a new acquaintance.

Communication is **symbolic** because symbols stand for something else. Symbols in interaction involves language as a major one together with those as postures, gestures, facial expressions, tones and stress, etc. which constitute a meaning-loaded system. However, the participants may have different interpretations of these symbols due to cultural and personal experiences. As Anderson stated, "Language symbols are no more consisting or precise than the experience, values, and belief system of the people using them." Although all cultures use language as symbols and the language used is discretionary and subjective, the meaning assigned to the symbols depends on who uses it for what purposes.

Communication is **irrevocable** as illustrated by a Chinese proverb to the point, "A harsh word dropped from the tongue cannot be brought back by a coach of six horses." There is no "delete" key in communication, and what is said has produced an effect on the communication even though apology may be extended for what is said a second ago.

Communication is **self-reflective** because human beings are able to think about oneself in relationship with others and with the world in reflection of the present, past and future. Samovar thinks that in communication, the ability of reflectiveness enables one to be both the participant and observer at the same time so that one can watch, evaluate and alter his performance. But reflection in intercultural communication varies across cultures with the Western tending to focus on "self" and the group-oriented ones on " others".

Communication brings about a **consequence** as people communicate with purposes to fulfill their needs. Intentionally or unintentionally, the messages communicated produce changes in people, leaving an effect on someone else and modify the behaviors of the Sender and Receiver. These changes can be overt, convert, unconscious or biological as shown in Figure 2.3.

```
1 -------------------25 ---------------50 ---------------------75 ----------------100
      overt              convert            unconscious           biological
```
Figure 2.3 Communication Responses (Samovar, 2017)

D. Does Communication Always Work?

Communication is imperative and indispensable that sometimes it's assumed that communications is omnipotent. However, communication is so complex that there are **some misconceptions** as Samovar summarized in the following.

"All of problems can be solved through communication." History and practice has taught humans that it is not true at all times between nations or countries; otherwise there had not been the world wars or regional conflicts. It is same as the interpersonal relationships, as between couples, among friends or family members. Misunderstanding and conflicts are part of life as Wood stated, "Not all societies think it wise or useful to communicate about relationships or to talk extensively about feelings. Just as interpersonal communication has many strength and values, it also has limits and its effectiveness is shaped by cultural contexts."

"The message one sends is the message received." In any communication, "the thoughts" or "the intended meanings" constitute the message that a sender attempts to convey to the receiver, but how the receiver would perceive the meaning of the message sometimes remains problematic as "the meaning" depends on the cultural context together with the experience of the people involved. And it will become even more problematic in intercultural communication when it may involve in different "meanings" in terms of the sender or receiver, thus it requires clarification, negotiation and confirmation in the process.

"Some people are born effective communicators." It is true that some people seem to possess a facility and personality as a successful communicator who feels comfortable with people around, skillful at public speeches and good at persuading others. But what is also true is that every individual can develop the basic skills as an equally effective communicator by learning to comprise, showing empathy and listening intently.

Test Your Reading 2

Decide whether the statements are True (T) or False (F).

(1) As long as we use the same language, we will mean the same thing by the same words. (   )

(2) For better communication one may focus more on speaking than listening to others. (   )

(3) Contextualization in communication means the meaning of messages depends on where and how it is said, who said it and to whom it is said. (   )

(4) In group cultures people would reflect more on the others than themselves in communication. (   )

(5) As long as we try hard enough to communicate, problems will be solved. (   )

III. Understanding Culture

Activity 4

Try to answer the questions by studying the pictures (Figure 2.4).

(1) What do you mean when you speak of "cultural differences"?

(2) Does culture mean the same in "tea culture" "campus culture" or "the Chinese culture"?

Figure 2.4 Various Cultures

A. What Is Culture?

Globalization and technology have brought about more contact between people from different cultures and "culture" has been mentioned more often at many occasions, having people look more into it than ever before.

Culture is so familiar that people use it in many meanings. For example, one is "cultured" if he can read and write, meaning literacy; and someone who is artistically talent in Chinese painting and calligraphy is also depicted as "well-cultured". With the increasing Confucius Institutes abroad, Chinese culture becomes popular along with "Chinese tea culture" and "Chinese liquor culture" (Chinese Baijiu Culture) frequently mentioned as part of the Chinese culture. Besides, "corporate culture" "campus culture" "local culture" or "pop culture" is discussed at high frequency. In learning a foreign language, one is often advised to learn more about culture of the target language, and the expressions like "American culture" "German culture" or "Russian culture" sounds so familiar that one seldom ponders what culture is.

Apparently the meanings of "culture" in the above examples are different in specifying dimensions in context, but they share something in common. Scholars in anthropology, linguistics, literature, philosophy and history have been trying to define culture from diverse perspectives in various ways and there are over 250 definitions of culture, and some of the concepts and definitions are as follows:

E. T. Hall holds that "Culture is man's medium; there is not one aspect of human life that is not touched and altered by culture. This means personality, how people express themselves, including shows of emotion, the way they think, how they move, how problems are solved, how their cities are planned and laid out, how transportation systems function and are organized, as well as how economic and government systems are put together and function."

Clyde Kluckhohn once stated, "By 'culture', anthropology means the total life way of a people, the social legacy the individual acquires from his group. Or culture can be regarded as that part of the environment that is the creation of man."

The dimensions above cover some aspects of culture, focusing on materials, institutions and values, but more on the visible aspects that are apparent and unique to some specific cultures (Figure 2.5). And the most accepted definition of culture in general is the total life way of a people, which consists of what the people have, what they do and what they think about.

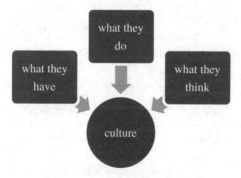

Figure 2.5 Elements of Culture

To understand more about culture, one may look into more details of culture from the following perspectives.

In terms of "what they have", it refers to the material culture of both the spiritual and physical ones. The achievements of education, history, geography, intuitions, literature, arts, music, etc., are referred to as high culture, or big "C" (Culture). The physical ones like architectures, gardens, animals and plants, the way of life are referred to as small "c" (culture), which entails the dress, food, holidays and etc.

Activity 5

Work in groups to add more in the table what you know about some of big

"C" or small "c" of the following countries to find out what knowledge of a specific culture plays an essential part in intercultural communication (Table 2.4, 2.5).

Table 2.4 Examples of Culture of Big "C"

	China	France	Japan
Education	Imperial Examination system		
History		The Great French Revolution	
Institutions	System of People's Congress	Democratic Republicanism	Constitutional Monarchy
Geography	The Great Wall, the Huangshan Mt.		Mount Fuji
Literature	The four masterpieces	*Les Miserables* *The Red And The Black*	
Arts	Calligraphy, Beijing Opera	Paintings & sculptures	Ukiyoe (浮世绘)
Music	Chinese Folk Music		

Table 2.5 Examples of Culture of Small "c"

	China	Korean	the USA
Dress	Cheongsam (旗袍) Chinese tunic suits (中山装)	Hanbok (韩服)	
Food	Hot Pot, Beijing Roasted Duck	Kimchi (泡菜) Korean barbecue	Hamburg Hotdogs
Holidays	the Spring Festival the Qingming Festival the Dragon Boat Festival the Mid-Autumn Festival	Lunar New Year Hansik	Christmas Thanksgiving Day Halloween Valentine's Day
Architecture	the Forbidden City the Summer Palace Suzhou Lion Grove		
Plants & Animals			
Customs			Tipping

In terms of "what they do", it refers to the institutional culture which concerns the ways of how they manage their life, educate their offsprings, settle disputes and communicate with others. For example, in China, the National People's Congress (NPC) and the Chinese People's Political Consultative Conference (CPPCC) are the fundamental political system while the United Kingdom owns the Houses of Commons and the House of Lords, and the United States has the House of Representative and House of Senate. "What they do" in a certain culture tells its people the rules and norms they follow when they handle their life like education, marriage, business and so forth at the national, provincial, municipal or local level. There are other ways that people handle their life in family and among friends and relatives as well, which are part of the ways of life in personal relationship. For example, how are children raised and how are the old treated? Who will pay for the wedding expenses? How do people deal with the critical patients or the dead? Answers to these questions vary greatly in each culture in spite of some similarities.

Activity 6

Work in groups to find out the similarities and differences among the countries (Table 2.6).

In terms of "what they think", it is related to the most important part of culture, i.e. the values, which are known as the core of culture. Values of a culture are the essential parts, which consist of worldviews, beliefs, perceptions and attitudes of the people in the culture. Values determine how people think of the world and the gods, what people believe to be true and right, and how they should live in relation to nature, human, etc. Among all of these, what people think as true serves as the basis of culture, directing what people do and have as their culture. Usually what people have in a culture is seen from language, dress, food, holidays, customs and etiquette, which is known as the visible culture. But the invisible culture is where values rest and result in the visible ones, that is, what people think tells what they do and what they have in life therefore.

Table 2.6 Examples of Institutional Cultures

	China	German	Australia
Education	School starts at 7 years old, with 6 years in primary school, 3 years in junior school as 9-year compulsory education and 3 years in senior school before the National College Entrance Examination.	12 years of compulsory education is implemented, and the high school level is divided into two directions, i. e. vocational and higher education. As a federal country, the education system is complex with each state has its set of education with the 12-year compulsory education.	
Judiciary	The Chinese judiciary includes civil, administrative and criminal systems with the Supreme Court, the provincial courts and local courts. The people's mediation system is a characteristic the Chinese judicial system		
Economy	The Chinese economic system at the present stage is a socialist market economic one, which is characterized by public ownership as the main body and the development of various ownerships	Mixed market economy with the private-owned enterprises as the main body.	

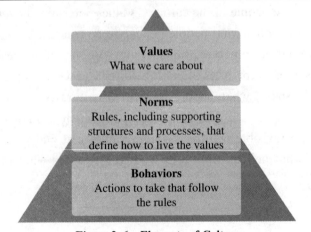

Figure 2.6 Elements of Culture

People are culture animals and at the same time each individual is unique as a result of the personal experiences, family and educational background, social contacts with others or critical events in life, therefore he/she shares similarities of human nature, national culture, regional culture, ethnical culture, gender culture on one hand, and owns his/her personalities at the same time, distinguishing him/her from others, as shown in the graph.

Activity 7

Identify your cultures.

> The following graph shows how culture affects individuals. Take yourself as an example for your own cultural stories to identify the cultures you are affected by. Your writing may include but is not limited to where you were born and studied, who brought you up, what proverbs you learned in life, what impressed you critically in your experience, what books you have read, what you are told constantly to do or not to do, or why you keep some hobbies or habits, etc., Then find out what is specific that makes you different from others in corresponding context, such as when studying abroad, applying for a job, or acting as a daughter / son at home, etc.
>
>
>
> Figure 2.7 How Culture Affects Individuals

In consideration of culture and communication, the definition advanced by Triandis can be referred for consideration, which states that "Culture is a set of human-made objective and subjective elements that in the past have increased the probability of survival and resulted in satisfaction for the participation in an ecological niche, and thus became shared among those who could communicate with each other because they had a common language and they lived in the same time and place."

Test Your Reading 3

Decide whether the statements are True (T) or False (F).

(1) Culture is the total way of life for some people, which they think normal and right. (   )

(2) Values are what people think right in a culture and can be observed by what they do and say. (   )

(3) To dress in red for good luck is an example of what Chinese people believe. (   )

(4) The Great Wall, the Terra-Cotta Warriors in Xi'an and the wall paintings in the Mogao Caves are what the Chinese people have as culture. (   )

(5) It is the universally accepted cultural value that "Follow her father before she marries; follow her husband after she marries and follow her son after her husband dies". (   )

B. What Are the Characteristics of Culture in General?

Culture tells its group members what to do, how to handle the problems and conflicts, and what their goals are in lives so that the needs of its members are satisfied even though their ways are different. In this sense, they therefore share some features in common.

To be an effective intercultural communicator, one has to look into a series of characteristics that all cultures have in common for the following reasons. First, learning about these characteristics help appreciation of importance and influences of culture on human behaviors, i.e. understanding why people do in this way rather than the other. Then, these shared characteristics of all cultures facilitate to sense the strong connection between culture and communication as "culture is communication", so as to understand how culture affects the way that people behave in culture, or in other words, from communication one learns about the culture of the communicator. At last, by looking into the features of culture, one is given the opportunity to think about his/her own culture, which is usually taken for granted as Hall said, "... my friends and colleagues from foreign culture taught me so much about my own culture."

Culture is shared. Nolan holds that "Culture is a group of worldview, the way of organizing the world that a particular society has created over time. This framework or web of meaning allows the members of that society to make sense of themselves, their world, and their experiences in the world." This process is a shared set of ideas, values, perceptions, and standards of behaviors, which make people in the culture to understand each other by predicting how others are likely to behave in a given context, and knowing how to react accordingly in the "normal" way. For example, when receiving a visitor in China, either at work or at home, it is courteous to treat him/her with a cup of tea even though the offer is usually declined definitely.

Activity 8

> Make a list of some shared beliefs or behaviors as Chinese people, and the longer the list, the better. You may start with what people do on holidays, for example, to warship family ancestors during the Spring Festival; or what your mother constantly tells you to do or not to do, for example, cold food is bad for health; or what is believed and practiced as normal, for example, the elders should be treated with respect and care. Or what are the traditions in your family or at your hometown to do something, for example, to celebrate the Spring Festival, or to have a wedding ceremony? etc.

Culture is transmitted from generation to generation. Culture is shared in the form of materials and ways of life guided by a set of values and beliefs because it has been passed on for generations. For a culture to endure, it is vital and prominent to share its main messages and elements among its present generation, making sure it is taught, practiced and delivered to the future generations so that the genes of the culture will survive. For any culture, this process is a kind of cultural inheritance, and the heritage consists of the major beliefs and behaviors that may have evolved long before each new generation, thus our culture, said by Matsumoto and Hwang, determines what it means to be a husband or wife, child, work colleague, acquaintance, or even a stranger.

Culture is transmitted both in conscious learning at school and unconscious acquisition at home by means of communication. For example, when a baby learns to wave a "good-bye", to use chopsticks, or to experience *zhuazhou* (抓周), and the essential cultural values continue to be reinforced as they share holidays with their family members. Just as Samovar believes, so strong is the need for a culture to bind each generation to past and future generations that it is often asserted that a fracture in the transmission process would continue to a culture's extinction. Moreover, communication is the basic means that transmits culture from the past to the future, so does from one place to another.

Culture is based on symbols. Communication is essential in transmission of culture and symbols are the means of communication. Language is one of the most important symbols both in writing and speaking to symbolize objects and thoughts, allowing people to package, store and transmit them, therefore to learn a language is one of the ways to enter the corresponding culture. In addition to language, a flag, a sign, a color, plants and animals, food, dress, statues, religious icons, gestures or postures are culturally-loaded symbols. The capacity of humans to think symbolically and express those symbols allows culture to be transmitted from generation to generation. For example, the color of red is the favorite one for the Chinese people, thus it is named "Chinese red", and the same is true of the Irish green to the people of the Republic of Ireland, which was originated by St. Patrick from the color of clovers, and has been one of three colors, green, white and orange, of the Irish flag.

Activity 9

> It's accepted that Chinese characters, calligraphy, silk, tea, the Great Wall, Terra-Cotta Warriors, Chinese medicine, etc. are the traditional Chinese cultural symbols. "高铁、共享单车、电子支付、快递" are regarded as the new symbols of China. Would you translate the Chinese terms into English?

Culture is learned. Culture is not innate or born with, instead, it is transmitted. Culture is learned when one grows up as part of his socialization who internalizes the shared and symbolized thoughts and actions as direct implication of communication.

Culture is learned in many ways that people are not aware of. A baby is born with no cultural elements, but the way he is delivered, taken care of and fed are decided by the family he/she is born into; the way he is talked to, the sound and actions interacted with him/her are culture-loaded. He/she learns to greet people with a bow, a kiss, a touch of nose, a hug or a smile as unconscious learning of culture, which he/she internalizes by practicing habitually and takes with him/her all life as part of his/her culture. As one grows up, his/her parents, grandparents and people in the culture teach him/her how to survive by taking care of him/her, teaching him/her knowledge and skills to cope with environments, to communicate with the people, and most importantly, influence his/her ways to see the world, to settle disputes and think and express himself/herself appropriately and acceptably in the culture. In a word, one learns how to satisfy his/her needs in every way unique to the culture.

Case Study 1

Study the following to find out what element of culture is taught in the following contexts?

(1) A Chinese child is told to begin eating after the oldest one has begun.

(2) An American boy was reminded to get in the elevator after ladies.

(3) An Arabian father reads the Kohan to his son and daughter.

(4) An Indian child lives in a home where the women eat after the men.

(5) Chinese children help preparation of the Spring Festival.

(6) A Japanese girl attends tea ceremony classes.

(7) When a child finds money on the playground, his parents ask him to return to the Last and Found.

(8) A child was told to finish the food he/she ordered.

> (9) A Chinese child is educated to give out his favorite toy to the visiting peer.
> (10) Children prepare birthday presents to Mum with the help of Dad.

Of all the contexts, parents, care-takers or the family members are teaching some aspects of their culture either in words or by behaviors. Interestingly enough, some of cultures are taught consciously, and most of them are transmitted unconsciously. Consequently, it's in the cultural context that children acquire the values and practice the norms. The aspects of culture are taught as follows: (1) Respect for the old; (2) "Ladies first"; (3) Worship of the God; (4) Gender roles; (5) Traditions; (6) Patience, self-discipline and ritual; (7) Honesty; (8) Responsibility of taking the consequences of decision; (9) Maintaining face for harmonious relationship; (10) Love and appreciation.

And there are more objects and behaviors that teach one of his/her culture. A baby is a silent observer and an active participants in the culture as everything around makes up a cultural context, everyone interacted is a culture teacher, and the ways that people live, work and play serve as teaching instruction. For example, dining at a round table for the Chinese, five prays a day for the Muslim, wine for the French, gardens for the Japanese, totems for the African and symphonies for the German are all lessons that share, transmit and restore culture heritance.

The ways that one learns his/her own culture are various. Informal learning usually takes place in life through interactions, observation and imitation. For example, babies in some cultures learn about kissing when being kissed by parents; worshiping and praying by going with parents to temples or churches, shaking hands, bowing to each other or hugging and air kissing as greetings. More culture learning takes place in social institutions as formal teaching. When a child goes to school, he/she is more exposed to the home culture by learning language, history and other courses accumulated as culture inheritance. The native language or the official language teaches him/her the thinking patterns, values, beliefs, perceptions and attitudes more than the meaning of the words, rules of grammar and the rhetorical devices. They also learn about the history of culture through folktales, legends and myths so that cultural identity is reaffirmed and the cultural values are reproduced for further transmission.

Activity 10

> Find out the values, language and history of the Chinese culture that you have learned by listing the courses that you took in primary, junior and high school and in college.

In addition to formal teaching, a child learns about his/her culture through proverbs about worldviews and values to shape his/her attitudes toward life and death, gods and people, work and leisure so as to evaluate as to what is good or bad, ugly or beautiful, right or wrong, true or false, etc. For example, in Chinese culture, red color is the symbol of happiness and a sign of good luck, therefore a wedding ceremony is expected to be highlighted with red color.

Activity 11

What values are transmitted in these proverbs?

> (1) Time is money.
> (2) God helps those who help themselves.
> (3) A man's home is his castle.
> (4) East and west, home is the best.
> (5) Don't cry over the spilt milk.
> (6) 养儿防老。
> (7) 人要脸,树要皮。
> (8) 不孝有三,无后为大。
> (9) 一个兄弟三个帮。
> (10) 水滴石穿。

The art of a specific culture is both the method of passing on culture and a reflection of that culture because people throughout the world feel "a strong historical, emotional and spiritual attachment" to their art forms as its cultural identity and heritages, therefore visiting a national or local museum is an effective and direct way to learn about a culture and its history. The statues of

Greek, the paintings by Leonardo DaVinci, the precious relics discovered in the Sanxingdui Cultural Ruins, including gold, bronze and jade articles, pottery and many other excavated artifacts, tell stories of culture, history, the way of life and the values of its people.

Art is a vital conduit of the important message of any culture. For example, India has had an artistic tradition for religious purposes by employing gods and goddesses to fuse spiritual messages with its varied aspects of culture; the Islamic art with its emphasis on shape, form, design style and calligraphy instead of people, landscapes or other representation of reality, is unique in expressing its values in contrast to Catholic tradition by wide use of Christ, the Virgin Mary and the saints. The Chinese art is believed to represent Buddhist and Taoist concerns with the mind in meditation, with the relative insignificance of human striving in the great cosmos, and with the beauty of nature.

Culture is shared through art, and the same is true of media. The types and formats of media are far more numerous, such as traditional media like newspapers and magazines, broadcasting, television and movies. Thanks to the Internet, new forms of media like Wechat, Meta (formerly known as Facebook), YouTube and blogs or Vlogs and Tik Tok represent the culture in the form of language, music, dress and thinking patterns and values. For example, *Old Friends*, *Games of Thrones*, *Downton Abbey* and *The Crown* tell stories of American and British society and culture. With advanced communication technology, different cultures are spread worldwide, facilitating people to know more about one's own culture by learning about cultures of the others from advertisements on television, TV series, movies, and streams on Internet.

Culture is dynamic. Culture is subject to change as it does not exist in a vacuum and is constantly affected by overt and covert factors in the interaction with other cultures. These changes can be external and compulsive such as invasions or wars. For example, the Japanese culture is seen in the regions where was once occupied by Japanese troops during World War II. And the increasing contacts with other cultures due to globalization and technology result in more changes in culture even though the changes are superficial and slow. The superficial ones are usually related to dress, food or entertainments. For example, cheongsams (*qipao*, 旗袍) as daily clothing for females in Hong Kong were replaced by the casual Western clothes in the 1970s. However culture resists changing as it needs to endure but at the same time it changes to adapt to the trend and environment in order to retain the genes to be transmitted to future generation.

There are many factors bringing about changes to culture, among which innovation and diffusion are the major ones. Samovar difines innovations as the discovery of new practices, inventions, tools or concepts that may produce changes in practices and behaviors for a particular culture. He thinks that innovations are related to technologies but in most cases, new concepts, new ideas and new forms of art and new processing and producing are considered innovations as well. Samovar defined diffusion as a mechanism of change that is seen by the spread of various ideas, concepts, institutions and practices from one culture to another. Diffusion is considered by Samovar as cultural borrowing ever since culture has existed, which has enriched cultures in many ways in a form of universal of life. Examples of diffusion are tea from China to Europe, tomatoes and pomegranates from Arab to China, hamburgers of McDonald and KFC all over the world, Korean fashions, Japanese animations, Disney movies, Italian pizzas, education of major English speaking countries, just to name a few.

In spite of changes in the style of life, each culture resists changes to its fundamental worldviews and values so as to survive. The changes mentioned above usually are concerned with the exterior or the visible part of culture refraining damages to the core values. For example, a Chinese is not likely to think and behave like an American as a result that he/she uses an iPhone or a Mac, instead he still remains filial to family and observes the Confucius thinking in life and work because values and behaviors associated with such things as ethics and morals, definitions of the role of government, the importance of family and the past, religious practices, the pace of life, folklore, and attitudes towards gender and age are so deeply embedded in a culture that they persist generations after generations. For example, it has been a new custom to enjoy the Spring Festival Gala on the eve of the Chinese New Year with family members but the essence of family union and harmony remain unchanged.

Test Your Reading 4

Decide whether the statements are True (T) or False (F).

(1) Culture is learned by reading books, watching movies, attending schools except experiences at home or communication with others. (   )

(2) People from the same culture understand each other easily because they share the values and information of the culture. (   )

(3) Values of culture are transmitted in the ways of greeting people, treating visitors, getting married, being treated as new mothers, or the funeral customs. (   )

(4) Language and communication styles reveal cultural values and thinking patterns. (   )

(5) Culture remains static as it is transmitted for generations. (   )

C. What Are the Elements of Culture?

Culture is made up of visible elements and invisible ones (Figure 2.8). The visible ones include food, dress, shelters, work, games, holidays, customs, etc. that can be seen apparently. There are also some elements which are distinctive from other cultures and can be seen with careful observation, such as family relationships and friendship, defense, social control, perceptions of illness, sexual taboos, forms of governing, social harmony, gender roles, purpose in life, etc. And there are invisible elements such as worldviews, religions, history, values and language as "what they think", which determine

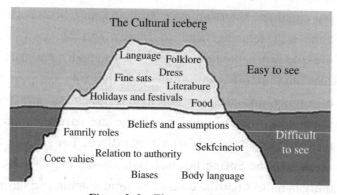

Figure 2.8　Elements of Culture

the visible one as "what they have" and "what they do", making one culture different from others.

As far as the invisible elements are concerned, they are the fundamental basis how one culture is distinct from the others. Worldview, values, religion, history, social organizations and language are the prominent elements of culture.

Samovar sums up that worldview provides some of the unexamined underpinnings for perception and the nature of reality as inexperienced by individuals who share a common culture. Bailey defined that "Worldview is the way a people interpret reality and events, including their images of themselves and how they relate to the world around them." The worldview of a culture functions to make sense of life when it is perceived as meaningless or disordered, but Hall points out that "Like the air we breathe, worldviews are a vital part of who we are but not a part we usually think much about."

Religion is closely related to worldview in helping understand the universe, natural phenomena, the meaning of life and death, relationship between people, etc. Ferraro and Andreatta hold that the religion of a culture functions in many ways as social control, conflict resolution, reinforcement of group solidarity, explanations of the unexplainable and emotional support and it provides its people with a set of values, beliefs and guidelines ranging from business practice to personal behaviors in life philosophy and daily practice. Examples of beliefs in the Chinese community demonstrate how philosophies determine behaviors in that people are influenced by Confucianism in valuing high of education, Taoism in governing by doing nothing that goes against nature, Buddhism in one good turn deserves another and so forth.

History of a culture provides its people with stories about the past which serve as lessons on how to live in the present. By learning the history of a culture, its members are cemented to have "a common culture", which tells them where they are from, what are important in life and what they are proud of so as to create a sense of belonging, solidarity and shared identity. History teaches generations with proverbs in "taking history as a mirror you will know what to do".

Values, according to Newman, "represent the general criteria on which our lives and the lives of others can be judged. They justify the social rules that determine how we ought to behave. In other words, values provide its members with guidelines on what is deemed right or wrong in relationship with specific behaviors. For example, the old are highly respected and taken care of in Asian, Mexican and American Indian cultures but not the same in modern American culture as the youth is highly valued in the United State. These rules tell their people what to do and how to do, what is expected in personal relationships and how others are treated. For example, offers of gifts or help have to be repeated three times before it is accepted or declined for the sake of courtesy in China and other collective Asian cultures, but in the United States, the answer to "would you like something to drink?" may keep a Chinese thirsty for hours as Americans take what one says as what he means. It is, therefore, reasonable that some misunderstandings take place in intercultural communication as people involved may hold different values, and thus what people do is closely related to their values.

Social organizations or structures are the various social units within each culture, such as family, government, schools, business forms and other social networks. These organizations are the products of the worldview, values and religions for the need of interdependence of its members to survive. It is in these organizations that its members learn the values and behaviors of the culture to satisfy their basic needs. For example, extended families in some cultures serve as major function of child-rearing while in other cultures children are taken care of in nuclear families; some cultures have kings and queens and others have presidents or prime ministers. In these organizations individuals are expected to behave on his/her assigned roles and responsibilities in accordance with its values and social norms.

Language is another indispensable element of culture, which represent values, thinking patterns and life styles of a specific culture. When a baby is born, he/she is born into his/her culture environment in which he/she learns the language, by which he/she learns more about religion and philosophy, worldviews and values of his/her culture directing his/her normal behaviors on the daily basis as Barley and peoples conclude,

"Language underlies every other aspect of a people's way of life —
their relationship with natural environment, family life, political
organizations, worldview, and so forth. Most socialization of children

Module One   Basics of Intercultural Communication   73

depends on language, which means language is the main vehicle of cultural transmission from one generation to the next."

It explains the process that one learns about a new culture at the same time when he/she picks up a new language.

To sum up, people are cultured animals with specific symbols to share and a common language to communicate with each other at the same time and place. With the same culture, people are informed of knowledge regarding life, therefore to reduce confusions and help to predict what to expect from life. And the elements that compose culture are worldviews, religions, history, values, social organizations and language, among which the values make cultures different from each other. Different as culture is, the central characteristics of culture are that it is shared, learned and transmitted from generations to generations and culture is based on symbols and it is dynamic.

Test Your Reading 5

Decide whether the statements are True (T) or False (F).

(1) When one travels to another country, he experiences its food, clothes, artifacts, music, architectures, and ceremonies as the visible elements of culture. (   )

(2) One will learn more about the political, economic or educational system by studying or working in an alien culture. (   )

(3) The judicial system of a culture can be learned either by reading books or resolving problems or conflicts in a different culture. (   )

(4) There are usually not many cultural problems in intercultural marriage as long as the couple can speak the same language and love each other. (   )

(5) Language is the only symbol that presents the culture and its values. (   )

Activity 12

Culture is sometimes compared to an iceberg, some of which is visible, but much of which is difficult to see, or invisible.

(1) Look at the list of components of national culture, and tick "√" in one or two of the three categories with your reasons.

A. things which you can recognize quite easily

B. things which take you some time to recognize

C. things which you recognize only when you are very familiar with a culture

(2) Are any of these more important than others in understanding a particular national culture with which you are familiar with?

(3) Add any other elements in Table 2.7 which you think are important in defining a national culture you know.

Table 2.7 Defining A National Culture You Know

Components of National Culture	A	B	C
1. artifacts (art and architecture)			
2. balance between work and home			
3. corruption			
4. democracy			
5. directness of speech in business			
6. driving habits			
7. emotion shown in public			
8. family life, gender(roles of males and females)			
9. greetings			
10. humor			
11. organization of companies			
12. personal friendship			
13. physical gestures			
14. press and other media			
15. punctuality in business			
16. social life (public and private)			
17. social organization and class			

Module One Basics of Intercultural Communication   75

Continued

Components of National Culture	A	B	C
18. treatment of outsiders/foreigners			
19. values and beliefs			
20. school systems			

IV. High-context and Low-context Cultures

As shown in the interactive communication model, the receiver's responses are based on the decoding of the message he/she receives, therefore the meaning of communicated information is more than the linguistic meaning but is more concerned with the context.

A. What Is the Relationship between Context and Communication?

Context is the major factor that decides the meaning of the message. **Context** is defined by Hall as "the information that surrounds an event." In other words, the context is the situation together with other elements of communication in which communication occurs. According to Edward T. Hall, communication works with culture to determine the meaning of the message. As he says "communication is culture," and communication can be classified into high-context communication and low context communication.

In **high-context communication**, information is shared and the meaning of the message is decoded according to the participants, the relationship of the participants and the context. In high context communication, less verbal expressions are employed as more information are shared and transmitted in the context. Contrast to high-context communication, in **low-context communication**, more explicit expressions are employed with less relation to participants, the relationship between them and the context. The message is explicit and clear. Information is needed verbally.

The following Figure 2.9 is the continuum bar of high/low-context cultures by Edward T. Hall:

Figure 2.9 High/Low-Context Cultures (Hall, 1976)

Erin Meyer specified cultures based on Hall's bar of high/low-context in the following Figure 2.10.

As shown in the bar, there is no distinct turn of high/low-contexts as there is no absolute high/low-context in any culture. Apart from the extreme high/low-context cultures, there are more cultures in between which prefer the middle context, i. e. either high or low context. Hall describes other characteristics of high/low-context culture, which reveals the beliefs, values, norms and social practices of the cultural system in the use of convert or overt messages, the importance of in-groups and out-groups, and the culture's orientation of time.

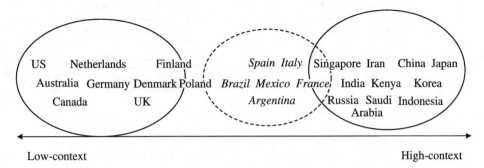

Figure 2.10   High/Low- Context Cultures (Meyer, 2015)

Case Study 2

What did the Malaysian mean to say?

> Read the conversation to see the characteristics of high/low-context culture communication.
> Malaysian: Can I ask you a question?
> European American: Yes, of course.
> Malaysian: Do you know what time is it?
> European American: Yes, it's two o'clock.
> Malaysian: Might you have a little soup left in the pot?
> European American: What? I don't understand.
> Malaysian: (Becoming more explicit since the colleague is not getting the point) I will be on campus teaching until nine o'clock tonight, a very long day for any person, let alone a hungry one!
> European American: (Finally getting the point) Would you like me to drive you to a restaurant off campus so you can have a lunch?
> Malaysian: What a good idea you have!

The dialogue illustrates that the reaction in high-context cultures are more likely to be reserved and the reaction in low-context cultures are more explicit, direct and easily observable as the purpose of communication in high-context cultures is to promote and sustain harmony among people while communication in low-context cultures aims to convey explicit meaning and concise information as shown in Table 2.8.

Table 2.8 Characteristics of High/low- Context Cultures

High-Context Cultures	Low-Context Cultures
Covert and implicit	Overt and explicit
Messages internalized	Messages plainly coded
Much nonverbal coding	Details verbalized
Reactions reserved	Reactions on the surface
Distinctive in-groups and out-groups	Flexible in-groups and out-groups
Strong interpersonal bonds	Fragile interpersonal bonds
Commitment is high	Commitment is low
Time is open and flexible	Time is highly organized

The importance of in-groups and out-groups is another characteristic of high/low-context cultures. In high-context cultures, the meaning of message is embedded in the rules and rituals of situations, in which there are expectations of behaviors and verbal responses for in-group members to follow. For example, in response to compliment in China, one is expected to decline it instead of accepting it with "thank you".

Moreover, in high-context cultures, group responsibilities and loyalty to the group take precedence over one's own interest. Orientation to time is the last characteristics that high/low-context cultures differ. In high-context cultures, time is regarded more open, less structured, and ready for the immediate needs of people. People are more flexible to changes to accommodate the hierarchy and harmonious relationship as the Chinese saying goes "Plans can never keep pace with changes." On the contrary, in the low-context cultures, time is highly structured as commitment to long-term relationship is lower and one has to concentrate more on explicit messages.

What has to be noted is that high/low-context cultures are comparative and specific context in any culture is not static, rather, it changes when the relationship or topic alters. For example, the Chinese generally belong to high-context culture but communication between family members on daily basis is more likely to be low-contextualized.

Test Your Reading 6

Decide whether the statements are True (T) or False (F).

(1) High/low-context cultures are defined by Edward T. Hall to compare cultural differences in terms of communication. (   )

(2) There are usually no problems of communication if both parties are from the same context culture, for example, the low-context culture as they employ more direct and explicit way of communication. (   )

(3) There would be more problems in communication of different context cultures if they are not aware of the differences, for example, a German and a Korean. (   )

(4) In high context cultures, the speaker is obliged to express himself clearly and explicitly. (   )

(5) In high-context communication, repeated denials of compliments are regarded as appropriate social norms, which may be inferred as fishing more positive comments. (   )

Activity 13

Read the following to learn about communication styles.

> Select the characteristics for each set of parameters that best describes your own communication style. And then do the same for another person you are familiar with, preferably someone from another culture, either national or corporal, regional or ethnical, male or female, etc.
> **What is your communication style?**
> People communicate in different ways, here are some sets of parameters which help identify communication styles.
> Systematic/organic: Some people like to present information, or deal with topics, in a systematic, sequential manner. Others prefer to explore things randomly, relying on instinct or experience to help them touch upon the major areas.

Direct/diplomatic: Some people go straight to the point of a communication, with no time spent on introduction, preparation or formality. Others will spend time on social talks or on related matters before moving to the central point.

Formal/informal: Some people use formal and possibly complex language as opposed to a more relaxed, familiar and friendly style; the tone of voice can be distant or intimate.

Inductive/ deductive: Some people make a suggestion or state an idea, then explain or justify it; others will present information first, then draw a conclusion or recommendation from it.

Head/heart: Some people rationalize and speak objectively and reflectively and others speak instinctively, following their feelings.

High-context/low-context: Low-context communicators state the message simply and clearly, with no redundant material; for high-context communicators, the situations, surroundings and other associated details are an important part of the communication.

Colleague/friend: Some people treat others as colleague whom they have a strictly professional relationship while others assume that most other people are their friends, and treat them as such.

B. "What Do You Mean" in Communication

An effective communication lies in the shared purpose of communication, mutual understanding between the participants and instant response in addition to good use of language since the meaning of communicated message is determined by the context, i.e. the information that surrounds an event. The following question may help in understanding what is said in terms of cultural, physical or personal context.

"Is it in the same cultural context or is it an intercultural one?"

"What is the special context? Is it in a classroom, at home, at business or others?"

"Who are the participants and what are their relationships? Are they friends, strangers, or others?"

In consideration of the above, the following will help one clarify the meaning in communication, which is referred to utterance meaning, speakers meaning and hearer's meaning as the meanings in communication:

The utterance meaning is what an utterance normally means, i.e. what is said in language. The speaker's meaning is what the speaker has intended to convey by way of utterance meaning, i.e, what the speaker wants to say. The hearer's meaning is what the hearer has understood on the basis of the utterance meaning, i.e, what is interpreted by the hearer.

Activity 14

What did Zixin mean to say? Why did he say in this way?

> On a weekend morning, Zixin shouted to his mother, "It's Saturday" when she intended to wake him up at nine o'clock.
> What did Zixin want to tell his mother in the sentence of "It's Saturday"?

Listening attentively to what is said for what it is meant is even more important since meaning in communication is determined by the social and cultural context, which is ignored by unskilled intercultural communicators, who would like to interpret the meaning with his/her cultural and social rules. For example, a Chinese student may speak to the international teacher to show his concern, "Put on more clothes as there is a temperature drop," however it will be interpreted as interference of privacy.

Test Your Reading 7

Decide whether the statements are True (T) or False (F).

(1) In intercultural communication, context determines the meaning of the words in the language used by both parties. (   )

(2) Context reveals more what is said than the language itself does. (   )

(3) As long as the same language is applied, misunderstanding occurs as result of language proficiency. (   )

(4) The meaning of what is said is determined by who the speaker is, what the context is and how it is said. (   )

(5) People would like to interpret what is said in the ways that complies with their own cultural norms. (   )

V. Extended Reading

Archaeological Find in Sanxingdui Casts New Light on Ancient Rituals
(*China Daily*, June 17, 2022)

An exquisite and exotic-looking statue recently excavated from the Sanxingdui site in Guanghan, Sichuan province, may offer tantalizing clues to decoding the mysterious religious rituals surrounding the famous 3,000-year-old archaeological site, scientific experts said. A human figure with a serpent-like body and a ritual vessel known as a zun on its head, was unearthed from the No. 8 "sacrificial pit" from Sanxingdui. Archaeologists working on the site confirmed on Thursday that another artifact found several decades ago is a broken part of this newly unearthed one.

In 1986, one part of this statue, a man's curving lower body joined with a pair of bird's feet, was found in the No. 2 pit a few meters away. The third part of the statue, a pair of hands holding a vessel known as a lei, was also recently found in the No. 8 pit. After being separated for 3 millennia, the parts were finally reunited in the conservation laboratory to form a whole body, which has an appearance similar to an acrobat.

Two pits full of bronze artifacts with a bizarre appearance, generally thought by archaeologists to have been used for sacrificial ceremonies, were accidentally found in Sanxingdui in 1986, making it one of biggest archaeological finds in China in the 20th century. Six more pits were found in Sanxingdui in 2019. Over 13,000 relics, including 3,000 artifacts in complete structure, were unearthed in the excavation which started in 2020.

Some scholars speculate the artifacts were deliberately smashed before being put underground in sacrifices by the ancient Shu people, who dominated the region then. Matching the same artifacts recovered from different pits tends to lend credence to that theory, the scientists said. "The parts were separated before being buried in the pits," explained Ran Honglin, a leading archaeologist working on the Sanxingdui site. "They also showed that the two pits were dug within the same period. The finding is thus of high value because it helped us better know the relations of the pits and the social background of communities then." Ran, from the Sichuan Provincial Cultural Relics and Archaeology Research Institute, said many broken parts may also be "puzzles" waiting to be put together by the scientists. "Many more relics may be of the same body", he said. "We have many surprises to expect."

Figurines in Sanxingdui were thought to reflect people in two major social classes, differentiated from each other through their hairstyles. Since the newly found artifact with the serpent-like body has a third type of hairstyle, it possibly indicated another group of people with a special status, the researchers said. Bronze wares in previously unknown and stunning shapes continued to be found in the pits in the ongoing round of excavations, which is expected to last until early next year, with more time needed for conservation and study, Ran said.

Wang Wei, director and researcher at the Chinese Academy of Social Sciences' Academic Division of History, said studies of Sanxingdui were still at an early stage. "The next step is to look for ruins of large-scale architecture, which may indicate a shrine," he said. A construction foundation, covering 80 square meters, was recently found near the "sacrificial pits" but it is too early to determine and recognize what they are used for or their nature. "Possible discovery of high-level mausoleums in the future will also breed more crucial clues," Wang said.

Post-class Tasks

Self-test Tasks

1. Answer the questions in your own words.
   (1) What is the factor that indicates an effective communication?
   (2) What are the communicative characteristics of high/low-context

cultures?

(3) Will communication do everything? Why or why not?

(4) Explain "people engage in communication for a variety of purposes."

2. Describe the process of communication in your own words.

Group Work

1. What are the "meanings" of the Sender and Receiver in the following conversations.

> A Chinese met a British on campus in China. The Chinese greeted the British with "Have you had lunch?" And the British replied, "Not yet."
> What was the meaning of the Chinese?
> How did the British interpret it?

2. Role-play the following case to find out:

(1) What did Litz want to know? How did her mother-in-law interpret the dialogue?

(2) Why was there this misunderstanding?

(3) How would Litz do in this situation?

(4) Who else would have helped to prevent it from happening? In what ways?

> Litz, a Finnish, who married a Chinese doctor, told the story of misunderstanding between her mother-in-law and her.
> My husband and I had long wished to bring his mother to stay with us for a while. Last summer, after we redecorated our house, we invited her over. You can well imagine how happy my husband was! And I was just as happy. I know being filial to parents is a great value Chinese people cherish. As a wife of a Chinese man I try to be as filial as my husband.
> Two days after my mother-in-law's arrival, I talked to my husband while his mother was sitting in the garden enjoying the sunshine.
> Litz: Dick, how long is your mum going to stay?

> Dick: I don't know. I haven't asked her.
>
> Litz: Why not ask her?
>
> Dick: What do you mean by asking her?
>
> Litz: I mean what I said. Just ask her how long she's going to stay.
>
> My mother-in-law overheard our conversation, and decided to leave for China the very afternoon. I had never expected that her visit should be so short! I tried very hard to persuade her to change her mind, but in vain.
>
> (Adapted from *Bridge between Minds: Intercultural Communication* by Wang Rong & Zhang Ailin)

Telling China's Stories

One of your net friends in Israel is visiting China and he/she is coming to your city next week. Think about what you are going to let him/her know about some local culture in your city. Try to find out the cultural values by introducing some culture symbols, such as food, holiday customs, proverbs in local dialect or local memorable sites, etc. Mind the etiquette related to religions practice as your friend is from Israel.

My Learning Reflection

1. What have I learned about Chinese cultures or myself?

2. What have I learned about other cultures?

3. What impressed me most in this chapter?

4. What still confuses me?

Chapter 3　Cultural Patterns

> **Learning Objectives**
>
> - To identify the kernel elements of culture and major culture patterns;
> - To compare Chinese culture with some others with cultural patterns;
> - To tell Chinese stories with cultural confidence.
>
> **Pre-class Tasks**
>
> - Read the textbook and watch the concerned clips in *xuexitong* (学习通).

Ⅰ. Lead-in Tasks

Activity 1

Discuss the quotes in groups to answer the questions:
(1) What are the functions of values?
(2) What are the relationship of values and behaviors?

> The definition of a society is shaped by its values, which define its ultimate goal.
>
> Henry Kissinger
>
> Values are not just words; values are what we live by. They're about the cause that we champion and the people we fight for.
>
> John Kerry

> The values that we hold inform our principles. The principles that we hold inform our actions.
>
> Frank Matobo

II. Understanding Values as Core of Culture

In additions to the visible differences in language, food, dress and holidays, culture functions to their people with elements of worldviews, perceptions, beliefs, values, religions and attitudes as the kernel. And instruments are needed to compare cultures to see how they are different in terms of worldviews, values, religions, history and language as mentioned previously.

There are as many definitions of worldview as those of "communication" and "culture". Worldview is a culture's orientation towards gods, humanity, nature, questions of existence, the universe and cosmos, life, death, sickness, and other philosophical issues that influence how its members perceive the world. In other words, worldviews are the unified, shared outlook on the world that guides people in their actions on earth. Samovar says, "what one person might call religion or world view, another might call philosophy."

As there are many different worldviews, learners of the English language in China are usually confronted with two major ones, which are closely related to the Chinese culture and the Western culture or culture of major English-speaking countries, i.e. the holistic and dualistic worldviews respectively.

The holistic worldview is featured with the concept of "one" "blending" "harmony" and "wholeness" as the ancient Chinese proposition states that "*Tao* (道) consists of *Yin* and *Yang*" in *The Book of Changes* (about 600 B.C.) and Lao Tze developed it in *Tao Te Ching* in that

> "One is the child of the divine law.
> After one comes two,
> after two comes three,
> after three comes all things.

Everything has a bright and a dark side,
co-existent in harmony.
People dislike to be lonely and worthless,
But rulers call themselves the sole and unworthy.
So things may gain when they seem to lose,
or lose when they seem to gain.
I will teach what others teach me.
The brute will die a brutal death.
I will teach this as a lesson."

(Translated by Xu Yuanchong)

Chang Tze (369—286 B.C.) furthered the idea by saying that "One reality is all men, gods and things; complete all-embracing and the whole; it is all-embracing unity from which nothing can be separated." In addition, Confucianism, which is the dominant ideology in the Chinese culture seek the proper way for all people to behave with the purpose of promoting harmony in personal relationships. When it comes to the relationship of the human and Nature, the Man is proposed as part of the Nature, which is regarded as a whole.

The dualistic worldview, on the other hand, is characterized with the view of division which was explicitly stated by Plato, who conceived of "reality as consisting of two parts. The lower part included material things. The higher part consisted of the ideas on which material things were always patterned …". Aristotle continued this view by dividing the world into two opposite parts, i.e. "elements" and "forms", "realities" and "reasons", "matters" and "forms". And other European philosophers like Descartes and Hegel consolidated the theoretical basis through notions like "the matter" and "the mind", and "real objects" and "absolute spirits'. In other words, the Man and Nature are separated rather than related which can be analyzed one by one; and each individual is thus regarded independently as one and the other, thus being on one's own is fundamental.

Case Study 1

What culture values are revealed in the Traditional Chinese Medicine

(TCM)?

> Chris is one of the international teachers in a Chinese university who has just come to teach English in China for a few months. One day, he woke up with a stiff neck on the right and went to class uncomfortably. When he went to the clinic for medications, one of the physicians suggested that he try the Chinese Traditional Medicine (TCM).
>
> Dubiously he went to the Department of TCM. The TCM doctors examined his neck and prescribed him with massage therapy. To his surprise, the masseur relaxed those tense muscles on the left instead of on the right, explaining that the TCM takes the human body as whole, thus the pain on the right is cured on the left, headache is treated with a foot massage and some miscellaneous diseases are dealt with comprehensive treatments.
>
> Thirty minutes later, Christ found pain on his neck reduced with relaxed muscle on his right back, finding TCM amazing to his knowledge.

This case shows the worldviews in the treatment of human bodies. Different from the Western medicine which mainly treats each organic illnesses individually in part, the holistic and alternative medicines focus on the whole body as a system affecting one another. The Holistic worldview is widely applied by the Chinese in many ways in dealing with problems.

Samovar defined that perception is how one makes sense of the world and how one constructs the reality. To survive, people engage in managing the stimuli considered important by selecting, organizing and interpreting information from many resources. As culture is the most influential in shaping an individual, the relevant sociocultural factors, such as belief, values and attitudes provide a framework for understanding the meaning of the reality, thus perception is formed.

Culture determines both the categories we use and the meanings we attach to them. For example, people from China, Japan and Korea, who concern more for positive, enduring interpersonal relations, prefer indirect communication between valued associates and would have the negative and adverse information couched in ambiguous terms. Americans, on the other hand, tend to expect direct, forthright communicative style and would have frank exchange of ideas and animated debates at meetings as they focus more on the event or problem rather than personal relations. And in many instances, one's culturally-based perceptions are maintained in the form of beliefs and values, which work in combination to form cultural patterns.

Samovar thinks that a belief is the concept or idea that an individual or group of people hold to be true and is reflected in one's actions and communication behaviors. And the beliefs shared by a group of people will come to norms, or values which will transmit from generation to generation. For example, Chinese people believe that boiled warm water keeps people healthy from diseases and they would have thermos with them at work and on trips, and visitors are treated with hot water as social norms. Another example is in the Asian, African and Latin American cultures, the elder is believed to be experienced and resourceful, thus they are respected and taken care of.

Beliefs represent the subjective convictions in the truth of something with or without proofs which are learned and subject to cultural interpretations. Beliefs and the cultural values may be different, which may shape the worldviews and manners of communication.

Values are formed on beliefs. Although each individual may have a set of values, there are values that permeate and characterize a culture, known as cultural values, which provides, as noted by Samovar, "a set of guidelines that assist the culture's members in deciding what is good or bad, desirable or undesirable, right or wrong, and appropriate or inappropriate in almost context of human activity." Values of a specific culture establish the expected, normative modes of behaviors for its members and institute the criteria to judge people's conduct.

Values are learned as culture is learned, and they are hidden and interrelated to make up the basis for its people to cope with the surroundings and relate with each other as the cores of culture. In intercultural communication, it happens that one is likely to apply his/her criteria to people from other cultures with different values, which may lead to misunderstanding, confusion or even conflicts. For example, the ways of rearing children and taking care of the old are quite different across cultures as the result of varied values between individualism and collectivism. Therefore, it's helpful for an intercultural communicator to keep in mind that, "if you consider the other person strange, they probably consider you strange".

Behaviors are the outward manifestations of the internalized beliefs and values. In other words, one behaves as a result of his/her values, which are based on his/her beliefs. For example, Asian females tend to protect their fair skin from the sun by using sunscreen, wearing a hat and long-sleeved shirts or with umbrellas on sunny days because it is believed that people who have fair skin are more beautiful. And beliefs and values also influence individual's communication behaviors. For example, people of collectivist culture tend to communicate in implicit and indirect way as they believe in interdependence with harmonious interpersonal relationship.

Test Your Reading 1

Decide whether the statements are True (T) or False (F).

(1) There are many worldviews in the world as people and culture are different in perceiving the world. (   )

(2) The holistic worldview is held by the Chinese people as the only right one to cope with the world and people. (   )

(3) The worldviews, values, beliefs and attitudes of a culture will shape the perceptions of individuals by means of social and cultural events. (   )

(4) An individual who does not stay late believes in "Early to bed and early to rise makes a man healthy". (   )

(5) That "Harmony at home brings prosperity" leads to support and tolerance among Chinese family members as values. (   )

Ⅲ. Value Orientations to Compare Cultures

Cultures are studied in value orientations or culture patterns, which is defined by Samovar as an umbrella term "to describe collectively those cultural values that characterize the dominant group within a culture". With the help of cultural patterns in the study of intercultural communication, dissimilar cultural values can be identified and examined with a systematic structure. The instruments in use are Gelfand's Tight and Loose Cultures Dimensions, Kluckhohn's Cultural Orientations, Hofstede's Cultural Dimensions, Minkov's Cultural Dimensions and Hall's High-Context and Low-Context Orientations.

A. Tight and Loose Cultures Dimensions

Tight and Loose Cultures were originated by Gelfand, an American anthropologist in 1950's, which have been recently proven by means of quantitative evidences to substantiate the classifications. **Loose Cultures** are characterized by relatively weak social norms and considerable tolerance of deviance from expectations. **Tight Cultures** will exhibit strong established societal norms and a low level of tolerance for deviations from accepted behaviors.

Table 3.1 Tightness Scores for Thirty-Two Countries/Regions

SCORE	COUNTRY/REGION	SCORE	COUNTRY/REGION	SCORE	COUNTRY/REGION
1.6	Ukraine	5.4	Spain	7.5	Germany (E.)
2.6	Estonia	5.6	Belgium	7.8	Portugal
2.9	Hungary	6.0	Poland	7.9	China
3.1	Israel	6.3	France	8.6	Japan
3.3	Netherlands	6.3	Hong Kong (China)	9.2	Turkey
3.4	Brazil	6.4	Iceland	9.5	Norway
3.7	Venezuela	6.5	Germany (W.)	10.0	Korea
3.9	Greece	6.8	Austria	10.4	Singapore
3.9	New Zealand	6.8	Italy	11.0	India
4.4	Australia	6.9	United Kingdom	11.8	Malaysia
5.1	United States	7.2	Mexico	12.3	Pakistan

In Table 3.1, the lower-numbered scores are those favoring looseness; a higher score denotes a preference for tightness. For example, in the United States, which is numbered 5.1, handshaking is preferred as social norms without very many differences on who initiates it or how long it lasts in consideration of status or titles. But in Japan, which is 8.6, there are distinctive norms for societal protocols that govern social interactions between individuals, for example, there are rigid sets of procedures of greetings as to who bows first, how low and for how long, depending on the interactants' status. Therefore, the American culture can be described as being looser than the Japanese culture, or the Japanese culture is tighter than the American culture.

The Tight and Loose Cultures Dimensions process the advantage of being easily understood as it's concerned with the social interaction norms in personal communication, which is more visible in cultures. From the tight cultures to loose ones there are more in between, and it goes without saying that there are more aspects that distinguish one cultures from another either in the tight one or loose ones, which justify more concise orientations to look into the cores of cultures, i.e. the values.

The Tight and Loose Cultures Dimensions concerns the general trend of cultures rather than the personal traits in the corresponding ones.

Test Your Reading 2

Decide whether the statements are True (T) or False (F).

(1) The cultural pattern of Tight and Loose cultures by Gelfand focuses on the dimension of the social norm in personal communication in comparing cultures. (   )

(2) Cultures are compared because they shared some similar features in common. (   )

(3) From Table 3.1, it is found out that the Italian culture scored at 6.8 is looser than the Chinese culture scored at 7.9. (   )

(4) The cultural pattern by Gelfand can be applied to two individuals from different cultures in a specific manner. (   )

(5) Any individual from the UK is more tolerant and easy-going than one from Japan. (   )

B. Kluckhohn's Cultural Orientations

Kluckhohn's Cultural Orientations is one of the well-accepted cultural patterns, advocated by American anthropologists Florence Kluckholm and Fred Strodtbeck in the 1950s. They hold that individuals in all cultures would deal with five basic questions as to what is important as guidelines in their lives, which all human societies are confronted, yet solutions to them are varied. These five questions are referred to as "value orientations" as follows.

What is the character of human nature (the human nature orientation)?

What is the relation of humankind to nature (the man-nature orientation)?

What is the orientation towards time (the time-orientation)?

What is the value placed on activity (the activity orientation)?

What is the relationship of people to each other (the interpersonal relational orientation)?

Answers to these basic questions are classified in Table 3.2 for better understanding cultures.

Table 3.2 Five Value Orientations by Kluchhohn and Strodtbeck

Orientation	Value and Behavior Range		
Human Nature	Basically Evil	Mixture of Good and Evil	Basically Good
Human and Nature	Subject to Nature	Harmony with Nature	Master of Nature
Sense of Time	Past	Present	Future
Activity	Being	Being-in-becoming	Doing
Social Relationships	Authoritarian/Hierarchy	Group	Individualism

Human Nature Orientation is the basic and most important because answers to it determine how individuals live their life and the way they treat others. Some cultures believe that people are intrinsically evil for some religious reasons, they therefore have to achieve goodness by means of working hard, self-control, education and self-disciplines, and that's why laws, rules and regulations are needed to monitor, manage and restrict human behaviors as they cannot be trusted for their own resources. Cultures believing evil human nature are generally related with the societies of Judaism, Christianity and Islam. For example, the Seventh Commandments in *The Bible* tends to keep people from doing evil. Another example is the restrictive views found in parts of Islam world, where it's imbued that people are to have a pendant for evil and cannot be trusted to make correct decisions, social institutions are therefore designed to monitor and manage behaviors of its members. *Good and evil* human nature describes the beliefs that people are born with both good and evil characters corresponding the good and evil part of the universe. For example *Yin and*

Yang in Taoism and the infinity system of opposing elements and forces in balanced dynamic interaction. The good and evil are believed to coexist in human but each of them periodically takes turns at dominance according to circumstances. What people should do is to control the evil and release the potential of good. It's also believed that as humans are born with propensity for good, they are likely to become good through learning and education. Interesting enough, Samovar found in 2017 that Americans, who used to hold evil nature, now have come to believe good-and-evil nature of humans since last century. The strong belief of inner goodness of human nature is best illustrated in Confucianism and Buddhism in the Eastern cultures. "Human nature is originally good" is what most Chinese people believe. A culture of this kind believes in the goodness of human nature. Buddhism also maintains that one is born pure and good but the evil people around make him going from the good to evil. And that's why parents would like children to have good-natured peers and educated in good schools by good teachers so as to maintain the goodness, refraining them from being affected by the objective evils. "Don't learn to be evil!" is what children are advised, and parents would feel pity if their children have been found guilty. As a result of this belief, the solution to crime in society is the comprehensive efforts to re-educate the criminal from the evil to good as goodness is the essence of human nature.

Man/Nature Orientation concerns the relationship of human beings with nature, which characterizes how different cultures relate and interact with nature. Humans as subject to nature are at one of the scale viewing that humans are subject to nature. Cultures holding this orientation believe that there is a magic force in nature that determines the fate of people, which cannot be overcome, controlled and have to be accepted. Indians, the Aboriginal people in Australia and some Southern Americans tend to have "oneness" with the world, helping create a vision of world operating in harmony and people would accept things as what they are. In these societies, improvements are less encouraged and innovations are rare.

Harmony with nature is the middle or cooperative view well-accepted by East Asians. Human beings are regarded as the integrated part of the universe with nature, which either should be subdued or controlled. The Chinese believes that man and nature are in one and that people should do whatever to keep harmony with nature rather than to exploit or remold it to his own desires and needs. China, Japan, Thailand tend to have this view guiding their life in harmony with nature, one's body in harmony with his mind and personal relationships in harmony as well.

Master of nature is the view at the other end of the scale which sets a clear separation between humans and nature. And humans are entitled to direct the forces of nature to their advantages, conquering and changing nature by means of science and technology. Western Europeans and Americans tend to have this orientation, "taming" the wildness and "conquering" the space for human benefits.

Time Orientation is one of the imperceptible cultural perspectives towards time, demonstrating the greatest differences in the respective values placed on the past, present and future, i.e. how time is viewed. Past Orientation refers to the past-oriented cultures in which history, established religions and tradition are most valued, and it's deeply believed that contemporary perception of decision-making, human actions and determination of truth should be guided by what had happened in the past. In China, there is a saying that "take the history as a mirror to see what to do for the future". India has the similar saying that "learn about the future by looking at the past." Samovar concludes that cultures characterized with rich traditions usually have a strong orientation towards the past. The Great Britain adheres to its history by remaining monarchy and taking pride in its historical achievements. France is another example of past-oriented culture by "tending to see things in their historical context and relate contemporary events to their origin".

People from the past-oriented culture are likely to value history and tradition very much, and the old age is respected as it means wisdom with more knowledge and experiences related to time. In China, there are sayings like "an old at home is like a treasure of a family" and the old is very much respected. People with past orientation are proud of the long history and cultural traditions and individuals therefore enjoy being treated as the old. In addition, hierarchy is another feature of past orientation culture. For example, in Korea and Japan, elders and seniors are respected both in words and in behaviors.

Present Orientation holds that the present and here is what people can take control of as the past has gone and the future is ambiguous, unpredictable and out of the control. People from the present orientation cultures tend to enjoy living at the moment, having a causal, relaxed and easy life style, like the Filipinos and Latin Americans, Mexicans and some African Americans. They would work enough to pay for what is needed, leaving less as savings. They won't have long-term goals as tomorrow is not reliable when today is only what can be enjoyable and pleasant as described as "Fasting comes after feasting".

Future Orientation is characterized with the beliefs that the future is better and grander than the present or past because the future is yet to come when people have more to do for control of it. In the future-oriented cultures, changes, improvements, innovations are encouraged as they are under the control of human beings. That "do something to improve it" is a feature of this orientation, therefore, something new, something effective, something more productive is what people seek for. But in these cultures the old age is regarded negative to be "useless" or "valueless" while the young is reckoned promising and valuable, thus optimism are the hallmarks of this orientation, therefore people don't like to be treated as the old, trying to stay "young and energetic' as long as possible. People with future orientation tend to have short-term goals for immediate outcomes and prefer direct communication.

Activity Orientation reveals the attitude towards activities and action, affecting the perspective of work, efficiency and time, such as the pace of life, decision-making or action-taking. It is also related to one's identity as to who he/she is or what he/she does.

Being Orientation refers to the spontaneous expression of the human personalities which accept people, events, and ideas as flowing the moment. They value personal relationship more than accomplishments, taking long hours in conversation with family members and friends. For example, Mexicans enjoy the moment of being with companions. People holding being orientation are usually present-oriented as well. What's more, one's own and others' titles, status or background are more concerned in interpersonal relationships, i. e. who he/she is is more important than what one does, therefore communication is mainly depends on relationships in terms of titles and background.

Being-in-becoming focuses on the ideas of improvement and growth. People holding this kind of orientations value spiritual life than material one, emphasizing activities that improve themselves in mediation and contemplation.

Hinduism and Buddhism are examples of this king.

Doing Orientation pays a lot more attention to actions and activities in which accomplishments are measured by external standards of individuals, such as cars, houses, yachts and so forth. People believing in doing are usually quick in decision-making and action-taking with immediate outcomes. Americans are characterized most by doing orientation with life being in constant motion. They change jobs frequently for better opportunities, travel for new scenes and seeking for potentials, without being bothered by moving from one place to another.

Social Relationships is the fifth orientation in Kluckhohn and Strodtbeck scale for cultural comparisons, which indicates the relationship between people in different cultures. In some ways, social relationship is correlative to the mood of communication of the culture as well.

Authoritarian/Hierarchy refers to ordering relationship in a society where everyone is assigned to his/her position of privileges and obligations. It is true that there is no society without hierarchy but the difference lies in whether hierarchy is emphasized or how much is emphasized. In such a culture, people act and interact according to what he/she is, accepting what is expected from him/her without feeling unequally treated. Generally a small number of people is more privileged while more are underprivileged.

In societies that hierarchy is assigned by races, ethnic groups or inheritance from family, the social position of people is more rigid and is less likely to change. If the criteria are based on financial ownership or educational background, there are more possibilities for people to change their social status. For example, from the Imperial Examination System to the modern College Entrance Examinations, China has had a long history of upgrading one's social status by education.

Group Orientation cultures prefer interdependence within the group. The group can be the extended family, a clan or a tribe, or it also can be a school one attends, the course class one takes, or the profession one belongs to. Within the group, one feels secured, comfortable and dependable. The group is what one can turn to for support and help in difficulty and need, and at the same he contributes to the group with loyalty and obedience. Group-oriented cultures see a clear separation of in-groups and out-groups, and communication differs greatly between the two. Within the group, humility and harmony are encouraged, but hostility and competition is as plain as the nose on one's face, which explains why on some occasions people would like to be involved into groups for some reasons.

Individualism is another type of interpersonal relations compared with the first two. In the individual-oriented societies, people live on autonomy, free to decide on one's own business and take consequences of his/her decisions. As there is also hierarchy in any society, inequality does exist in some field or occasions, but people would like to minimize the impact of it as much as possible. For example, in the United States, people prefer to communicate on the basis of first names instead of addressing with ranks or titles except the specific one, such as Doctor, Professor, Lawyers or General, etc., just to name some of them.

To sum up, the cultural orientations by Kluckhohn and Strodtbeck deal with various relationships, such as human to nature, person to person, person to activity and person to time, of which are based on the nature of human beings. When different cultures are compared to these orientations, correlations are found. On the other hand, it has to be noted that these orientation are relative and changing over times, and can not be taken as absolute features of a culture or individuals, which otherwise will lead to stereotypes.

Test Your Reading 3

Decide whether the statements are True (T) or False (F).

(1) Kluckholm's Cultural Orientations are likely to describe national cultures in regard with the core values of culture. (   )

(2) Human nature is what one is born instructively as being good, evil or both good and evil. (   )

(3) Future-oriented cultures tend to take "doing" as prominent in planning for future and achieving goals. (   )

(4) In terms of social relationships, the group-orientated people tend to treat each other more equally. (   )

(5) People from doing-oriented culture tend to be future-oriented as well. (   )

Activity 2

Identify the following Cultures in terms of Kluckholm's Cultural Orientations, and compare any two of the three, for example, China with India or the US, or the US with India. Write your answers in Table 3.3.

Table 3.3 Identify the Cultures

Orientations	China	the United States	India
Human Nature			
Human-nature Relationships			
Sense of Time			
Activity			
Social Relationship			

C. Hofstede's Cultural Dimensions

Hofstede's Cultural Dimensions has been a well-accepted cultural pattern for many years. Geert Hofstede, a Dutch social psychologist conducted a statistical survey of cultural values based on data of IBM employees from 50 countries and 3 geographical regions. These countries and regions were assigned a rank of 1 to 50 in four identical value dimensions, i. e. individualism/collectivism, uncertainty avoidance, power distance and masculinity/femininity. Later a fifth dimension, long/short-term orientation was added with a subsequent study over 23 countries. The country rankings of his study offer a clear picture of what is more valued in each culture, making it easier to compare values across cultures.

What has to be kept in mind is that Hofstede's cultural orientations are more at the national level than an individual level, namely, they characterize dominant cultures in corresponding society. In addition, Hofstede's cultural orientations are more related to communication in workplace, which is a bit alien to social encounters.

Individualism/collectivism is very much observed in previous studies in the name of "individual orientation vs. group orientation" or "individualism vs. collectivism" as the fundamental concepts to understand and explain the social life. Variations of these values are seen in family structures, classroom activities, organization management and interpersonal relationships, etc. What is special about Hofstede's individualism/collectivism continuum is shown in his Individualism/Collectivism Index, where two or more subject cultures can be compared in ranking numbers. Anderson finds "Collectivist cultures emphasize community, collaboration, shared interest, harmony, tradition, the public good, and maintaining face. Individualistic cultures emphasize personal rights and responsibilities, privacy, voicing one's own opinions, freedom, innovation, and self-expressions."

As shown in Table 3.4, the lower the number, the more the country prefers individualism, and a higher number means the country tends to be more collective. For example, in the United States where individualism prevails, individual interest goes first, and the organization or coworkers are the secondary consideration, which explains why Americans change jobs often for better wages or to advance one's career. Conversely in Japan and other Asian countries, loyalty to organization is more expected and appreciated traditionally. But it is changing with globalization and acceptance of individualism among new generations in the traditionally collectivist cultures, such as Japan and China.

Table 3.4 Individualism/Collectivism Values for 53 Countries and Regions (IDV)

RANK	COUNTRY/REGION	RANK	COUNTRY/REGION	RANK	COUNTRY/REGION
1	the United States	19	Isreal	37	Hong Kong (China)
2	Australia	20	Spain	38	Chile
3	Great Brain	21	India	39~41	Singapore
4/5	Canada	22/23	Japan	39~41	Thailand
4/5	Netherlands	22/23	Argentina	39~41	West Africa
6	New Zealand	24	Iran	42	El Salvador
7	Italy	25	Jamaica	43	Korea
8	Belgium	26/27	Brazil	44	Taiwan (China)
9	Denmark	26/27	Arab Countries	45	Peru
10/11	Sweden	28	Turkey	46	Costa Rica
10/11	France	29	Uruguay	47/48	Pakistan

Continued

RANK	COUNTRY/REGION	RANK	COUNTRY/REGION	RANK	COUNTRY/REGION
12	Ireland	30	Greece	47/48	Indonesia
13	Norway	31	Philippines	49	Colombia
14	Switzerland	32	Mexico	50	Venezuela
15	Germany	33~35	Yugoslavia	51	Panama
16	South Africa	33~35	Portugal	52	Ecuador
17	Finland	33~35	East Africa	53	Guatemala
18	Austria	36	Malaysia		

From Table 3.4 it is seen that a majority of the world's population live in collectivistic societies where group interests take precedent over those of individual. In collectivist cultures, interpersonal relationship form a rigid framework that distinguishes in-groups and out-groups, and people rely on in-group for financial, emotional and any other support, and at the same time they feel obliged to provide the same to other members of the group, such as families, tribes, clans or organizations.

People in collectivistic societies are usually born into extended families, clans, tribes, and child-rearing is the obligation of the big family. They exchange their allegiance for support and protection. Group membership is emphasized and the individual is emotionally and physically reply on the institution and organization which may sometimes affect one's private life. As the Chinese proverb says, "No matter how stout, one beam cannot support a house", and the collectivist cultures depend on in-group decision and benefits as well. The mood of communication in collectivistic cultures tends to stress harmony and face instead of information exchange and persuasion.

Collectivism is contextual in such cases as in classroom activities or healthcare institutions. For example, in the classroom, there are more group activities than individual ones who are aimed for harmony and cooperation instead of competition. Continuous visitors of family members, colleagues or friends will show up in the wards when one is hospitalized. Collectivist cultures share joys and sorrows in most cases. A sense of "collective grief and guilt" may hang over when disasters take place and rescue support will follow in rows, for example, the Japanese earthquake and tsunami in 2011, the tragic ferry sinking in Korea and the 512 Earthquake in China.

Test Your Reading 4

Decide whether the statements are True (T) or False (F).

(1) Hofstede was the first one who compared Individualism verse Collectivism. (   )

(2) Hofstede's Cultural Dimensions are characterized with the indexes to rank the countries and regions in the corresponding dimensions. (   )

(3) Collectivist values are demonstrated in many aspects, one of which is the different ways of communication between in-groups and out-groups. (   )

(4) Sharing of joy and sorrow together with physical items is considered as one of features of individualistic cultures. (   )

(5) According to the index of IDV France is more collectivist than Australia. (   )

Uncertain Avoidance is defined by Hofstede as "the extent to which the members of a culture feel threatened by ambiguity or unknown situations". In other words, uncertainty avoidance means how much people would tolerate or do to prevent the possibilities of future changes.

Ambiguity is the root of uncertainty which creates anxiety, and the essence of uncertainty is a subjective experience or a feeling, which can be personal and also be shared with other members of a society. Therefore, feelings of uncertainty are learned, reinforced and transmitted. Human beings have been attempting to alleviate anxiety and reduce uncertainty by technology, laws, rules or religions so that people feel that they would control the future. Feelings of uncertainty and ways of coping with them are cultural heritages of societies, and the degree of uncertainty avoidance varies across cultures.

In Table 3.5, the lower numbered countries are those that tend to dislike uncertainty, and those with higher numbers usually feel comfortable with uncertainty and ambiguity. In other words, high uncertainty avoidance cultures attempt to reduce unpredictability and ambiguity through intolerance of deviant ideas and behaviors, emphasizing consensus, resisting changes, and adhering to traditional social protocols. People in these cultures tend to suffer relatively high level of stress and anxiety, "what is different is dangerous." They would do whatever they can to reduce uncertainties, having rules to follow so as to have things under control. For example, Greece is ranked top one and is famous for its legal institutions at its early ages; Japan, ranked the 7th is a country with many formal social protocols to regulate how people will behave in every social interactions. Switzerland as the 33rd is skillful in producing clocks and watches and Germans ranking 29th are strict with schedules and punctuality.

Table 3.5 Uncertainty Avoidance Values for 53 Countries and Regions (UAV)

RANK	COUNTRY/REGION	RANK	COUNTRY/REGION	RANK	COUNTRY/REGION
1	Greece	19	Israel	27	Australia
2	Portugal	20	Colombia	38	Norway
3	Guatemala	21/22	Venezuela	39/40	South Africa
4	Uruguay	21/22	Brazil	39/40	New Zealand
5/6	Belgium	23	Italy	41/42	Indonesia
5/6	El Salvador	24/25	Pakistan	41/42	Canada
7	Japan	24/25	Austria	43	the United States
8	Yugoslavia	26	Taiwan (China)	44	Philippines
9	Peru	27	Arab Countries	45	India
10~15	Spain	28	Ecuador	46	Malaysia
10~15	Argentina	29	Germany	47/48	Great Britain
10~15	Panama	30	Thailand	47/48	Ireland
10~15	France	31/32	Iran	49/50	Hong Kong (China)
10~15	Chile	31/32	Finland	49/50	Sweden
10~15	Costa Rica	33	Switzerland	51	Denmark
16~17	Turkey	34	West Africa	52	Jamaica
16~17	Korea	35	Netherlands	53	Singapore
18	Mexico	36	East Africa		

On the other hand, the low uncertainty avoidance cultures tend to easily accept the uncertainty inherent in life, being more tolerate of the unusual and not preferring the structure associated with hierarchy. They are flexible in time arrangements and much less constrained by social protocols. "What is different is curious" is their general attitudes towards something unexpected. For example, in the United States which is ranked 43th, multiculturalism is appreciated as there are cultures of different races and ethics, with varied religions even though there is a generally accepted American culture. Singapore is another example in Asia whose population is consisted of Chinese, Malays, Indians and Eurasian, and therefore Confucianism, Christianity, Islam, Taoism, Buddhism and Hinduism are popular. In terms of education, Drzewieck found that the high uncertainty avoidance culture prefer to have structured learning situations, firm timetables and well-defined objectives.

Power Distance is defined by Hofstede as "the extent in which the less powerful members of institutions and organizations within a country expect and accept that power is distributed unequally." In other words, power distance concerns how people expect and accept inequality of power in their culture. As a measurement of authority and control over others, power distance is depicted as "high or low" and "large or small" ones, and it has to be noticed that it is not absolute but relative in a continuum as shown in Table 3.6.

Table 3.6 Power Distance Values for 53 Countries and Regions (PDV)

RANK	COUNTRY/REGION	RANK	COUNTRY/REGION	RANK	COUNTRY/REGION
1	Malaysia	18/19	Turkey	37	Jamaica
2/3	Guatemala	20	Belgium	38	the United States
2/3	Panama	21~23	East Africa	39	Canada
4	Philippines	21~23	Peru	40	Netherlands
5/6	Mexico	21~23	Thailand	41	Australia
5/6	Venezuela	24/25	Chile	42~44	Costa Rica
7	Arab Countries	24/25	Portugal	42~44	Germany
8/9	Ecuador	26	Uruguay	42~44	Great Britain
8/9	Indonesia	27/28	Greece	45	Switzerland
10/11	India	27/28	Korea	46	Finland
10/11	West Africa	29/30	Iran	47/48	Norway
12	Yugoslavia	29/30	Taiwan (China)	47/48	Sweden
13	Singapore	31	Spain	49	Ireland
14	Brazil	32	Pakistan	50	New Zealand

					Continued
RANK	COUNTRY/REGION	RANK	COUNTRY/REGION	RANK	COUNTRY/REGION
15/16	France	33	Japan	51	Denmark
15/16	Hong Kong (China)	34	Italy	52	Israel
17	Colombia	35/36	Argentina	53	Austria
18/19	El Salvador	35/36	South Africa		

In Table 3.6, the lower the number, the corresponding country is more likely to be a higher power distance culture, and a higher number is more likely to be associated with low power distance cultures. What has to be noticed is that power distance, same as the other cultural dimensions, is relative in comparison with others in a continuum.

Gudykunst believes that individuals from high power distance cultures accept power as a part of society. As such, superiors consider their subordinates to be different from themselves and vice versa, and they feel obliged to have authority to make decisions and have more privileges, i.e. something more and better. On the other hand, their subordinated accept the same and feel comfortable with it. People in the culture of high power distance are educated that people are not equal in terms of family names, education, genders, ages, profession and organizational positions and are ranked by societal hierarchies. Usually there is centralization of power in family or other institutions where power is distributed in line of authority and decisions are made by men.

On the contrary, Hofstede found that individuals from culture of low power distance would treat people more equally, thinking that inequality in society should be minimized. In low power distance cultures, there are many laws, regulations and rules to follow so as to avoid human factors to much extent. Decision-making are made on the basis of consensus and consultations with proposals being discussed and debated thoroughly. In social life, people usually feel uncomfortable with privileges, feeling shamed of preferential treatments. And in the low power distance cultures, there is distinction between work and leisure as privacy is respected as individual rights.

High and low power distance can be seen in education sectors. Usually in high power distance cultures, education is teacher-centered with students listening attentively to teachers. Comparatively, in low power distance cultures, classroom is student-centered, with more activities to students' interests and needs, encouraging listening to others and expressing one's own.

Test Your Reading 5

Decide whether the statements are True (T) or False (F).

(1) According to the index of UAV, high uncertain avoidance cultures tend to be in low tolerance of ambiguity and changes. (　)

(2) Feelings of anxiety and attempts to control them are associated with culture, which is instinctive. (　)

(3) In higher power distance cultures, students are expected to listen attentively to teachers in the classroom who are respected without questioning. (　)

(4) Lower power distance is illustrated by student-centered education with autonomous learning and less emphasis on right/wrong answers. (　)

(5) Both the dimensions of power distance and uncertainty avoidance are referred to in comparison of cultures with continuum. (　)

By **masculinity / femininity** Hofstede refers to the degree to which masculine or feminine traits are valued or revealed in cultures. All cultures consist of men and women, who are often referred to as males and females for their biological distinct, i.e. "the sex difference". And in each culture there are social, cultural determined roles for males and females known as "gender roles" and the corresponding traits and behaviors known as masculine and feminine.

In the common trend among most cultures, men are supposed to be more concerned with achievements in career, and they are more likely to be assertive, competitive and tough. Women, on the other hand, are more concerned with taking care of the home, children and people in general, they, therefore are supposed to take the tender roles. Male achievements reinforce muscular assertiveness and competitiveness and female care reinforces feminine nurturance and concern for relationships, which means the masculine or feminine traits respectively.

Of course, which behaviors are considered feminine or masculine differ not only in traditional but also modern societies, leading to gender dominance in professions. For example, women dominate as doctors in Russia, as dentists in Belgium, and shopkeepers in parts of West Africa, but men dominate as typists in Pakistan and sizable share of nurses in Netherlands. Female managers are rare in Japan but more in the Philippines and Thailand.

According to Hofstede, a society is masculine when emotional gender roles are clearly distinct: men are supposed to be assertive, tough, and focused on material success whereas women are to be more modest, tender, and concerned with the quality of life. A masculine culture is usually male-oriented where achievements emphasized, such as higher social status, financial incomes, bigger houses or fancy cars, or even attractive females, and women are in a supportive position for men's success and there are fewer women are in workforce. On the other hand, a famine society is one where emotional gender roles overlap: both men and women are supposed to be modest, tender and concerned with quality of life. A feminine society promotes sex equality, maintaining that men and women own the equal position and rights for social progress and quality of family life. In other words, men do not have to be assertive and they also assume nurturing roles. In feminine cultures, there are more women in workforce, some of whom may occupy higher position as well. Table 3.7 shows how much masculine values are stressed across countries and regions.

Table 3.7 Masculine Values for 53 Countries and Regions (MAS)

RANK	COUNTRY/REGION	RANK	COUNTRY/REGION	RANK	COUNTRY/REGION
1	Japan	18/19	Hong Kong (China)	37/38	Spain
2/3	Austria	20/21	Argentina	37/38	Peru
2/3	Venezuela	20/21	India	39	East Africa
4/5	Italy	22	Belgium	40	El Salvador
4/5	Switzerland	23	Arab countries	41	Korea
6	Mexico	24	Canada	42	Uruguay
7/8	Ireland	25/26	Malaysia	43	Guatemala
7/8	Jamaica	25/26	Pakistan	44	Thailand
9/10	Great Britain	27	Brazil	45	Portugal
9/10	Germany	28	Singapore	46	Chile

Continued

RANK	COUNTRY/REGION	RANK	COUNTRY/REGION	RANK	COUNTRY/REGION
11/12	Philippines	29	Israel	47	Finland
11/12	Colombia	30/31	Indonesia	48/49	Yugoslavia
13/14	South Africa	30/31	West Africa	48/49	Costa Rico
13/14	Ecuador	32/33	Turkey	50	Denmark
15	the United States	32/33	Taiwan (China)	51	Netherlands
16	Australia	34	Panama	52	Norway
17	New Zealand	35/36	France	53	Sweden
18/19	Greece	35/36			

As shown in Table 3.7, the lower the number, the more it is classified as one that owns more masculine traits; and the higher scores are those that tend to have more feminine traits. For example, Japan ranks the first as a very masculine nation where material success of males is stressed at work while obedience and nurturing nature are expected from females who usually quit jobs after getting married. In contract, in the countries like Norway, Sweden, Denmark, it is not unusual for the husband to stay at home taking care of babies while the wife works as a high official to earn the bread. Samovar found that, in the early 19th century, Swedish women were able to trade and sell; women in Norway were granted six weeks of maternity leave more than 100 years ago. In Finland, women had the right to vote and stand for election in 1906. In the following ten years, women in Norway, Denmark, Iceland and Sweden also obtained such rights. After the 1970s, Nordic countries successively implemented the minimum proportional system, stipulating that women should account for a certain proportion in national institutions, generally at a minimum of about 40%. After the general election in Sweden in 2010, women occupied 45% seats in the Parliament. In 2019 the present Finland government elected a female premier with 46% females in the Parliament while in 2018, women sit 20% in the US Congress, and 17.1% and 10.2% in Korea and Japan, which are at the top of masculine rankings.

Gender gap as the impact of masculinity/femininity can be measured by economic participation and opportunities, educational attainment, health and survival and political empowerment. Hausmann found that in 2013, the political empowerment report assessing 136 countries showed that Iceland, Norway, Finland, and Sweden were ranked the top four while the United States was 23, Mexico 68, Italy 71 and Japan 105.

Masculinity and femininity is not absolute but relative in comparison of two or more cultures. Similarly, regions or cities can also be masculine or feminine within a country. Think of Shanghai and Harbin, which is more feminine? Which is more masculine? The differences take place in many families as well, i.e. some families are more masculine while others are more feminine.

The same is true of social institutions. Masculinity and femininity as culture traits can be seen in family, school and workplace. The stability of gender roles is learned in family as the initial part of socialization. For example, in the male-oriented culture, most women want male dominance. In education, the masculine society transfer the role of father to the teacher at school, and students are rarely praised in face. For example, in China, "A teacher for a day is a father lifelong" is an often-quoted saying for centuries showing respect to teachers. Criteria for evaluating both teachers and students differ between masculine and feminine cultures. In a masculine society, teachers' brilliance and academic reputation and students' academic performance are major factors while in feminine one, teachers' friendliness and students' social skills and adaption plays a big role. In a feminine society, a large amount of shopping is done by the husband or husband and wife together while in masculine one, shopping is generally by the wife. And a car is regarded as a sex and status symbol in masculine culture, which is under the decision of the male sovereign, and they would prefer to have one more car, a luxurious one. But in feminine culture, a car is a necessity of live and is usually shared by husband and wife.

Masculinity and femininity affect the way of handling conflicts in workplace. In the masculine cultures like the United States, Britain or Ireland, conflicts should be resolved by a "good fight", while in feminine cultures such as Netherlands, Sweden, and Denmark, they prefer to resolve conflicts by compromise and negotiation. In addition, organizations in the masculine culture stress outcomes and reward it on the basis of equity, i.e. to everyone according to one's performance. Organizations in the feminine culture are more likely to emphasize the process with reward on equality, i.e. to everyone according to need.

Test Your Reading 6

Decide whether the statements are True (T) or False (F).

(1) Masculinity/femininity refers to the gender roles that males and females play in cultures. (   )

(2) Muscular cultures tend to be task-oriented and outcome-based, pursuing physical achievements. (   )

(3) A femininity society is more likely to be less distinctive in gender roles, encouraging equality between genders. (   )

(4) There seems to be higher power distance between males and females in femininity cultures. (   )

(5) The degree of masculinity or femininity affects the ways the females are treated in family or at work. (   )

Long and Short-Term Orientation is the fifth dimension added to the previous ones for more Eastern values from data on Chinese Value Survey (CVS), which is also known as Confucian work dynamism. The study was replicated and extended from data of the World Values Survey (WVS) on more countries with disclosure in 2010 by Minkov and Hofstade as " a universal dimension of national culture, underpinned by concepts that are meaningful across the whole world".

According to Hofstede, the long-term orientation "stands for the fostering of virtues oriented toward future rewards in particular, perseverance and thrift." And the opposite pole, the short-term orientation "stands for the fostering of virtues related to the past and present in particular, respect for tradition, perseverance of face, and fulfilling social obligations."

As shown in Table 3.8, China and other Eastern Asian countries rank high on the dimension, suggesting a long-term orientation. Continental European countries average in the scores while Anglo, African, and South Asian countries score lower for short-term orientations. In other words, the higher scores, the cultures tend to focus on the future rewards. What has to be noted is that the LTO dimension is definitely not Confucianism as not only the Asian countries but non-Confucian countries like Brazil or India are also ranked high for long-term tendency.

Table 3.8 Long-Term Orientation Index Values for 39 Countries and Regions (LTO)

RANK	COUNTRY/REGION	SCORE	RANK	COUNTRY/REGION	SCORE
1	China	118	20~21	Slovakia	38
2	Hong Kong (China)	96	22	Italy	34
3	Taiwan (China)	87	23	Sweden	33
4~5	Japan	80	24	Poland	32
4~5	Vietnam	80	25~27	Austria	31
6	Korea	75	25~27	Australia	31
7	Brazil	65	25~27	Germany	31
8	India	61	28~30	Canada (Quebec)	30
9	Thailand	56	28~30	New Zealand	30
10	Hungary	50	28~30	Portugal	30
11	Singapore	48	31	United States	29
12	Denmark	46	32~33	Great Britain	25
13~14	Netherlands	44	32~33	Zimbabwe	25
13~14	Norway	44	34	Canada	23
15	Ireland	43	35~36	Philippines	19
16	Finland	41	35~36	Spain	19
17~18	Bangladesh	40	37	Nigeria	16
17~18	Switzerland	40	38	Czech Republic	13
19	France	39	39	Pakistan	0
20~21	Belgium	38			

According to the study by Hofstede, long and short-term orientation cultures show themselves in the family, school and workplace. For example, marriage in long-term cultures tends to be regarded as a pragmatic, goal-oriented arrangement. And the old age in high LTO society is an enjoyment and tends to begin earlier, i.e. people enjoy being treated as the old. But in low LTO societies, getting old tends to be delayed as late as possible as it is regarded negatively. In high LTO societies, presents for children such as toys are chosen for the purpose of education or training but parents of low LTO societies pick up presents for love and fun. The major features of the long-verse-short-term orientation are summarized as follows.

Table 3.9 Major Differences between Long-term and Short-term Orientation Societies in General Norms (Hofstede, 2001)

Short-term Orientation	Long-term Orientation
Efforts should produce quick results	Perseverance, sustained efforts toward slow results
Social pressure towards spending	Thrift, being sparing with resources
Respect for traditions	Respect for circumstances
Concern with personal stability	Concern with personal adaptiveness
Concern with social and status obligations	Willingness to subordinate oneself for a purpose
Concern with "face"	Having a sense of shame

High LTO cultures value perseverance and persistence for the goal when the low LTO cultures are likely to have immediate rewards. For example, Chinese students exert efforts to prepare for the college entrance examination for 12 years. In high LTO societies, family and work are not separated and family enterprises are normal with long established relations.

The rate of imprisonment is another evidence of long-verse-short-term orientation in attitude to crime. The long-term orientation solution to crime is to reform criminals and recycle them into productive citizens as described to "turn over a new leaf" because collectivist culture would like to see the crime as a problem whose causes need to be corrected. In individualistic culture people tend to treat criminals as problem, locking them away in prison for punishments.

Hofstede's Cultural Orientations have been widely critiqued for his Western bias and the workplace-oriented data. With the follow-up studies, this cultural pattern has been accepted in cultural studies, media, business and management.

Test Your Reading 7

Decide whether the statements are True (T) or False (F).

(1) Marriages in LTO cultures tend to be more practical, emphasizing more materials, such as decent residences, luxurious cars and splendid wedding ceremonies. (   )

(2) In low LTO cultures people tend to rank pursuit of individual interest before financial rewards in career planning. (   )

(3) People in the high LTO cultures tend to spend what they have for enjoyment while those from the low LTO would save money for the future. (   )

(4) Most of the LTO cultures are the Asian ones where Confucianism is highly valued. (   )

(5) The practice of "reforming the criminal to productive citizens" in high LTO cultures is correlated with the belief in good human nature. (   )

Activity 3

Identify the following Cultures in terms of Hofstede's Value Orientations based on the corresponding indices and compare any two of the three, for example, China with the UK, or the US, or the US with the UK. Write your answers in paragraphs.

Orientations	China	the US	the UK
Individualism-Collectivism			
Power Distance			
Uncertainty Avoidance			
Masculinity-Femininity			
Long-term/Short-term Orientations			

D. Minkov's Cultural Dimensions

Minkov's Cultural Dimensions are based on the statistical analysis of data from the large public databases to identify four bipolar national cultural dimensions by Michael Minkov, a Bulgarian scholar. They are industry verse indulgence, monumentalism verse flexumility, hypometropia verse prudence, and exclusionism verse universalism. The first two are based on the data from the World Values Survey, (known as WVS, a global research project that explores people's values and beliefs, and how they have changed over times and what social and political impact they have), and the other two dimensions are related to data from the United Nations, the World Health Organization, the Transparency International and WVS. As the dimension of hypometropia verse prudence is concerned with physical conducts with little impact on communication, the other three are illustrated hereafter.

Industry verse indulgence considers the priority of work and leisure in national cultures. Evidently, most underdeveloped nations place high priority on industriousness or hard work while those countries with developed economy prefer more leisure than work, which is the indication of any improved economy where people would value more enjoyment of life over work. Table 3.10 shows Industry versus Indulgence Order Ranking Scores (IIS).

In Table 3.10, the high-numbered scores are seen as favoring industrious traits, and the lower scores denotes a preference for indulgent traits. Apparently in the economically underdeveloped culture, people tend to work longer hours with less consumption on personal hobbies or leisure, and are likely to be more thrift in spending. In contrast, people from an indulgent society would place more on sense of freedom and personal enjoyment by means of leisure time and getting together with others. For example, as the second large economy in the world, China had been known as an industrious culture and hardworking and thrift are admirable traditional elements of the Chinese nation. Chinese people used to work six days a week since 1949 and now the Chinese enjoy more leisure life since the 5-day week was adopted from May 1, 1995. And in addition to the Spring Festival, more individual-owned shops would be closed on such traditional holidays as the Dragon Boat Festivals, the Qingming Festival and the Mid-autumn Festival for family union and leisure enjoyment.

Table 3.10 Industry versus Indulgence Order Ranking Scores (IIS)

SCORE	COUNTRY/REGION	SCORE	COUNTRY/REGION	SCORE	COUNTRY/REGION
1000	China	625	Poland	321	Slovenia
968	Vietnam	625	South Africa	316	Argentina
900	Korea	609	Georgia	251	Colombia
883	India	600	Iran	250	Switzerland
869	Indonesia	563	Jordan	228	Mexico
864	Moldova	548	Turkey	213	Chile
827	Romania	527	Serbia	213	the United Kingdom
826	Russia	489	Brazil	196	Australia
744	Bulgaria	463	Italy	167	New Zealand
739	Ukraine	455	France	124	Uruguay
705	Morocco	402	Nigeria	84	Finland
700	Egypt	399	the United States	71	Netherlands
653	Iraq	395	Germany	0	Sweden
636	Zimbabwe	372	Spain		
627	Taiwan (China)	343	Japan		

Table 3.11 shows a comparison of values across industrious and indulgent cultures. There are exceptions when economy develops people remain industrious, for example, in Japan and Korea, overtime work is generally accepted as part of corporate culture, but young people in Korea are trying to shift from long working hours to reduce stress.

Monumentalism verse flexumility is another cultural dimension identified from WVS data by Minkov. By "Monumentalism", Minkov describes cultures "that exhibit individuals with a high level of self-pride along with 'unchangeable identities, strong values, unshakable beliefs, and avoidance of personal duality and inconsistence." According to Minkov, "flexumility", a combination of "self-flexibility" and "humility", characterizes those cultures "that typically exercise humility and situational flexibility, and that easily adapt to changing conditions" shown in Table 3.12.

Table 3.11 Selected Characteristics of Industrious and Indulgent Cultures

Industrious Cultures	Indulgent Cultures
Hard work over leisure	Leisure over hard work
Thrift important	Thrift less important
Economic development most important	Economic development less important
Not fully in control of life	Mostly in control of life
Unhappiness and dissatisfaction with life	happiness and satisfaction with life

Table 3.12 Selected Characteristics of Monumentalism and Flexumility Cultures (Minkov, 2011)

Monumentalism	Flexumility
Self-pride/self-promotion	Humility
Self-concept is consistent/fixed	Self-concept is flexible / fluid
Truth is absolute	Truth is relative
Feelings and expressions equivalent	Feelings and expressions may differ
Religion is important; can be dogmatic	Religion less important
Interpersonal competition valued	Interpersonal competition problematic
Lower educational achievements	Higher educational achievements
Strong defense of one's opinion	Compromise is best
Difficulty in adapting to another culture	Easily adapting to another culture
Direct, forthright negotiating style	Indirect, conflict avoiding negation styles
Suicide unacceptable	Suicide acceptable
Low number of women in workforce	High number of women in workforce

In consideration of the traits, scores are calculated to illustrate the tendency of Monumentalism verse Flexumility based on data from WVS. The higher-numbered scores are seen preferring monumentalism traits and the lower score favoring flexumility traits. For example, Arabian countries are scored higher on monumentalism scale which shows that religion is a central part of life. The United States is ranked middle in the scale, indicating individuality is more valued by encouraging younger ones for his/her American Dreams. The lower-numbered countries like Japan or Korea, interpersonal competition is less encouraged and compromise is best, preferring indirect and conflict-avoidance style of communication, and suicide is accepted as personal tactics without being condemned for religious reasons. In other words, the lower score in monumentalism means higher scores in flexumility on the other end.

Table 3. 13   Monumentalism and Flexumility Scores for 43 Countries and Regions (MFS)

SCORE	COUNTRY/REGION	SCORE	COUNTRY/REGION	SCORE	COUNTRY/REGION
1000	Egypt	571	Argentina	276	Moldova
997	Iraq	564	Chile	265	Bulgaria
955	Jordan	527	India	242	Switzerland
908	Nigeria	521	Romania	191	Russia
890	Morocco	505	Poland	184	Sweden
811	Zimbabwe	492	Uruguay	175	Ukraine
747	Iran	436	Australia	165	France
736	South Africa	427	Spain	119	Netherlands
668	Turkey	423	Vietnam	99	Germany
667	Colombia	388	New Zealand	43	Korea
662	Georgia	359	Serbia	40	Japan
659	Mexico	354	the United Kingdom	16	Taiwan (China)
623	Indonesia	352	Italy	0	China
614	Brazil	340	Slovenia		
572	the United States	312	Finland		

The third dimension is **Exclusionism verse Universalism**, which resembles more like individualism and collectivism by Hofstede's Cultural Dimensions in workplace. Exclusionism verse universalism concentrate on the way of how people treat each other in cultures in terms of its national wealth or the economic development. Exclusionism refers to those cultures in which personal interactions is strongly influenced by group membership while in universalist cultures relationship is established and maintained on the individual basis.

Table 3.14 Selected Characteristics of Exclusionist and Universalist Cultures (Minkov, 2011)

Exclusionist	Universalist
Relationships based on group relationship	Individuality
Close-knit extended family	Nuclear family common
In-group members favored over out-group members	Everyone should be treated equally
Frequent group discrimination	Group discrimination minimized
Agreementare flexible	Agreements normally adhered to
Weak safety procedures	Strict safety procedures
Low environment concerns	High environment concerns
In-group communication clear; out-group communication can be ambiguous	Clear communication with everyone; ambiguity avoided

The characteristics of exclusionism and universalism in Table 3.14 show the different attitudes and behaviors from the corresponding cultures. Minkov studied the correlations and ranked the scores as shown Table 3.15.

Table 3.15 Exclusionist and Universalist Scores for 43 Countries (EUS)

SCORE	COUNTRY	SCORE	COUNTRY	SCORE	COUNTRY
1000	Ethiopia	681	Mexico	395	Hungary
949	Iraq	664	Philippines	382	Chile
872	Morocco	640	Vietnam	333	Japan
858	Egypt	631	Russia	311	Spain
849	Saudi Arabia	615	Brazil, China	274	Portugal
815	Kyrgyzstan	585	Turkey	262	Ireland
803	India	579	Colombia	237	the United States
791	Zambia	557	Bosnia	170	France
773	Venezuela	554	Croatia	120	Germany
756	South Africa	542	El Salvador	119	Australia
733	Uganda	529	Poland	107	Canada
727	Jordan	507	Bulgaria	57	the United Kingdom
724	Bangladesh	476	Korea	34	Norway
718	Azerbaijan	425	Italy		
710	Guatemala	397	Singapore		

In Table 3.15, the higher numbered scores are those favoring exclusionism and the lower score denotes a tendency for universalism. For example, the higher scored ones like Ethiopia, Egypt, India are less developed economically while the lower scored ones such as Italy, Japan, the United States, Germany, Australia and Canada are more developed economies which are also considered to be more individualist. Therefore in exclusionism cultures people rely on more in-group ties for favors, preferential treatments and assistance when in need, conversely member of universalistic cultures tend to treat everyone the same with no regard on group affiliations.

Test Your Reading 8

Decide whether the statements are True (T) or False (F).

(1) Minkov's Cultural Dimensions are featured with the extreme comparison of cultures in four dimensions on the basis of databases of values. ( )

(2) The dimension of hypometropia verse prudence concerns with the physical ways of communication.

(3) In terms of Industry verse Indulgence, cultures with higher numbers tend to be thrifty and long-term oriented, working harder for future happy life. ( )

(4) In terms of labor forces, cultures of Monumentalism prefer more females working outside families for religious or traditional reasons. ( )

(5) Cultures of Flexumility seem to be of high-context communication styles, meaning by what is said. ( )

(6) Exclusionism verse universalism correlate with the dimension of social relationships by Kluckhohn and Strodtbeck in treatment of in-groups and out-groups. ( )

(7) Based on the EUS, there are more extended families in Saudi Arabia than in Australia. ( )

(8) Exclusionist cultures are more flexible in agreements as in low uncertainty avoidance.

Activity 4

Work in groups to identify the following cultures in terms of Mincov's Cultural Dimensions based on the corresponding indices and compare any two of the three, for example, China with Russia, or the US with Russia. Write your answers in Table 3.16.

Table 3.16 Identify the Cultures

Orientations	China	the US	Russia
Industry vs. Indulgence			
Monumentalism vs. Flexumility			
Exclusionism vs. Universalism			

E. Face and Facework

Face and Facework was developed by Ting-Toomy, which high scores the role of "face" and "facework" in intercultural communication. According to Ting-Toomy, face is the metaphor for the self-image that one wants to project to others, or in other words, face is one's public identity. Since face is how others sees, it can be acquired, maintained or lost in social interactions, thus the process of which is defined as Facework.

Researches by Ting-Toomy have shown that people from all cultures strive to "maintain and negotiate face in all communication situations.", and face and facework vary across cultures. In individualistic cultures one's face is derived from his own efforts and independent of others, without much reliance on group affiliation for his identity or social support, thus resulting in a direct and forthright communication style, such as " tell me what you really think" and "don't hold anything back". Samovar found that sometimes harmonious interpersonal relations may become secondary to frankness. However, in collectivist cultures, much more concern goes to other's face as group membership is normally the primary source of identity and status. Establishing and sustaining stable, harmonious relationships with in-group members is of great value and Gao and Ting-Toomy found that gaining and losing face is connected closely with issues of social pride, honor, dignity, insult, shame, disgrace, humility, trust, mistrust, respect and prestige. And extreme politeness and positive interpersonal relationship are of importance in face-saving, thus leading to indirect styles of communication in much regard of contexts.

Face and facework is represented in the ways of how cultures view and approach conflicts. There are three face concerns during a conflict situation according to Face Negotiation Theory by Ting-Toomy, which are "self-face", where the individual is concerned for his/her own face; "other-face", which concerns on the other person's face; and "multi-face", which encompasses both parties in the conflict.

Facework are noticeably influenced by different values on face, face components and face management. For example, when confronting conflicts, collectivists are more likely to be inclined to avoidance and obligating measures as a result of concern for mutual face, other's face and how one's action may affect others. Individualists, however, are more concerned with self-face, and prefer confrontational and solution-oriented approaches. This difference is apparent with the fact that there are more lawyers and frequent lawsuits in the US while in Japan and China disputes are often resolved through intermediaries.

The cultural patterns discussed have shown that cultures could be compared from various value dimensions on the basis of the similarities of cultures. For example, the Tight and Loose Cultures Dimensions is more likely related to what people do in social life while high/low-context cultures concern about the communication style between cultures. Kluckhohn's Cultural Orientations focus more on national values while Hofstede's Value Dimension are more related to international workplaces. And Mincov's Cultural Dimensions add more to Kluckhohn's in understanding perceptions of life, attitudes towards personal relationship and ways to tackle problems in life. Hall's high/low context orientations describe the degree to which individuals rely on internalized information.

What have to be noted is that these perspectives are related to each other in intercultural communication as culture and communication are inseparable. With the help of these instruments, cultural traits could be found out from what people do, facilitating to interpret the cultural values in communication.

Test Your Reading 9

Decide whether the statements are True (T) or False (F).

(1) There are variations concerning how people from different cultures value face and facework. (   )

(2) Generally speaking, collectivist cultures relate one's face to his/her groups for dignity and pride or disgrace and humiliation. (   )

(3) People from individualistic cultures concerns "self-face" and "multi-face" of the communicators. (   )

(4) Conflicts in Asian cultures are likely to be settled through mediations and compromises between the two sides as a result of face concern. (   )

(5) Both Americans and Chinese are sensitive of self-face, other-face and multi-face within their own cultures but more awareness and attention are required in the intercultural context. (   )

Ⅳ. Case Studies of Specific Cultures

Cultures are similar as they share commonalities in characteristics as discussed in previous chapters. As Hall says "culture is communication and communication is culture", cultures can be understood in comparison with help of cultural patterns.

Case Study 2

Study the following cases to list the differences in attitudes and responses to understand the cultures.

> A. Alice is a mother of three boys, John, Alex and Eric. One day she took several apples from the refrigerator, holding the biggest one in her hand before the boys scrambled for it. "Each of you is entitled for this only one, but who is going to have it? Now I have divided the lawn into three pieces and the first one who finishes mowing the lawn is going to have it." Then the boys rushed out to start mowing, and John finally got the apple as a winner.
>
> B. Kong Rong was one of the kids in an ancient Chinese family. One day when the kids were offered pears, Kong Rong took the smallest one, giving the biggest one to the elder and the bigger one to the younger brother, explaining "I decline the bigger one as I am elder than the youngest, and my elder brother deserves the biggest as I am younger." Kong Rong thus has been praised for centuries in China.

Case Study 2 illustrates the values of individualism and collectivism in the forms of open rules for equality and privileges for ages, and rewards on competition and intentions for harmony respectively.

In the American culture, individualism is encouraged for self-reliance, self-responsibility and self-esteem. These boys are equal in the family and each of them is entitled to have the biggest apple, it's therefore Alice assumes it unfair for her to decide who has it. To get the apples as fair reward, obligations are demanded to mow the lawn effectively so that competition is encouraged. At the same time the rules are open and voluntary, i.e. any boy may choose to give up the opportunity for the fine apple, which is the consequence of his own decision. It appeared that every boy has tried hard and John finally won the apple as reward of his work.

Kong Rong has been praised for his respect to the elder brother and love for the younger one as the traditional Chinese values of collectivism. In the Chinese family power distance among siblings is expected and respected due to gender and age. Kong Rong gave the biggest pear to elder brother because the elder one "deserves" privileges for his elder age. On the other hand, Kong Rong himself "deserves" the bigger one as he was elder than the younger one while he gave up his bigger pear to the youngest, leaving the smallest pear to himself. Compared with the American sibilings, Kong Rong voluntarily declined the pear he deserved out of the internalized value of harmony without any open requirements, i. e. what Kong Rong valued was the harmonious relationship among brothers rather than the pear.

Case Study 3

Find out the reasons that made Hollis bewildered and dismayed.

> Hollis was a successful American who was thinking of expanding his business in Asia. Grant was a Thailander who was one of college buddies of Hollis in the United States. Hollis and Grant had been in touch by emails and phones after graduation. Knowing that Grant was also doing business, Hollis told Grant that he wanted to set up a joint venture in Thailand. Grant was very much interested in the idea, looking forwarding to Hollis' visit to Thailand.
>
> The second day after Hollis arrived in Thailand, Grant treated Hollis in a decent restaurant with several of his business associates who would like to meet Hollis. The dinner went on well and Hollis was pleased with the exotic food and Grant and his friends were delighted as well, trying to find out more about Hollis' plan and his business. Memories of the college days lingered on Hollis, and he brought up several incidents he considered humorous and memorable, one of which was a time when Grant was trying to ridicule a professor. He elaborated on Grant's seemingly ridiculous antics and kept commenting, "You should have seen your face!"
>
> Hearing the mention of that sad incident, Grant got blushed, and the others were not laughing as Hollis had expected. The topic was immediately shifted and they left soon after with nobody mentioning the next meeting. Hollis was bewildered and dismayed.

Case Study 3 concerns face and failure of facework in intercultural communication. Face can be gained, maintained or lost due to words or behaviors as it is the self-image or one's public identity that one would like others to have in social interactions. Although Hollis and Grant are both successful in business in the States and Thailand who used to be college friends in the United States, business protocols together with Thai culture were expected with special concern of face in the presence of Thai business people when Grant received Hollis in Thailand with his business associates.

Hollis was bewildered because he didn't know that his recollection of the college life had mad Grant loss of face. Intimate friends as they were in college, Hollis should not have mentioned the incident about Grant in the United States, which made Grant embarrassed, which may result in unhealthy business relationship because one's face is related to his group and others in collectivist cultures. By making Grant lose his face, the face of his friends and even the face of Thailand were damaged as well, and the Thai business people would reckon that Hollis is unfriendly to Grant and their people.

Besides, what happened in the American college at that time may seem normal because it is common for students and teachers to have jokes after class due to shorter power distance between them. But in the Asian culture, the similar behavior would be unacceptable as teachers and professors are widely respected and appreciated.

Hollis was dismayed as he didn't realize what went wrong. According to the high/low context culture communication by E. T. Hall, Thailand, as one of Asian cultures, was influenced by Confucianism and belongs to high context culture, in which communication is more implicit with fewer words and nonverbal messages play a key role. Grant and his friends did not say anything even though they were offended, and they left without mentioning meeting again meant no chances of cooperation. On the other hand, Hollis, from the United States, is used to the low-context communication, and would like to say what it meant, thus he didn't get the message of the Thais.

Case Study 4

Explain to Amanda the cultural reasons for Xiao Mei's hospitality.

> Xiao Mei shared a room with Amanda when she was studying in New York. Yi Han, one of Miao Mei's friends, went to share the bed with Xiao Mei when she visited the Big Apple.

> For the first three days, Xiao Mei showed Yi Han around in the city, going shopping and treating her with the local delicacies without attending her lectures and ignoring her assignments. Amanda was unhappy with one more person in the room but tried to be as nice as she could because she and Xiao Mei had been getting along well.
>
> On the evening of the fourth day, Amanda joined the Chinese girls at dinner. Yi Han was very much impressed with New York, and Xiao Mei seemed as pleased as well. Amanda asked Yi Han about her schedule in New York before Xiao Mei stopped her, but she didn't expected what Yi Han said, "I'm enjoying myself here, and I haven't thought about leaving so far." To her more surprise, Xiao Mei paid the bill by herself even though Amanda insisted on going Dutch.
>
> Seeing the weary and worried look of Xiao Mei, Amanda was puzzled as she knew Xiao Mei had to take part-time jobs for her living expenses and tuitions and she studied hard so that she could return to China upon her graduation.

Case Study 4 shows differences of individualism and collectivism in terms of hospitality, sense of time, and privacy in intercultural communication. Amanda was puzzled because Xiao Mei treated Yi Han with her time and money wholeheartedly regardless of her own schoolwork. On the part of Xiao Mei, she believed in the Chinese saying that "it is always a pleasure to greet a friend from afar" and took it as priority to receive her friends. In the collective cultures, in-group members are supposed to be interdependent and help each other when needed. To show hospitality and intimacy, the host is expected to entertain visitors with accommodation, food and sightseeing together with gifts when leaving. The host is also expected to spend time with the visitor all day long as the round-the-clock company, leaving no privacy for both. Besides, it's regarded rude to require into the plan of the visitor as it would be taken as an hint to expel guests and it's why Xiao Mei tried to stop Amanda from asking for Yi Han's schedule.

On the part of Amanda, she is from the individualist culture where each individual is educated to be independent and take care of his/her own business, for example, one would travel alone, reserving hotel rooms, booking tickets and touring the city with maps without interfering others too much. Amanda was puzzled at the fact that Yi Han has no definite plan for her trip, which is contrary to the individualist culture where one would inform the host of dates of his arrival and departure for the convenience of the host. In addition, Americans would treat friends as well but they would share expenses for most cases for equality and independence, but Yi Han did not pay her meals even though Xiao Mei had to live on less money.

Case Study 5

Choose the best answer from the choices for each question.

> Tom Bancroft, the top salesman of the Midwestern US area, was asked to head up a presentation of his office equipment firm to a Latin American company. He had set up an appointment for the day he had arrived, and then began explaining some of his objectives to the marketing representative sent to meet him at the airport. It seemed that the representative was always changing the subject and he persisted in asking lots of personal questions about Tom, such as his family, and his interests.
>
> Tom was later informed that the meeting has been arranged in several days later, and his hosts hoped that he would be able to relax a little first and recover from his trip, having some sightseeing and enjoying their hospitality. Tom responded by saying that he was quite fit and prepared to give a presentation the very day, if possible. The representative seemed a little taken aback at this, but said he would discuss it with his superiors. Eventually, they agreed to meet with him, but at the subsequent meeting after chatting and some preliminaries, they suggested that since he might be tired they could continue the next day after he had some time to recover.
>
> During the next few days, Tom noticed that though they had said they wanted to discuss details of his presentation, they seemed to spend an inordinate amount of time on inconsequentiality. This began to annoy Tom as he thought that the deal could have been closed several days ago. He just didn't know what they were driving at.

1. What confused Tom's?

A. The Latin American company is investigating Tom and his firm for sufficient information so as to make sure it is a good deal.

B. Latin Americans prefer leisure to work, spending more time on enjoyment.

C. The Latin American company is playing games with Tom as they are not interested in his office equipment.

D. Tom is more interested in the completion of deal while the Latin American company intends to establish good relationship in the course of the business.

2. What are the possible reasons for the differences?

A. Tom is homesick and would like to go back as soon as possible while the Latin American company would like to show their hospitality.

B. Tom is task-oriented with separation of work and leisure while the Latin American company is relation-oriented for business.

C. Tom does not enjoy the sightseeing so much without his family.

D. The Latin American company does not want to do business with Tom but they won't tell him in a direct way.

V. Extended Reading

Chinese Art vs. Western Art: A Comparison

There are many complex factors that come into play during the development of an artistic tradition, such as the histories and philosophies of the involved artists. When comparing the Chinese and Western art, the differences are evident in the medium, composition, perspective, and tone. While most of the Chinese art was used to represent a specific way of expressing landscapes, the Western art was directed at accuracy.

The differences between the two are believed to have originated from the philosophies underlying them. For example, Chinese art was mainly driven by **Buddhism and Taoism**, which targeted the eternal expression of sceneries. On the other hand, the Western art, borrowed more from the Christian philosophy, is targeted to present accuracy, while scenes were seen as mirrors of the nature of God.

A Closer Look at the Chinese Painting

In most **traditional Chinese paintings**, artists used brush dipped in pigments and then applied on silk or paper. Then, the finished work was hung or kept as scrolls. They were also used on lacquer-ware, walls, and porcelain. Taking a closer look at the works of art in China, say from the Han to the Tang Dynasties, one can see detailed portraits of courts showing emperors and the royal lifestyle. During the era, artists started adopting the free-form style of **landscape painting** that later dominated traditional Chinese art. From these early works of art to later developments, the effects of Confucianism and Buddhism that targeted to demonstrate the harmony between nature and humans were very strong. Because of this, artists were able to focus more on emotions and personal feelings when presenting landscapes.

The dominance of landscape painting resulted in the development of more Chinese symbols, including water, clouds, trees, rocks, and people. When these symbols were used, the artists rarely included color or shade to show landscape elements, such as nighttime or daytime. Instead, they used symbols, such as the moon, to indicate it is nighttime.

A Comparison of Western and Chinese Art

Now that you have a brief view of how the Chinese art developed here, is a head-to-head comparison with Western arts:

• **Representational vs. Expressive Art**: Chinese art was used to depict nature, and in most cases, took an imaginative, unique, and expressive method to represent what people could see in nature. This is in line with the **Taoist principle** of living in harmony with nature. In contrast, the Western painting was more representational, using things such as lighting and shapes to denote accuracy.

• **Fixed vs. Dynamic Perspectives**: Most traditional Chinese paintings frequently used dynamic perspectives that helped the viewer to get a clear sense of movement without including realism. However, the Western perspectives took a more fixed approach to create a sense of realism. It is like a photo representation.

• **Minimalism vs. Shading**: Chinese artists used brushstrokes that help them to generate the minimalist outlook and personal feelings. On the other hand, Western arts relied on technical brushstrokes that help to render shading of the item being painted.

As you can see, there is so much difference in the representation of the Western and Chinese art. In both cultures, the main determining factor is the underlying philosophy.

Post-class Tasks

Self-tests Tasks

1. Answer the questions in your own words.

(1) Culture is similar and culture is different.

(2) What are cultural patterns? How are they helpful in understanding cultures?

(3) How does a study of cultural values help you understand other cultures?

(4) What cultural values help explain why face is more important in Asian societies than in the United States?

2. Decide whether the statements are True (T) or False (F).

(1) The cultural patterns discussed in Chapter 3 are the only ones available in studies of intercultural communication. (   )

(2) Some of the cultural patterns are not applicable to practice as the result of the fact that culture is changing. (   )

(3) Cultural patterns can not be taken for all cases as cultural are different in some ways or others.

(4) One can not learn about his/her own culture with help of these cultural patterns.

Group Work

1. Examine the concept of high/low-context cultures. What problems can you anticipate when you are communicate with someone who holds a different context orientation?

2. List the advantages on how a study of cultural values helps you understand other cultures with examples.

3. Values guide what people do as the kernel of culture, and they change with times as well, even though not very much. A comparison of what different generation do provides some clues of these changes. The following is a list of fundamental and basic values for Chinese people revealed in a survey of Chinese values in the early 1980s.

(1) Discuss in groups and decide five values that you think are still important today, and five ones that you believe have changed.

(2) Discuss with your parents or grandparents to find out what they believe the five most important ones and compare with yours (you don't have to agree with each other but you have to give reasons to defend your choices).

Fundamental and basic values for Chinese people (with no particular order).

① filial piety　　　　　　　　　　　　服从、孝敬、尊崇、赡养父母
② industry (working hard)　　　　　　勤劳
③ tolerance of others　　　　　　　　容忍
④ harmony with others　　　　　　　随和
⑤ humility　　　　　　　　　　　　　谦虚(贬己尊人)
⑥ observance of rites and social rituals　礼仪
⑦ loyalty to superiors　　　　　　　　忠于上司
⑧ reciprocation of greetings, favors and gifts 礼尚往来
⑨ kindness (forgiveness, compassion)　仁爱(宽恕、人情)
⑩ knowledge(education)　　　　　　学识(教育)
⑪ moderation, following the middle way 中庸之道
⑫ solidarity with others　　　　　　　团结

⑬ sense of righteousness　　　　　　　正义感
⑭ self-cultivation　　　　　　　　　　修养
⑮ ordering relationships by status and
　　observing this order　　　　　　　尊卑有序
⑯ benevolent authority　　　　　　　恩威并重
⑰ personal steadiness and stability　　稳重
⑱ non-competitiveness　　　　　　　不重竞争
⑲ resistance to corruption　　　　　　廉洁
⑳ patriotism　　　　　　　　　　　爱国
㉑ sincerity　　　　　　　　　　　　诚恳
㉒ keeping oneself disinterested and pure　清高
㉓ thrift　　　　　　　　　　　　　　节俭
㉔ patience　　　　　　　　　　　　耐心
㉕ persistence　　　　　　　　　　　耐力（毅力）
㉖ sense of cultural superiority　　　　文化优越感
㉗ repayment of both the good or the evil
　　that another person has caused you　报恩或报仇
㉘ adaptability　　　　　　　　　　适应环境
㉙ prudence(thoughtfulness)　　　　　小心（谨慎）
㉚ trust-worthiness　　　　　　　　　信用
㉛ having a sense of shame　　　　　知耻
㉜ courtesy　　　　　　　　　　　　有礼貌
㉝ contentedness with one's position in life　安分守己
㉞ being conservative　　　　　　　　保守
㉟ protecting your own "face"　　　　要面子
㊱ close, intimate friendship　　　　　知己之交
㊲ chastity in women　　　　　　　　贞洁
㊳ have few desires　　　　　　　　　寡欲
㊴ respect for tradition　　　　　　　尊重传统
㊵ wealth　　　　　　　　　　　　　财富

Telling China's Stories

　　Education has been highly valued in the Chinese history for thousands of years. As the third generation of your family, write a report on your family education by interviewing the first and second generation, i. e. your grandparents and your parents about their school experiences in terms of the school systems in China. You may include the resumption of the national college entrance examination in 1977, enrollment expansion in higher education in 1999 and your preparation for the National College Entrance Examination (NCEE).

My Learning Reflection

1. What have I learned about Chinese cultures or myself?

2. What have I learned about other cultures?

3. What impressed me most in this chapter?

4. What still confuses me?

Module Two

Cultural Differences in Intercultural Communication

Chapter 4 Verbal Communication

Learning Objectives

- To identify major differences in lexical, syntax and discourse of the English and Chinese languages;
- To apply English as lingua franca for effective and appropriate intercultural communication;
- To help people of different cultural backgrounds as interpreters in intercultural communication.

Pre-class Tasks

- Read the textbook and watch the concerned clips in *xuexitong* (学习通).

Ⅰ. Lead-in Tasks

Activity 1

Study Table 4.1 and guess the meaning of each word.

Table 4.1 Guess the Meaning

Words	Meaning	Language
biladi gujarati		Indian
gatto		Italian
kotka		Bulgarian

		Continued
Words	Meaning	Language
kocka		Czech
Kissa		Finnish
dieKatze		German
paka		Swahili
gato		Spanish
koyangyi		Korean
ねこ		Japanese
cat		English
猫		Chinese

From Table 4.1 we can found that the relationship between the selected symbol and the agreed meaning is arbitrary in each language, as Solomon and Hyperlink believe that "because there is no inherent reason for using a particular word to represent a particular object or idea. In this way, language is said to be the arbitrary vocal symbol, which implies that language consists of speech sounds (e.g. sounds produced by using speech organs) based on the social agreement or convention. It is thus concluded that a certain word has a meaning because the language users have given it. But at the same time it is also true that when someone selects a particular word or phrase, he or she may not be using it precisely in the same manner as someone else, which is often the case when the language is employed as a foreign language.

Activity 2

Paraphrase the following sentences.
(1) "The limits of my language are the limit of my world." (Ludwig Wittgenstein)
(2) "By words the mind winged." (Aristophanes)

As has shown in the quotes, one's thought is expressed with the help of language and at the same time one can perceive the world with language as well. In addition, one's language and thought are closely related, exerting influence on each other, i. e. language and what and how people think are corresponding.

Increasing globalization has made English a lingua franca as means of communication between people speaking vernaculars that are not mutually intelligible and more meanings for the same word are built into the communication experience which may bring about confusion, misunderstanding or even conflicts in intercultural communication. Hence for English language learners in China, concise comprehension of language and culture will facilitate communication, as said by Rita May Brown, " Language is the roadmap of a culture. It tells you where its people came from and where they are going."

II. Understanding Language

A. What is Language?

Language is a medium that helps transmission of thoughts and feelings between individuals. Moreover, it is the tool for people to connect and bond with each other. Same as culture, language is defined in many ways by various scholars.

Case Study 1

Listed are some definitions of language by linguists or philosophers. Compare them and find out what are in common in these statements and conclude your own definition of language in Table 4.2.

Table 4.2 Definitions of Language

Names	Definitions of language	Key words/phrases
Aristotle	Language is a speech sound produced by human beings to express their ideas, emotions, thoughts, desires and feelings.	

Names	Definitions of language	Key words/phrases
Saussure	Language is an arbitrary system of signs constituted of the signifier and signified. In other words, language is first a system based on no logic or reason. Secondly, the system covers both objects and expressions used for objects. Thirdly objects and expressions are arbitrarily linked. And finally, expressions include sounds and graphemes used by humans for generating speech and writing respectively for communication.	
Sapir	Language is a purely human and non-instinctive method of communicating ideas, emotions, and desires through a system of voluntarily produced sounds.	
Bloomfield	The totality of the utterances that can be made in a speech community is the language of that speech community.	
Noam Chomsky	Language is the inherent capability of the native speakers to understand and form grammatical sentences. A language is a set of (finite or infinite) sentences, each finite length and constructed out of a finite set of elements.	
Lyons	According to Lyons, languages are the principal systems of communication used by particular groups of human beings within the particular society of which they are members.	
Encyclopedia Britannica	Language is a system of conventional or written symbols through which human beings as members of social groups and participants in its culture, communicate.	

In these definitions, there are such words or phrases as "a system" "symbols" "signs" "communication" "humans" "community", etc., which indicates the major features of language as means of human communication. Therefore Samovar defines language as "**an organized system of symbols, both verbal and nonverbal, used in a common and uniform way by persons who are able to manipulate these symbols to express their thoughts and feelings.**"

Language is what everyone takes for granted in communication. Schultz and Lavenda noted, "All people use language to encode their experiences, to structure their understanding of the world of themselves, and engage one another interactively."

As David Crystal puts it, "We look around us, and are awed by the variety of several thousand languages and dialects, expressing a multiplicity of world views, literatures, and ways of life." People with different mother tongues would not communicate successfully, and they resort to English as a lingua franca (ELF). For instance, a Danish tourist in Athens asking a Greek passerby for directions; co-players from Germany, China and Hungary sending each other online messages about the team strategies in the game. In each of the cases they communicate in ELF.

English as a lingua franca enables people to understand one another regardless of their cultural and ethnic backgrounds, which makes communication a lot easier and efficient in intercultural communication. As mentioned in Chapter 1, more than 372.9 million people in the world has been speaking English as their first language in the Inner Circle, and almost half a billion people are using English as their second language in the Outer Circle. In addition, English has been used in foreign affairs, economy, trade and education as the first foreign language of many countries in the Expanding Circle.

Against the background of globalization and Chinese culture going global, understanding of the differences and characteristics between English and Chinese will avoid misunderstanding in multicultural workplaces or in daily interactions.

B. What Are the Components of Language?

Linguists have traditionally analyzed language in terms of several subfields of study including phonetics and phonology, morphology, syntax, semantics and pragmatics, among which basic sounds (phonology), the way words are formed (morphology), meanings in language (semantics) and grammar (syntax) are so crucial and varied between English and Chinese that it is a must for English learners to deal with (Figure 4.1).

A good mastery of a language begins with correct pronunciation and accurate meanings in context. If one language does not have similar sounds in another language, it is difficult for speaker to hear and pronounce them correctly. In fact, it is audible to notice difference in sound between two languages, and discrepancies in meanings and sentence structures deserve more consideration. For this reason, it is hard for some English learners in China to distinguish "thank" /θæŋk/ and "sank" /sæŋk/ in English because there is no /θ/ in Chinese. The same is true for learners of the Chinese language to pronounce the tones of Chinese characters in *ma* for 妈, 麻, 马, 骂.

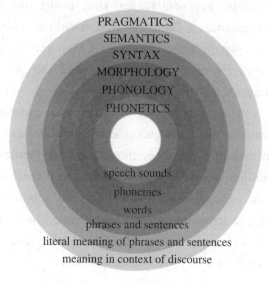

Figure 4.1　Components of Language

Vocabulary is regarded as the basic elements for construction of sentences, paragraphs and discourses, which deserves attentions as well. Because language is arbitrary as symbols, meanings of words can be related in different language to some extent in examples of tables for 桌子, males and females for 男女, and universities for 大学, etc. In the meantime, a single language owns some vocabulary expressing its unique culture as well, but there may be no equivalents in another language, for example, sofa in English or *zhuazhou* (抓周) in Chinese. Interestingly, there are diverse meanings even in the same expressions. For example, "girls" in English refer to female juveniles while the same word is applied to unmarried females in China.

Sentences in each language are constructed based on the rules to combine words for sentences, sentences for paragraphs and discourses, which is known as grammar. Grammar reveals the thinking patterns in regard to how people perceive the world, and how they relate to each other. For example, English sentences are different from Chinese ones in many ways, one of which is the sentence relationships known as hypotaxis for English and parataxis for Chinese. Besides, punctuation marks differ in each language as part of grammar for concise and concrete meanings.

In view of the above, a good mastery of a specific language involves pronunciation, vocabulary and grammar, which are the fundamental elements of any language. To learn a foreign language therefore entails efforts in distinguishing similarities and differences between the new one and one's mother tongue in comparison of these elements.

C. What Do Humans Do with Languages?

Language is essential and central to human lives for its function of communication and is arguably the cultural tool that sets humans apart from any other species. By around four years of age, each normally developing human child is a linguistic genius. Nevertheless, people carry on learning their mother tongue throughout their lives in many ways. Then what else do people do with languages?

Language is the media of recording the history of cultures. Notched sticks, knotted animal hair, scribed or incised tablets, carved or incised bones and shells, painted or scraped rocks i.e. all were media for the storage of information. Among the earliest known forms of data storage are the images carved in stone or painted upon the walls of caves.

Activity 3

Think about the other media to store information in addition to language.

Pictographic images gradually became more abstract and evolved into alphabets prior to historical times. When people first began to write, they drew small pictures to represent the objects. This is called picture writing, and it was very slow because there was a different picture for every word. Egyptian Hieroglyphics are an example of a highly developed form of picture writing (Figure 4.2).

Oracle bone script (Figure 4.2) was an ancestor of modern Chinese characters engraved on oracle bones i.e. animal bones or turtle plastrons used in pyromaniac divination i.e. in the late 2nd millennium BC, and is the earliest known form of Chinese writing. Since the identification of oracle bones in the late 1800s, researchers have attempted to decipher their inscriptions. The carvings reveal much about life in China during the Shang Dynasty over 3000 years ago. They record important events, and offer glimpses of the lives and beliefs of the elite members of society.

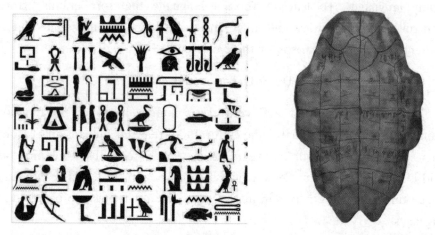

Figure 4.2　Egyptian Hieroglyph (left) Oracle Bone Script (right)

Language is crucial and capable of performing various functions. In addition to storage of information and means of communication, human beings employ language as means of learning and reasoning. For example, language facilitates people to think, imagine, propose, discuss and argue for new ideas as in the design, possibility, production and accessibility of concept cars. In addition, Samovar holds that language functions as social interaction, social cohesion and cultural identity in communication.

Social Interaction

People live with language. In other words, language serves as a special type of social interaction in helping individuals to interact with others in their life, i.e. chatting with friends and family members, discussing at class, asking a passer-by for directions, etc. Moreover, language allows people to express their wishes, feelings, likes, dislikes and ideas. And people use language to buy groceries in the supermarket, to get a job, to hire or fire an employee, to buy train tickets, to think, to store information in computer and to send texts on WeChat, etc. Over time, languages have been passed down verbally through generations and eventually reduced to a form of written records, which allows a group of people to maintain a record of their cultural values and expectations.

Social Cohesion

Language works as the means in helping individuals to form social groups and to engage in cooperative efforts. With a shared language, a group of people could preserve a record of the past events, passing on their traditions. For example, the merits of traditional Chinese culture, such as *dao*（道）, *de*（德）, conscience（良知）, *ren*（仁）, sincerity（诚）, *zhongyong*/golden mean（中庸）are popular in China, so is it in the Southeast Asian with many overseas Chinese speaking Chinese dialects. In addition, Japan and Korea worship Chinese culture and thus some Chinese characters and similar pronunciation can be found in their languages.

Cultural Identity

Language is the major mechanism through which individual or group identity is constructed. As each individual belongs to many types of social groups, such as families, occupations, age groups, clubs and organizations or the sociological class, they interact by means of language on the basis of mutual understanding and expectations. For example, a dialect helps one to get connected with townsmen associations far away from home. To promote economic and cultural exchanges among all the Chinese ethnicities and regions for the unified identity as Chinese, *Law on the Standard Spoken and Written Chinese Language of the People's Republic of China* (《中华人民共和国国家通用语言文字法》) went into effect as of January 1, 2001 in which the State popularizes *putonghua*（普通话）and the standard Chinese characters so that Chinese people can understand each other in the same language. And at the same time, language policies, such as bilingual education, i. e. *putonghua* together with the ethnic minority language or the ethnic minority dialect, are implemented to maintain the ethnic cultures of the autonomous regions for the diverse ethnic identities in China. The same is true of French people who believe so strongly in the value of their language and the need to keep it pure that in 1635 they established the Académie Française to regulate and standardize their language.

These cases demonstrate that language is the major mechanism through which cultural identity of individuals and groups is constructed for senses of belonging and loyalty. In other words, identities will exist until they are enacted through language to unite people by reinforcing group identification accordingly. Nelson Mandela, the former President of the South Africa once said, "If you talk to a man in a language he understands, that goes to his head. If you talk to him in his language, that goes to his heart" as the language binds people together.

Language or dialects help people to bridge contacts with others. Urbanization in recent decades has brought people to big cities in China where they can't use dialects but have to use *putonghua* as means of communication. But they would usually shift *putonghua* to dialects when they go back hometown for the Chinese New Year or at reunions with fellow-townsmen, where dialect is the only choice of means for communication. Think about the occasions when Chinese meet together outside of China, what language would they speak?

To sum up, language is a distinctly human activity that aids the transmission of feelings and thoughts from one person to another as a primary means of communication, which is a dynamic and systematic process in which meanings are created and reflected in human interactions with symbols, therefore language functions in making sense of complex and abstract thought.

Test Your Reading 1

Decide whether the following statements are True (T) or False (F).

(1) Language is a product of human life and record of culture. (　)

(2) A local dialect is one of varieties of a language as language consists of pronunciation, vocabulary and grammar. (　)

(3) People use language in many ways except thinking and reasoning. (　)

(4) Humans live with language as a means of survival, establishing identities and reinforcing sense of belonging and maintaining culture genes. (　)

(5) Speaking the same language makes people feel connected and close. (　)

(6) Esperanto, a man-made world language, does not take the place of English as lingua franca because there is no specific culture is attached to it. (　)

(7) Language represents its culture in the way that it reflects the thought because it shows how people classify and what is important to them. (   )

D. What Are the Characteristics of Language?

Some characteristics are shared for all languages in common. According to Yule, first of all, language and culture are inseparable as a means to store information of culture and pass it down to future generations through a characteristic process called cultural transmission. It is from oracle bone scripts that the history of Chinese culture is estimated and the new archaeological findings in Sanxingdui （三星堆） supplement more detailed evidence to depict Chinese culture in social life, economy and interpersonal relationships.

Then language contextualizes and is contextualized. In other words, language functions in the context related, which determines the meanings of the language concerned. For example, the meanings of word "remove" differs in a sign on the wall of a laundry room reading, "when light flashes, remove clothes" from one in a hospital "remove clothes when being examined", and to be more specific, meanings of words depend on the context where the interaction takes place. It is also true that contexts tailor the language use as well. For example, a teenage will talk with his or her peers in language different from what he/she communicates with his/her parents or teachers.

Finally, language is a part of culture and the channel of culture. According to the Endangered Languages Project by UNESCO, there used to be over 7000 languages in the world, more than half of which will die out by this century and 80%~90% in the next 200 years, and on average a language dies every two weeks. When a language is lost, so is an integral part of a culture's identity. Every language has an exclusive form of cultural, spiritual and intellectual expression. As these forms of expression are misplaced, so is a sense of its people's belonging. When a language vanishes, part of its speaker's history does too, limiting the amount of information linguists can learn about it. China is endeavoring to revitalize local dialects in some regions of China, like Guangdong and Shanghai. By preserving these dialects, China will ensure that many aspects of its rich cultural heritages, such as its music, literature, and customs will endure well into the future.

III. Relationship between Language and Culture

Language is one of the most important elements of any culture and plays a vital role in it. Compared as a living organism, language is metaphoric as flesh while culture as blood, which indicates that without culture, language will die or vice versa, as shown in the Australian and American continents where hundreds of native languages disappeared with colonization by Europeans. In another metaphor, communication is the swimming pool where culture is taken as "water", language itself therefore is the swimming competence.

Culture makes communication possible as it tells people what is expected and how to react in response in communication as part of culture as E. T. Hall holds that "culture is communication". In each society or community, there are established rules and norms for interactions between its group members, by which its offspring are trained to learn and internalize as part of culture. For example, presents are not expected to be accepted after refusals for at least three times, neither are to be opened in the presence of the giver in most Asian cultures. And some Africans, Latin American and Arabian cultures follow the same way, failure of which is considered impolite. On the contrary, in many European countries people would willingly accept gifts with much appreciation, opening it right away. Each of the interactions is accompanied with the conventional expressions as well, which makes communication effective and appropriate.

A. Why Is Cultural Competence Significant in Communication?

In addition to the primary mastery of a new language, one has to have adequate cultural knowledge of the language concerned as language and culture are inseparable.

In terms of language learning, there are two categories of errors in general, linguistic ones and pragmatic ones. The former errors are those related with inaccurate pronunciation, for example, mistaking "th" for "s" in pronunciation, or inadequate use of vocabulary, or failure in grammar, for example, zero use of articles of "the" or "a" where there is expected, or the improper use of numbers or persons in "she" for "he", or inconsistency of tenses in sentences, such as "He teach English in a university." or "We have gone to the park." which will not obviously ensure communication to much extent, thus being tolerated.

The latter ones refer to those related to knowledge of target culture, etiquette practice of social interactions, or nonverbal behaviors, which will result in misunderstanding, unfriendly relationships or conflicts as the result of cultural differences in communication.

Case Study 2

> At one of receptions by a Sino-Spanish joint venture in China, Lilly, a Chinese employee greeted Bella, the Spanish manager in Marketing, complimenting her new dress. Bella replied to this praise with a smile and "thank you".
> What surprised Bella next is the question: "Where did you get it?"
> Bella excused herself to talk with others with a long face, leaving Lilly at a loss.

This case illustrates the consequences that pragmatic errors may bring about. When a linguistic error presents the fact that the speaker is not fluent in the language, pragmatic errors will be interpreted as imperfect personal qualities, leading to poor judgments as being dishonest, rude, uncooperative, impolite or deceitful, which will in return affect relationship and communication.

Globalization and technological development offer excellent potential for individuals and institutions to communicate with people from different cultural backgrounds in English as lingua franca, who unconsciously behave on the basis of their culture norms. Therefore, knowledge of language and communication together with cultural repertoire regarding more specific countries and regions turns out to be essential in intercultural communication, thus intercultural communication awareness (ICA) should well be developed.

Activity 4

> Share in groups your failures of communication due to pragmatic errors. You may tell about personal experiences or retell stories from family members or friends or plots from movies or TV series.

B. What Does Sapir-Whorf Hypotheseis Suggest?

Sapir-Whorf Hypothesis is formulated by Edward Sapir and his student Benjamin Whorf, which indicates the relationship between language and thought. Sapir believes that language and thought are interwoven in some way, and people are affected by the limitations of their language, i.e. human beings are trapped by language as the mental prison and are unable to think freely due to confined vocabulary. This is the basis of the linguistic determinism, also known as the strong version of this hypothesis.

Sapir noted, "Human beings do not live in the objective world alone, nor alone in the world the social activity as ordinarily understood, but are very much at the mercy of the particular language which has become the medium of expression for their society ... The real world is to a large extent unconsciously built up on the language habits of the group. No two languages are ever sufficiently similar to be considered as representing the same social reality. The worlds in which different societies live are distinct worlds, nor merely the same world with different labels attached."

The principle in Sapir's view lies in that what one thinks is fully determined by their language. Whorf, one of the students of Sapir, developed this idea which states:

"…. the background linguistic system (in other words, the grammar) of each language is not merely a reproducing instrument for voicing ideas but is itself the shape of ideas, the program and guide for the individual's mental activity, for his analysis of impressions, for his syntheses of his mental stock in trade."

Therefore the principle in Whorf's idea holds that the difference in language reflects the varied views of different people.

Case Study 3

Study the following kinship vocabulary in English and Chinese and think about the possible relationship between language, thought and communication.

uncles	叔叔、伯父、舅舅、姨夫、姑父
aunts	姨妈、姑妈、婶婶、伯母
grandparents	爷爷、奶奶；外公、外婆（姥爷、姥姥）
grandchildren	孙子、孙女；外孙、外孙女

These Chinese terms indicate different paternal or maternal relationships together with ages and seniority as well while English equivalents are more simple with status of a generation in the family. In the Chinese culture, paternal and maternal relationship is distinct both in language and communication. For example, "uncles" are the terms applied to those who are brothers of mothers and fathers in English, including the in-laws, i.e. husbands of sisters of both mothers and/or fathers. But in the Chinese language brothers of fathers are referred to as *shushu*（叔叔）for younger ones or *bofu*（伯父）for elder ones, indicating ages and seniority respectively, but brothers of mothers, either younger or elder, are called *jiujiu*（舅舅）without differentiation in ages. "Aunts" in English are the sisters of both fathers and mothers, inclusive of the in-laws as well, i.e. wives of brothers of fathers and/or mothers. Again in the Chinese language, *gugu*（姑姑）is termed for both younger and elder sisters of fathers and *yima*（姨妈）for sisters of mothers' with no regard to ages. But *shenzi*（婶子）and *bomu*（伯母）are addressed to wives of brothers of fathers corresponding younger and elders ones while *jiumu*（舅母）are wives of mothers' brothers. It's clear that power distance between males and females is emphasized for authority and seniority on the paternal side with delicate terms for intimacy. Terms of *waisun*（外孙）and *waisunnv*（外孙女）obviously exhibit more remote relationship than those of *sunzi*（孙子）and *sunnv*（孙女）. In this way, language users are trained to distinguish close and distant interpersonal relationships and in turn affect cognition of relationship and communication.

To sum up, both the linguistic determinism and the linguistic relativity illustrate the relationship between language and thought in the ways how people are affected by the language used. In spite of the fact that Sapir-Whorf

Hypothesis has been questioned as there have not yet been sufficient evidences proving that language affects thinking patterns, it's generally agreed that each language does represent experiences of its users which in turn affect their perceptions of the world and their behaviors and communication.

C. How Is Language Related with Thinking Patterns?

Different nations and cultures have their own thinking patterns due to historical backgrounds, religious beliefs, traditional customs, psychological characteristics and values, etc. Therefore, the ways people express their thoughts reveal the way how they perceive the world and how they relate to and communicate with each other.

Synthetic Thinking vs. Analytic Thinking

The general perception of the world is the fundamental philosophy of culture in relation with human beings and among people, which is reflected in its language, interpersonal relationship and the way of communication. Synthetic thinking is based on the holistic worldview, which emphasizes "wholeness" and integrated nature of the world and events. For example, the Chinese culture has been influenced mainly by such religious and philosophical systems as Confucianism, Taoism, and Buddhism, which profoundly affect Chinese people's way of thinking. Chang Tze (369—286 B.C) developed the concept of the Tao by saying that the "One reality is all men, gods and things; complete all-embracing and the whole; it is and all-embracing unity form which nothing can be separated." He also believed that the Man is part of the Nature. And Confucianism as the dominant ideology in China trains people to behave for the purpose of promoting harmony as the world and its components are not many things but one reality. Therefore Chinese people would think and behave in consideration of overall situation for the purpose of unity and integrity. For example, the Traditional Chinese Medicine (TCM) takes a human body as a whole system when there is something wrong in one of his parts, and that is why a foot massage works well for a severe headache, thus synthetic thinking is in practice.

Traditionally, the Western thought pattern follows such famous Greek Western philosophers as Plato and Aristotle who express the idea of "subject and object are separated". They believe that the nature and the cosmos were cognitive objects of humans, and that the fundamental task of humans was to comprehend the cosmos and conquer the nature. The Man and the Nature are antitheses among the permanent contradictions. Contrary to the Chinese view of "unity of the Man and the Nature", the Western philosophy is basically dualism, which definitely makes two opposites, separating a subject from an object, the Man from the Nature, spirits from materials, thoughts from existence, the soul from the body, phenomenon from essence. As a result, they tend to emphasize the parts of the whole rather than the whole itself as one. They tend to split an object into various parts for analysis rather than to take it as a whole for synthesis. For example, doctors of the Western medicine would cure headache to rid pains at head by checks and trials where analytical thinking is applied to the specific components of the human body. Same as in regards to "time", the English expression follows such an order of minute, hour, date, month, and then the year. And in terms of "place", the English expression follows such an order of a street, a city, a province (or a state) and then the country.

By synthetic thinking, Chinese people tend to lay emphasis on commonalities among people or objects so that differences are ignored for the sake of harmony either as interpersonal relationship or relationships among nations, regions, ethnicities so that Chinese people are entitled as friendly and peace-loving. On the contrary, analytic thinking prefers to go into details by classifications and comparisons, stressing on differences, sometimes going to extremes, such as either A or B, black or white, right or wrong, which may lead to conflicts with less tolerance.

Activity 5

Translate the addresses into either Chinese or English and figure out the thinking pattern.

(1) The University of Manchester, Oxford Rd, Manchester, M13 9PL, UK
(2) 中国北京市海淀区西三环北路 2 号　北京外国语大学英语学院华裔美国文学研究中心华飞　邮编 100081
(3) Your home address or cyber shopping address

Abstract Thinking vs. Image Thinking

Abstract thinking is considered to be one of the prominent characteristics in the Western culture, which derives from the ancient Greek and Roman traditions. In the process of exploring the objective world, the Western people aim at finding out the essence and origins of the world. They try to make the abstract generalization with taxonomy by figuring out the common traits among all kinds of concrete objects. They emphasize analysis and fieldwork in favor of components and rations. Consequently, they have developed the tradition of thinking logically and abstractly. The wide use of prepositions is an example to show the abstractness in English. For example, the phrase "to cut it with a knife" means "to cut something by using a knife". Here the preposition "with" is used instead of the concrete verb "use", and the same is true for "a lady in black". Another example is the English alphabetical letters which do not represent any images compared with Chinese characters, though it is said that the original English letters used to be pictograms as well.

Comparatively, image thinking is one of the most apparent characteristics of traditional Chinese culture. *The Book of Changes* (《易经》) seeks for the origin of Chinese culture by "observing the images". Traditional Chinese medicine advocates the principle of "viewing the appearance colors" to diagnose a disease. Therefore Chinese people tend to be inclined to extract an image from an object to express their feelings and thought. They believe that images are more expressive than words, concealing the very meaning with vivid symbols as "the true meaning lies in the outside world". Chinese people have thus formed the custom of expressing ideas by metaphors, similes, and allegories. They would employ every known device to make opinions plain and meaningful by comparing it to something else. There are many Chinese words and idioms with figurative comparison for concrete and sensible ideas. For example, the metaphor of "鸦雀无声" implies that a sudden silence falls when noise cannot be heard because "鸦" (ravens) and "雀" (sparrows) are birds characterized by their constant chirping of sounds, which is an unusual situation. Same as the example of "掌上明珠", for a beloved daughter in the eyes of her parents as "pearls in one's palm", the combination of the two Chinese words "明珠" and "掌上" respectively as metaphors of images.

Image thinking is more often applied in Chinese arts and artworks as well.

For example, Chinese paintings are more likely to present comprehensive descriptions of broad scopes of mountains, rivers, clouds, birds, trees, flowers, bamboos and stones, etc. as images for imagination. Together with poetry, calligraphy and stamps, a piece of Chinese painting is therefore appreciated as a whole rather than in fine details. On the contrary, the Western paintings are more dedicated to vividness and reality of objects (Figure 4.3).

Figure 4.3   Chinese Painting (left) and Western Painting (right)

Linear Thinking vs. Circular Thinking

It's generally agreed that Westerners prefer linear thinking while Chinese prefer circular thinking in contrast. Linear thinking is also called deductive reasoning which starts out with a general statement, or hypothesis, examining the possibilities to reach a specific, logical conclusion from outcomes to reasons, from the small to the big with help of generality to understand particularities. Westerners tend to think in linear because they are good at analyzing and reasoning. Influenced by individualism, Westerners are encouraged to express their opinions directly, so they prefer a clear and direct way of communication, which can be found in the idioms like "call a spade a spade" "Don't beat about the bush", etc. Linear thinking as a form of logical reasoning is widely applied as shown in the menu of computers or smart phones.

Circular thinking is also called inductive thinking or particular-general thinking. Induction refers to the process in which conclusion is inferred on the basis of facts or from the particular to the general. The circular reasoning is more favored by the Chinese who are influenced by the traditional Chinese culture because they focus on integrity and depend on intuitions. In China, Confucianism has been prevalent for thousands of years, and the doctrines of Confucianism such as tolerance, benevolence, and politeness have exerted a strong influence on the Chinese so that people tend to be moderate and reserved in communication.

Activity 6

Here's a quiz to determine your thinking style (Table 4.3). Imagine yourself facing a challenge. Does Column A or Column B feel like the best way to proceed?

Table 4.3 Determine Your Thinking Style

Column A	Column B
1. Define the goal	1. Gather and welcome everyone affected
2. Develop a strategy	2. Ask each person to express their feelings
3. Make a plan	3. Interactively share information
4. Set time lines, costs, tasks	4. Recognize a pattern, follow an idea
5. Activate the plan	5. Give language to what is meaningful
6. Measure progress	6. Respond to the information and redesign

Objective Thinking vs. Subjective Thinking

"Being objective" refers to a mind-independent reality, meaning that an objective feature of the universe is something that does not rely on personal beliefs of anyone else or feelings of the matter. In the Western culture, the object is thought to be separated from the subject, and "the Heaven and Man are opposite". Therefore objective thinking takes an object and/or the nature as the core with observations and researches, emphasizing that it is only by paying more attention to the natural objects that the Man will know about the Nature so as to conquer the Nature. Influenced by such beliefs, Westerners would act as observers, probing into details as objects, which results in the English language with frequent applications of inanimate subjects (无灵主语) or impersonal subjects (物称主语), including material objects, abstract concepts and nouns (nominalization) derived from verbs or adjectives.

Instead, "unity of the Man and Nature" prevails in the Chinese culture. Chinese is more likely to regards the Man (the subject) as the center and the starting point of the cosmos, focusing on subjectivity of human beings and the beliefs are commonly accepted by Chinese people, such as "Heaven and earth were born at the same time I was, and the ten thousand things are one with me."("天地与我并生,而万物与我为一"《庄子·齐物论》). It is under the long-term influence of such beliefs that subjective thinking, as the representative in Chinese culture, came into being. Subjective thinking is also embodied in the Chinese sentences as in the animate subjects are frequently referred to. For example, the Chinese would say "我突然想到了一个好主意", in which "我"（I） as the subject, while in English "A good idea suddenly occurred to me" presents the objective thinking. For the same reason, "it" is often employed as the subject in English as in "It's a good idea to call her before you go".

Activity 7

Study the following sentences for language difference in terms of thinking patterns in Table 4.4.

Table 4.4 Language Difference in Terms of Thinking Patterns

Sentences	Language features	Thinking patterns
My total ignorance of the connection must plead my apology. 恕我孤陋寡闻,对此关系一无所知。		
My conscience told me that I deserved no extraordinary politeness. 凭良心讲,你待我礼貌有加,我却受之有愧。		
Specialties in colleges and universities should be adjusted and teaching methods improved. 必须调整高等院校的专业设置,改进教学方法。		
The resistance can be determined provided that the voltage and current are known. 只要知道电压和电流,就能确定电阻。		
It is a good horse that never stumbles. 人有失误,马有失蹄。		
It is in the hour of trial that a man finds his true profession. 人总是在面临考验的关头,才发现自己的专长。		

Ⅳ. Language Use in Intercultural Communication

English as a lingua franca is widely applied in daily communication or in business context between people or institutes with different cultural backgrounds, but misunderstanding may occur because language is unavoidably affected by culture at the lexical, syntactic, discourse and pragmatic levels.

A. How Is Culture Expressed in Words?

As pronunciation is notably different in each language, meanings of words are sometime taken for granted that they are equal when translated. However, it is not true as the result of cultural differences in thinking patterns.

Non-equivalence in Lexical Meanings

In terms of the word meanings in two languages, there are varying degrees of equivalences in consideration of cultural influence. There are terms of total equivalents, zero equivalents, partial equivalents, superficial equivalents or several equivalents in corresponding language. The following are discussed on the basis of the English and Chinese language as examples.

Total equivalents are the terms of full degree of equivalence in both languages, i. e. the terms in one language have exact or near equivalents in another language. Terms of total equivalents are found when individuals start learning to express the same meaning in the corresponding language as the native one. For example, kids are interested in repeating "apples" "balls" "boys and girls" when they begin learning English, and foreigners first learn to say "你好" "谢谢" and "再见" when they are in China. Total equivalents are usually those referring to the natural objects, scientific or technical words, for example, a cat, a rose, rain, air, phones, etc.

Zero equivalents are terms of vacant degree of equivalence in another language, referring to those objects, ideas or concepts to which there are no corresponding words found in another language. For example, there is nothing like sandwich, sofa and coffee in Chinese culture, or *fengshui*(风水) and *junzi* (君子) in English either. Examples of this kind are *qi* (气) and *jingluo*(经络)

in the Traditional Chinese Medicine, varieties of noodles in Italian or sausages in German as they are representations of the unique cultural phenomenon of the language. Therefore these terms are referred to as "zero equivalents" and are usually expressed by way of transliterations or interpretations.

Superficial equivalents are the terms that seem to have the same linguistic meanings in both languages while the cultural connotations vary a lot. For example, "爱人" in Chinese is often applied to one's spouse, especially those of the educated. If translated into "lover" in English, it refers to the extramarital relationship instead of "husband" or "wife". Another example is "girls" or "ladies" in English which differ in maturity, independence and behavioral appropriateness in addition to ages when referring to females, but in the Chinese language, they are generally classified by marital status. Terms such as cadres and "干部", peasants and "农民", propaganda and "宣传", materialism and "唯物主义", intellectuals and "知识分子", play and "玩" are where cultural confusions or misunderstanding would arise.

Partial equivalents are those terms which express the overlapping meanings of words in both languages. In other words, these equivalents are equal in meanings to some extent or different interpretation as result of cultural values or practice. For example, "family" in English usually refers to the nuclear household in most cases with two generations as parents and children, meaning "小家庭" while in the Chinese language, nowadays it means the same in most cases, but it's more generally applied to the family clan with more generations and branches including remote relatives as in "family history" (家谱) "family business" (家族企业) and "family temples" (祖祠), etc.

More equivalents are terms with more similar words to context in either language with distinctions. A good example of this category is the kinship terms in Chinese which are found fewer equivalents in the English language as the result of the distinctive form of Chinese address for paternal and maternal relatives. The English equivalents of "爷爷、奶奶/阿公、阿婆""姥姥、姥爷/外公、外婆" are generally addressed as grandfather and grandmother, and same is true of uncles and aunts for "叔叔、伯伯、舅舅" and "姨妈、姑妈、舅妈、婶婶" in Chinese.

Activity 8

Study the words and classify them into the categories of equivalence that they best fit in Table 4.5.

> water, sky, rain, snow, computer, clone, science, democracy, freedom, privacy, family, wife、husband, jacket, teachers, colleagues, grandmother,grandfather, uncles, aunts.
> 三伏、节气、经络、抓周、风水、家族、夫人、太太、妻子、先生、老爷、爱人、爷爷、奶奶、叔叔、伯伯、舅舅、姨妈、姑妈、外套、书套、教师、导师、同事、同行。

Table 4.5 Equivalence of Words

Degree of equivalence	Examples of words
Total equivalents	
Zero equivalents	
Superficial equivalents	
Partial equivalents	
More equivalents	

Words with Culture-specific Concepts

The degree of equivalents at the lexical level stems from the cultural connotation in the language concerned. And the words with cultural specific concepts may work as communication barriers as well, which entail vocabularies in relation to color, animals and plants as well.

Connotations of Words

Colors are culturally loaded in expressing mourning, happiness, anger, sad or fear but they may have opposite connotations for people from different areas or countries. Some of color connotations are shared, for example, the colors of traffic lights are universal. But there are variations as well. For example, in China, "红色" (red) is associated with joyful events, such as weddings, celebrations of starting business, Chinese New Year and anniversaries while the same color may stand for danger, violence or bloodshed in Western cultures.

Case Study 4

> Mr. Murphy, an Irish professor who used to teach in one of the universities in Beijing visited China years later after he returned to Ireland. He was welcomed by his former colleagues and students when he was in Beijing, meeting old friends, enjoying the local food and sightseeing the new look of the city. On the day when he set off home, he left a farewell present as a token of appreciation at the airport to Professor Wan, one of his Chinese colleagues. To a surprise of Professor Wan, he found a baseball hat in light green color! After a second thought, Professor Wan smiled.

In general, "green" stands for vitality and life, and it is the joyful color in Ireland, especially on St. Patrick's Day when people dress in green with various shapes of green hats! In this case, Professor Murphy takes it for granted that Chinese people would like the Irish green baseball cap because Irish people are keen on sports and green color is the symbol of Irish culture while he doesn't know the cultural connotation of "the green hat" in Chinese culture. Professor Wan was surprised at the present as he knows well how Chinese people would feel, seeing people wearing green hats. But he smiled later because he realized the cultural meaning of the green hat with the help of his intercultural competence.

Colors are applied for metaphors as well. For example, in China, "红眼病" is the metaphor of envy while in English, "green with jealousy" bears the same meaning. The white wedding dress symbolizes purity and holiness in the West while the same color stands for condolence in most of Asian cultures.

Activity 9

Work in groups to find out the color connotations in other cultures in comparison with Chinese customs in Table 4.6.

Cultural connotations are expressed in plants and animals related vocabularies. Culture teaches people values by means of metaphors, proverbs and images in literature and daily expressions which are familiar to its people but sometimes sounds different to the ears of other cultures.

Table 4.6 Color Connotations

Colors	Chinese Connotations	Other Cultures	Connotations
red		Russia	
yellow		Japanese	
green		Irish	
white		English	
yellow		English	
black		English	
blue		English	

Activity 10

Work in groups to find out the connotations of plants and animals in other cultures in comparison with Chinese customs in Table 4.7.

Table 4.7 Connotations of Plants and Animals

Plants/Animals	Chinese Connotations	Other Cultures	Connotations
bamboos		English	
orchids			
plums			
pines			
chrysanthemums		European	
foxes			
monkeys			
bats		English-speaking	
owls			
dogs			
tigers			
peacocks			
oxen			

In addition to these connotations, the concept in question may relate to philosophical schools, abstract or concrete concepts, social customs or even food, which are often referred to as "culture-specific". For example, there were no equivalents in Chinese for the words such as democracy, science and rights, etc. until they were translated from Japanese into Chinese in the modern times. Similarly, there are no equivalents in English for such Chinese terms as "躺平"(to lie flat; to be a couch potato), "双减"(double reductions; to ease the burden of excessive homework and off-campus tutoring for students undergoing compulsory education), "强国有我"(We are ready to build a powerful China) etc. The "speakers" (of the House of Commons/Representatives) find no equivalents in languages such as Chinese, Russian or Arabic. It is often translated into Chinese as "议长", which does not reflect the role of the Speaker of the House of Commons as an independent person who maintains authority and order. There are examples of concrete concepts in Chinese, which are unknown to English speakers, such as "知行合一" (unity of knowledge and action), "居安思危" (be on alert against potential danger when living in peace), "道法自然"(Dao operates naturally), "脏腑"(zang-fu organs) etc.

Test Your Reading 2

Decide whether the following statements are True (T) or False (F).

(1) As vocabulary is the basis for constructing sentences and paragraphs, it's good enough to know the meaning of words by looking up English and Chinese dictionaries. (   )

(2) Reading in English is regarded as the best way to expand vocabulary and learn about cultures. (   )

(3) In the Chinese culture, the bird owl is a symbol of misfortune but in other cultures it represents intelligence and wisdom. (   )

(4) Westerners believe that peacocks strut their heads and show off their beauty by waving their crowns and spreading their tails from time to time, which is the expression of "pride" and "vanity", for example, "as proud as a peacock", "a peacock in his pride" and "play the peacock", etc. (   )

(5) The pine tree as metaphor of longevity is widely applied in the world. (   )

B. How Are Thinking Patterns Revealed in Sentences?

The way of thinking is indicated in construction of sentences as a result of cultural values, therefore each language tends to have the specific ways to organize the parts of sentences. For example, verbs of German are usually delayed at the end of sentences, and personal pronouns as objects in French tend to be before verbs, etc. As far as English and Chinese languages are concerned, there are differences that deserve attention in communication.

Hypotactic Structures vs. Paratactic Structures（形合与意合）

The major syntactic difference in English and Chinese is what is known as hypotactic and paratactic structures. Sentences in English tend to be in hypotactic structure, in which clauses are arranged depending on relations or constructions through linguistic forms, such as conjunctions, adverbs and prepositional phrases. On the other hand, sentences in Chinese are likely to be in the paratactic structure, where clauses are arranged one after another without connectives showing relation between them through semantic ties.

Table 4.8 Hypotactic Structure in English vs. Paratactic Structure in Chinese

After peaceful reunification, Taiwan will enjoy lasting peace **and** the people there will live **in** peace **and** contentment. 和平统一之后,台湾将永葆太平,民众将安居乐业。
We must put **into** action the thought **on** foreign affairs **and** work continuously **to** create an external environment favorable **for** realizing the Chinese Dream **of** national rejuvenation **and** building a global community **of** shared future. 我们要全面贯彻落实新时代中国特色社会主义外交思想、不断为实现中华民族伟大复兴的中国梦、推动构建人类命运共同体 创造良好外部条件。
The world is undergoing a scale **of** change unseen **in** a century, **and** Macao is facing new internal **and** external dynamics. **In** this context, the new MSAR government **and** all sectors **of** Macao need **to** stand taller **and** look farther, brace **for** potential risks even **when** the going is good, break new ground **while** keeping **to** the right path, **and** be results- oriented **and** hard-working. I encourage you **to** build **on** what Macao has accomplished **and** take all undertakings **in** the MSAR to the next level. 面对世界百年未有之大变局,面对澳门内外环境新变化,澳门特别行政区新一届 政府和社会各界要站高望远、居安思危、守正创新、务实有为,在已有成就的基础上推动澳门特别行政区各项建设事业跃上新台阶 。

In consideration of communication, the hypotactic structure coincides with the low-context culture, which prefers more specific information with explicit expressions on the part of speakers/writers to make themselves understood, while the paratactic structure conforms to the high-context culture where the listeners/readers are responsible for the interpretation of what is said with implicit expression, the fewer the better. For example,"你听懂了吗?"is more common in Chinese, which is " Have I made myself understood?" in English.

Compound Sentences vs. Simple Sentences

There are more compound structures in English than in Chinese which demonstrate one of the major differences between the two. Compound structures are known as the tree structure, where there is a basic sentence structure of the subject and verbs, from which all other constructs sprout out without affecting the expansion of the branching ones in the forms of noun clauses or relative clauses. On the contrary, there are more simple sentences, usually short ones in the Chinese language, known as the bamboo structure, where sentences or phrases go one after another like bamboo joints. Sometime subjects are missing in the sentences as it's taken for granted as in the high-context culture communication.

Table 4.9 Compound Sentences vs. Simple Sentences

Compound Structure(as a tree)	Simple Sentences (as bamboos)
He told me what had happened when he got to the building where he used to work for years.	他告诉我,那天楼里出事儿了,他在那儿工作了多年。
He jumped to rush into the bathroom, **where** he looked though the wound, a towel in hand.	他跳起来,跑到卫生间,拿起毛巾,仔细查看脸上的伤口。
Researchers looked at data from 30,000 adults followed for an average of 17 years and found that each additional half an egg per day was significantly linked to a higher risk of heart disease and death.	研究人员观察了3万名成年人,跟踪时间平均达17年,数据显示,每天每多吃半个鸡蛋,心脏病和死亡的风险显然更高。

Head-weight Placements vs. End-weight Placements

English and Chinese are different in where the key words are placed. Head-weight in sentence features prominently in English with the key words at the beginning of the sentence followed with attributes, especially the longer ones. In the Chinese language, the key words are delayed further away after the attributes.

Table 4.10　Head-weight Placements vs. End-weight Placements

Head-weight Placements	End-weight Placements
Michelle Wu, who entered public service out of frustration with the obstacles that her immigrant family faced, will be the next major of Boston, pledging to make the city a proving ground for progressive policy.	因对自身移民家庭所面临的困难感到沮丧,**吴弭**进入了公共服务领域。她将成为下一任波士顿市长,并承诺将这座城市变成进步政策的试验场。
This is **the book** that my sister brought me on my birthday.	**这本书**是我姐姐送我的,我生日那天买的。
I **don't agree** to this plan **for** three reasons.	……(基于上述三点),所以,我对上述计划持**保留意见**。
He was absent **because** he caught a cold.	他因感冒缺席。

In both English and Chinese, conclusions, judgments, consequences and facts are weighted as the main part of sentences, but English and Chinese differ in placing these components. In the English language, points of view, judgments and consequences usually appear at first of the sentences or at the beginning of paragraphs. In compliance with head-weight writing in English, attributive and adverbial clauses are to follow after the main sentences as back modifiers for a pre-emptive strike. In comparison, the Chinese ones are usually delayed at the end of the paragraphs and the attributive and adverbial as front modifiers are placed ahead of the key words, expecting the effect to make the finishing touch.

Language reveals the thinking patterns as in the above example. The head-weight way of writing in English results from deductive thinking and inductive thinking contributes to the delayed key words in sentences or conclusions at the end of writing in Chinese.

Impersonal Statements vs. Personal Statements

As observers of the Nature, Westerners prefer to probe into details as objects, thus the English language tends to describe the "facts" with frequent application of inanimate subjects (无灵主语) or impersonal subjects (物称主语), including material objects, abstract concepts and nouns (nominalization) derived from verbs or adjectives.

As the result of objective thinking, "it" is more often than not employed in English to comply with inanimate subjects or impersonal subjects.

Table 4.11 Impersonal Subjects vs. Personal Subjects

Impersonal Subjects	Personal Subjects
The past four decades have seen great changes in modernization in China.	四十年来，**中国的现代化**发生了巨大变化。
A report was presented by the Mayor at the conference on the ecological development and evaluation of this area with the implementation of the new law.	会议报告中，**市长**阐述了该地区实施新法规后的生态发展与评估情况。
This is an objective for which we should never relax our efforts, nor should our future generations.	**我们**要紧紧扭住这个总任务，一代一代锲而不舍干下去。
It would take a universally trusted organization with sophistication in health, technology and diplomacy to get countries to agree on global standards.	要让**各国**就全球标准达成一致，需要一个在卫生、技术和外交方面都很成熟，且受到普遍信任的组织。

Passive Voices vs. Active Voices

In the English language, frequent use of inanimate subjects or impersonal subjects result in the corresponding application of passive voices so that subjectivity is avoided and the point of view in the third person highlights objectivity. For example, instead of indicating "people think that …", "it is generally accepted that …" is preferred. Here are some more examples in this regard.

Table 4.12 Passive Voices vs. Active Voices

Passive Voices	Active Voices
The study was written by people with financial links to Woebot.	但是这项研究（的论文）是由与 Woebot 有利益关系的人撰写的。
Mental-health apps were designed to be used in addition to clinical care, not in lieu of it.	心理健康应用程序旨在用于临床护理之外，并非取而代之。
Studies find moderate amounts of black coffee have been shown to lower the risk of certain diseases.	研究表明，适量的黑咖啡可以降低患某些疾病的风险。

In view of what is discussed above, the different ways in expressing ideas in sentences deserve attention when communicating in English. In other words, sentence patterns are the verbal expression of the thinking patterns as its cultural values.

Test Your Reading 3

Decide whether the following statements are True (T) or False (F).

(1) The Chinese language is more likely in the paratactic structures with more short sentences and fewer conjunctions to indicate the logical relationship of sentences. (   )

(2) The English sentence is like a tree with many branches from a truck as the main structure with many clauses. (   )

(3) To organize the Chinese ideas into the English structure what one has to do is to translate it into English in the same order of the Chinese. (   )

(4) The Chinese language tends to delay the key words with modifiers ahead of it while the English prefer to highlight the key words first with long modifiers following afterwards. (   )

(5) Narration in the third person is more usual in English writings with the inanimate subjects or impersonal subjects as a result of dualistic worldviews to separate the Man from the Nature. (   )

C. How Are Thinking Patterns Displayed in Discourses?

Detective stories by Agatha Christie are well-known for "deductive reasoning" in finding out murderers, for example in *Death on the Nile* and *Murder on the Orient Express*. Then what is deductive reasoning and what makes it different from inductive reasoning?

Case Study 5

Identify the differences of following reasoning. Do you agree with the statements? What is the logic in it?

> A. All men are mortal. Harold is a man. Therefore, Harold is mortal.
> B. I have seen four students at this school leaving trash on the floor. The students in this school are disrespectful.

Deductive reasoning sometimes is confused with inductive reasoning, and vice versa. It is important to learn the meaning of each type of reasoning so that proper logic can be identified.

Deduction/Deductive Reasoning（演绎法）

Deductive reasoning is a type of logical thinking that starts with a general idea and reaches a specific conclusion. It's sometimes is referred to as top-down thinking or moving from the general to the specific. A common example is the if/then statement. If A = B and B = C, then deductive reasoning tells us that A = C.

Table 4.13 Examples of Deductive Reasoning

Logically sound ones
A. All dogs have ears; golden retrievers are dogs, therefore they have ears.
B. All racing cars must go over 80MPH; the Dodge Charger is a racing car, therefore it can go over 80MPH.
C. Christmas is always on Dec. 25th; today is Dec. 25th, therefore it's Christmas.

Induction / Inductive Reasoning（归纳法）

Induction is reasoning from a specific case or cases and deriving a general rule. It draws inferences from observations in order to make generalizations. You may have come across inductive logic examples that come in a set of three statements. These start with one specific observation, add a general pattern, and end with a conclusion.

Deduction and induction by themselves are inadequate to make a compelling argument. In deduction, a "top-down" process of understanding whether or not an assumption is true, there are no place for observation or experimentation, and no way to test the validity of the premises. But induction is driven by observation, going from the specific to the general, and it never approaches actual proof of a theory. Therefore an effective paper should include both types of logic to make itself more logical and persuasive (Table 4.14).

Table 4.14 Examples of Inductive Reasoning

Stages	Example 1	Example 2
Specific observation	All of my white clothes turn pink when I put a red cloth in the washing machine with them.	Baby Jack said his first word at the age of 12 months.
Pattern recognition	My white clothes don't turn pink when I wash them on their own.	All observed babies say their first word at the age of 12 months.
General conclusion	Putting colorful clothes with light colors causes the colors to run and stain the light-colored clothes.	All babies say their first word at the age of 12 months.

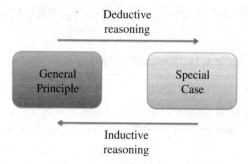

Figure 4.4 Deduction and Induction

Test Your Reading 4

Identify whether the discourse patterns of the statements are in deduction (D) or in induction (I).

(1) All men are mortal. Joe is a man. Therefore Joe is mortal. If the first two statements are true, then the conclusion must be true. (   )

(2) Bachelors are unmarried men. Bill is unmarried. Therefore, Bill is a bachelor. (   )

(3) To get a Bachelor's degree at the Utah Sate University, a student must have 120 credits. Sally has more than 130 credits. Therefore, Sally has a bachelor's degree. (   )

(4) This cat is black. That cat is black. A third cat is black. Therefore all cats are black. (   )

(5) This marble from the bag is black. That marble from the bag is black. A third marble from the bag is black. Therefore all the marbles in the bag are black. (   )

(6) Two-thirds of my Latino neighbors are illegal immigrants. Therefore, two-thirds of Latino immigrants went to the US illegally. (   )

It is generally agreed that discourses are the linguistic structures above sentence levels. To be more exact, it concerns with the ways how to get one's ideas to others with extended texts, the use of language and structures. Examples of discourses can be in any of written or spoken forms, such as novels, letters, stories, chapters, articles, argumentation, jokes, dialogues, sermons, prays, speeches, conversations, interviews, business dealings, lectures and etc. While written discourses involve writers and readers, a spoken discourse is a joint product by the participants more than the speaker and listener as a communication process, which explains at best complexity of communication across cultures.

Discourses are conditioned by cultural values and thinking patterns as the way of communication in the language concerned, and the style of discourse is expected in the respective culture when communicating, i.e. how something is stated is related to how it is understood and responded in terms of communication styles and thinking patterns. Therefore, in addition to correct use of the grammar of a language, the cultural factors affect the way of getting across the meanings, which may result in unexpected or even shocking responses from the reader or listener. To be more exact, when one communicates in English as lingua franca, he/she is expected to employ the language in the way as it is so as to maintain the accepted logic and styles of the language in coherence and cohesion.

Activity 11

Study the following spoken presentations in Table 4.15 at a business meeting between a Chinese and an American. Decide which one might have been delivered by the Chinese and which by the American with reasons.

Table 4.15 Spoken Presentations

Presentations	Speakers	Styles of Discourse
A. Because most of our production is done in Hong Kong, and it's not certain how the situation right now will last, and since I think a certain amount of caution in committing TV advertisement is necessary because of expanses. So I suggest that we delay making our decision until after the Legco makes its decision.		
B. I suggest that we make our decision until after Legco makes its decision. That's because I think a certain amount of cautions in committing TV advertisement is necessary because of expense. In addition to that, most of production is done in Hong Kong, and it's not certain how the situation right now will last.		

 The Chinese applies the inductive pattern of discourse which is characterized by "topic-delayed" structure in which reasons or elements are given in consideration of the comprehensive picture before the main idea is presented. On the contrary, the American expresses his idea in the deductive pattern which is characterized by "topic-first" structure by stating the main point with a topic sentence followed by the supporting information and reasoning.

 Generally the deductive pattern is more prevalent in the West and the inductive one is more popular in most Asian cultures as the result of worldviews and values. In terms of language use and communication, Westerners prefer to state their ideas and attitudes more directly as they belong to low-context culture. When they communicate with Chinese, it would be hard for them to get the main point as the inductive discourse is not what they expect, i.e. the topic sentence is delayed as a conclusion at the end. However, it's comparatively easy for Chinese to get the point of the deductive discourse on the basis of good mastery of English.

Case Study 6

Try to give advice to Wu on each of the specific criticism from the company by finding out the problems of verbal communication of Wu in the Swedish company.

> Wu has just started working for a Swedish company which has extensive commitments in China. A large part of his work concerned advising his expatriate colleagues on Chinese business practices, which involves both writing reports and recommendations and addressing at meetings.
>
> Wu has always researched his topics thoroughly and tried to make his presentations as clear as possible. However, he gradually became aware that something was wrong. It often seemed that nobody listened to him and his advice was ignored. When he spoke at meetings, he felt that people were impatient and uninterested in what he had to say. He got more and more unhappy and began to feel that his colleagues were not interested in his opinions because he was Chinese. This he thought was racism.
>
> There is policy of annual review in this company, which meant every staff member met with the managing director once a year to discuss his / her progress. When it was time for Wu's review, he was given a copy of assessment on his performance. He was praised for his hard work but was criticized with the following: arguments were often unfocused and speeches lack clear direction when speaking at meetings; written reports contain too much irrelevant materials; in both speaking and writing, material is poorly organized with important recommendations often appearing only at the end of the report; Wu often appears uncertain about the points he wants to make.

Hard as he worked for success, the annual review by the company showed that there were problems in communication, which need to be improved. It is obvious that Wu was admitted to the company as he is fluent in English and knowledgeable about Chinese business practice, which is the basis for large part of his work. In fact, the problem that Wu met with the Swedish company stems from the ways of expressing oneself in discourse with cultural differences.

"His arguments were often unfocused and speeches lack clear direction when speaking at meetings" because he has been trained as a Chinese to express himself in the topic-comment structure in sentences and discourses, i. e. the topic part lists persons, objects or concepts and the comment part develops the topic part. And this structure often goes with inductive format by moving from specific details to generalities, i. e. the speaker or author would present the relevant situation with the topic in his mind. He develops on the hidden topic until the last when the topic finally appears. On the contrary, his expatriate colleagues are trained for deductive discourse in topic-first structures. In other words, they are accustomed to discourses which begin with a general topic sentence and then systematically restrict its meaning by presenting more details at several levels, which is referred to as a direct or linear approach.

He was also criticized that "his material is poorly organized in both speaking and writing with important recommendations often appearing only at the end of the report" because his way of inductive approach is contrary to that of his colleagues who prefer deductive pattern in which topic sentences with opinions or recommendations are presented at the beginning and followed by statistics and information to support the opinions and recommendations. Wu was assessed that "he often appears uncertain about the points he wants to make" because of modesty and humility of the Chinese culture by use of such terms as "maybe" or "perhaps" etc. to avoid assertiveness for harmonious relationship, which appears uncertainty instead of modesty to his colleagues, and he may also appeared lack of confidence due to body language such as fewer eye contacts or affirmative gestures in his speech.

In addition to the above, he is from the high-context culture and he gave some relevant information about the situation as background for his further expositions with his hidden topic, which is different from the habit of his colleagues who are used to low-context communication with explicit expressions. As a result, his audience couldn't follow his thought in his speech because Wu's speeches sounds "unfocused without clear directions" and his writings appear "badly organized", and his advice was ignored because he didn't seem confident in what he said.

To improve the situation for better performance, Wu has to adapt to the communication styles in speeches and writings of his colleagues in the company.

He needs to know more about the different thinking patterns, styles of discourses, and the use of language. For example, deductive patterns are recommended for direct and clear direction of points; topic sentences are necessary for concise and logical organizations of the materials to support his points of view and recommendations are to be presented at the beginning, etc. Wu is expected to apply terms with concrete and specific meanings to avoid ambiguity. In addition, to comply with the verbal changes in discourse and use of language, nonverbal behaviors with assured looks and assertive signs at meetings are recommended.

It has to be noted that it is general for Westerners to think in a linear approach and communicate in a deductive pattern and most of the Asians prefer the inductive way of reasoning in most cases, but it is not absolute in either case as language is contextualized. For example, the deductive way of writing is more accepted in Chinese academic writings, such as journal papers and dissertations.

V. Working as Interpreters

Interpreting is the mechanism to help those who are not capable to communicate with people from different cultural backgrounds in a foreign language, and interpreters are fundamentally linguistic and cultural analysts in intercultural communication. Therefore, linguistic and cultural knowledge are vital to the work of the interpreter. Ideally, interpreters are balanced bilinguals, who are capable of transferring meaning between languages and cultures. Being bicultural is just as important for qualified interpreters as being bilingual, for bicultural individuals have naturally absorbed the sensibilities and nuances of two cultures and have inherent abilities to mediate between them. Dr. Holly Mikkelson from the Monterey Institute of International Studies states: "In all of their work, interpreters must bridge the cultural and conceptual gaps separating the participants in a meeting."

A. What Is Language Competence?

Most people don't realize the extent to which knowledge and vocabulary an interpreter needs in his/her native language. Michelle Hof, a professional conference interpreter and trainer who runs a blog called *The Interpreter Diaries*, writes:

> *"As an interpreter, you need to be able to express yourself well in many different registers and have access to a broad active vocabulary covering different fields. Just growing up speaking a language does not automatically mean you will have these skills. I see it all the time in the early days of a course, when students can't seem to stop themselves from talking like they do to their friends in the bar and start sounding like interpreters."*

Interpreting competence refers to a set of knowledge and skills that are required for an interpreter to perform an interpreting task. Current research often but not always distinguishes it from interpreter competence. Where it does, the assumption is that interpreting competence is mainly concerned with core elements associated with bilingual or translation competence, such as knowledge of both languages and transfer skills. And that's just what is needed for the interpreter's native language. The website of the International Association of Conference Interpreters (AIIC) states that, to be an interpreter, one's "understanding of the language should be comparable to that of an educated native speaker of the same language."

Interpreters need to have an exhaustive grasp of the language they interpret for. This sounds obvious, but it's not always the case. When an interpreter is working in the field, they probably don't have time to refer to an encyclopedia or a dictionary. An extensive vocabulary and excellent written and verbal communication skills are a must. An interpreter should be able to speak just as well, and preferably better than a native speaker. Superior grammatical knowledge and the ability to interpret idioms, nuance and metaphors in conversation is essential for to effective communication.

B. What Are Cultural Considerations in Interpretation?

Interpreters should not only be very familiar with more than one language, but they should also have a cultural understanding of the languages they interpret for. This is the ability to detect certain nonverbal cues or customs that are specific to a particular group of people or geographical place. Having a strong grasp on cultural norms will help an interpreter better convey what a non-native speaker is trying to get across. Ethnicity, history, religion, and nationality are crucial elements that make up a culture. In regions around the world there are cultural diversities and conflicts that can affect how interpreters do their jobs.

The California Healthcare Interpreters Association explains the role of the interpreter as cultural clarifier/ mediator as follows:

The cultural clarifier role goes beyond word clarification to include a range of actions that typically relate to an interpreter's ultimate purpose of facilitating communication between parties not sharing a common culture. Interpreters are alert to cultural words or concepts that might lead to a misunderstanding, triggering a shift to the cultural clarifier role.

Interpreters need to be culturally competent and develop a thorough understanding of the target language and cultural background, awareness and sensitivity in order to effectively communicate messages from the source language to the target language audience.

Due to the fact that connotation in language involves the deep structure of words and expressions that are strongly associate with the culture, it can be problematic during intercultural exchanges. Some words in English and Chinese are identical in the denotative meaning but different in the connotative or affective meaning due to cultural differences. For example, "凤凰" or "凤", is an imaginary bird symbolizing a good omen particularly closely associated with the Chinese culture as "凤凰来仪" and "跨凤乘鸾". A phoenix is an imaginary bird that burns itself to ashes every five hundred years and is then born again in the west culture by contrast. Moreover, "phoenix" tends to collocate with "king", usually a male, according to the British National Corpus (BNC, 英语国家语料库), whereas "凤凰" is usually seen as a female in the Chinese culture as "凤冠霞帔". On the surface, both are imaginary birds in ancient mythology, but differ in their connotative meanings.

More examples can be found in those culture-loaded words. Due to the religious and cultural differences, it is advisable to adopt functional equivalence to achieve a fluent and transparent style in interlingual transfer while keeping the precise meaning of source language speaker. For example, right off the bat

（立刻、马上），off one's own bat（经过努力），as poor as a church mouse（一贫如洗、穷得叮当响），like a duck to water（如鱼得水），cast pearls before a swine（对牛弹琴），beauty lies in the eyes of the beholder（情人眼里出西施），a cat-and-dog life（吵吵闹闹的日子），meet with one's Waterloo（惨遭失败）.

C. What Does "Mindfulness" Mean for Interpreters?

Successful intercultural communication depends on verbal communication, i. e. the language spoken, and also on non-verbal communication, like the context, body language and the relationship with time, personal space and authority. Suggestions by Samovar are as follows.

Preparing Yourself for the Interpreting Task

It is a truth universally acknowledged that an interpreter must be prepared for an interpreting assignment.

First, interpreting of any kind is not simply about knowing languages; that's just a prerequisite for a job that's all about conveying what a speaker says. Within the communication process, a language is no more than raw material waiting to be formed into the message. Interpreters must have a complete grasp of subject matter and the context they are working in so that they can perform the task successfully.

The complexity and challenges of interpreting lie in a finished product of message greater than the sum of its parts, such myriad resources as knowledge on culture and subject matter, contextualization, rapid analysis, cohesion, subtlety of expression, correct terminology come into play, which brings us back to preparation because that is the stage during which all these elements are readied. Compare it to the research a scholar does before sitting down to write, or think of the accomplished speaker you've invited who expressly gets ready to address the audience — that's part of what has made him or her successful. Here are a few suggestions on preparing yourself for the interpreting task at a conference:

- On the basis of the conference documents and your own research, prepare your own multilingual glossary for the meeting. Never be a terminology freeloader, relying on others to do the work. Glossary preparation is an important learning process, the main point of which is to help you understand and memorize the terminology.

• The agenda may not seem like much but it's chock-full of information. It shows how the meeting is organized, schedule, speeches/presentations, discussion and breakout sessions, etc.

• Any background material made available to participants, especially information on the purpose of the meeting, should be made available, as it will help put things in context and construct mind maps.

• Having a single contact person on each side is advisable. It is a good idea to have distributed to all the speakers, through the conference organizer or secretariat. It is also good practice to visit the conference hall the night before the conference, to make sure that the technical set-up is satisfactory, and, when mobile booths are being used, that they are positioned properly in the meeting room with a direct view of the speaker and of the projection screen.

• A pre-meeting briefing/Q & A session can be advantageous, especially if the topic is highly specialized. A well-organised briefing, i.e. one attended by experts, preferably covering the working languages of the conference, and by the interpreters, who have studied the conference documents and done background research in advance, can greatly improve interpretation performance.

• Thorough preparation helps interpreters deal with the unexpected, not just during speeches but also throughout discussion and Q & A sessions.

Interpreting Taboos

A taboo, according to the *Oxford Advanced Learners Dictionary* (OALD) is "a cultural or religious custom that does not allow people to do, use or talk about a particular thing as people find it offensive or embarrassing." As for taboo words specifically, they are defined by the OALD (ibid) as "words that many people consider offensive or shocking, for example because they refer to sex, the body or people's race". One classification by Abrantes of taboo topics divides them into:

  a. Fear based topics (Death, diseases)
  b. Shame based topics (Sex and bodily functions)
  c. Politeness based topics (insults)

For example, when dining at a Chinese table, one should never leave chopsticks standing straight up in the bowl of rice, which is considered as very bad table manners in China. According to Chinese taboos, this act is said to bring bad luck as the chopsticks in rice look are similar to the tombstone in the graveyard. Just put them down on the table when not using them. However, the same never happens in the English speaking countries. This change in the status of what is nowadays considered to be taboo, and what is not, demonstrates the rapid changes within different societies; it also highlights one of the difficulties in interpreting taboos since an interpreter needs to stay abreast of what is currently acceptable and what is not.

Paying attention to, and applying guidelines on interpreting taboo, will not only lead to a more accurate, faithful and efficient interpreting, but once the interpreters understand why people swear and use bad language it will help them realize when a situation is threatening to get out of hand. For example, in mental health assignments, where the gradual increase in bad language may indicate a negative change in the patient's mental status that may lead to disruptions and maybe even violence. Training interpreters who aim to work in the health sector to be aware of those signs means they will ensure they interpret those "bad" words appropriately hence allowing the healthcare worker to make an informed decision on the gradual deterioration of the patient.

Using Feedback Effectively

Feedback takes place when interpreters receive comments on their performance, both positive and negative, which will get them to know where to improve in order to give a better quality interpretation next time.

When it comes to giving and receiving feedback, the interpreting profession, along with many other industries, has yet to standardize an approach. There are many reasons for this, but the reality is that from one assignment to the next, we interact with one another in a variety of ways. As a result, after the completion of an interpreting assignment, colleagues ask us for feedback but don't really mean it. Ask us if they can share an observation and then proceed to dance around the issue; invite our observations in a judgmental tone that implies an error in our decisions, behavior, and/or interpreting product; or without regard for the emotional impact, "let us have it" because their heart is in the right place but their soft skills leave something to be desired.

One way to ensure interpreters keep working on their skills is to get feedback through clients, organizers interpreted or practicing with other interpreters who can give each other feedback, focus on specific skills and monitor their progress. Another way to get feedback would be to take part in a project such as Interpretime Bank where interpreters earn listening hours by giving feedback to others who will then do the same for you.

Paying attention to the speaker's any minor facial expressions, pause, revision or a hand signal that he or she needs a longer gap in simultaneous interpreting also is a must. In reality, when interpreters are working it can be difficult to get this level of detailed feedback — a client will rarely tell you that your décalage was slightly too close on that last presentation, or your booth partner may not want to discuss anything work related once the assignment is over. However, interpreter should be self-monitoring as interpreting, and at the end of the assignment or during a lunch break, you can note down how you feel it is going, what elements you struggled with and what you feel you did well.

Ⅵ. Extended Reading

Kiwi students show language skills
(*China Daily*, August 18, 2021)

Thirty-four secondary school students from across New Zealand showed off their Chinese proficiency in the annual Chinese Bridge competition held on Aug 8.

Due to the COVID-19 pandemic, 15 junior high school students and 19 senior high school students participated in the 14th Chinese Bridge Chinese proficiency competition for secondary school students via videolink. Hosted by Confucius Institute at the University of Canterbury, the theme of the contest was "fly high with Chinese".

Dong Zhixue, education counselor at the Chinese embassy in New Zealand, said at the opening ceremony that the Chinese teaching program this year has been facing a lot of difficulties due to border closures that prevent the arrival of more Chinese language teachers. However, students have still made lots of progress, as indicated by the number and quality of contestants in this year's competition. Dong encourages Chinese learners to become "friendly ambassadors of China-New Zealand people-to-people exchanges", making positive contributions to promoting China-NZ educational exchanges and enhancing friendship between the two countries.

Chinese Consul General Wang Zhijian says the Chinese proficiency level of the students has been increasing year by year. "Learning Chinese well will not only open doors to China's long and rich history and culture, as well as help make friends with 1.4 billion Chinese people, but will also enable you to become successful in your career development," Wang says, adding that China is the biggest trade partner of more than 120 countries and regions, including New Zealand.

Andrew Turner, deputy mayor of Christchurch, says despite current restrictions, the relationship between China and New Zealand is growing in tourism, education, trade, cultural and people-to-people exchanges. "There will definitely be big opportunities in the future for people who have the skills to build bridges between New Zealand and China," Turner says.

Post-class Tasks

Self-test Tasks

1. Decide whether the statements are True (T) or False (F).

(1) A good mastery of a foreign language alone ensures effective intercultural communication. (   )

(2) Intercultural competence involves helping others to communicate effectively with people from different cultures by interpreting. (   )

(3) Each word in a language has its corresponding equivalent in another, which make intercultural communication easier by knowing more words of them. (   )

(4) Human beings remember and think with help of their brains, and they express their ideas with help of language in the same way. (   )

(5) The English and Chinese languages are different in pronunciation and vocabularies but not the sentence structures and discourses. (   )

(6) Thinking patterns of a culture is reflected in sentences and discourse as

cultural influences. (　)

(7) Euro-Indian speakers tend to think analytically with deductive reasoning, which differs from the Asian people. (　)

(8) English language learners have to adjust to the hypotactic sentences and the deductive discourse for better communication because language and culture are inseparable. (　)

(9) In addition to good mastery of languages, interpreters are required to be culturally aware and sensitive in thinking and nonverbal messages. (　)

(10) Cultural taboos are identical in all cultures, which deserve attention of interpreters in intercultural communication.

2. An English visitor in China is treated by his/her Chinese host at a restaurant, how will you introduce to the visitor the Chinese dishes, such as "红烧狮子头""回锅肉""糖醋排骨" and "佛跳墙"? Do you find the equivalents for them in English? What would you do?

Group Tasks

1. Discuss with your partners the difference between Parataxis and Hypotaxis by filling in the blanks with appropriate prepositions, conjunction and connectives, change the forms where necessary.

(1) someone wants (2) learn (3) another culture, it is easy (4) go (5) a website (6) pick up a book (7) offers a general background (8) a country (9) commonly either lists (10) provides concise paragraphs (11) how (12) culture differs (13) others. Usually, these "differences" focus (14) such basics (15) greetings, introductions, business protocols, dress, food, punctuality, gender issues, important holidays, (16) similar topical subjects. This information is essential (17) gaining an appreciation (18) how a culture can differ (19) your own (20) offers little (21) no actual understanding (22) the causes (23) underlie those differences. (24) other words, they seldom provide insight (25) what we consider (26) be a fundamental part (27) learning (28) other cultures — understanding why cultural differences exist. (29) an appreciation (30) why members (31) another culture have beliefs (32) behaviors (33) differ (34) your culture's, you can inadvertently fall (35) the trap (36) simplistically viewing

those differences (37) exotic, strange, oppressive, (38) even misguided.

2. The president of a Chinese university presented a horse-themed Wuhu Iron Picture (芜湖铁画) as a gift to a Noble Prize winner from the United States. As an interpreter, how would you deal with the cultural message when facilitating intercultural communication for the participants?

Telling China's Stories

China owns a recorded history of over 3000 years, in which language has played an important role for development and communication with other cultures. One of your net friends got interested in the Chinese culture and is going to take courses of the Chinese language, but he/she is a bit afraid of complexity of the Chinese characters.

Write him/her an email about the rough history of the Chinese language, focusing on the language reforms since 1949 with the campaign to eliminate illiteracy (扫盲运动), the national policy to promote *putonghua* (推广普通话政策), to simplify the traditional Chinese characters (简化繁体汉字), maintain and create minority languages (保护创设少数民族文字), etc. under the *Law on the Standard Spoken and Written Chinese Language of the People's Republic of China* (《中华人民共和国国家通用语言文字法》). In addition, with the Internet and use of computers, the input methods of the Chinese character have facilitated communication between human and machines as well as the learning of Chinese characters.

My Learning Reflection

1. What have I learned about Chinese cultures or myself?

2. What have I learned about other cultures?

3. What impressed me most in this chapter?

4. What still confuses me?

Chapter 5   Nonverbal Communication

Learning Objectives

- To master the definition, functions and characteristics of nonverbal communication;
- To identify apparent nonverbal means for effective communication across cultures on the basis of similarities and differences;
- To apply and respond to nonverbal approaches appropriately in communication by observation, interpretation of nonverbal messages.

Pre-class Tasks

- Read the textbook and watch the concerned clips in *xuexitong* (学习通).

Ⅰ. Lead-in Tasks

Activity 1

Answer the following questions.
1. The idea that "time is money" may be good for a business. Is it good for a society in general?
2. As a learner of the English language, try to recall your learning experience or your life to identify how you change the perception of time by shifting the language you think in.
3. The party was over. An American wanted to say goodbye to his Italian

friends. But when he intended to shake hands for goodbye, his Italian friends kissed him on both cheeks. He felt stunned and was at a loss of what to do. Try to help the American out of the trouble and confusion.
4. What effects has COVID-19 brought to contact cultures and non-contact cultures?

The replies to the above questions may vary due to personal experience but reflections on the replies lead to the topic of this chapter, i.e., what else helps express one's feelings, thoughts or implied meanings and intention in addition to the language itself? Is there "silent language" in communication?

Ⅱ. Understanding Nonverbal Communication

Language is the tools that human beings communicate generally with, either in spoken or written forms. In addition to language, there are other means applied to transform information in communication, such as eye contacts, smiles, gestures, which are known as nonverbal behaviors. Accordingly, nonverbal communication takes place when nonverbal messages are sent and understood by means of human body instead of language.

A. What Is Nonverbal Communication?

Communication is a process in which meanings are created and exchanged with symbols, and these "symbols" can be in vocal or written languages, or by physical behaviors with messages which create and exchange meanings either consciously or unconsciously in communication. Therefore, Samovar defined that "nonverbal communication involves all those nonverbal stimuli in a communicating setting that are generated by both the source and his or her use of the environment and that have potential message value for the source or receiver. Basically, it is sending and receiving messages in a variety of ways without the use of verbal codes (words)."

The key elements in nonverbal communication are similar to those in verbal communication except that the message is sent and received with the help of "the environment", i.e. in what context the specific communication takes place, and where the meanings of the message actually determined. And what is equally important is who is involved in the context of interaction as culture is the vital factor in the meanings. For example, a smile means happiness and friendliness in most cases across cultures, but it functions differently when a Japanese lady was talking with a smile about the loss of her daughter in a flood.

The nonverbal stimuli include the factors that participants of communication make use of to convey messages, which are generated with the help of their facial expressions, gestures or postures, dress and hairstyles, or even perfume and/or jewelry. What are often ignored are the environmental aspects, i. e. the use of time and the use of space. The "potential message values" are those hidden, implied, intended meaning that the Sender would like to transform by any other means without words, which are to be interpreted and responded to by the Receiver. However, meanings of nonverbal messages are sometimes blurred, misleading or disputing in intercultural context due to different cultural values and communication customs. Therefore, nonverbal behaviors are meaningful messages when they are observed, interpreted, understood and responded to with feedback in the cultural context.

Activity 2

What is emphasized in the following passage?

> In public speakings, it is important for speakers to make sure that facial expressions are communicating emotions, moods, or personality traits that their audience will view favorably, helping achieve the goals.
>
> In order to set a positive tone, a speaker will, before starting the speech, briefly look at the audience and smile to communicate friendliness, openness, and confidence. If the speaker is not bored, a slack face with little animation may lead an audience to think that the speaker is bored with his own speeches, which is not likely to motivate the audience to be interested.

What's more, it is necessary to make sure that the facial expressions of the speaker match the content of the speech. When delivering light-hearted or humorous ideas, a smile, bright eyes, and slightly raised eyebrows will nonverbally enhance the verbal messages of the speaker. When delivering serious or somber content, a furrowed brow, a tighter mouth, and even a slight head nod will enhance those messages. If the facial expressions and speech content are not consistent, the audience would become confused by the mixed messages, which would lead the audience to question honesty and credibility of the speaker.

Case Study 1

Read the conversation and answer the following questions.

A: I'm telling you that the girl totally winked at you.

B: Really? I didn't know her. Ah, I got it. She must have seen the extra-big hamburger in my hand!

Question 1: Why did that girl wink at B?
Question 2: Did B understand what that girl meant to him?

This case shows the differences between the nonverbal behavior, nonverbal messages, and nonverbal communication. Speaker A reminded Speaker B that a girl winked at Speaker B. "Winking" is a nonverbal behavior, which conveys some information or message from the girl. But Speaker B does not understand the girl's nonverbal message; thus, this nonverbal behavior is meaningless to Speaker B and there is no nonverbal communication between the girl and Speaker B, which is the process in which nonverbal behaviors are used.

It has to be noted that there are some other similar terms in studies of intercultural communication, such as nonverbal codes, nonverbal cues, etc., referring to nonverbal behaviors or messages, which are used interchangeably.

Case Study 2

Study Figure 5.1 to classify the categories of nonverbal communication.

Figure 5.1 Categories of Noverbal Communication

  The picture indicates that nonverbal communication involves elements more than communication with language does. In the picture, there are seven types of factors, namely, personal appearance (attire), proxemics (space and distance), chronemics (time), kinesics (facial expressions, movements, gestures), haptics (touch), vocalics (paralanguage) and physical environment.

  To look into these behaviors or factors that people communicate with, there are three categories, i.e. body language, paralanguage, and environmental language. Generally, body languages are those messages sent by means of human body, such as facial expressions, gestures or postures and touches, or elements related to human body, such as dress, perfume, jewelry, shoes and handbags. Paralanguages concern with how voice is employed for complicate and delicate meanings together with or without language, such as intonations or stresses, just to name a few. Environmental languages refer to the silent factors in communication, i.e. the use of time and use of space. Figure 5.2 illustrates these three categories.

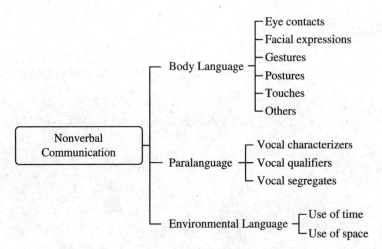

Figure 5.2 Classification of Nonverbal Behaviors

As shown in Figure 5.2, body languages include eye contacts, facial expressions, gestures with fingers, hands and arms, postures of the physical body, touches between or by people, and other accessional details of the body showing cultural traits like ethnicities, religions, personalities, occupations, education or ages.

Paralanguages are related with the communicative characteristics of the voice and use of voices, which includes the linguistic elements of speech, vocalization, and silence/pauses. Vocalization can be divided into three categories, i.e. vocal characterizers, vocal qualifiers and vocal segregates. Silence is the extreme application of mute situation, which is regarded as an effective means in communication with cultural variations.

Environmental languages refer to the biological and psychological settings related to cultural values, which shed effect on communication. There are many kinds of environmental languages, such as time, space, colors, signals and architecture, among which the use of time and space is less imperceptible without sufficient attention.

Test Your Reading 1

Decide whether the statements are True (T) or False (F).

(1) Personal appearance doesn't matter in communication. (   )

(2) Proxemics is the nonverbal communication factor about time. (   )
(3) Haptics refers touches in nonverbal communication. (   )
(4) The paralanguage is concerned with body movements in communication. (   )
(5) Environmental languages refer to the biological and psychological settings related to cultural values. (   )

Activity 3

Read this same phrase with a different stress to take notice of the meanings that are changed by the way (Figure 5.3). Pay attention to the way of your vocalization and silence or pauses.

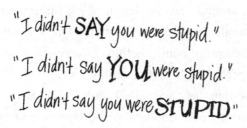

Figure 5.3 Read the Same Phrase with A Different Stress

B. What Do Nonverbal Behaviors Function in Communication?

People communicate with the help of language consciously as means both in speaking and writing, and nonverbal behaviors can be taken as the silent language which share the same function to convey meanings and messages, sometimes unconsciously.

Activity 4

You are going to have a job interview. Discuss the following questions with your peer students.

> (1) How are you going to appear for the job interview?
>
> (2) Why do you have to do much about your appearance before an interview?
>
> (3) How would you behave in terms of standing or sitting position? Where are you going to put your hands? How are you going to use your voices?
>
> (4) What messages will be sent to the interviewers through your appearance and behaviors?

Nonverbal behaviors matter because what people do is powerful and expressive more than what they say, which accounts for the majority of what is heard and understood by communicators so as to persuade, confuse and empower the people around, just as shown in job interviews.

Nonverbal elements function in exchange of information in regard of regulation, substitution, contradiction, repetition, accentuation and complementation together with verbal expressions.

Regulation functions of nonverbal behaviors are applied to manage communication by means of paralanguage, gestures, and eye contact to make the cooperative communication under control. For example, nodding, or/and direct eye contacts indicate that communication channels are open or one's turn to talk. For example, silence is required when the index finger is put across lips and traffic is directed with gestures.

Substitution works in communication when performance takes place of words. For example, one is apt to enlarge his smile, throwing his arms to greet one of his old friends, substituting the words for the same feeling.

Contradiction refers to mixed messages resulting from conflict of verbal messages opposite to nonverbal ones. For example, one is saying that he/she is relaxed and at ease with his/her voice quavering and his/her hands shaking. Contradiction occurs when nonverbal actions send opposite signals from the literal meanings in the verbal messages. Contradictory information is confusing and even hurting. For instance, it is sarcasm to say with a disgusting look, "What a *flavorful* meal" when the food tastes bland.

Repetition offers a better chance to understand the verbal message with nonverbal behaviors simultaneously. For example, one points to the direction saying, "The new dining hall is south of the library." Actually, the nonverbal conduct repeating the verbal messages are those that could stand alone if the verbal messages were not present. For example, one may point to the chest to indicate "me" instead of saying "me".

Complementation means adding more information by actions to what is said. For example, a pat on one's should together with a smile expresses additional appreciation than "I'm pleased with what you have done."

Accentuation upgrades complementation by emphasizing something more. In other words, accentuation adds intensity or power to verbal information while complementation supports its meaning. Facial expressions and paralanguage reinforce the emotional states people convey through verbal communication and to accent verbal communication, and gestures help describe an unfamiliar space or shape in the ways that words alone cannot. For example, one smiles bigger and holds them tight, saying loudly "I'm so glad to see you again!" with excitement when meeting with old friends.

To put it simple, repetition, complementation and accentuation have a progressive increase in their roles of exchanging information.

Activity 5

Identify the functions of the behaviors in the following contexts.

> (1) At a party, John said to his friends that he was fine with the party and enjoyed himself, but he did not eat or drink, nor talk with anyone.
> (2) At a meeting or seminar, people often use gestures to excuse themselves not to disturb other attendees.
> (3) A speaker is requiring responses when he raises pitch or intonation at the end of a sentence in a speech, or invites clapping by the audience when he lowers the pitch by the end of the sentence.
> (4) One is likely to say "two hamburgers!" holding up two fingers for "two" at the same time when ordering in McDonald's.
> (5) Someone is supported and encouraged by his friends with hugs, crossed arms and cheers in a competition.

> (6) Someone speaks loud at a fast pace across the stage with noticeable gestures and postures in a campaign.

C. What Are the Characteristics of Nonverbal Communication?

Activity 6

Observe one scene in your daily life, for example, when you buy your breakfast, get your package, or ask your teacher a question, etc., and discover whether people exchange nonverbal messages consciously and frequently or not.

People use nonverbal communication whether they know it or not. Every day they respond to thousands of nonverbal cues and behaviors including postures, facial expressions, eye gaze, gestures, and tones of voice.

Anthropologists estimate that language accounts for 35% of communication, while cultural factors as nonverbal messages, basic cultural assumptions and values affect the other 65%.

That "actions speak louder than words" underscores the importance of nonverbal communication in essence because it supplies valuable information about a situation including how a person might feel, how someone receives information and how to approach a person or group of people. Paying attention to and developing the ability to read nonverbal messages is an invaluable skill people can leverage at every stage of their career.

Nonverbal communication is omnipresent and universal. Communication takes place everywhere and similar messages in behaviors (i.e. smiling, frowning, laughing, and crying) make communication possible.

Nonverbal communication reflects one's internal state. Nonverbal messages are more reliable than words because most of nonverbal actions are not easily controlled consciously, which explains nonverbal information stands out when verbal and nonverbal messages contradict each other.

Nonverbal communication is responsible for one's first impression. Most of the time people are no more conscious of interpreting nonverbal signals than they are conscious of breathing. They consistently find that nonverbal messages more powerful, when presented with both verbal and nonverbal messages.

Nonverbal communication is open to many interpretations. The same nonverbal behaviors contain multiple meanings. For example, smiles may mean "I'm feeling content", "I can't believe you just did that", "How do I get out of this conversation?" etc. People can never be sure that others understand the meanings they intended to express with their nonverbal behaviors. And these meanings are culturally based, which increases the possibilities of misunderstanding.

Nonverbal communication is learned and rule-governed as part of culture. Although much of outward behavior is innate, such as smiling, people are not born knowing the communication dimensions associated with nonverbal messages. They acquire such knowledge from other people around them. Human beings all laugh, but their culture teaches them when, to whom, how much and under what circumstances they may laugh.

Test Your Reading 2

Decide whether the statements are True (T) or False (F).
(1) Nonverbal communication is universal. (   )
(2) Nonverbal behaviors cannot reflect one's internal state. (   )
(3) One's first impression relies on nonverbal behaviors to some degree. (   )
(4) One kind of nonverbal behaviors only has one interpretation. (   )
(5) Nonverbal communication is not culture-loaded. (   )

III. Nonverbal Messages in Intercultural Communication

Similarities of nonverbal communication in essences promote cultural integration and human civilization in many ways as elements of nonverbal communication are universal and identifiable across cultures, such as happiness, sadness, fear and anger, which can serve as the basis for intercultural communication.

However, different cultures rely on disparate systems of nonverbal communication. In other words, what is acceptable in one culture may be considered obscene or improper in another, and accordingly nonverbal behaviors may be likely to be misinterpreted and lead to communication obstacles or breakdowns in international interactions. Therefore, people should avoid interpretation of nonverbal messages of others in the ways that they do in their own cultural groups.

Case Study 3

Study Figure 5.4 to find out what are the similarities and differences in the ways to count from 1 to 10 with fingers across cultures.

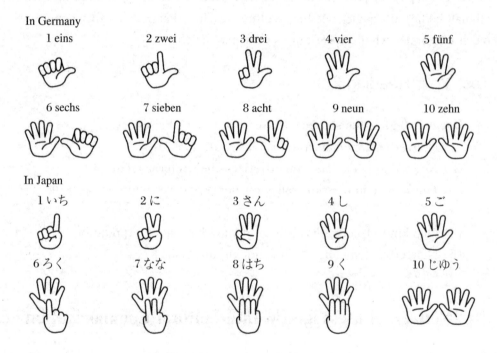

Figure 5.4 Counting from 1 to 10

Generally, it is natural for most of Chinese count 1～5 from the index finger, then the middle one, the ring finger and the pinkie before the thumb, so do Anglo-Saxons, while Europeans start counting with "1" on the thumb, "2" on the index finger, and "3" on the middle finger and so on. To indicate "2" with fingers, Chinese prefer the index and the middle ones, so do 96% of Anglo-Saxons while 94% of Europeans will be holding up the thumb and index finger, which appears to be "8" for Chinese.

It may appear surprising to note that people count by starting from different fingers for 1~4, and even more ways to present 6~10 across Asian to Europe, but interesting enough, in almost every culture, "5" is displayed with the open palm of hand. Therefore, in terms of equivalence as verbal communication, nonverbal behaviors fall in four categories, i. e., same behaviors for same meanings, same behaviors for different meanings, different behaviors for same meanings, and unparalleled behaviors and meanings.

Apparently, it is optimal in intercultural communication when both parties share some of meanings with same behaviors like "5" displayed with an open palm while it is somewhat "disastrous" when same behaviors for different meanings. For example, the sign of "thumb-up" is complementing and encouraging in China, and a sign for a free ride in the United States, Australia and New Zealand, but it is insulting in Iran and Iraq as the middle finger in Europe and Russia. That is why more knowledge and practice of intercultural communication will facilitate to learn more nonverbal messages.

A. Body Languages

Body language refers to those messages sent from or associated with human bodies, including eye contacts, facial expressions, gestures, postures, touches, appearance and accessories. And body language is reliable for accurate information as "your body does not know how to lie".

Eye contact is one of the primary ways that human beings gauge interest or disinterest, but it is valued and interpreted differently from culture to culture.

Direct eye contacts are favored in some cultures as proper attention, confidence and honesty but taken as a challenging or offensive conduct in others. For example, in the US and the Latin America, it is regarded as a sign of disrespect and a suspicious look if someone is not looking at the other person in the eye in conversation as expressed in that "he/she doesn't dare to look me in the eye, or he/she is hiding something", thus there is an English saying "Don't trust anyone who won't look you in the eye".

On the contrary, some other cultures like Asian, Middle Eastern, Hispanic and Native American do not take frequent or close eye contacts in the same way. Rather, direct eye contact is taken as a rude and offensive expression. In China, children are told not to look at the elders or the respected directly when talking. Students are usually not expected to have direct eye contact with teachers, tending to look away or looking down. Moreover, in the Eastern cultures females are not expected to have eye contacts with males as it implies power or sexual interest. However, economic development and cultural exchanges have seen some changes in the use of eye contact in communication in the younger generations.

Many cultures believe that direct eye contact from a child to an adult is an act of disrespect or defiance which is not allowed. For example, in Ghana, Guinea, Bissau, the Philippines, some Hispanic countries, and the Appalachian Mountain areas in the US, a child is more likely to be punished if he/she looks into an adult. Instead, looking down is taken as sign of respect for younger ones to the elder.

In Asian cultures, prolonged eye contacts are overwhelmingly offensive, which are avoided at all costs. For example, in Japan, speakers are supposed to look at the neck of the listener or elsewhere instead of into his/her eyes. In Arabian cultures, males show compliment to females by avoiding looking into their eyes because the otherwise could be interpreted as a physical attack.

Besides, winking is a kind of eye contacts which means differently across cultures. Generally, it is impolite to wink at others in Hong Kong, Tunisia, and Bangladesh, and it is assumed vulgar to wink at the opposite sex in Nepal, Paraguay and Australia, and Chinese people take winking negatively, especially between opposite genders. In addition, winking may serve as signals as well. For example, children will leave when they are winked at in Nigeria. There are more connotations of winking in the U.S. For example, a wink may mean one of the following depending on the context and relationship of the communicators: "We are having fun, aren't we?" "The person over there is ridiculous, don't you think so?" "It's a secret between us" "I like you" or "I want to get sexually close to you."

Test Your Reading 3

Decide whether the statements are True (T) or False (F).

(1) Direct eye contacts are favored in the United States. (　)

(2) In Ghana, a child is more likely to be punished if he looks into an adult. (　)

(3) In China, children are encouraged to look at the elders or the respected directly in talking. (　)

(4) In European cultures, prolonged eye contacts are overwhelmingly offensive. (　)

(5) It is assumed vulgar to wink at the opposite sex in Nepal. (　)

Facial expressions show feelings, attitudes and emotions as faces are the most expressive part of the human body.

Meanings of some of facial expressions are acknowledged all over the world, and their meanings are commonly understood everywhere. However, there are differences in perception and use of facial expressions. For example, too much facial expression is taken as superficiality in some places whereas in some it is taken as cowardice or weakness. Generally, people from the United States show emotions more than their Asian counterparts. In some Asian cultures, being expressionless or poke-faced is a sign of maturity and a neutral smile is appropriate in social events.

Smiling is universally accepted as the sign of happiness and pleasure but may connote either positively or negatively in some cultures. In the United States, smiling is natural and ubiquitous, usually showing pleasure and friendliness. In Thailand smiling also means happiness and respect. And in Latin America, people frequently smile to express their gratitude and willingness to help others. Though it is common for Americans to smile freely at strangers as greetings, in Russia the same is considered strange and even impolite. Similarly, a smile is not necessarily an expression of joy or friendliness in China or Japan; rather, one may smile to cover up anger, embarrassment or suffering. In Korean culture, people smile less since it often means the person is shallow. And many Scandinavians smile rarely or hide from facial expressions because it is considered timid and weak to show emotions. There are gender differences in use of smiles as well. Generally, females smile more and are more likely to return others smile than males. Table 5.1 illustrates some cultural connotations of smiles in some cultures.

Table 5.1 Connotations of Smile across Cultures

Cultures/Countries	Frequency	Positive Interpretations	Negative Interpretations
the US	A lot	Happiness, agreement, friendliness	/
Thailand	A lot	Happiness, respect	/
Latin America	Frequently	Thank you. Please. How may I help you?	/
China	Often	Happiness, agreement	Embarrassment, apology, shyness
Japan	Often	Happiness	Frustration, anger, sadness, disagreement, embarrassment, discomfort, apology, shyness
Korea	Less		Shallowness
Europe	Less	Happiness	/

Other facial expressions are sucking lips and sticking the tongue out, which are interpreted differently in many cultures. For example, sucking lips in Chinese culture means gusto and enthusiastic enjoyment while in British culture it means that there is no taste. It is common for Asian females and children to stick their tongues out accompanied by a shrinking neck when they find their words or deeds inappropriate or embarrassing, which is regarded as kind of cute and adorable. In Polynesia, people stick out their tongue to greet others. But the same behavior is taken either as childish and immature or as a rude expression with denigration and disrespect in the UK and the US.

Test Your Reading 4

Decide whether the statements are True (T) or false (F).
(1) Generally, people from the United States show emotions more than Asians do. (   )

(2) In Russia, smiling at strangers is considered as greetings. ( )

(3) Many Scandinavians often smile and don't hide from facial expressions. ( )

(4) Sucking lips in British culture means that there is no taste. ( )

(5) Stick the tongue out is taken either as childish and immature or as a rude expression with denigration and disrespect in the UK and the US. ( )

Gestures are movements of fingers, hands and arms applied to illustrate, emphasize or accompany the meaning of the verbal message, which are common in communication in all cultures. For example, hand gestures are likely to indicate the size or shape of an object and some gestures own a specific agreed on meaning, for instance, rolling hands over and over in front of the body says "move on." Some gestures are used subconsciously. It is no surprise that people still gesture when having an animated conversation on the phone even though the other person cannot see them.

Gestures are essential in communication as they may mean drastically different across cultures. Sometime it is hard for outsiders to figure out their meanings.

Head movement is one of gestures. In many cultures of the Middle East and Bulgaria, the direction of the head movement for "yes" is just the opposite of that in almost any other cultures. How confusing is it to see that somebody smiles with his/her head moving "no". In such cases definite verbal message of "yes" or "no" is absolutely required to avoid confusion. Americans nod to agree with what a speaker is said, or a way to show that he/she is actually listening, but a slight upward nod in Greece, Iran, and Italy shows "no" and Bulgarians nod up and down to indicate dislike. Lebanese inhabitants show "no" by an upward movement of the head or raised eyebrows, sometimes accompanied by tongue clicking.

Activity 7

Fill in Table 5.2 to summarize the cultural connotations of head movements.

Use of one's left hand may be problematic in intercultural communication as a result of ways of living. It is fine for most of people to hold an item or doing something with their right or left hands. But there are places in the US and in wide portions of Africa, Asia and the Middle East, where the use of the left hand is still traditionally mired with personal hygiene connotations. It is considered unclean to hand objects to people with a left hand. Therefore, it is a big no-no for someone to receive something, such as a gift with a left hand. A left handshake is also forbidden in the Middle East, the North and sub-Saharan African nations.

Table 5.2 Cultural Connotations of Head Movements

Cultures/Countries	Head Movements	Cultural Connotations
The Middle East	Shaking heads	
Greece, Iran, Italy		No
Bulgaria	Shaking heads	
		Dislike
Lebanese	One downward nod	
		No
America	Nodding	

Waving goodbye is straightforward, unlikely to offend someone in the USA. But in areas of Europe and South America, this gesture means "no" instead of farewell.

The middle finger is one of the most offensive expressions in most Western cultures. For example, in the US, it is offensive to "flip the bird", i.e., pointing or jabbing the middle finger upward. But in China the middle finger is what Chinese people usually point with without any ill will among themselves but may appear offensive to those from other cultures.

Test Your Reading 5

Decide whether the statements are True (T) or false (F).

(1) In the US and in wide portions of Africa, Asia and the Middle East, it is considered unclean to hand objects to people with a right hand. (   )

(2) A left handshake is forbidden in the Middle East, the North and sub-Saharan African nations. (   )

(3) The gesture of waving goodbye just means farewell in areas of Europe and South America. (   )

(4) In China the middle finger is what people usually point with without any ill will. (   )

The "OK" sign is a universal gesture by making a circle with a hand, i.e., touching the thumb to the index finger in most cultures but its meaning varies from culture to culture. Throughout the UK and the US, it means "OK" showing approval, agreement or understanding. Traditionally, it also represented the figure of three in many Western countries, and a way to indicate the number seven in China. However, in Japan, the okay sign means money, which may be confusing to those who interpret it as okay in business since the Japanese may think of bribery.

In addition, the OK gesture is interpreted negatively in some cultures. For example, when a French is praised for his excellent cooking with this sign, he would be very much irrigated as it means "zero" or "worthless" rather than "fine" or "OK" in France. And in such Mediterranean countries as Greek, it implies homosexuality. Moreover, in Brazil, the okay symbol is equivalent to the middle finger in the U.S., which is seen as highly offensive and should definitely be avoided.

Activity 8

Fill in Table 5.3 to summarize the cultural connotations of OK gesture.

Table 5.3 Cultural Connotations of OK Gesture

Cultures/Countries	Cultural Connotations
The UK, the US	
Many Western countries	
China	
Japan	
France	
Greek	
Brazil	

With different cultural connotations, it is necessary to use the following hand gestures in Figure 5.5 cautiously during the process of intercultural communication.

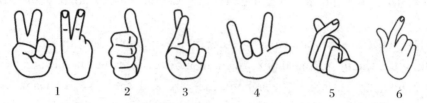

Figure 5.5 Hand Gestures

Number 1: the Victory Sign

Originally "V" stood for "victory" and now it is used as the "peace sign." Sometimes when people are trying to evoke hippies, and it is such an iconic part of taking pictures in their daily life. Thus, the victory sign seems to have a positive connotation everywhere until it is flipped around.

The reverse victory sign shows defiance and contempt the same significance as the middle finger when it is shown with the back of hand facing others. It is interpreted as an insult by some nations of the Commonwealth, such as South Africa, India and the UK. Therefore, it is necessary to ensure to have the palm heading away from the body before doing the V sign.

Number 2: the Thumb-up Gesture

It is common in many countries equally as an "OK" for positive connotations, indicating that something is good or well done in many cultures, such as in Chinese culture. Hitch-hikers employ it for a free lift in places strongly influenced by the British culture, such as the US, Australia, South Africa, the Singapore and New Zealand. However, it means "Up yours!" in Greece, Latin America, the Middle East, Russia. And in Italy, Greece, Iran, and Iraq, this is an insulting gesture since it means to sit on the thumb and possibly spin in some parts of the world.

Number 3: the Gesture of "Crossed Fingers"

It usually hopes for good luck or best wishes in English-speaking cultures for those starting off or going to competitions, examinations or job interviews, which is used by saying "I cross my fingers for you" for good luck. But this does not mean the same in every culture. For example, it represents the figure "10" in China, a white lie in Germany and the UK, but an extremely offense in Vietnam.

Number 4: the Horn Gesture

The distinctive horn gesture by the fans of the Beatles, i.e., extending one's index and pinky fingers while jumping up and down, are popular among fans when their most iconic songs are played. However, the horn gesture bears obscenity in Italy, known as "la corna", and "el cornudo" in Colombia, both meaning "the cuckold" and that one's partner is cheating on him/her, the same as the green hat in China.

Number 5: the Finger Heart Gesture

Americans have such a sign for money. But, in Korea it will not be related with one who is obsessed with money but one who is romantic as this gesture indicates "love".

Number 6: the Gesture of Curling the Index Finger

In the US, curling the index finger toward the body with the palm face upward is a common gesture to beckon someone to come. But it has a very negative connotation in China, Japan, Singapore and other parts of the East Asia and in the Philippines; one may be arrested for use of it.

Test Your Reading 6

Decide whether the statements are True (T) or False (F).

(1) In some nations of the Commonwealth, such as South Africa, India and the UK, the reverse victory sign is interpreted as an insult. (   )

(2) The thumb-up gesture in Italy, Greece, Iran, and Iraq means OK. (   )

(3) The "crossed fingers" represent the figure "10" in China, a white lie in Germany and the UK, an extremely offense in Vietnam. (   )

(4) The horn gesture, popular among rock music fans, has negative connotations in Italy and Colombia. (   )

(5) The finger heart gesture indicates money in Korea. (   )

(6) The gesture of curling the index finger has a very negative connotation in China, Japan, Singapore and other parts of the East Asia and in the Philippines. (   )

Case Study 4

Observe Figure 5.6 to learn more about cultural connotations of gestures.

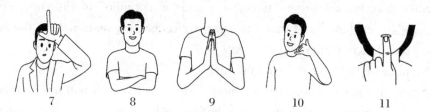

Figure 5.6 Hand Gestures (continued)

Number 7: the "L" Gesture

This sign in front of one's forehead as the initial of "Loser" indicts that the sports team sucks in the US and the American continent. Yet, this gesture in horizontality means the figure "8" in China.

Number 8: the Gesture of Crossed Arms

In the US, this may be a mild sign of meanness or rage since that is how many people instinctively rest their arms. However, it is best to avoid this gesture entirely in Finland, which can mean people are causing trouble or starting a war.

Number 9: the Pray Gesture

When Americans pray, they sometimes place their palms near the chest. However, in Nepal, India and Pakistan, it is a traditional and friendly way to greet someone or say goodbye.

Number 10: the Phone Call Gesture

In the US, people take their thumb and pinky finger and put their hand up to their ear like a receiver to mime a phone call. But in Hawaii, this sign means "relax" while in Germany it means they are trying to order a beer.

Number 11: the Shh Gesture.

When people hope others to keep quiet, they often put their index finger on their lips to illustrate "shh" in China and many other cultures. However, in Greek, if people put the index finger on the lower lip, they actually hope to be with others for a while since they have something to say.

Test Your Reading 7

Decide whether the statements are True (T) or False (F).
(1) The "L" signs in front of one's forehead mean winners. (   )
(2) The crossed arms in Finland are a mild sign of meanness or rage. (   )
(3) In Nepal, India and Pakistan, the pray gesture is a traditional and friendly way to greet someone or say goodbye. (   )
(4) People in Hawaii use the phone call gesture to order a beer. (   )
(5) The shh gesture in Greek means to be quiet. (   )

Moreover, people in different cultures have varied amounts of gestures. Some cultures use gestures more than others. For example, the Italians find it a great disadvantage if they are unable to use their hands when they are speaking. The Irish people, with their tradition of dancing with arms stiffly at their sides, use far less hand movement.

Case Study 5

Study the amounts of gestures in some cultures in Table 5.4 and think about who is most likely to make this table?

Table 5.4 Gestures in Some Cultures

Cultures/Countries	Frequency of Gestures
the US	Moderate
France, Italy, Spain, Greece, Middle Eastern countries, most of Central and South African countries	More
England, Germany, Switzerland, Asian countries	Less

Obviously, this table is made by Americans since the amounts of gestures in the US. is evaluated to be "moderate", while that of other countries is thus either "more" or "less" because the American culture is taken as the standard to judge the amount as an example of ethnocentrism which should be avoided in intercultural communication.

Postures are the ways that people sit or stand and how open their body to others around them, which convey a lot of information about attitudes and emotional states. For example, leaning the upper body toward a speaker indicates intense interest, and putting hands on the hips is a nonverbal cue that people are subconsciously to make them look bigger and show assertiveness. The pointed elbows prevent others from getting past easily, which also a sign of attempted dominance or a gesture as a warning for action. In terms of position of sitting, leaning back shows informality and indifference, and straddling a chair is a sign of dominance, but also some insecurity because the person is protecting the vulnerable front part of his or her body.

Physical postures are also quite different across cultures. The most common example is the habit of many American executives to rest with their feet on their desk, which in Asia, the Middle East, and Europe is considered highly offensive.

In Asia and the Middle East, a straight and balanced posture prevails as a respectful norm. In Japan, sitting cross-legged is seen as disrespectful, especially in the presence of someone older or more respected while sitting with crossed legs is common in the North America and European countries. In the Middle Eastern cultures, it is offensive and insulting to cross an ankle over a knee, displaying the sole of the shoe while talking to another person.

Case Study 6

Analyze Figure 5.7 and identify what is inappropriate with the people in it.

Figure 5.7 What Is Inappropriate?

In Figure 5.7, the businessman in the suit on the left is sitting cross-legged, crossing an ankle over a knee, and displaying the sole of the shoe while he is talking to the person in white on the right. But the businessman is unaware that he has committed a major gaffe due to his posture, since he is smiling confidently. On the other hand, it can be seen that conducting business may become more difficult and complicated from the serious and unhappy facial expression of the man in white on the right. Thus, it is necessary to be aware of the posture in communication with people from other cultures to avoid intercultural misunderstanding.

Touches are the contacts on some parts of the human body with others as means of communication. To what extent it is considered acceptable to be "touchy-feely" also varies from country to country. Edward Hall proposed that cultural norms are one of the most crucial factors in determining social distances and touches between people. He believed that there were two groups of cultures i.e. "contact cultures" and "non-contact cultures" or high/low contact cultures depending how much and how often one is offended by being touched.

People from higher contact cultures would stand closer to each other and speak louder, making more eye contacts and incorporating touches on each other more frequently. Examples of high contact cultures include hugs, pats on shoulders of others, hand in hand with others, etc. accompanied with verbal expressions in cultures from the Middle East, Latin America and Southern Europe. Conversely, people from lower contact cultures may stand further away when talking, who would maintain fewer eye contacts and usually steer clear of touches. It has been suggested that people from lower contact cultures tend to rely on verbal communication and have greater visual needs. In other words, in higher contact cultures frequent and close touches are consider appropriate. In the Latin American, the Arabian and Southern European cultures like France and Italy, face to face communication is preferred with more physical touches and eye contacts at higher voices. Lower contact cultures include China, Japanese, Thailand and the Philippines, the UK, Netherlands, Finland, Germany, Australia, the US and New Zealand, where interpersonal distance in communication is farther away with fewer bodily touches at lower voices.

The major difference between high and low contact cultures is the amount of body language employed in communication. For example, the French and Italians tend to continually touch each other as they talk, while the British would avoid touching others at any time unless it is on a sports field in front of a large audience. Intimate embracing by British, Australian and New Zealand sportsmen is copied from South American and Continental sportsmen who embrace and kiss each other after a goal is scored, which will continue in the dressing rooms. The moment when the Aussies, Brits and Kiwis leave the field, they revert to the "hand off-or else" policy.

Touches are also related to who and where to touch as well. Thus, it is not surprising that an innocent hug made headlines around the world in 2009 when Michelle Obama, the former first lady of America, broke the royal protocol by putting an arm around Queen Elizabeth on her visit to Britain (Figure 5.8)!

Figure 5.8　An Innocent Hug

Table 5.5 lists cultures where touches are acceptable or avoided.

Table 5.5　Touch or Non-Touch Cultures

Don't Touch	Do Touch
German	India
Japan	Turkey
England	France
the US & Canada	Italy
Australia	Greece
New Zealand	Spain
Estonia	Middle East
Portugal	Parts of Asia
Northern Europe	Russia
Scandinavia	

Activity 9

Table 5.6 are some ways of greetings. Match A and B to see how well you know about different greetings, especially the touching.

Table 5.6 Ways of Greetings

A	B
Europeans and Americans	Touching their heart, mouth and forehead
American youths	Shaking hands with their right hands
Chinese	Joining their hands and bowing their heads in respect
Muslims	Putting the right hand over the left and bowing slightly
Hindus	Greeting each other with the expression, "Give me a five!"

Handshakes are acceptable almost everywhere, even between strangers. For example, a handshake in the US or the UK may be considered appropriate for meeting someone new. With globalization, handshakes have become more popular in most of intercultural communication for greetings and farewell while specific greetings in some cultures are kept, for example, bows in Japan or joining hands together by Buddhists in many countries. It deserves attention to know that handshakes are not acceptable in the Islamic cultures between opposite genders for greetings or farewells.

Cheek-kissing as one of the French customs for greetings is mostly restricted among friends, closer acquaintances and family members, so is Latin Americans with a minor degree of relational closeness. However, genders matter more because cheek-kissing often happens between a woman and a man or women but rarely between two men. In contrast, in certain Arabian, African, and Asian countries, men publicly hold hands or show physical affection as signs of brotherhood or friendship, which may suggest a romantic relationship in other parts of the world. Figure 5.9 shows that Pakistani President Asif Ali Zandariit is holding a hand with Iranian President Mahmoud Ahmadinejad, as sign of mutual respect, which does not work in the US or the UK.

When a kiss on both cheeks is common in France, close touches such as kissing on the cheek, patting on the shoulder, embracing, or touching other bodily parts are not so much accepted for many people in Asia and other parts of the world since such behaviors are interpreted as an offense or even a violation of one's private space.

Figure 5.9　A Sign of Mutual Respect

Patting on one's head also has different meanings depending on cultures. Patting on the head can be tabooed in some Asian countries such as Thailand as the head is taken to be sacred, but is seen as a sign of affection in China, Japan or Korea. The Middle Eastern countries take touches between people from opposite genders as bad characters. In China babies are touched on the face for affection while in the United States, parents do not like their babies to be touched except family members.

Test Your Reading 8

Decide whether the statements are True (T) or False (F).

(1) High contact cultures include Chinese, Japanese, Thailand and the Philippines, the UK, Netherlands, Finland, Germany, Australia, the US and New Zealand. (　　)

(2) Low contact cultures include the Middle East, Latin America and Southern Europe. (　　)

(3) Handshakes are not acceptable in the Islamic cultures between opposite genders for greetings or farewells. (　　)

(4) Cheek-kissing often happens between a woman and a man or women

but rarely between two men. (　)

(5) In Arabian, African, and Asian countries, men publicly hold hands or show physical affection as signs of brotherhood or friendship. (　)

(6) Patting on the head can be tabooed in some Asian countries such as China, Japan or Korea as head is taken to be sacred, but is seen as a sign of affection in Thailand. (　)

B. Paralanguage in Intercultural Communication

Paralanguage refers to the non-speech sounds by speakers to modify the meaning of their message, which also vary across cultures. Vocalization can be divided into three categories, i.e., vocal characterizers, vocal qualifiers and vocal segregates.

Vocal characterizers include yawning, laughing, crying, yelling, whining, belching, and moaning to convey meanings to an audience, which are comparatively uncomplicated to infer. For example, it is time to leave when the listener yawns. And **vocal segregates** include such sounds as "un-huh" "shh" "uh" "oooh" "mmmh" or "humm", to convey messages about internal feelings as dissent or pleasure, which requires efforts to figure out in practice for foreign language learners.

Vocal qualifiers include such elements as tones, tempos, rhythms, resonance, pitch and volume for expression of strong emotions. Meanings by volume of speech as a vocal qualifier vary across cultures. Generally, Asians and Europeans speak at lower volumes than North Americans do while Asians tend to control themselves from shouting as they are taught since childhood. And in Saudi Arabia, speaking loudly conveys authority but speaking softly expresses submission. Americans, on the other hand, are more perceived as brash for their loudness by Europeans. And British speakers show anger by raising volume, but Indian English speakers command attention with loudness.

There are significant **pitch** differences across cultures. For example, Japanese females adopt an extremely high pitch, separating themselves acoustically from Japanese males, whereas for English speakers, the male pitch is less ditterentiated from the female pitch.

Speaking rates also demonstrate intercultural differences. The Finnish language is spoken more slowly than other European languages, leading to the perception that the Finnish people themselves are "slow". Some people have a similar perception of the Southern drawl accent in the United States.

Even intonation can cause confusion and misunderstanding in intercultural communication. For example, the Indian and Pakistani employees in a cafeteria at London's Heathrow Airport were perceived by the airport staff to be quite rude because they failed to use a rising intonation with the word "Gravy". The fact that the Asian employees' intonation fell at the end was interpreted by the British diners that it as "Gravy. Take it or leave it!" as the falling intonation was seen as abrupt and rude. In British English, the rising intonation with "Gravy" implies a polite question, as in "Would you like gravy?"

Test Your Reading 9

Decide whether the statements are True (T) or False (F).

(1) Generally, Asians and Europeans speak at higher volumes than North Americans do. (   )

(2) In America, speaking loudly conveys authority while speaking softly expresses submission. (   )

(3) British speakers expose anger by raising volume while Indian English speakers command attention with loudness. (   )

(4) Korean females adopt an extremely high pitch, separating themselves acoustically from Japanese males. (   )

(5) The Finnish language is spoken more slowly than other European languages, leading to the perception that the Finnish people themselves are "slow." (   )

Case Study 7

This is the cover of *Learn to Be Silent* by Ma Xiaomin (Figure 5.10). What message does the cover convey?

The book cover demonstrates that the quality and competence to keep silence is learned and trained characters and virtues as part of culture. In Chinese culture, silence is taken as wisdom and inner peace, exhibiting tolerance and respect; therefore it is positively valued as in "Speech is silvery,

Figure 5.10   Book Cover

and silence is golden."

Silence communicates even more as an extreme form of paralanguage in mute as it implies a variety of meanings to different groups of people all round the world. Silence is interpreted for face-saving, conveying positive or negative emotions, communicating consent or dissent, marking approval or disapproval, or for social bonding or alienation depending on communication contexts.

Differences in silence are most pronounced between high-context and low-context cultures. A high-context culture is one in which meaning is inferred from the context or setting instead of the words used. The contextual cues include social status, social relationships, setting and non-verbal behaviors like eye contacts, facial expressions, body languages, and the use of silence are relevant in interpreting messages. Silence is a sign of respect, contemplation, and thoughtfulness since it allows others to express themselves without interruption or embarrassment, thus more positively valued in China, Japan and Korea. In China, silence can be used to show agreement and receptiveness. In many cultures, a question will be answered only after a period of contemplative silence. In Japan, silence from women can be considered an expression of femininity.

On the other hand, Western cultures, especially the North America and the UK, tend to view silence negatively. In their interactions at work, school, or with friends, much silence makes people uncomfortable, which is often perceived as a sign of inattentiveness or disinterest. Differences in the use of silence can lead to negative stereotyping.

Varied cognition of silence would result in problematic situations. For example, Greeks regard silence as refusal, whereas Egyptians use silence to convey consent. When Egyptian pilots requested permission to land their planes on Greek territory, the Greek traffic controller did not respond, which the Egyptians interpreted as consent and proceeded to land. The Greeks interpreted this action as a direct contravention of their refusals.

Activity 10

Fill in Table 5.7 to summarize different cultural connotations of silence.

Table 5.7 Cultural Connotations of Silence

Cultures/Countries	Cultural Connotations
China, Japan and Korea	
China	
Japan	
North America, the UK	
Greece	
Egypt	

C. Environmental Language

Environmental language refers to the messages sent and understood with the help of the factors related to the biological and psychological environment in regard with culture itself. There are many kinds of environmental languages, such as time, space, colors, signals and architecture, among which the use of time and space is prominent as a way to communicate nonverbally.

Proxemics is the study of how space and distance influence communication, which measures physical distance between people in communication.

Use of space is one of the means of human communication. The personal bubble is a metaphor of the size of one's "personal space" which is culturally and contextually determined. The radius of the personal space is personal distance as an imaginary bubble around oneself for the comfortable distance between oneself and other people or objects. According to the American anthropologist Edward Hall, people are actually enveloped by bubbles of four different sizes, each of which applies to a different set of potential interlopers (Figure 5.11).

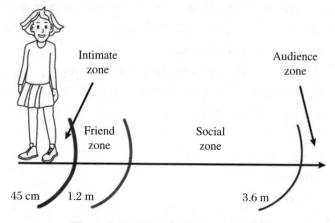

Figure 5.11 Distances between People

The average sizes of personal bubbles of Americans are as follows.

The intimate zone ranges between 6 and 18 inches (15 cm~45 cm), which is reserved for those who are emotionally close with, where lovers or spouses, children and parents, intimate friends, family members, close relatives, or pets are welcome and one feels comfortable and secured. People feel uncomfortable, and their body reacts protectively when a stranger, someone they do not know well, or someone they do not like, enters this space.

The personal/friends zone extends between 18 inches and 48 inches (46 cm~1.22 m), which is the most comfortable for personal conversations for most Western cultures. Friends and acquaintances occupy this zone comfortably, especially during informal conversations but strangers are strictly forbidden. For example, when one steps too far into the space, the other may feel threatened and the same is true when one stands outside of the space, the other may feel rebuffed. It is a distance that people stand from others at cocktail parties, office parties, social functions and friendly gatherings.

The social zone goes farther between 4 and 12 feet (1.22 m~3.6 m), where people stand away from strangers. In this zone, people feel comfortable conducting routine social interactions with new acquaintances or total strangers, for example, the plumber or carpenter doing repairs around their home, the mailman, the barista at Starbucks, the new employee at work and the person whom people do not know very well.

The public/audience zone spreads over 12 feet (3.6 m), when one is speaking to an audience in a formal setting. The distance between him/her and the first row is taken as the public space in which the speaker will feel intruded upon and communication cramped for any closer interspace, and any farther away with make him feel harder to connect with the audience due to distance.

It has to be noted that Hall's study is more related to Americans, and distances between people also vary across cultures. For example, Chinese people tend to have a shorter distance for person/friend relations or social occasions.

Test Your Reading 10

Fill in the blanks in Table 5.8 of proxemic distances of Americans.

Table 5.8 Proxemic Distances of Americans

Space	Distance	Examples
Intimate distance	15 cm~45 cm Ankle space/elbow space	
Personal distance		Friends and acquaintances
Social distance	1.22 m~3.6 m More than an arm space	
Public distance		An audience in a formal setting

Activity 11

How do you describe the relationships of these people in terms of space (Figure 5.12)?

Figure 5.12 Relationships of People in Space

These four distinct zone distances can be applied in places such as Australia, New Zealand, Great Brian, Northern Europe, Scandinavia, Canada, Iceland and Singapore. The personal space actually differs great between cultures as the result of high contact or low contact cultures vary. Generally speaking, people from the high contact culture tend to have a smaller space or closer distance in communication while those from the low contact culture prefer the opposite. The following graph demonstrates the relationship between culture and personal space, which is informative to understand spatial language in communication.

As shown in Figure 5.13, Latin Americans and Arabs are likely to have the smaller personal space than the French and Americans. Germans prefer even bigger personal bubbles than Americans and the Japanese have the biggest one.

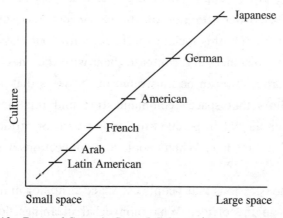

Figure 5.13 Personal Space in Several Cultures (Varner & Beamer, 2008)

Each person has varying comfort levels of personal bubbles which differ from culture to culture. For example, in Romania, the average personal distance kept with strangers is 4.6 feet, but 2.5 feet in Argentina. Likewise, in Saudi Arabia, a distance of 3.2 feet is proper even with closer friends or families, which is a suitable distance with strangers in most countries, such as Mexico and Norway.

In Latin America and the Middle East, the acceptable distance is much shorter than what most Europeans and Americans feel comfortable with. This is why an American or a European might wonder why the other person is invading his/her personal space by standing so close, while the other person might wonder why the American/European is standing so far away: "Are they trying to run away or what?"

This is one of the reasons why Asians, Europeans or Americans would look at each other with suspicion when negotiating business as the Europeans or Americans would refer to the Asians as "pushy" and "too familiar" and the Asians would think of the Europeans or Americans as "cold" "stand-offish" and "cool". Lack of awareness of Intimate Zone variations between cultures will lead to misconceptions and inaccurate assumptions about one culture by another.

Case Study 8

Watch the video clip "Invading Personal Space in Public Social Experiment". Focus your attention on the passengers' reactions when the lady came closer to them. Do this social experiment with your classmates to identify your four personal distances and compare them with the ones in the US.

Personal relationship can be illustrated in the ways that space shows up in common metaphors that space, communication and relationships are closely related. For example, when people are content with or attracted to someone, they are "close" to him/her. When people lose connections with someone, they are "distant."

Think of the occasions that people use space at home, in meeting rooms, in automobiles, or in the office. What nonverbal meanings do others perceive about the owners from these spaces? What nonverbal meanings are the owners of these spaces trying to send or how they keep them?

The expected amount of personal space varies depending on settings and is somewhat culture-specific, which indicates values in terms of personal relationships and power distance, etc.

Figure 5.14 are diplomatic meetings of Russian President Putin, one of which is with Emmanuel Macron, the President of France who is holding the rotating presidency of the European Union, and the other with Tokayev, President of Kazakhstan. Apparent are the relationship and attitudes of Putin held towards them.

Figure 5.14   Relationship in Personal Space

Activity 12

Study the sitting positions of talk shows in Germany, the United States and China for values revealed in Figure 5.15.

Figure 5.15   Sitting Positions of Talk Shows

Activity 13

Study the power distance revealed in the following sittings (Figure 5.16).

Figure 5.16 Power Distance in Sittings

Use of time also promotes human communication. Chromatics is the study of how time affects communication. There are profound cultural differences in how people think about, measure, and use their time. The passage of time is universal and inevitable, but is experienced by different cultures, which may lead to confusion, especially in overseas travelling, or socializing or doing business with someone with different perception of time.

Time orientation is included in Kluchhohn and Strodtbeck's Value Orientations as one of the features that unveil cultural values towards time, which influence their ways of communication. In the framework, culture is classified based on the perceptions of time as the past-oriented, the present-oriented, or the future-oriented, which result in corresponding use of time. For example, in many Arab and Latin American cultures, time is used more loosely, and punctuality is not necessarily a goal to achieve. The expression "Indian time" refers to "the perception of time that is circular and flexible". But, In the US, high value is placed on being on time, and punctuality is responded more positively. Time orientation does not static as culture is changing. For example, increasing Chinese are more sensitive to time with the Reform and Opening-up Policy and globalization, and it seems that Chinese culture has become more present or future oriented which used to be regarded as past-orientated.

Edward Hall promoted time-related cultures in *The Silent Language* in terms of use of time, i.e., the monochronic and the polychronic, which is also abbreviated as the M-timed and the P-timed accordingly. "Monochronic" means essentially doing one thing at a time while "polychronic" is characterized by several events happening simultaneously. Table 5.9 lists some features of the M-timed and the P-timed.

Table 5.9 Features of the M-timed and the P-timed

The M-timed	The P-timed
Time is linear and sequential	Time is cyclical and concurrent
Doing one thing at a time	Doing many things at once
Concentrating on the job	Being easily distracted and subject to interruptions
Taking time commitments seriously	Considering time commitment an objective to be achieved, if possible
Time is a precious and tangible commodity that one cannot afford to waste	Life is unpredictable and distractions are part of it
Being low context and individualistic	Being high context and collectivist
Schedules are important	Relationships are more important than task outcomes
Being committed to job	Being committed to people and human relationships
Adhering to plans	Changing plans often and easily
Being concerned about not disturbing others; following rules of privacy	Being more concerned with people close of them (family, friends, close business associates) than with privacy
Showing great respect for private property	Borrowing and lending things often and easily
Emphasizing promptness	Basing promptness on the relationship
Being accustomed to short-term relationships	Having a strong tendency to build lifetime relationship
Emphasizing more details	Emphasizing fewer details
Being more independent	Being more interdependent

Test Your Reading 11

Decide whether the statements are True (T) or False (F).

(1) Culture is classified into the past-oriented, the present-oriented, or the future-oriented in the framework of Time orientation by Edward Hall. (　)

(2) Kluchhohn and Strodtbeck promoted time-related cultures by the monochronic and the polychronic in terms of use of time. (　)

(3) North America, Israel, Germany, Switzerland, and North European countries are regarded as monochronic cultures. (　)

(4) Polychronic cultures include most Latin-American, Southern European, Asian and African countries and most of tribal communities around the world. (　)

(5) Monochronic cultures are usually collectivistic, preferring high-context communication while polychronic ones are more likely to be individualistic in low-context communication. (　)

Activity 14

Read the paragraphs and analyze what view of time these peoples show.

> A. An Australian once visited Fiji island and asked me when the stores were open, since it was afternoon and he hadn't seen a store open yet. Taken aback at what seemed a stupid question, I told him the obvious truth, "They're open when their doors are open." When I walked away, I realized it was a question I would have asked myself when I first arrived on Fiji.
>
> B. The idea of being late versus keeping time for the summit may differ widely between an Arab businessman and a North American one. The American might far less tolerant of the late arrival of the Arabian. However, the might be offended by the American's insistence on punctuality or on getting right down to business because the Arabian would generally prefer talking with his colleagues before cutting a conversation short to make an appointment.

Activity 15

Answer the following questions.

> (1) Suppose your American friend invited you to his/her party at half past 7 the day after tomorrow. When are you going to get there? Are you going to arrive before 7 o'clock to help your friend with the party? Or 5~10 minutes later to avoid being the first visitor? Or after 8 0'clock to be the VIP?
>
> (2) What do you mean by being "on time" or "on punctuality" when a conference is scheduled to begin at 9:00 am in China? A business appointment at 9:30 am in the US? An official appointment at 10:00 am in Columbia?

Ⅳ. Extended Reading

Commentary: Rediscovering China Through the Winter Olympics
(Xinhua, February 22, 2022)

Beijing, Feb. 22 (Xinhua) — As the Beijing Winter Olympics came to an end, the world has an opportunity to rediscover China — a confident, calm and determined nation that is ready to move forward.

In the summer of 2008, Beijing proved to the world that the most populous country in the world could successfully host the Olympic Games. However, 2022 is not 2008: the unprecedented COVID-19 pandemic is continuing, and there has been resistance from some Western countries seeking to "politicize" the Winter Olympics. Many asked whether China would be able to run the Winter Olympics well amid multiple challenges at home and abroad. Now China gives the world a resounding answer, based on living facts rather than deliberate eloquence. Some Western countries have always been afraid that China would become superior to them in terms of development, and have repeatedly used the

Olympics to play some despicable political games, pointing fingers at China.

As the Olympic Charter states that "the practice of sport is a human right," the Olympic spirit, which embodies mutual understanding, friendship, solidarity and fair play, should not have been tainted by political manipulation. The Winter Olympics is a competitive platform for athletes, not a stage for politicians to gain political capital. China's attitude of ignoring political noises is simply the best response to it, and it also reflects its firm confidence in its own path.

During the Games, the daily number of newly diagnosed COVID-19 cases in the world was shocking. It was not easy to ensure that athletes from all over the world continue to fully enjoy the competition at the Beijing Winter Olympics. Under such circumstances, Beijing had achieved "zero growth" of positive cases during the Games. This is the result of the implementation of various pandemic-prevention measures, and the contribution of Chinese pandemic-prevention staff.

In the face of such a severe pandemic, China has successfully hosted the Winter Olympics with composure. Isn't this an excellent illustration of how China copes with risks and challenges calmly today?

Through Beijing 2022, the world could see further evidence of a more eco-friendly Beijing and China. Many sports facilities and venues built for Beijing 2008 were remodeled for Beijing 2022. The "Water Cube," the National Aquatics Center in downtown Beijing, was turned into an "ice cube" hosting events including curling. More stunning is the Big Air Shougang venue, which was repurposed from a steel mill. Through this whimsical creation, China simultaneously retained the capital city's industrial memory and made an eye-catching feature for the Winter Olympics.

Only a few new competition venues were built for Beijing 2022, which followed an eco-friendly approach. For the first time at the Olympic Games, all Beijing 2022 venues were being powered with renewable energy, with solar and wind as the primary energy sources.

This "green, inclusive, open and clean" Winter Olympics has now ended. With confidence and calm, China is now embarking on a new journey of achieving higher, faster, stronger goals — together with the rest of the world.

Post-class Tasks

Self-test Tasks

1. Answer the questions in your own words.

(1) Compare different classifications of cultures: contact culture vs. noncontact culture, monochronic culture vs. polychronic culture, high-context culture vs. low-context culture. What is the relationship between them?

(2) The personal presentation, style of dress, and surroundings such as a dorm room, an apartment, a car, or an office send nonverbal messages about one's identities. Analyze some of the nonverbal signals that your personal presentation or environment that appear to others. What do they say about who you are? Do they create the impression that you desire?

2. Analyze the following statements to identify which nonverbal elements are involved in each statement.

(1) Someone might cross his arms if he is feeling angry or nervous.

(2) Sitting still and paying attention at a meeting conveys respect and attention.

(3) Someone slouches himself on his shoulders when he feels tired, frustrated or disappointed.

(4) Someone in the United States might display a "thumbs up" to communicate confirmation or that they feel positively about something.

(5) You might stand two to three feet away from a new contact to respect their boundaries.

(6) You might speak quickly if you are excited about something.

(7) Someone might raise their eyebrows and open his eyes widely if he feels surprised.

(8) Someone may convey disinterest or disrespect by looking away from others or at the ground or the phone.

(9) You convey support or empathy by placing your hand on the shoulder

of one of your friends.

(10) Distance produces beauty.

3. Decide whether the statements are True (T) or False (F).

(1) Nonverbal communication varies from culture to culture. (　)

(2) Every culture has developed a formal way to greet strangers to show hospitality. (　)

(3) OK sign means "something worthless" in Japan. (　)

(4) The Chinese tend to speak in lower voice than the English when they make speeches or deliver a lecture, or talk with each other, or make a phone call. (　)

(5) It is considered rude to point with the index finger in most Asian cultures. (　)

(6) Hispanics, people of Eastern European descents, Italians, the French, Arabs, and Jews belong to low contact cultures. (　)

(7) The M-timed schedules several activities at the same time and they are more flexible. (　)

(8) There are many factors that affect personal space among people, such as genders, ages, cultural settings and relationships to the talking partners. (　).

4. Fill in the blanks in the following passage.

Benefits of Effective Nonverbal Communication

Communication skills consistently ranked among the top skills most commonly listed in new job postings by employers in 2020. Having strong communication skills is essential for building both personal and professional relationships. There are several ways _____ communication can improve people's communication skills.

• Communicate _____. People may also use nonverbal communication completely to communicate with others. For example, if someone is explaining a sentiment the other person admire and agree with, he or she might nod his or her head up and down to express solidarity. Using hand gestures to indicate the importance of an idea may tell the listeners to pay attention to and remember a key point.

• Communicate _____. People's body language may also intentionally or unintentionally express the current condition. For example, people may pick up nonverbal cues that they are being dishonest, unengaged, excited or aggressive.

• Convey _____. People can also use nonverbal communication to show their feelings, such as disappointment, relief, happiness, contentment and more.

• Showcase _____. Nonverbal communication is a great way to show who a person is. For example, a kind and optimistic person might frequently smile with open body language and offer friendly touches.

Group Work

1. Role-play the following case to find out:
When a Japanese and an American are talking, the two will slowly begin to move around the room, the American moving backwards away from the Japanese and the Japanese moving forward. If we look at a video of this phenomenon replayed at high speed, it gives the illusion that the two men are waltzing around the room with the Japanese leading.

(1) What did the Japanese want to do? How did the American interpret the behaviors of the Japanese?

(2) What did the American want to do? How did the Japanese interpret the behaviors of the American?

2. Answer the questions by thinking about how you communicate with your classmates (Figure 5.17). Try to be as honest with yourself as you can. Read the definitions under each scale and circle the number that shows how you would like to communicate. Then go and show your partner what you have scored and vice-versa; jot down where you believe that person should have placed themselves and then show each other and discuss.

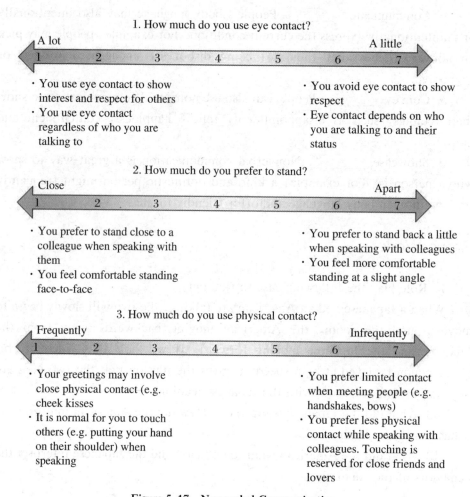

Figure 5.17 Non-verbal Communication

Telling China's Stories

Read the following passage and write a passage on the environment of your hometown or any place in China, which demonstrates some characters of Chinese culture. Then share your passage with your classmates.

Chinese *Fengshui*

Fengshui, which means wind and water, is the ancient Chinese art of living in harmony with our environment. *Fengshui* can be traced as far back as the Banpo dwellings in 4000 BCE. The ideas behind *Fengshui* state that how we use our environment and organize our belongings affects the energy flow (chi) of people in that space, and the person/people who created the environment. The inclusion or exclusion, and placement, of various objects in our environments are used to create a positive impact on others. The theory is to use the five elements of metal, wood, water, fire and earth to design a space. *Fengshui* is applicable to cities, villages, homes, and public spaces.

The Temple of Heaven in Bejing, China is an example of *Fengshui* architecture. To keep harmony with the natural world, the Temple houses the Hall of Annual Prayer which is comprised of four inners, 12 middle, and 12 outer pillars representing the four seasons, 12 months, and 12 traditional Chinese houses.

My Learning Reflection

1. What have I learned about Chinese cultures or myself?

2. What have I learned about other cultures?

3. What impressed me most in this chapter?

4. What still confuses me?

Chapter 6　English and Chinese Literature

Learning Objectives

- To identify basic similarities and differences of English and Chinese poetry and novels;
- To analyze the hidden origin in the differences from cultural dimensions;
- To develop cultural confidence in Chinese literature and intercultural perspective.

Pre-class Tasks

- Read the textbook and watch the concerned clips in *xuexitong*（学习通）.

Ⅰ. Lead-in Tasks

The following quoted part is chosen from the poem "To Autumn" written by John Keats, a great English Romantic poet. And the Chinese version is translated by a Chinese scholar, Zha Liangzheng（查良铮）.

Activity 1

Read them out loudly to sense rhythmic tempo. Then talk with your partner and report your understanding to the class, paying more attention to the underlined parts.

> **To Autumn**
>
> John Keats
>
> Sea <u>son</u> of <u>mists</u> and <u>me</u>llow <u>fruit</u>ful <u>ness</u>
> Close <u>bo</u>som <u>friend</u> of <u>the</u> ma<u>tu</u>ring <u>sun</u>
> Con <u>spi</u>ring <u>with</u> him <u>how</u> to <u>load</u> and <u>bless</u>
> With <u>fruit</u> the <u>vines</u> that <u>round</u> the <u>thatch</u>-eves <u>run</u>
>
> **秋颂**
>
> 约翰·济慈
>
> 雾气洋溢、果实圆熟的<u>秋</u>
> 你和成熟的太阳成为伙<u>伴</u>
> 你们密谋用累累的珠<u>球</u>
> 缀满茅屋檐下的葡萄藤<u>蔓</u>
>
> （查良铮译）

You might have sensed the different features in the two versions of the poem. Actually, English and Chinese poetry have different ways of deciding the rhythm. In English poetry, the different arrangement in stressed syllable and unstressed ones can decide the rhythmic patterns. The underlined parts in the four lines should be stressed and the rest should not, thus form the poetic rhythm. In each line, there are five stressed and five unstressed syllables, and these syllables are alternatively arranged to achieve certain kind of rhythmic tempo. Quite differently, the rhythm of Chinese poetry is decided with *si sheng* （四声）, four changes in tones, and *ping ze* （平仄）. In each line, every Chinese character is well arranged according to its sound, i.e. the first, second, third or fourth tone, and the specific changes in the line. The difference in the rhythm in English and Chinese poetry is caused by the different systems of phonetics and writings, living environments, ways of thinking and cultural inclinations.

As shown in the poetry, literature conveys the implications of cultures. Different cultures have their different ways of expressing and presenting, which can be helpful to see into the inner quality of the culture. Poetry and novels, together with other genres of literature serve as an effective approach to recognizing differences and similarities in both English and Chinese literature and culture. Therefore, this chapter will set about analyzing their differences and similarities, figuring out the barriers of Chinese learners to understand English literature and culture, and bridging the gap between the two cultures to pave the way for an effective intercultural communication.

II. English and Chinese Poetry

Literature, as the most important carrier of culture, has been considered as an essential representation of a country or region, and is viewed as a unified demonstration of culture in the form of language. Classic literature consists of such genres as poetry, novels, drama, prose, short story, and so on. Among them, poetry and novels can be considered as the major instruments to demonstrate the close relationship between language and culture. Due to word-formations and syntax, poetry and novels in English and Chinese present different faces to the world, showing respective society and reality to its best in contexts, exposing the inner heart of the people and expressing subtle emotions and feelings. A comparative study of literature thus can be an effective way to see into the hidden cultural connotations, which may benefit in language use, appreciation of the core of culture in terms of the worldviews, values, perceptions and beliefs of the nation or countries concerned.

Poetry in literature, as the art of language, expresses the highest qualities in the most refined language, thus is known as "a temple of words" and would be the most effective vector of language and culture as well. Poetry is a literary genre different from prose or any other writing as it is either in metrical pattern or in free verse. There are diverse definitions on poetry both in English and Chinese. According to Merriam-Webster dictionary, poetry is a composition in verse, something suggesting a poem (as in expressiveness, lyricism, or formal grace). Ancient Chinese scholars believe that poetry is where the will is, as in "where there is a will in heart, and it is poetry in speech"(在心为志,发言为诗).

Traditional English and Chinese poems share some features in common. Both of them follow certain metrical and rhythmic patterns, telling stories or expressing emotions. Diverse as the forms are, poetry is characterized by a highly developed artistic form and by the use of heightened language and rhythm to express an intensely imaginative interpretation of the subject. Poets also express individual feelings through poetic lines, extending their emotions and ideas to a lager sphere, both socially and geographically.

In both English and Chinese, poetry can be categorized into different types, according to the numbers of words in a line and the total numbers of all lines in a poem. In English poetry, there are epics, ballads, sonnets, hymns, limericks, Haiku and many other types. Traditional Chinese poetry owns five-characters octaves（五言律诗）and seven-characters quatrains（七言绝句）. Traditional poems usually follow metrical patterns, rhythmic schemes, and rhyme patterns, employing mainly images and rhetorical devices for sound, such as assonance and consonance, to create its unique artistic atmosphere.

A. What Are the Rhythmic Patterns in English and Chinese Poetry?

Many differences exist inevitably between traditional English and Chinese poetry due to the language systems, which also demonstrates more hidden and delicate features in the two cultures. Thus, the differences in rhythmic patterns can be of great significance in understanding English and Chinese cultures, from which different cultural inclination will be shown.

English poetry, especially traditional poetry, demonstrates its cultural essences, for poetry has long been cherished by men of letters as a treasure of culture. English poetry makes use of five basic rhythms, which are of different arrangements of stressed and unstressed syllables. Among them, four types are frequently-used, which include iamb, trochee, dactyl and anapest. The iamb is most commonly used. It consists of two syllables, the first of which is unstressed, while the second is stressed. A trochee has two syllables, the first of which is strongly stressed, while the second syllable is unstressed. The dactyl is made up of three syllables, the first of which is stressed, and the remaining two are unstressed. The anapests are total opposite to dactyls in that the first two syllables are unstressed and the last one is stressed. The patterns of stressed and unstressed syllables in each meter partly decide the rhythmic pattern of the poem (Table 6.1).

Table 6.1 Rhythmic Patterns in English Poetry

Feet	Features	Examples of Words
Trochee	stressed syllable followed by an unstressed one	custom
Iamb	unstressed syllable followed by a stressed one	describe
Spondee	equal stress for both syllables	bicycle
Dactyl	stressed syllable, followed by two unstressed ones	cupcake
Anapest	two unstressed syllables, followed by a stressed one	understand

To identify the rhythmic pattern of a poem also needs the number of the meter in each line. Types of metrical feet in one line also help to create poetic meters, and repetitions or regular occurrence of the type of meter contributes to the rhythm of the whole poem. The times of the repetition will decide the numbers of meter. And the numbers of a poetic meter is usually labeled with Greek suffixes. Mono-meter is for one foot, and diameters are for two feet. The following words can express different numbers in Chinese in terms of meter (Table 6.2).

Table 6.2 Basic Meters in English Poetry

Di-		两	
Tri-		三	
Tetra-		四	
Penta-	meter	五	音步
Hexa-		六	
Hepta-		七	
Octa-		八	

In conclusion, the rhythm of English poetry is decided by the type and the number of meters. To identify the type of the meter, one needs to identify the arrangement of stressed and unstressed syllables. Then, check the whole poem and see if all, or at least most of the lines are in the same or similar pattern by counting the numbers of the meter in one line. Lastly, the rhythm will be confirmed by combining the type and the number of the meter. The following lines from "Sonnet 18" by William Shakespeare demonstrate how the rhythmic and metrical pattern can be decided in English poetry.

Shall I/ compare/ thee to/ a sum/mer's day?
Thou art/ more love/ly and/ more tem/perate:
Rough wind/ do shake/ the dar/ling buds/ of May,
And sum/mer's lease/ hath all/ too short/ a date.

The rhythm of English poetry is determined both by the stressed and unstressed syllable and the times it occurs. In the above example, "Shall I" in the first line takes two syllables, and the first unstressed and second stressed. The word "compare" also has two syllables, and the unstressed one is followed by a stressed one. This pattern is known as "iamb". In each line of the sonnet, iamb occurs five times, thus this is called "pentameters". And all the following lines in the sonnet are in similar pattern. Therefore, the rhythm of the sonnet is in "iambic pentameter".

Case Study 1

The following stanza is taken from poem "I Wandered Lonely as a Cloud" by William Wordsworth. Read it aloud to figure out the metrical and rhythmic features in the poem. Is it iambic pentameter or some other kind of pattern?

> I wandered lonely as a cloud
> That floats on high o'er vales and hills,
> When all at once I saw a crowd,
> A host of golden daffodils;
> Beside the lake, beneath the trees,
> Fluttering and dancing in the breeze.

This poem follows the rhythmic pattern of iambic tetrameter, i. e. four iambic meters in each line. And in each of the two syllables, the first is unstressed and the second is stressed, therefore is called iamb. There are four meters in the first line, and in each meter, there are two syllables, the first unstressed and the second stressed, which is called iamb. Therefore the rhythmic pattern of the poem is roughly decided as iambic tetrameter, which means that each line has four ("tetra") iambic meters.

In view of the above, the metrical and rhythmic pattern of the first two lines should be divided like this:

"I wan|-dered lone| -ly as | a cloud
That floats | on high | o'er vales | and hills."

The iambic pentameter is the most popular and influential rhythmic pattern in English poetry. In the 2nd line, "o'er" is used instead of the more common one "over", to fit the need of assignment of music foot. Otherwise, the second line will have five meters, which will leave the rest of the lines in rhythmical disorder. To sum up, the rhythmic features in English poetry are decided by the regular occurrence and the number of the syllables.

The phonetic system of Chinese language is based on four tones, *Si Sheng*. Chen Yinque(陈寅恪)thought that the four tones of the Chinese language came into being because of the "reading in Chinese" of sutra and the introduction of the theory of "tone" in ancient India. The first tone is Level tone, the second Rising tone, the third Falling-rising tone and the fourth Entering tone. In the ancient Chinese poetry, rhythm was created according to Level and Oblique tone, in Chinese *ping ze*. Level tone(平)includes the first and the second, while Oblique tone(仄)includes the third and the fourth. A good line should have the musical tones of words fall in with the established patterns. In the rhythm there was not regulating Levels and Oblique tones but four tones before the Tang Dynasty.

$$\left\{\begin{array}{l}\text{平}—\text{平声}(1、2\text{声})\\\text{仄}\left\{\begin{array}{l}\text{上声}(3\text{声})\\\text{去声}(4\text{声})\\\text{入声}\end{array}\right.\end{array}\right.$$

Figure 6.1 *Ping Ze* and *Si Sheng*

The rhythm in traditional Chinese poetry is determined by the alternate occurrence of *ping ze*, which is based on arrangements of four tones. That is to say, the combination of *si sheng* and *ping ze* basically shapes its rhythm. For every single Chinese character in a poem, there should be one tone among the four tones, and this tone can be settled as *ping* or *ze*. The Chinese classical poetry emphasizes rhythms, Levels and Oblique tones, as well as word matching. This forms the poetical antithesis（对仗）, the rhythmical basis for the poem. It is a matching of both sound and sense in two lines or sentences, usually with the matching words in the same part of speech. The neat antithesis

(对仗工整) in antithetical couplet are highly valued. Classical Chinese poetry also strives to have harmonious tonal patterns, cadences and intonations, with double tone and vowel-rhyme. The following two lines by Wang Wei (王维) are an example of tones and rhythms in Chinese poems (Table 6.3).

Table 6.3 Examples of Tones and Rhythms in Chinese Poems

诗句		拼音		四声		平仄	
大	长	da	chang	4th	2nd	仄	平
漠	河	mo	he	4th	2nd	仄	平
孤	落	gu	luo	1st	4th	平	仄
烟	日	yan	ri	1st	4th	平	仄
直	圆	zhi	yuan	2nd	2nd	平	平

As shown in the above lines, in the first line there are five characters with five tones, which are the fourth, fourth, first, first and second. And they are categorized in the rhythm of *ze ze ping ping ping* (仄仄平平平). These five characters of the second line also have five tones, which are the second, second, fourth, fourth and second and in the rhythm of *ping ping ze ze ping* (平平仄仄平). According to *si sheng*, the two lines are labeled with Arabic numbers, 44112 and 22442. Then it's found by contrast that the two lines are parallel word by word, the first one in the first line to the first one in the second line, and the second in the first line to the second in the second line. The two lines will be in 4-2, 4-2, 1-4, 1-4, and with a 2-2 beat as a rhymed ending. That is to say, the first and second tones are usually put against the third and fourth tones. As for *ping ze*, the two lines are in 仄-平, 仄-平, 平-仄, 平-仄, with 平-平 as the rhymed ending. This explains how the rhythmic effects in the Chinese poetry are created according to *si sheng* and *ping ze*.

Case Study 2

The rhythm of the following two lines can also be shown with *si sheng* and *ping ze*. Read them aloud to analyze the rhythmic feature.

> 山行(节选)
> 杜牧
> 远上寒山石径斜，
> 白云深处有人家。

In *pinyin*, the lines are read: *yuan shang han shan shi jing xia, bai yun shen chu you ren jia*. If they are labeled in Arabic numbers, they are the patterns of 4422242 and 2214422. If contrasted word by word, the first one in the first line to the first one in the second line, and the second in the first line to the second in the second line, and so forth, the tones in Chinese characters should be as follows: 4-2, 4-2, 2-1, 2-4, 2-4, 4-2, and 2-2. When put in *ping ze*, they will accordingly be: 仄-平, 仄-平, 平-平, 平-仄, 平-仄, 仄-平, 平-平.

Si sheng and *ping ze* are the fundamental base for the phonetic system of Chinese poetry and the rhythm of Chinese poetry depends on the inner quality of Chinese language, or rather, Chinese characters as each Chinese character processes an autonomous field of shape, sound and sense. Therefore, characters in Chinese poetry show more than English words, and it is impossible to restore the exact phonetics of ancient Chinese language, especially how to articulate certain Chinese language.

Test Your Reading 1

Decide whether the following statements are True (T) or False (F).

(1) A trochee has two syllables, the first is strongly stressed and the second unstressed. (   )

(2) An iambic foot has three syllables, all being unstressed. (   )

(3) The rhythmic pattern of English poems is decided by the number of the meters. (   )

(4) Chinese *si sheng* includes the following four types: rising, falling, level and decreasing. (   )

(5) Iambic pentameter is the most popular and influential rhythmic pattern in English poetry. (   )

B. What Are Images in English and Chinese Poetry?

The image is the center of poetry and is also one important factor to demonstrate aesthetic quality, with which the artistic conceptions are well-constructed. The image is not merely a picture, but an interpretation of reality in its metaphoric and symbolic dimensions. Both the English and Chinese poetry attach more significance onto images.

Modern English poems would focus less on the strict rhythms than on images. Famous examples include Walt Whitman, Emily Dickinson, Ezra Pound, E. E. Cummings and many others. Free as they are, meaning and artistic conceptions they convey are clear and evident. The unity and richness in meaning and artistic conception are achieved through images both in the English and Chinese poetry. Noticeably, many English poets turn to Chinese poetry for inspiration. For example, Robert Frost absorbed nutrition from the Chinese poetry and philosophy, and E. Pound has a keen interest in traditional Chinese poems and even employs some of Chinese techniques in his writing. The Imagism movement, led by E. Pound in 1910s, brought the English poetry to an influential revival.

Images have to be constructed by the use of the language, the specific words. English words are formed with letters, and letters, if taken out of words, will be of no sense. Contrast to the Chinese characters, there is no unity of shape, sound and sense in English words. Thus, they need more words to describe the target they intend to convey. In general, the English language expresses meanings with a series of similar words for same ideas or objects, avoiding repetitions of a single word presenting an object, especially for images in the poem, which is regarded as the most compact artistic form. The following poem is written by Ezra Pound, in which images contribute to the building-up of the girl and the love the speaker has for her.

Activity 2

Read the poem aloud to find out the impressive image (or images) and share your points with your peers.

> **A Girl**
>
> The tree has entered my hands
> The sap has ascended my arms,
> The tree has grown in my breast-
> Downward,
> The branches grow out of me, like arms.
>
> Tree you are,
> Moss you are,
> You are violets with wind above me
> A child-so high- you are,
> And all this is folly to the world.

  With the hypotactic structures, English poems are not likely to present an object directly by listing one or more words since the English language is weak in unity of sound, form and meaning. The meaning blank between the lines in English poems is comparatively short, leaving less space of imagination for the reader. Consequently, poetry tends to depict a direct and immediate object with more words to convey what the poet intends to express. Modern poets also attempt to revolutionize the way of the poem writing, like E. E. Cummings and E. Pound, who have made some changes, which do not change the whole map of the English poetry.

  Images in Chinese poems are presented directly with fewer words compared to English ones. Sometimes, the artistic conception of the poem is based on listing or the juxtaposition of images, and the conception is constructed and appreciated with the help of information internalized and shared in the same culture. Contrary to English poems with sufficient information for interpretation in the low-context culture communication featured in linear thinking pattern, the reader is responsible for interpretation of the Chinese poem as a product of high-context culture, filling the gaps of words with intuition and imagination.

  Many traditional Chinese poems have been translated into English by famous scholars in China and abroad, and the English versions offer good examples to look into the differences in Chinese and English language and culture.

The Chinese poem *Tian Jing Sha*: *Qiu Si* (《天净沙·秋思》) by Ma Zhiyuan (马致远) in Yuan Dynasty(元朝), is well-known for its ample images. Compare the translations in terms of patterns and rhymes to find out the omissions, additions and transmissions from the paratactic to hypotactic for images and meanings based on both high and low context communications.

Activity 3

Study the English versions of the Chinese poem for the images in them.

天净沙·秋思
马致远
枯藤老树昏鸦，
小桥流水人家，
古道西风瘦马。
夕阳西下，
断肠人在天涯。

Tune: Sunny Sand- Autumn Thoughts	To the Tune of Sky-Clear Sand
Over old trees wreathed with rotten vines fly evening crows; Under a small bridge near a cottage a stream flows; On ancient road in the west wind a lean horse goes. Westward declines the sun; Far, far from home is the heartbroken one. By Xu Yuanchong （许渊冲译）	Withered vine, old tree, a raven at dusk crows Tiny bridge, thatched cottages, the streams flows Ancient road, bleak wind, a bony steed slows. The setting sun in the west glows, The sorrow of the heart-broken traveler grows. By Zhou Fangzhu （周方珠译）

The gap between the original poem and the English version lies in the different qualities in expressions of the two languages. Images, listed one by one, can be presented and conveyed immediately in the Chinese characters. Therefore, translating Chinese poems into English ones is challenging, which entails to bridge the gap caused by the different qualities in two languages, for something may be lost, or hard to be conveyed totally in the other language. And "something" here originates constitutionally from the language and the logical and thinking characteristics behind it as Chinese poems tend to leave more space for imagination by readers. Therefore, Chinese language can list images by posing several notional words, creating the poetical sphere directly and immediately. In this way the artistic conception in a Chinese poem lasts for a long time, and readers will infer endless new meanings every time they come to it.

Figure 6.2 *Tian Jing Sha*: *Qiu Si*

  The above example shows to its deep the features of the thinking pattern in Chinese and language. Things in the poem can be inter-related with something outside the poem. To read Chinese poetry it needs a dialectical or circular thinking. Readers can easily form the relations between the images in the poem "Tian Jing Sha" as the Chinese language or characters present images. Moreover, Chinese poems, by taking advantage of the Chinese language, build up a powerful space of this artistic conception. In *kuteng* （枯藤）, *laoshu* （老树） and *xiaoqiao* （小桥）, *ku* （枯） in English means "wither'd", both *lao* （老） in English means "old" and *xiao* （小） in English means "tiny", all refer to feelings of loneliness, painful annoyance and bitter sorrow, contributing to the atmosphere of sorrow running through the whole poem. And Chinese readers can fill the blank of relevance by themselves to appreciate this unique emotion. It can be seen that Chinese culture tends to be in circular or interdependent way of thinking to perceive the world around. Table 6.4 illustrates the major differences of English and Chinese poetry.

Table 6.4 Features of English and Chinese Poetry

	Lines	Meters	Rhythms	Images	Communication Styles
English Poems	Numbers of lines: stanza, ballad, quatrain, sonnet, octave, tersest, and sestet ...	Numbers of meters: mono-meter, trimesters, Tetrameter, pentameter ...	Occurrence of stressed & unstressed syllables. iambic, trochaic ...	Expository, more words in details featured, hypo-tactic forms	Low-context communication
Chinese Poems	Most popular types: five-character Octaves, or seven-character Quatrains (五言或七言诗)	Changes of sound: Level, Rising, Falling-Rising, Entering, known as Si Sheng	Regular use of tones, the unity of sound patterns, Ping Ze	Compact, brevity, concise, fewer words, para-tactic forms	High-context communication

One of the reasons why such poetic forms in English as couplets, tercets, quatrains and sestets can be formed is that English word may have several syllables and they can be united with syllables from the following word(s) for a complete meter. In other words, the lines in a traditional English poem may vary in forms for the format of a poem, creating more variations. Poets therefore are free in writing poems, with diverse combinations of the rhythmic foot and the number of meters.

On the contrary, the Chinese characters, as a picture in its origin, achieve the unity of sound, form and meaning by a settled existence and tones. A single Chinese character will be the unity of sound, form and meaning, each of which may have different components. The reader assembles the series of impressions into a whole piece in a very direct way. Many poems contain allusions of people and events in the Chinese history, making a challenge for non-Chinese to understand these poems. For example, a word may have a form, with more than one sound, thus indicating more than one meaning. Given the same numbers of words in characters, Chinese poems tend to have more implications. In addition, its sound is unnecessary to be divided and reunited with that of other characters in the same line, thus there being the patterns of five-character (五言) and seven-character (七言) as the most structural and most commonly used poetic forms.

In the early years of the 20th century, China turned to the Westernization, learning from the Western countries in many ways, and new forms of poems came into being and the free choice of expressions have enriched the ways of presentation in Chinese poems, which focus more on meanings than formats. The Chinese language belongs to a character-based writing system instead of an alphabetic system, though the language has changed a lot, the modern Chinese people are still able to read most of the ancient poetry. Since the pronunciation of words has changed a lot, the rhymes or tonal rhythms are also likely to change and even lose. But the meanings of the characters haven't changed that much, although modern readers may get the meaning other than the ancient author intended. And all this provides the basis of getting acquaintance of traditional Chinese poetry.

There exist ancient Chinese poems nowadays, and the modern Chinese people remain keen on them as the essences of Chinese culture and language. For example, in 2016 the Chinese Poetry Conference was designed with the basic purpose of "appreciating the Chinese poetry, tracing Chinese cultural genes and tasting the beauty of life". Since its launch in 2016, it has become one of the most popular programs, sharing the beauty and interest of poetry through the competition, appreciating the wisdom and feelings of the ancient Chinese to cultivate the soul and the knowledge of poetry. With its seventh season in 2021, it has become a linguistic and cultural brand activity that leads the mass communication and promotion of Excellent Traditional Chinese Culture and the practice of the Socialist Core Values. And a wave of poetry culture, naturally also attracts the attention of classical culture fans from all over China. At the same time, Chinese poetry has gained audience through modern media and technologies, for example, BBC(British Broadcasting Corporation) has edited series of documentaries on Chinese poems or poets, one of the most celebrated one is Du Fu (杜甫), a well-known poet in the golden period of Chinese Poetry, of the Tang Dynasty (唐朝).

A close look at the differences in English and Chinese poems will lead to a better understanding of the cultures. Chinese culture demonstrates another color of unity, induction and synthesis. The Chinese language, with the unity of shapes and images, and sometime tones, is the language of description. And some Chinese characters are poetical in describing the world and conveying richer meaning with fewer characters, i.e. fewer characters, more meanings. Accordingly, Chinese culture is of general description and induction. In addition, Chinese language, as the unity of sound, form and meaning, expresses the world in an economical way, leaving more gap for readers to fill in. This actually mirrors the circular or dialectical way of thinking. Chinese culture thus tends to focus on the harmonious relationship between the Man and the world, and the Man can only find his dwelling in a harmonious world. This is a synthetic way of perception, viewing the world as an organized whole. Chinese poems, mainly about mountains and water, actually reflect the Chinese mindset, expressing a wish of living harmoniously with the surroundings.

Both English and Chinese poems demonstrate the corresponding cultures in language use, thinking patters and communication styles in addition to the aesthetic philosophy in worldviews and values as shown in Table 6.5.

Table 6.5 Cultural Elements in English and Chinese Poetry

	Language	Logic	Thinking Patterns	Communication
English culture	Analytical	Deduction	Linear	Low-context
Chinese culture	Descriptive	Induction	Circular/dialectical	High-context

The table illustrates the major cultural patterns revealed in the form of poetry which facilitate to comprehend cultural differences beyond words and rhymes. As a matter of fact, it helps one to have a good understanding of cultures by appreciating world literature as a whole so that a global mindset will be formulated to carry out intercultural communication.

III. English and Chinese Novels

Novels reflect common life in daily language and the culture behind it, catering the need of ordinary people and serving as the stock of vocabulary of the times. Most novels are concerned with ordinary people and their problems in the societies in which they find themselves. Culture is also found in novels. As a matter of fact, novels, especially some classics, present most important and delicate aspects of the culture and provide readers with a new way of seeing the world.

There are many different genres of novels, each of which demonstrates its unique way of writing, such as experimental novels, realistic novels, short stories, romantic novels, autobiography and semi-autobiography, fantasy, sentimental novels, speculative fictions, even genre fictions, etc. In order to improve intercultural communication competence, novels of very well-known and representative ones are selected to figure out some distinct differences between Chinese and English novels so that the hidden cultural cores in English and Chinese culture will be revealed.

To illustrate the major features of the English and Chinese novels, *Robinson Crusoe* by Daniel Defoe and *A Dream of Red Mansions* by Cao Xueqin (曹雪芹) are chosen from a cultural dimensions respectively as the representatives of English and Chinese novels. These two novels were written in different ages with its different cultural backgrounds and plot-lines, but they both serve to reflect the hidden part of the corresponding cultures distinctively and directly. *Robinson Crusoe* is regarded as the first English novel, which indeed contains some of basic common features that English novels may share with some fundamental cultural codes with which English culture is born (Figure 6.3). This novel mirrors the real colors of English culture, embedded with a great significance on reflecting the social and mental reality of English people of the times.

Figure 6.3 *Robinson Crusoe*

The Four Literature Masterpieces of China (中国四大名著) cannot be avoided when illustrating Chinese novels. One scholar once commented as follows.

> Four long fictional novels are usually thought to be the best novels in Chinese literature. What all four have in common is that they were written in a spoken language of their times unlike most ancient literature that was written in the literary classical language. Also, all four have disputed authorship. The four works were seminal for the development of Chinese societies in past eras. They were widely read by the literati and administrative rulers and contained philosophical ideas, history, and ideas about human society, family life, and politics that defined part of the world view of the literate and politically influential.

These novels, namely, *Journey to the West* (《西游记》) written by Wu Cheng'en (吴承恩), *A Dream of Red Mansions* (《红楼梦》) written by Cao Xueqin (曹雪芹), *Romance of Three Kingdoms* (《三国演义》) written by Luo Guanzhong (罗贯中), and *The Water Margin* (《水浒传》) written by Shi Nai'an (施耐庵), reflect the basis of Chinese culture and tradition to its best. Among them, *A Dream of Red Mansions* plays an irreplaceable role in presenting the core of the traditional Chinese culture, many aspects of which are shown in the novel in line with daily life, either socially, historically, politically, or economically. This novel is therefore the best way to get acquainted with Chinese culture.

Among many differences in English and Chinese novels, the narrative point of view and features in characterization are of significance in understanding the differences existing in the two cultures.

A. What Are Differences in Narrative Points of View in English and Chinese Novels?

The narrative point of view tells who is telling stories and how he or she does it, providing an effective way of seeing into the inner heart of the narrator, and the author as well. The approach, as the research target of narration, actually helps to expose the physical and mental space to the readers.

Generally speaking, English novels tend to employ the first-person narrative to tell the story. In a narrative or mode of storytelling, the narrator appears as "I", recollecting his or her own part in the events related, either as a witness of the action or as an important participant in it.

The term "the first-person narrative" does not mean that the narrator speaks only in the first person, and usually he/she discusses other characters with this technique. Examples include such early works in English literature as *Robinson Crusoe* and *Moll Flanders* by Daniel Defoe, *Pamela* by Samuel Richardson's or *Tristram Shandy* by Laurence Stern. Herman Melville's *Moby-Dick* begins with "Call me Ishmael", a clear sign of the first-person narrative, and *Jane Eyre* by Charlotte Brontë also has a first person narrator. Jane Eyre told her own story both as the central character and the narrator.

The novelists intend to help the readers experience the events in the novel just like he/she is one part of the protagonist, attracting them into the place along with the characters in the story. This narration provides a better way to the inner heart of the characters and thus also explained why Stream of Consciousness has been so popular in modern English novels. Many famous writers, such as James Joyce, Virginia Woolf, William Faulkner, and Marcel Proust, etc., employed this writing technique, which can be evidently found in many modernists' novels, for example, *Ulysses* by James Joyce, *Mrs. Dalloway* by Virginia Woolf, and *Ambassadors* by Henry James. Sometimes the whole novel is just a monologue of the hero in the story. The narrator notes down his/her thinking to presents it without any difficulties. The novelists seem to be totally indulged into this technique to conduct the story-telling inside the mind of the protagonist. This method pays attention to the inner heart of the character, to the nature; it remains a way of portraying the individual, which goes deeply into his/her inner mind, creating a wider room for the characterization of the characters.

Activity 4

You are given 10 minutes to discuss the following questions with your learning peers. Try to get the points that he/she presents, and organize them in two paragraphs before reporting to the class. "What is the cultural inclination of Robinson Crusoe, both as the central protagonist and the novel?"

> "I was born in the Year 1632, in the City of York, of a good Family, tho' not of that Country, my Father being a Foreigner of Bremen, who settled first at Hull: He got a good Estate by Merchandise, and leaving off his Trade, lived afterward at York, from whence he had married my Mother, Relations were named Robinson, a very good Family at Country, and from whom I was called Robinson Keutznaer; but by the usual Corruption of Words in England, we are now called, nay we call our Selves, and writer Name Crusoe, and so my Companions always call'd me."

Robinson Crusoe holds an important position in the development of English novels. As much information was provided under the considerably longer original title *The Life and Strange Surprizing Adventures of Robinson Crusoe, of York, Mariner: Who lived Eight and Twenty Years, all alone in an un-inhabited Island on the Coast of America, near the Mouth of the Great River of Oroonoque; Having been cast on Shore by Shipwreck, wherein all the Men perished but himself. With An Account how he was at last as strangely deliver'd by Pirates*, the story is told from the viewpoint of "I", making the novel look more like an autobiography. Although the novel might be realistic as Daniel Defoe meant it to be, it is fictionally told by "I", Robinson Crusoe himself. The long explanation of the title provides more information about the novel and the intention of the author. This way of writing coincides with the low-context culture in expressing individualism by providing explicit information in the form of "I" perspective.

However, Chinese novels use a different perspective. In general, early Chinese novels are mainly told from the third-person point of view, or in third-person narration. According to Shen Dan(申丹), this is to be accounted for by the fact that this genre developed directly from storytellers' scripts. Because of the direct contact between the storyteller and the audience, oral narration does not accommodate first-person narration. In the third-person narrative mode, the narrator refers to all characters with third person pronouns like he, she, or they, instead of the first- or second-person pronouns. This makes it clear that the narration develops without a narrator who is identified and personified as a character within the story. In comparison to stories with a narrator, the third-person narration is described as having an anonymous narrator. The third-person narrative can be subdivided as a third-person omniscient narrator or a limited narrator. The former one conveys information from multiple characters, places, and events of the story, including any given characters' thoughts, while the latter expresses in the knowledge and subjective experience of the only character. The third-person narration, both limited and omniscient, became the most popular during the 20th century.

This form of narration owns multi-level benefits while the third-person view enables the narrator to stay away or keep some distance from the actual location of the occurrence, providing a more objective view to the story, thus adding more credibility of his/her narration. In this way different point of views will bring up different color to the stories.

It should be noted that all the Four Literature Masterpieces mainly take the third-person omniscient narrative as the main method of telling stories.

Case Study 3

Read the following to note in which person the narrative it is.

> 列位看官:你道此书从何而来？说起根由虽近荒唐,细按则深有趣味。待在下将此来历注明,方使阅者了然不惑。原来女娲氏炼石补天之时,于大荒山无稽崖炼成高经十二丈,方经二十四丈顽石三万六千五百零一块。娲皇氏只用了三万六千五百块,只单单剩了一块未用,便弃在此山青埂峰下。(《红楼梦·第一章》)
>
> Readers, can you suggest whence the story begins? The narration may border on the limits of incoherency and triviality, but it possesses considerable zest. But to begin.

Generally, novelists may take a more eclectic method with more than one narrative, but Chinese novelists tend to employ the third person narrative. The third point of view presents an objective narration, which also forms a relation to the thinking patterns, setting a certain distance from the happening to gain an objective view to it. The third person is giving a more general and collective view, seeing more similarities from differences. To be objective, Chinese thinking patterns tend to be dialectical interdependence, seeing the bad in the good, or the negative in the positive, or vice versa. The Chinese ways of thinking focus on changes, contradictions and relations, seldom drawing a clear cut line, thus novels reflect the same.

B. What Are Different in Characterization in English and Chinese Novels?

Characterization refers to the way of building the character figures in the story. Characters, as the projection of the readers and the author, stand as the eternal representative of the Man, thus as the agent of a culture. Characterization makes cultural codes more clear and persuasive.

Characterization is a popular literary device to highlight and explain the details about a character in a story. It has direct or explicit, indirect or implicit characterizations. Characterization builds up vivid characters for the story and the readers, showing opinions of writers to the society and the world, thus reflecting the culture the writer lives in and the character is put in.

As for characterization, English novels usually pay more attention to one single protagonist, conducting a psychoanalytical study of his inner mind and portray him or her as the center of the story. For example, in *Robinson Crusoe* its main focus is on Robinson Crusoe although the novel touches upon about ten characters. Other minor characters include Xury, Friday, Moorish patron, the sea captain, Spaniard, savages and black people. Xury is Crusoe's friend and servant, who escapes from the Moors. He is admirable for his willingness to stand by the narrator. However, he does not think for himself. Friday spends a number of years on the island with Crusoe, and even saves Crusoe from cannibalistic death. Moorish patron is Crusoe's slave master, and he allows for a role reversal of white men as slaves. The sea captain is one of the kindest figures in the story who embodies all the Christian ideals. Spaniard is one of the prisoners saved by Crusoe. And it is interesting to note that he is treated with much more respect in the mind of Crusoe than any of the colored people in the story. Savages are the cannibals representing the threat to Crusoe's religious and moral convictions and his safety as well.

The individual "I", here Daniel Defoe, or Robinson Crusoe in this novel was portrayed as a pioneer or a colonial explorer. And the story is also told from the perspective of the white colonial explorer.

The story of Robinson Crusoe is told from this perspective. It is the story of a white colonial explorer who got lost on a New World Island, found a slave, was relatively kind to him but nevertheless treated him as a sub-human brute with no human feelings at all. Friday is a chattel in the traditional story of Robinson Crusoe, just because he is black.

In the novel, Robinson Crusoe, as the white colonist, occupied the central position with all the other minor characters serving him and making his colony more acceptable and respectable for his countrymen and other white explorers, which reflects the importance of the individual and the culture of individualism.

Different from the English novels, Chinese novels mainly focus on the characterization of more than one character, sometimes a group of characters for a general picturesque view and thus presenting the collectivist quality. For example, the well-known four great classic works and many other Chinese novels have portrayed a group of characters, i.e. *The Water Margin* depicts one hundred and eight heroes with wonderful stories, which were interwove together as an organized unity, and can be read separately as well. *A Dream of Red Mansions*, the peak of Chinese novels, also characterizes many vivid characters.

Believed to be composed by Cao Xueqin, *A Dream of Red Mansions*, also called *The Story of the Stone*, or *Hong Lou Meng* (《红楼梦》), is one of the Four Literature Masterpieces of China. It was written sometime in the middle of the 18th century during the Qing Dynasty. The title of the novel has also been translated as *Red Chamber Dream* and the novel circulated in manuscript copies with various titles until its print publication in 1791. Long considered as a masterpiece of the Chinese literature, the novel is generally acknowledged to be one of the pinnacles of Chinese fiction. And the "Redology" is the field of study devoted its research focus exclusively to this work.

As the author details in the first chapter, the novel is intended to be a memorial to the women he knew in his youth: friends, relatives and servants. The novel is remarkable not only for its huge cast of characters and its psychological scope, but also for its precise and detailed observation of the life in the Chinese society in the18th-century. The novel offers a comprehensive picture of social and family life of the time, epitomizing the best part in Chinese culture. Cao Xueqin skillfully designed his story with vivid details in daily life, interweaving diverse aspects of the Chinese culture, such as traditional festivals, the Chinese medicine, social hierarchies, feudal authorities, political systems, traditional architectures, gardening and cooking, early education systems, clothes fashions, marriage customs, poetry and music and traditional dramas, health care and so on. The novel reveals a vivid picture of the rich and the time with a description of a group of characters with a "good" or "evil" personality and their different kinds of love. This story is a truthful cultural history and a kind of cultural criticism from the viewpoint of aesthetics.

The focus of *A Dream of Red Mansions* is on young Jia Baoyu（贾宝玉）, the gifted but obstinate heir of the clan. But in the novel, there are more than 30 main characters and more than 400 minor ones. Jia Baoyu, Lin Daiyu（林黛玉）, Xue Baochai（薛宝钗）, Shi Xiangyun（史湘云）and many other characters are inter-related with each other, forming a colorful and whole artistic space. This novel mainly covers Cao Xueqin's families, friends, relatives and servants in addition to many other characters from the four families of Jia（贾）, Wang（王）, Shi（史）and Xue（薛）. The novel narrates the love tragedy between Jia Baoyu and Lin Daiyu. Jia Baoyu, the Twelve Beauties in Jinlin（金陵十二钗）, and many others form a giant community. And among it, Jia Baoyu, the bearer of the divine Jade, as an important part in the family, is colorfully characterized based on the background of the Jia Family. The unsaid but strong interrelations between the Four Big Families go underneath the whole novel. The importance of the individual can only be valued in the community. Otherwise, the individual will be nothing. Chinese novels usually focus on more heroes rather than one, and that reflects a collective way of Chinese thinking.

Test Your Reading 2

Decide whether the following statements are True (T) or False (F).

(1) Generally speaking, English novels focus on the characterization of more than one, sometimes a group of characters, to form a general picturesque view. (   )

(2) Chinese is the language of description, and its culture is of general description and induction. (   )

(3) Generally speaking, English is the language of analysis, and its culture

is of specific analysis and deduction. (　)

(4) Chinese novels mainly focus on the characterization of more than one, sometimes a group of characters, to form a general picturesque view. (　)

(5) Generally speaking, English novels tend to employ the first-person narrative to tell the story. (　)

C. What Are Revealed as Cultural Values in Literature?

English novels, partly presented in the first-person narrative, focus on the individual, finding its position in English novels. The view of the first-person allows readers to see more into the mind of characters from a subjective view. Sometimes "I" am the person who takes part in the event. "I", as the central character, reflects the importance of the individual. Each individual, as a single and unique being in the world, is given a kind of divine power, performing the duty of the "God", telling the story, acting and behaving, and even making moral comment to guide readers. Thus, the quality in individuals or individuality is extracted from here and this, of course, also becomes one of the cornerstones of English culture. The focus on individuality certainly frees the Man from the bondage of the Nature. However, in the process of being freed, the Man is also thrown into a possibility of pride and individualism, thus acquires a fateful and dangerous situation of losing himself in the illusion of his own, ignoring the humble status before the almighty the Nature. However, when individuality becomes individualism, the value of the Man will face the danger of being distorted.

Chinese novels are found in both the third person narrative and group characterization. The third-person narrative provides an objective and omniscient view of the story and creates a controllable space between authors and readers, in which the narrator sees all the events from an omniscient and comprehensive view of point. This method intends to provide a more panoramic picture of the world in the novel. The wholeness and collectivism, as a very important aspect of Chinese culture, can be seen from it. Group characterization covers a group of characters, which also reflects the collectivism in the traditional Chinese culture. Individuals grow in the collectivism. Some specific demonstrations of collectivism are belonging to a community, cherishing the history, valuing the families, community and country. Chinese people tend to see the world as an interdependent community and everything is related. The view of inter-relations gives a different and unique way of view into the things. In this way, Chinese novels build personalities and identities into community and hopefully, establishing mutual relations among members, which are in accordance with the development of the whole world.

It should be noted that, both Chinese and English novels have undergone many deep and wide-spreading changes as time goes by, adopting more eclectic methods concerning the first and the third point of view and novelists have been trying to tell stories from the multiple views. Some modern English novels may focus on more characters like Chinese novels did before, becoming more collectivist; and some Chinese novelists may begin to turn their attentions to the first-person narrative and learn to revolve around one key characters, appearing more individualistic. It is not the ultimate goal to see the differences but to see through and beyond the differences for the purpose of intercultural communication. With the help of the intercultural approach for the very root of the narrating with the hidden core of English narration, it will be beneficial to view the Western culture on the basis of Chinese cultural standpoints for a better sense of an intercultural communication.

Chinese culture processes its unique qualities sharing common qualities with other cultures at the same time. The Chinese ways of seeing the world provides a beneficial and inseparable part to the wholeness of perception into the world. For example, Chinese novels are undergoing a process of assimilation and development and the Chinese writer Mo Yan（莫言）has won the 2012 Nobel Prize for Literature. He writes with hallucinatory realism, merging folk tales, history and the contemporary, which may be seen as a signal of world-wide recognition of Chinese culture, indicating the fact that different cultures own unique beauties, and when accepted and appreciated by others, the whole world would become a harmonious sphere of beauty. Chinese culture should also go international and spread its influence, facilitating the world to see the wisdom and charm of the Chinese nation and culture.

Table 6.6 demonstrates the major differences of the English and Chinese novels, on the basis of which sum up the similarities of the English and Chinese novels.

Table 6.6 Comparison of English and Chinese Novels

Novel	Narrative View	Feature	Characterization	Cultural Value
English	The First-person	Subjective and Psychoanalytical	A Central Hero, Single: One against All	Individualism
Chinese	The Third-person	Objective and Realism	Heroes, A Group of Characters: One in All, A Community	Collectivism

Activity 5

Read *Robinson Crusoe* and *A Dream of Red Mansions* for the social and cultural background to understand the people of the times concerned.

Activity 6

Read *The Tale of Genji* (《源氏物语》) by Murasaki Shikibu (紫式部) and *The Chrysanthemum and the Sword* (《菊与刀》) by Ruth Benedict in Chinese to understand the Japanese culture in its early stage, and compare it with *A Dream of Red Mansions* if you are interested.

Ⅳ. Literature Helps Cultural Fusion

Nowadays cultures communicate and assimilate in many ways and cultural fusion, as a global trend, happens anytime and anywhere. Same as no man is an isolated island, no culture can be isolated from other cultures. A culture needs to learn from other cultures and absorb more nutrients, forming a healthy relationship with them and keeping itself in the position of development.

The inclination of cultural fusion can be found in many aspects. For example, the Western food can be found in the Eastern countries, and paintings of the Western styles can also be appreciated in China. The facts that *The Three-Body Problem* won Hugo Award, and *Harry Potter* series have become popular around the world demonstrate that novels, poems, dramas, and other literature genres are undergoing a process of learning from each other and presenting from the other's point of view. That's why modern novels thus are selected for analysis on the basis of traditional novels in the West and China.

Novels in the modern times begin to absorb different writing skills. Modern writers from all over the world learn from each other and absorb whatever will benefit their own writings to make up good stories. Novels entail such good elements as subtle structure, vivid characterization, profound historical background and so on. Thus, the specific techniques which were thought to be used by a writer, or a group of writers, or the writers of a certain culture, will find their ways to other writers other than the original ones. This can be seen as a phenomenon of intercultural communication in the present globalization. When one intends to have more overseas readership, or more economical benefits and world-wide reputation, the output of novels must cater for the taste as many diverse readers as possible.

Two novels which are popular in China are chosen as examples of cultural fusion (Figure 6.4). The first is the science fiction *The Three-Body Problem* (《三体》), by Liu Cixin (刘慈欣), a Chinese novelist who is famous for his *The Three-Body Problem Series* (《三体系列》), i.e. *The Three-Body Problem* (《三体》), *The Dark Forest* (《黑暗森林》), and *Death's End* (《死神永生》). The other novel is *Harry Potter and the Sorcerer's Stone* (《哈利波特与魔法石》) by J. K. Rowling, an English novelist, in October, 1998.

Figure 6.4 *The Three-Body Problem* *Harry Potter and the Sorcerer's Stone*

With many differences in the plot, the historical context, character settings and themes, they share similar points of view, or the way of telling stories and characterization. Liu Cixin tells the stories in *The Three-Body Problem* in the third-person with limited omniscient narrative mode for at least two reasons. Similarly, the stories of *Harry Potter and the Sorcerer's Stone* are also mainly told from the perspective of third person, only with a slight change. Harry is the character whose thoughts, feelings, and experiences are revealed to readers. The narrator is omniscient at some odd points throughout the book, telling the reader what Harry is thinking or feeling.

As for characterization, both novels focus on more than one protagonist. Liu Cixin is far more interested in science than character development, and his heroes and villains are all thinly written. Liu constantly tells rather than shows when it comes to his characters' motivations. In *The Three Body Problem*, the major characters include Ye Wenjie, Wang Miao, Shi Qiang, and Mike Evans. There are also minor characters that influence the plot, such as Lei Zhicheng, Yang Weining, Yang Dong, and Ding Yi. These characters work together to create a vivid and imaginary world (Figure 6.5).

In the novel *Harry Potter and The Sorcerer's Stone*, three protagonists form the center of the story. The protagonist is in no doubt Harry Potter, who was orphaned as a baby when the dark wizard Voldemort killed his parents, Lily and James. Ron Weasley is one of Harry's best friends, along with Hermione Granger. Hermione, another protagonist, is a first-year student in Gryffindor with bushy brown hair, large teeth, and a bossy voice. Her desire to stand out and earn good grades perhaps stems from the fact that she is from a Muggle family and, like Harry, worries that she may not fit in with the other students or may feel that she is behind (Figure 6.6).

Figure 6.5　Ye Wenjie in *The Three-Body Problem*

Figure 6.6　Potter, Weasley and Hermione in *Harry Potter and The Sorcerer's Stone*

Table 6.7 Major Difference between the Two Novels

Novels	Major Characters	Minor Characters	Views of Narrative
The Three-Body Problem	Ye Wenjie, Wang Miao, Shi Qiang ...	Lei Zhicheng, Yang Dong ...	Third Person, Limited Omniscient Narrative
Harry Potter and The Sorcerer's Stone	Harry Potter, Ron Weasley, Hermione Granger ...	Rubeus Hagrid, Vernon Dursley ...	Third Person, Limited Objective Narrative

As shown in the table, authors of both novels have gone beyond their own cultural boundaries, integrating literature traditions with that of others for effective storytelling and character portraying. With more techniques employed by both English and Chinese writers, cultural fusion in literature has been a trend as writers intend to spread the influence of their works in regions with different cultures, which requires literature to have inborn functions of intercultural communication.

By reading literature of other cultures, Chinese readers are exposed to more diverse ways of life and various views of the world so that they would be able to sharpen their insights and develop abilities to embrace diverse views as a process of improving the competence of intercultural communication.

Cultural fusion helps people to communicate and learn from each other, which will better shoulder the responsibility to contribute to the well-being and development of the human being as Xi Jinping addressed at UNESCO on March 27 in 2014, "Civilizations are enriched by exchanges and mutual learning as exchanges and mutual learning among civilizations are an important driving force for the progress of human civilization and world peace and development".

Literature takes different ways of expressing perceptions into the reality, even in the similar genres, for example, poetry and novels reflect the differential features in a language, then in a culture with various views to the world and life, and the most importantly, the differential ideological systems in culture. Consequently, literature of different cultures provides potentials for one to be exposed to alien cultures and to see the world from the other viewpoint, with which one learns to understand the cultures more deeply by identifying these differences so as to develop an effective intercultural communication competence.

Communication between cultures in any forms would dedicate to bridging cultural gaps and differences and achieving a mutual understanding with each other. Only by this way can a harmonious world be expected, as Fei Xiaotong (费孝通) said, "achieving one's own goal yields gratification, lending a hand to consummate others' goal doubles satisfaction, goals of self and others can be unified, thus the world can be harmonized", as expressed in Chinese, "各美其美,美人之美,美美与共,天下大同". President Xi Jinping (习近平) has proposed to build a community of a shared future for mankind, a world of enduring peace, common security, common prosperity, openness, inclusiveness, cleanliness and beauty. Chinese people would stick together economically and respect cultural diversities, insisting on solving problems through dialogues in terms of security to protect the common Earth ecologically.

To sum up, cultural diversities in literature is one of the resources that learners of the English language would get access to, and with comparison of the Chinese literature they will develop competence and approaches of mutual understanding and communication across cultures.

Ⅴ. Extended Reading

Storyteller Hopes Tibetan Epic Tale Lives on in Harmony
(*China Daily*, August 17, 2021)

When storyteller Sithar Dorje closes his eyes to start singing and narrating *The Epic of King Gesar* (《格萨尔王》), he says he enters into another world where the king lives and he plays one of the fabled roles. The 32-year-old says he's able to recite more than 140 episodes of King Gesar's story, equal to several million words.

An inheritor of the Gesar epic tradition, which was inscribed on the UNESCO list of world intangible cultural heritage in 2009, Sithar Dorje works at the Gesar epic research center of Tibet University in Lhasa in the Tibet autonomous region. The storyteller and researcher tasks himself with the mission to preserve and spread the Gesar epic, a masterpiece that is regarded as an encyclopedia of ancient Tibetan society.

The longest epic in the world-dozens of times the length of Homer's Iliad, The Epic of King Gesar has been passed down orally through singers and storytellers on western China's Qinghai-Tibet Plateau. The legend of King Gesar can be traced back to the 11th century. It tells how the king, sent by god, banishes demons, helps the weak and unifies tribes. "It's a kind of Tibetans' 'live history'. People living on the plateau used to learn their history from the Gesar epic," says Xu Guangzhi, director of the Tibetology institute of Tibet University. Xu says because the epic has been mainly passed down orally, preserving the tradition is urgent as old storytellers are passing away.

In 1979, scholars from Tibet University set up a special team to record videos of a well-known storyteller Drakpa, who was already 72 years old. More than 1,000 hours of Drakpa's performing of the Gesar epic in his last eight years have been recorded and compiled into 26 books. Most storytellers of The Epic of King Gesar can't read or write, such as the legendary singer Drakpa. They can recite for days the king's tales, for which many Tibetologists have not yet found a reasonable explanation.

Currently, there are a few storytellers performing in teahouses in Tibet, especially in nomadic areas. Most of them are old and not formally educated. Sithar Dorje is the only one among the storytellers to obtain a master's degree. He says he learned narrating of the epic at the age of 9 after he had a long dream where he was led into the world of King Gesar. "The dream changed my fate. From then on, I decided to become a storyteller," he says. His hometown is Palbar county in Chamdo city, the same with the legendary storyteller Drakpa.

As a teenager he was in demand from wedding hosts and party organizers to perform the epic. Because of his talent in reciting the king's tales, Sithar Dorje has been funded by the region's government since middle school. He went to Tibet University in 2010, studying Tibetan history and literature. After graduation in 2014, he got a job at the Gesar epic research center in the Tibetology institute and furthered his study at the graduate school in Tibet University.

Currently, he records his performances several times a week and spends most of his time compiling recital episodes and doing research.

Sithar Dorje says the longest performance he ever offered was for a group of nomadic people and it lasted two days, with no sleep. Although he and a few storytellers are performing the epic which includes hundreds of myths, folklores, ballads and proverbs, it's still hard to pass it to the younger generations when entertainment options in the internet age are more attractive and diversified. In June last year, Sithar Dorje performed in a primary school in his hometown of Chamdo city, where the epic is taught. "We're trying to spread it in primary schools. Three schools are cooperating with us and it is going well," he says.

Xu, director of the Tibetology institute, says because the narrative is so vast and different storytellers have their own style, the compiling and translation work is huge. For the translation alone, 7 million yuan ($1.08 million) has been invested since 2006, part of the central government's 200 million yuan investment in the region's intangible cultural heritage protection, according to a government report issued in May. "Although it's a tough and huge project, we, together with the storytellers, will make our efforts to protect and spread the heroic Tibetan epic," says Xu.

Post-class Tasks

Self-test Tasks

1. Decide whether the statements are True (T) or False (F).
(1) A trochee has two syllables, the first being strongly unstressed and the second stressed.
(2) An iambic foot has three syllables, with all being unstressed.
(3) The rhythmic pattern of English poems is decided by the number of the meters.
(4) Chinese *si sheng* includes the four types: rising, falling, level and decreasing.
(5) Generally speaking, English novels focus on the characterization of more than one, sometimes a group of characters, to form a general picturesque

view.

(6) Chinese is the language of description, and its culture is of general description and induction.

(7) Generally speaking, English is the language of analysis, and its culture is of specific analysis and deduction.

2. Answer the Questions.

(1) What are the differences in culture can you see from English and Chinese language?

(2) How English and Chinese poems convey their meanings in a different manner, and what cultural implications behind it can you see through it?

(3) How do you think the language that you think and speak will affect your perception to the world?

Group Work

1. According to what you have read, talk with your partner about the cultural differences you can figure out in English and Chinese language.

2. Different cultural implications can be seen from the **narrative point of view and characterization** in Chinese and English novel, as have been examined above.

(1) Work with your partner for the cultural qualities with materials about these two aspects from Chinese literary classics.

(2) Share with the class to present with supporting details and PPT or make a video clip with explanation in English.

Telling China's Stories

One of the international students of your university, who is very much interested in the Chinese culture and contemporary China, asks you to recommend some Chinese novels to him/her. Which novels are you going to recommend? What will you tell him/her about the significance and the features of the novel(s)?

My Learning Reflection

1. What have I learned about Chinese cultures or myself?

2. What have I learned about other cultures?

3. What impressed me most in this chapter?

4. What still confuses me?

Module Three

Intercultural Communication Practice

Chapter 7　Intercultural Etiquette

Learning Objectives

- To recognize similarities of the culture-based functions of etiquette in intercultural communication;
- To construct repertoire of the major differences in etiquette across cultures;
- To adjust to cultural diversities in communication on the basis of awareness and tolerance.

Pre-class Tasks

- Read the textbook and watch the concerned clips in *xuexitong* (学习通).

Ⅰ. Lead-in Tasks

Case Study 1

Study the case to find out the functions of etiquette in life and work.

> A Chinese delegation of a potential business partner arrived at the US office but was not greeted in the lobby by a senior executive. The nonverbal message conveyed was interpreted by the Chinese that they were not sufficiently important to warrant being greeted by a senior executive. This type of mistake, though unintentionally can delay or even destroy a deal.

This case demonstrates how etiquette is a great lubricant for success in international business, and there are many cases that life is ruined by lack of etiquette as "Anyone who is not equipped with etiquette will not survive and any event that doesn't follow the protocols will not succeed" (by *Xun Zi*,荀子). To communicate effectively, appropriate etiquette is a must in addition to a good mastery of the target language and nonverbal behaviors.

Ⅱ. Understanding Etiquette

Etiquette is said to be the passport to one's success in establishing relations with others as well as in maintaining it in many cultures. Successful interactions with people from other cultures involve knowledge of rules of global etiquette to avoid inadvertently offending others in intercultural communication since manners and correct behaviors are learned rather than inherited. And learning correct behaviors in other countries is important to avoid personal and professional harassment as well because what is polite in a certain culture may be downright insulting in another.

Relationship building begins with communication. Either travelling to one country or hosting visitors from others, the first impression is decisive at the initial meeting and appropriate etiquette functions in maintaining relationships. Etiquette therefore is essential in setting up good relationships across cultures in addition to language.

But is there such a thing as international etiquette? Perhaps there is not. However, there are guidelines for universal etiquette that are applied around the world. For example, in terms of greetings and introductions, people shake hands moderately, err on the safe side of formality and avoid the use of given names. There are also suggestions on dining, oral and nonverbal behaviors, dressing, showing respect and avoiding gift taboos.

As etiquette varies across cultures in many aspects and it's almost impossible to know every detail of etiquette of each local culture, there are general principles to follow:

• Do as Romans do when you are in Rome;

- Follow the etiquette of the language that is used in the interaction. For example, the international students speaking Chinese are expected to follow the Chinese and the local etiquette;
- Observe what the host do and follow him/her.

III. Social Etiquette across Cultures

Socialization, which is how people interact with the world or culture around, is what makes life worth living. People learn the skills in their own culture from the time when they are born. When they switch to a new culture, what has become automatic in their home cultures may no longer work socially.

Effective communication matters the styles or modes that one expresses his/her ideas and information rather than the content itself and the goal of communication. To put it simple, it is related to "how" the content is communicated rather than "what" is said or "why" it is said. As far as communication is concerned, verbal and nonverbal means are both employed, and etiquette is the inseparable component in communication to support or enhance the efficiency of communication, or otherwise.

A. How Do People Address and Greet Others?

How to address the others appropriately to show respect is the first step to establish good relationships in communication either in home culture or across cultures.

Proper addressing includes the use of title which is the recognition of the social status of the people in accordance with the cultural norms. Courtesy titles such as Mr./Mrs./Miss/Ms. used with surnames is a common practice, and sometimes can also be used with official titles like Mr. President, Mrs. Ambassador, or Mr. Foreign Minister.

Procedural difference between cultures is the use of titles with first or last names. For example, unlike in the US where first names are used very soon after two people get acquainted, Germans use a title with family names when addressing someone in Germany till being told it's okay to use the first names.

Westerners are generally confused with the Asian names for first and family names. For example, President Clinton addressed Korean President Kim Young Sam's wife, Mrs, Sohn Myong-suk, as Mrs. Kim while he should have addressed her as Mrs. Sohn, since in Korea it is the custom for women to maintain their maid names and the same is true in China.

In the Chinese language, surnames, i.e. family names go first before given names, which is confusing for English speaking people. Therefore, to avoid confusion, it is considered as entirety both semantically and pragmatically in introduction of a Chinese by saying, " This is one of my friends. Her family name is Wu and given name is Li, and you can call her Wu Li."

Case Study 2

Translate the following into English.

> "您好！这是 王老师/张经理/胡教练/马记者/吴司机/薛主任/刘厂长"

In the Chinese language, it is polite to address someone by his/her position or profession with his/her family name, such as "王老师,张经理,胡教练,马记者,吴司机,薛主任,刘厂长" etc., which are unusual in the English-speaking countries or can not be translated equivalently to *Teacher Wang or *Manager Zhang. (Note: * means unacceptable in English). Consequently, when introducing someone in English, it's acceptable to say "This is Mr. Zhang, the Sales Manager," or "This is Ms. Wang, my English teacher."

There are some titles in English that can be used together with surnames as well as in Chinese, for example, Professor (教授), Doctor (博士、医生), President (主席), Prime Minister (总理), Governor (省长), Mayor (市长), General (将军), Colonel (大校), Major (少校), Lieutenant (中尉), Sergeant (中士).

Activity 1

Translate the titles with the help of dictionary and the Internet, paying attention to the equivalents of "副" in Chinese and English (Table 7.1).

Table 7.1 Translation of Chinese Titles

Chinese Administrative Titles	English Equivalents
部长	
委员长	
副主任	
副主席	
副部长	
副省长	
副秘书长	
副教授	

Same as the Chinese honorific address terms like "××先生" "×老" "××公", common English honorific terms such as Sir, Lady, Madam, Lord, etc., can either be used alone, for example, "Yes, Sir." and "No problem, Madam." or with the first name, for example, Sir Williams, Lady Gaga, Lord Henry, etc.

Kinship terms are used for those relations and affinities based on blood and marriage. Compared with European cultures, China has a distinctively amount of kinship terms to distinguish the relationship between paternal and maternal groups not only in genders but also in ages, which is complicated for nowadays younger generations. These kinship terms are also used fictively in the social relationships for closeness to make communicators esteemed and friendly as society is the magnified family in the view of the Chinese culture. For example, brothers and sisters, uncles and aunts, grandpa and grandma are often affiliated to profession terms to address someone at work, such as "警察叔叔" "护士姐姐" "医生阿姨", etc. However, these terms are confusing when they are translated into English because "Brothers or Sisters" are specifically used to refer to those who belong to the same religious groups in the form of "Brother John" or "Sister Rose", etc.

To sum up, attention is seriously invited when addressing someone across cultures in another language. And a good way to avoid embarrassment and confusion is to consult relevant resources beforehand, making sure to extend respect and friendliness. Table 7.2 shows some differences for references.

Table 7.2 Diverse Use of Titles

Cultures/countries	Use of titles	Examples
Latin Americans	Add mother's maid name to one's surnames	Maria Gomes Sanchez, Senorita Gomes,
Portuguese-speaking countries	Mother and father's names are reversed	
Iraq, India, African countries,	Titles are used with last names	
China, Japan, Korea	Titles are used with last names (Family names appear first)	Doctor Li, President Xu, Mr. Wang, the Sales Manager; But not * "Manager Wang"

As an essential part of daily communication, greetings in English and Chinese share similarities in functions of recognizing the existence of the others and extending respect and friendliness to establish and maintain social contacts. The differences lie in the sentences and responses according to the language used.

Case Study 3

Study the greeting and the response to them to find out the cultural reasons for them (Table 7.3).

Table 7.3 Greetings

Formal Greetings in English	Daily Greetings in Chinese
"(Good) morning/afternoon/evening", "How are you?" "How are things going?" "How are you getting on?" "How are things with you?" ...	——吃过了吗? (Have you had your meal?) ——散步去啊? (Are you going to have a walk?) ——拿快递啊? (Are you going to get your post?) ——上课去啊? (You are going to your lectures, aren't you?)

These questions are formalities which expect no answers. The usual reply would be "Fine, thanks" "So far so good, thank you" or "Good, thanks" and the similarities. People who are very close or familiar would use the informal greetings, such as "How are things?" "How is everything?" "How's life?" or simple "Hello" "Hey" or "Hi" with smile, and the same will be reciprocated as well.

The conventional Chinese greetings demonstrate concerns and care for others in order to keep harmonious social relationship for the sake of collectivist values, which involves daily details in consistent with the situation.

The greetings are extended in the form of questions or inquires which don't expect specific answers either, and the replies are generally affirmative or equivocal.

In intercultural communication, "Have you had your meal?" in English may be misunderstood as an intended invitation, and "Are you going to have a walk?" and the alike may sound offensive as invasion of privacy to those who are from individual cultures.

Test Your Reading 1

Decide whether the statements are True (T) or False (F).

(1) The appropriate way to address others varies across cultures but it's considered more polite to address someone on the basis of family names. (　)

(2) Terms such as "manager" or "teacher" can be used with family name for addressing, for example, Manager Wang or Teacher Xia. (　)

(3) In China, such kinship terms as Aunt, Uncle, Grandpa and Grandma are applied to those out of family relations for courtesy and respect. (　)

(4) Sister or Brother in the English speaking countries are applied in the same way as the Chinese use. (　)

(5) Chinese greetings reveal collectivist culture traits with close and harmonious relationship between people. (　)

(6) The reply to "How is your holiday?" expects descriptions of day-to-day events in the trip. (　)

(7) English versions of Chinese greetings can be equally used in intercultural communication. (　)

B. How Are Invitations Extended and Replies to them?

Invitations to social and business events constitute human life in all cultures. Invitations can be formal or informal both in written or oral forms. Most of formal invitations are in writing though some are in oral; in most cases informal invitations are in oral, both of which is socially culture-based.

Formal Invitations

Formal invitations are usually in written form both in English and Chinese for dinners, weddings, social or business celebrations. Formal invitations in English are written in the third person, indicating who will be invited for what event at what date and time with address, and the reply is usually expected for the host's convenience of preparation.

Example 7.1　A formal Invitation

Sally White and John White

Takes the pleasure to invite

Mr. & Mrs. Rosenberg

To a dinner

At 8:00 p.m. on 3 Oct. 2021 (Sunday)

At Harbor Restaurant.

R.S.V.P. (Tel: 010-54205599)　　　　　　　　Attire: Black Tie

Example 7.2　A Wedding Invitation

To compare with the Chinese invitations, the content is of no differences except that in the West, both husband and wife are more likely to be invited for social events even though the individual will be present for business events with colleagues, while in China it's more often than not that only husband or wife is invited for meals or social events unless specified.

In most English-speaking countries, the reply to the invitation is expected with "R. S. V. P." on the invitation, indicating "please reply" in French equivalent to "répondez, s'il vous plait" or "R. S. V. P. regrets only", which requires reply only when the invitee is unavailable. On the formal invitation, attire for the event, such as "White tie" "Black tie" or "Informal" is usually indicated.

To accept the invitation, it is appropriate to extend gratitude for the invitation and confirm the date, time and venue of the event and the invitees are expected to be present at the event on time unless something unexpected happens. For example, "Thank you so much for your kind invitation, and we are looking forward to seeing you at eight on Sunday."

In Example 7.1, a telephone call to respond the invitation is acceptable, but a written one is very formally appropriate either accepting or declining it. In China, written invitations usually are not expected to be replied in writing but it has become a trend that the invitee will notify the inviter if he/she won't attend the event either in person or by telephone.

To decline a formal invitation in English, gratitude is expressed before regretting being unable to be present without specifying reasons to avoid disclosure of privacy. An oral decline will be acceptable, for example, "Thank you very much for your invitation but it is a pity that we are not available that day due to previous arrangement".

Example 7.3 A Decline to An Invitation

Sept. 14, 2021

Dear Mr. and Mrs. Goodman,

We appreciate very much your kind invitation to the wedding reception of your daughter at the beach but deeply regret for inconvenience to attend due to previous event on the same day.

We sincerely extend our best wishes to the newly-wedded.

Sincerely yours,

Mr. & Mrs. Rosenberg

Formal invitations can be in written and oral form, and the reply to both can be oral. In China, the oral invitation is likely to be declined for the first time as a social protocol without specific reasons before it is accepted, which is taken as confirmation. If one has to decline an invitation, he/she tends to give detailed explanation at the cost of privacy leaks to indicate that it is against his/her will to do so in order to avoid offending the inviter for loss of face and to maintain the harmonious relationship without embarrassment to both parties.

A reply stating that "I'll try my best to come" may evoke different connotations between English and Chinese. In English it implies that the speaker sincerely will make efforts to go even though he/she may not be sure. But the same would sound insincere to Chinese because the statement is usually interpreted as a polite decline unless the inviter insisted on it, which sounds "very pushing" to the English speaking ears.

Invitations vs. Social Remarks

Social remarks sometimes may sound like invitations. Invitations with specific information, either written or oral, are formal and real as long as information of the event is explicitly expressed, which are taken seriously by both parties. Oral invitations can also be formal as they are usually extended among friends, colleagues or family members with specific information about the event, which is taken as actual ones.

To distinguish a real invitation from polite remarks, one has to be careful about the information concerned. In all cultures, social remarks of goodwill which don't contain definite information are not taken as invitations. For example, in China, nobody will take it seriously when someone tells him that "let's meet for a drink soon" or "Good to see you again! I'll invite you to dinner later."

Case Study 4

Read the dialogues and decide which one is a real invitation.
A Susan: It's nice talking with you. But I do have to go now.
    Lily: OK, we'll meet sometime soon.
  Susan: Sounds good. Why not meet for afternoon tea?
    Lily: Good idea. See you soon.

B Lily: I know you are going to China for further learning in two weeks.

    How about a get-together next week?

  Susan: So nice of you! I'd love to. How about Saturday?

  Lily: Fine! What would you like, Chinese food or something else?

  Susan: Anything is fine for me.

  Lily: Then, 6 o'clock at the Chinese Restaurant near the school.

  Susan: OK. See you then.

In Dialogue A, the event is mentioned without detailed information on exact date or venue, and it is taken as polite remarks rather than an invitation in the context. With specific time and date together with the name of a restaurant, Dialogue B presents an informal but real invitation, and they are sure to meet on Saturday because both parties are serious of it.

Informal invitations are usually in oral forms nowadays in intercultural communication with hasty pace of life and use of technology. Some of oral expressions for informal invitation are as follows (Table 7.4).

Table 7.4 Expressions of Informal Invitations

(1) Can you come over and join us tonight?
(2) I'd very much like you to come to home for dinner tonight.
(3) Shall we have a drink at the bar around the corner?
(4) We're having a party this Sunday. I hope you'll make it.
(5) Why don't you join us to the beach this weekend?
(6) Do join me for a coffee.
(7) We'd be delighted if you could spend Christmas with us.
(8) Would you honor us with a visit?
(9) If you could manage, we would like you to attend the speech contest on Monday evening.
(10) How about having a dinner at my home this Friday?
(11) I wonder whether it is OK for both of you to join us to the concert on Friday evening.

To show courtesy, oral invitations are stated in questions or in the subjunctive mood rather than the third person as the formal written ones (Table 7.5).

To accept an invitation, appreciation is extended and time and venue is confirmed. No specific reason is expected when an invitation is declined so as to avoid disclosure of one's privacy.

Table 7.5 Replies to Oral Invitations

Accepting an Invitation	Declining an Invitation
(1) Yes, I'd love to, thank you so much.	(1) That's very kind of you to ask, but unfortunately I already have a commitment then, and I am sorry I won't be able to go.
(2) Why not! I'd love to. It's so nice of you.	
(3) I would like nothing better, thank you!	
(4) I'd very much like to attend. Thank you!	(2) Much as I'd love to, I'm afraid I won't be free next Sunday.
(5) I'd very much like to but I'll be a little late, is it OK?	(3) What a pity! I'm afraid I already have something planned.
(6) It would be a great pleasure to have Christmas with you. It's so kind of you!	(4) Sorry I can't. But thank you anyway.
	(5) No, I don't think I can.
	(6) No, I won't be able to.
(7) What a wonderful idea! I'd love to spend the weekend with you!	
(8) Yes, I would love to and look forward to it.	
(9) I'd love, thank you very much.	
(10) Well, good for you! Yes, I'll come.	

Test Your Reading 2

Decide whether the statements are True (T) or False (F).

(1) Formal invitations are usually written in the third person with indication of attire and "RSVP". (   )

(2) Oral invitations are usually informal ones without mentioning time and venue. (   )

(3) Some remarks sound like an invitation in social interactions in all cultures. (   )

(4) To decline an invitation in individual cultures, one has to give detailed reasons. (   )

(5) In Chinese culture, one declines an invitation with external reasons for unavailability out of one's own control. (   )

Activity 2

How are you going to reply to the following invitation? Explain your reasons for your reply.

> Li Mei, a Chinese student helped a foreign male at a busy traffic center who looked like having trouble finding his way to his destination. He was appreciative and they had a friendly conversation and exchanged telephone numbers. He called her the next day, inviting her to go to his apartment at 9 p.m. that evening. She was unsure about what to do.

In addition to invitations, there are occasions when someone suggests a drink or a meal together, which has nothing to do with invitations. Misunderstanding may arise as hospitality of Chinese people is proverbial and some of them are not accustomed to "go Dutch" or "split the bill". As Chinese in this context, clarification of your intention is necessary when it happens.

Activity 3

Read the dialogue to decide how the bill is to going to be paid.

> Catharina and Mei are colleagues in a chemical joint venture in Thailand. Catharina is from France and Mei is from Xi'an in China. One day, they worked overtime for an emergency task.
> Catharina: Oh my! It's been so late! I'm so starving that I can eat an elephant!
> Mei: Me too. Let's get something to eat.
> Catharina: How about the French restaurant nearby?
> Mei: I'm afraid it has to to some place inexpensive as I don't want to spend too much on a late meal
> Catharina: Ok! Let's meet at McDonald's. (or: Come on! It's my treat!)

C. How Do People Say Goodbye?

When and how to say goodbye is difficult as it is a part of etiquette related to culture. Both in English and Chinese, there are expressions before one leaves, but there are some differences.

Case Study 5

Find out the differences in expressing the intention to leave (Table 7.6).

Table 7.6 Expressing the Intention to Leave

English Expressions to Say Good-bye	Chinese Expressions to Say Good-bye
(1) Well, it's a lovely party, but I'm afraid I must be going soon.	(1) It's late, and I'm leaving.
(2) It's nice to see your family again and I've been enjoying everything, but I don't want to hold you any longer.	(2) I have to go to work tomorrow and I have to go.
(3) It's late, I'm afraid I have to go in a few minutes.	(3) I'm going to get my kids home from my parents' and I do have to leave.
(4) I do enjoy the party, but I'm afraid that it's time for me to leave.	(4) I have to catch the last bus by 10:30, and I have to go.
(5) What a lovely party! But I have to go.	(5) I have a long way to go and it's time for me to go.

Generally speaking, parting constitutes two phases in social events, one of which is preparation for leaving; the other is to say goodbye and leave. In most European countries, the guest will indulge in a couple of minutes of small talks with appreciation and concise intention to leave. Then the host will see the guest to the door, saying "Thank you for coming, Good-bye!" and the door is shut at once, which would make Chinese feel uncomfortable.

In China, visitors are more likely to end the talk and stand up abruptly saying good-bye with some reasons. And the host will strongly insists on his/her staying longer while the guests move to the door saying, "请留步""别送了""回见", etc. In return, the host will see him/her beyond the door, sometimes to the gate or the bus stop, saying "请慢走""请走好""不送了"or "有空再来啊", etc. Sometimes Chinese farewells may last more than ten minutes or even longer with exchanges of appreciation, continued topics or a new one. The host will not shut the door, instead he/she sees the guest off out of sight.

In comparison, the emphasis of the two phases of farewell varies in China and some of the English-speaking countries, i. e. it takes longer time for Chinese people to say a good-bye before separating each other finally. In terms of language, appreciation for the event is extended with the intention to go without any reasons for the sake of privacy in individualist cultures while in China, objective reasons are stated for leaving. And the English-speaking visitors are likely to leave individually with quick goodbye while others continue enjoying the event, but the Chinese prefer to leave together simultaneously, ending the event all of a sudden.

Test Your Reading 3

Decide whether the statements are True (T) or False (F).

(1) There are two phases for farewell in all cultures, which vary in practice. (　)

(2) "请慢走" "请走好" "不送了" can be translated into English as " Please walk slowly" "Please go well" or " I won't see you off". (　)

(3) Chinese would feel unwelcomed when the door is shut with good-bye, which is the common practice in some cultures. (　)

(4) Saying good-bye together at an event is the tendency of the collectivist cultures. (　)

(5) Visitors are expected to explain reasons for leave at social events in most individual cultures. (　)

D. How Are Gratitude and Apologies Expressed?

Individualistic and collectivist cultures have different attitudes towards gratitude and apology in concept and vocabulary. In the individualistic cultures, one is supposed to be self-reliant and independent, taking care of everything by oneself, and any favor or help from others is a token of kindness and consideration of others, which are to be appreciated. Same as asking for help is interference of others' life and invasions of others' time and energy, and the word "please" therefore always goes together with a request. Consequently, words such as "thank you" and "please" are famed as the "magic words" in interpersonal relationships.

On the contrary, people in the collectivist culture tend to be interdependent, helping each other now and then. Doing something, minor or major, is taken as obligations for in-group members, which is not meant to be grateful. Therefore, "thank you" is rarely exchanged between husband and wife, parents and children, relatives or friends, but they would say "thank you" to strangers who are not obliged to be helpful. And people in the collectivist culture would also feel deeply grateful to superiors for their care and concern, which is regarded as grace and favor instead of obligations. Believing that "No words can express my thanks for your great kindness", people may be shy to express gratitude and would prefer to do something in return when needed.

Case Study 6

Study the case and answer the questions:
(1) How did this international teacher interpret the reply by the Chinese student?
(2) What was the appropriate reply in English in this context?

> A Chinese student spent several days helping the new international teacher in relocation on the campus for life and work by going to the offices, showing her around the university and getting her acquainted with the staffs and students, etc. The international teacher was very much grateful to the Chinese student.
>
> International Teacher: I do appreciate your time and efforts in helping me out these days. I really don't know how to thank you enough.
>
> Chinese student: It doesn't matter. It's my duty.
>
> On hearing it, the international teacher was stunned, feeling a bit unpleasant about it. It was several months later that she found out the differences in replies to gratitude between Chinese and English and understood what "It's my duty" means in the Chinese context.

Replies to gratitude in English are "my pleasure" "sure" "you are welcome" or "it's all right" etc. These replies to "thank you" such as "it's my duty" or "it's what I should do" (应该的), "never mind" (没关系), "don't mention it" "no problem" or "not at all" (别客气), etc. are confusing as they are appropriate in Chinese context but not the same in English.

People apologize for doing something wrong or offensive in all cultures but what is considered "not right" or improper is related to the values, beliefs and attitudes of the specific culture. For example, in China, questions about one's age, marital status, income used to be normal and proper, even as a token of concern from the superior to the subordinates, elders to the young, but in most of the European countries, the same is regarded as invasion of privacy, therefore "I'm sorry" is the appropriate reply to "... my father passed away when I was 10".

Both "I'm sorry" and "excuse me" can be translated into "对不起" in general in Chinese, but they are used in different context in English. To be specific, that "I'm sorry" is an apology after one has done something wrong, for example, "I am sorry that I am late", "I'm sorry to have spilt your coffee", or to show sympathy for bad news like "I'm sorry about your illness".

Table 7.7   Expressions of Apologies and Replies

Apologies	Replies to apologies
(1) I'm very/so/terribly/awfully/ extremely sorry for ...	(1) Apology accepted.
(2) I can't tell you how sorry I am for ...	(2) I forgive you.
(3) Please forgive me for ...	(3) There is no reason to apologize.
(4) I apologize.	(4) It's really not necessary.
(5) I must apologize for ...	(5) I understand it.
(6) I must beg to apologize for ...	(6) It's not your fault.
(7) I must make an apology for ...	(7) It doesn't matter at all.
(8) May I offer you my sincere apology for ...	(8) It's okay.
	(9) That's alright.
	(10) It's not a big deal.
	(11) Not at all.
	(12) That's all right.
	(13) It's nothing.
	(14) Forget it.

Replies by Asians to apology are likely to be considerate and generous as Asian cultures are much influenced by Confucianism which values much of harmonious relationships, being more tolerate of others, and trying to appear polite and friendly. For example, when one was late for an appointment and apologized by saying "I'm sorry I'm late because of the traffic," the other one would say, "It's OK. It happens."

It has to be noted that in the individualistic cultures, people tend to say "I'm sorry" or "excuse me" more often than those in the collectivist cultures where interdependence between people and obligations to each other are more expected and accepted. And it is rare for superiors to apologize to the subordinates, or elders to the younger ones, some males to females because of fear of loss of face, which doesn't mean that they don't feel sorry, but because they just don't verbally express regret or apology, and they would do something to make it up instead.

Activity 4

Study the replies to "Excuse me" for different contexts.

---

(1) A: Excuse me.
B: Yes? (With rising tone), Can I help you?
(2) A: Excuse me, may you let me pass?
B: Sure. I'm sorry (on your way).
(3) A: Excuse me for a moment.
B: Certainly.
(4) A. Excuse me (for sneezing, coughing, yawning, etc.)
B. Bless you.

It's customary to say "excuse me" when one can't help sneezing, coughing or yawning in the presence of others. Customarily, "bless you" is followed after one's sneeze but not cough or others in many cultures. "Gesundheit" in German, "alhamdulillah" in Arabic for "praise be to God", "live!" or "live well!" in Hindu, etc function the same. There are special sneezing responses for children. For example, in Russia, children are given the traditional response, "bud zdorov" for "be healthy" together with "rosti Bolshoi" for "grow big". In China, children will be wished with "百岁"after sneezing.

Test Your Reading 4

Decide whether the statements are True (T) or False (F).

(1) Gratitude is extended more often in individualistic cultures than in collectivist ones. (　　)

(2) In high-context cultures, gratitude is more likely to be extended by doing something rather than in verbal messages. (　　)

(3) "I'm sorry" and "excuse me" can be used interchangeably in all cases. (　　)

(4) It's universally polite to request with "please" and to appreciate with "thank you" for offers and help. (　　)

(5) One does not have to say "I'm sorry" for being late as Asians are more considerate in response to apologies. (　　)

E. How Are Compliments and Replies Expressed?

Complimenting in all cultures shares the functions of establishing relationship, maintaining solidarity, greeting, congratulating, appreciating, encouraging, softening criticism, starting a conversation or avoiding embarrassment, but the target topics and the semantic expressions vary in every culture.

Who is praised? In China people tend to compliment people with higher status to show respect, agreement and loyalty, and praise from superiors, parents or teachers are taken as encouragement and acceptance. Traditionally Chinese compliments are rarely extended to in-group people or peers in the presence of out-groupers. For example, parents would not praise their own children in get-together with friends or the extended family, or husband and wife would not express appreciation to each other in the face of others as the saying goes, "a wise wife won't praise her husband in public"（傻媳妇才当着外人夸老公）.

In the English-speaking cultures, people would like to compliment people around, especially those in the conversation. In most of the European countries, females are complimented more often than males, and it's considered polite to praise the wife of a friend or the host. But in China and Muslin cultures, it's a taboo to praise others' wives.

What is to be praised? It seems that cultures share similarities in praising females for appearance, dress and haircut, domestic arts while males are complimented for their abilities and achievements. In English, on greeting the other one, his/her appearance is commented positively, such as the look, clothes and accessories, jewelry and a watch, or a handbag, etc. But in Arabic and Asian cultures, it's inappropriate to praise appearance of other's wives.

Case Study 7

Compare the compliments and replies in English and Chinese (Table 7.8), paying attention to the cultural values revealed.

Table 7.8 Compliments and Replies

English compliments and replies	Chinese compliments and replies
(1) A. You look nice today! Any good news! B. Thank you very much!	(1) 甲:王教授的书法真不错! 乙:哪里! 哪里! 献丑了!
(2) A. You handbag goes well with your dress today! What a good taste! B. Thank you. I think so too.	(2) 甲:你家房子装修得真漂亮啊! 乙:过时了! 过时了!
(3) A. It's been long since we met last time. Your coat suits you very much. B. Yes it really flatters me.	(3) 甲:你烧的饭真好吃! 乙:家常菜,随便烧的!

In the above conversations, compliment is applied for greetings in the first one, and the other is for agreement.

In the recent decades females have become an increasing workforce in many fields, they prefer to be accepted for their abilities and achievements as well and some of them may feel disgraced when they are flattered for their physical appearances in business context.

How to reply to compliments? With English as lingua franca, people tend to reply to compliments with "thank you" but in each culture there are customs on how to reply to compliments. For example, in most of the European cultures, "thank you" is the most acceptable reply to compliments, and an agreement is also taken as a proper reply as shown in the above examples because it shows these two people have similar taste and it is a reciprocal compliment in return. But in China denial of the compliment is considered appropriate, especially on one's ability or achievements as it shows modesty and humility.

Misunderstanding in compliments and replies may take place in intercultural communication as a result of culture-based communication protocols. For example, when the humble and modest Chinese replies to compliments are translated literally into English, it may seem that the speaker is "fishing more compliments" or implies that he/she is overpraised, either of which is embarrassing to the one who gives the compliment.

Case Study 8

Why did the conflict occur in this conversation?

> One of the Chinese scholars to the United States was attending a reception with his wife. When both of them were introduced to the others, John, one of the participants praised his wife, "Your wife looks young and beautiful."
>
> As Chinese, the scholar was not pleased with the compliment of his wife but automatically replied in humility, " Where! Where!"
>
> John was surprised, and replied with embarrassment, "Everywhere!"

In Case 8, both the compliment and the reply to it led to cultural conflicts. In Chinese culture, it is customary to praise one's wife for her feminine virtues instead of appearances and that's why the Chinese scholar was unpleased. In addition, denials are expected as replies to compliments in Chinese for humble reasons and "哪里！哪里！" connoted denial instead of requiring more favorable remarks. On the part of John, he took it a courtesy to praise the appearance of a lady and didn't expect the denial as reply, which is literally interpreted as a request for explanation.

Table 7.9 Comparison of English and Chinese Compliments

English Compliments	Chinese compliments
I really enjoy the meal you prepared.	你做的饭真好吃！
I love your glasses.	你的眼镜真好看！
I like your jacket.	你的夹克真漂亮！
This is an impressive lecture.	您的课上得真好！

Some of the English compliments are misleading because they are more likely to be expressed in the first or third person while the Chinese ones are in the second person.

And praise in English usually begins with "I like …" or "I love …", which may sound like asking for what is praised to Chinese ears.

Case Study 9

> Julia is an international student from German in a Chinese University and Wu Wei is her study bud. They met on the campus after the May Day holiday was over.
>
> Julia: Good to see you again!
> Wu Wei: Hi, how is your trip to the Wolong Nature Reserve?
> Julia: It's wonderful! I can't believe that I saw pandas! Look at the video! How lovely they are!
> Wu Wei: They are adorable!
> Julia: Yes, they are! By the way, how is your holiday?
> Wu Wei: I went to Shanghai with my parents. We shopped till we dropped!
> Julia: Oh, yes! Is this the new bag you have? I just love it!
> Wu Wei: You do? Take it then!
> Julia: No! No! I don't mean it! I just find it pretty.
> Wu Wei: But I'm serious.
> Julia: …

This conflict arose as a result of the statement that "I just like it". On the part of Julia, it is a compliment with appreciation and agreement while to Wu Wei it sounds like an implied request. In the individualistic culture, personal properties are valued and people usually don't ask for something due to independence and self-esteem. In the collectivist cultures, properties are shared to some extent and the sense of sharing is a token of intimacy. On the other hand, Julia is from the low-context culture, and tends to communicate in a direct mood to mean what she says, i.e. she does appreciate the taste of Wu Wei. But Wu Wei is from the high-context culture, where people would try to figure out what the implied meaning of the speaker's words, she therefor assumes that Julia would like to have the bag because she says she likes it.

Test Your Reading 5

Decide whether the statements are True (T) or False (F).

(1) Compliments vary across cultures in terms of who is praised, what is praised and how it is praised, which deserve more attention in intercultural communication. (   )

(2) Compliments in English function as greetings, agreement and appreciation. (   )

(3) Denial as reply to compliments means asking for more praises in Asian cultures. (   )

(4) Nowadays more women would like to be praised for abilities and achievements rather than appearance. (   )

(5) The first and third person is more often used for compliments in English while the second person is preferred in Chinese. (   )

(6) European replies to compliments tend to express agreement, confirmation and appreciation while Asian ones tend to deny the same for modesty and humility. (   )

F. How Are Wishes of Visiting Expressed and Hospitality Shown?

Globalization has made it a customary practice to make appointments in advance for meetings or visits several days ahead, while there are still some cultural differences. For example, the Chinese request for visiting may sound like a command or a notice in the way that "I am going to see you on Sunday", by which he/she intends to say that "I would like very much to visit you sometime this week. Would it be convenient for me to go on Sunday?", or "I'd like to go and see you sometime. Would you be free one afternoon next week?'

Social customs on visits and hospitality from the host differ from culture to culture. For example, a Chinese "no" is confusing to people from other cultures. In China, visitors will be offered a cup of tea as a sign of friendliness and respect regardless of the procedural decline from the visitor, and "No. You don't have to bother yourself with that" will be confusing to English speakers because he/she can't figure out the meaning of "no" here for politeness. It will also be problematic for the Chinese visitor because he/she will suffer from thirst if he/she politely refused the offer that "Would you like something to drink?"

Hospitality is shown in various ways across cultures. For example, at a Western family dinner, people enjoy conversations at table while food is passed on around and everyone helps oneself by taking what he/she likes and is expected to finish what he/she has in his/her plate. On the contrary, it's hospitable and polite in China for the host to make sure the visitor is not starved by putting as much food as possible in the visitor's plate in spite of the refusal and it's acceptable for Chinese to leave the unwanted food on the plate. Therefore cultural clashes may occur when the cultural difference is not much noticed in intercultural communication.

For the sake of modesty and courtesy, Chinese hosts would say, "没有什么好吃的，随便吃吧！" when treating friends at home, which is contrary to the Western practice in " I have prepared all these for you and hope you will enjoy it!"

There are as many customary practices as cultures are, therefore it takes time to know all about them in details, but the comparatively efficient approach is to learn about the taboos of a specific culture so that the possible offense will be avoided to the most for the sake of friendliness and good relationship.

G. What Are Conversational Taboos?

Conversational taboos are topics considered inappropriate when conversing with people in one's own culture and with people in another culture (Figure 7.1).

Figure 7.1 Conversational Taboos

Case Study 10

> During a casual conversation, a businessman from Virginia, US, who was on his first trip to England, asked a man from Scotland about his wife and children. The US businessman was told it was none of his business. When asked about the weather, however, the man from Scotland talked incessantly.

In the United States, religion and politics are considered inappropriate topics as they are too controversial. Terrorism and disasters, such as September 11, 2001 are also inappropriate for small talks. Questions about one's income, how much one pays for clothes or personal belongings, why one is single, or why a couple does not have children are considered too personal. In Saudi Arabia, people avoid asking a man about his wife, or getting political discussions. It's same in Jordan that it's inappropriate to ask a man about his wife, and in addition, it's impolite to make negative remarks about the royal family. In Israel, politics and religion are not good topics either. In Egypt, personal questions should be avoided. In Iraq, personal questions and comments on birth control policies are not proper topics.

When talking with people from Nigeria, words like "witchcraft" "jungle" "hut" are to be avoided as they have negative connotations, implying that Africa is a backward country which in fact has advanced a lot and its people are proud of. In South Africa, such personal question as one's marital status should be avoided, and so is discussion on ethnic differences or politics. In Kenya, it's acceptable to ask about one's children but not the spouse; criticizing the government is not acceptable, either.

In Europe, topics concerning personal lives or questions as ages or marital status are taboos. In Spain, one's occupation is regarded as personal, thus should be avoided. Talking with Italians, comments on Mafia, Italian politics, taxes and religions are regarded inappropriate. In Britain, discussions on Scotland or Northern Ireland are avoided, so is the Royal family. In Europe as well as in any other country, good advice is to avoid any topic implying criticism of their country or government.

In Australia and New Zealand, the topic taboos include discussion of religion, politics, racial issues, treatment of the Aborigines, kangaroo population control or labor disputes. It's important to avoid speaking highly of Australia when in New Zealand and vice versa.

In Latin American countries, politics or religion are taboos in conversation in addition to personal questions. In Brazil, salary is regarded personal; criticism such as economic problems, social class differences and the government are to be avoided. In Bolivia and Colombia, drug policies or terrorism is not good topic for a conversation. In Chile, discussions of wars and comments about social classes are not good choices of topic.

What is a good topic in conversation may differ with cultures. It is a good rule to follow the lead of the host. And it is inappropriate to make derogatory remarks about any respect of the country, its government, its people and their customs or their sports teams.

Activity 5

List the taboo topics in China, in your provinces, city, or town. You may interview your grandparents or parents or turn to any resources on the Internet.

Activity 6

Fill in the table on taboo topics in common in Arabian world, Europe, Africa and Asia (Table 7.10).

Table 7.10 Conversational Taboos

Cultures/Countries	Taboos	Examples
the US	Religion, politics, personal questions	Terrorism, disasters, personal income, marital status, physical related topics (height, weight, body odor).
Saudi Arabia	Political or religious discussion, one's wife	
Egypt	Personal questions	

Continued

Cultures/Countries	Taboos	Examples
Jordan	one's wife, negative remarks on the royal family	
Iraq	Political or religious discussion, Personal questions, comments on birth control policies	
Nigeria	Avoid such words as "witchcraft, jungle, hut"	
South Africa	Personal questions, discussion of ethic differences or politics,	
Kenya	One's spouse, negative comments on government	
Europe	Personal life and personal questions	Spain: one's occupation Italy: Mafia, politics, taxes, religion England: politics, religion, comments on Scotland and Ireland, the Royal family
New Zealand, Australia	Political, religious and racial issues, treatment of Aboriginals	
Latin American countries	Political, religious issues, personal questions, criticism on the government,	Bolivia Colombia: drug policy, terrorism Chile: wars, social classes

IV. Extended Reading

Significance of Colors in African Culture

If you are familiar with African clothing, you may have noticed that the designs are rich, vibrant and colorful creations that shine. However, you may not be aware that colours are extremely symbolic in Africa and every color that is used in African fabrics has a deep history behind it. In this article, we will explore the true meanings behind colors, what each color represents and why this multitude of colors is so important in African culture.

In African culture, colors inherently have a symbolic nature in a variety of areas, including when rich and vibrant colors are used in African fabrics and African clothing. Colors can represent a variety of emotions, traditions and victories in the wake of struggles. For centuries, Africa has experienced turmoil followed by liberation and this is reflected in the colors that are intrinsic to African life. For example, in the various African nations & apos, flags are some of the most colorful of any continent.

The combination of reds, blacks, greens, whites and blues that are commonly found on the flags of African countries, each has its own symbolic meaning that is crucial to the citizens of every respective country. In the fashion industry, the symbolism of color is no less effective. African designers often use an array of colors and patterns to represent various states of energy and emotions that the wearer may experience. Colors have greatly impacted African clothing and both the traditional and modern African fashion industries as the meanings of colors have gradually evolved throughout history to create the rainbow of designs that are on offer today When you understand the true meanings behind the variety of African colors, you can choose the ideal fabrics, patterns and color combinations that will suit any specific occasion.

WARM COLOURS

Warm colors can make beautiful African outfits. They incorporate reds, oranges, purples and yellows and they are extremely bright and vibrant. African color combinations often engage these colors to make stunning outfits. The use of oranges, reds and purples in dresses can not only look incredible, but they also have profound meaning behind them. Warm colors are often used in Western Africa such as with the fabrics Berber, Bagola and Aso Oke.

PURPLE

African fashion often uses purple to symbolize the essence of femininity. It is a deep and rich color that represents the strong and beautiful nature of womanhood.

YELLOW AND GOLD

Yellow and gold can have a variety of symbolic meanings, including wealth and riches, spiritual purity, fertility, beauty and the precious nature of life.

COOL COLOURS

Cool colors include blues and greens and they are often representative of nature in African cultures. However, each individual color has its own specific meaning in African clothing. They are found in abundance in Sika & Apos, a Christine collection to represent emotions such as harmony, peace and love.

BLUE

Blue is the color of harmony and love, symbolizing the importance of peace and togetherness. It is often used in combination with other colors to create a rich tapestry of energy that has deep symbolism behind it. Blue fabrics are widely used in the Southern countries of Africa such as the Leteisi and Shweshwe.

GREEN

Green is a natural color that demonstrates growth. It can relate to the spiritual growth and development of an individual as well as the growth that takes place in nature, such as the agricultural rebirth of the land as the crops begin to bloom with a new season.

NEUTRAL COLOURS

African textiles commonly symbolically use neutral colors like white, black, grey and silver. Many of these colors are found in Sika & Apos; Sika & Apos; Femme Essence collection and they are interwoven with other symbolic colors from both the warm and cool shades of the color wheel. Neutral colors are often used within central Africa incorporated in the fabrics Ankara and Kuba Raffia.

WHITE

White is the color of purity. It represents cleansing and is often worn for festive occasions. It has an innocence to it that is representative of its pureness.

BLACK

Black color is often used for mourning, black has profound spiritual energy. The darkness of the color can also represent other meanings too, such as maturity.

SILVER

Silver is an extremely peaceful color that has associations with the moon. It represents a range of emotions like joy and peace.

Post-class Tasks

Self-test Tasks

1. Decide whether the statements are True (T) or False (F)
(1) For the benefit of the first impression, one should dress fashionably and beautifully to any social or business event. ( )
(2) Americans prefer to be addressed by first names for the sake of equality in most cases, so do Germans. ( )
(3) Most of Asians consider it polite and respectful to present and receive items with both hands, so do Muslins. ( )
(4) There is universal etiquette that functions the same in all cultures. ( )
(5) Generally etiquette is observed on the basis of the language applied in the communication so as to conform to the cultural norm. ( )
(6) When someone praises you by saying "I like your hat", you are supposed to give your hat to him/her as a gift. ( )
(7) When you are informed in Venezuela the meeting will begin at 10:30, you are to get there around 10:40. ( )
(8) You don't have to reply to a formal invitation with "R. S. V. P. regret only" if you are sure to attend it. ( )
(9) It is regarded rude to shake hands with A while signaling hello to B. ( )
(10) In the UK, the topic of Scotland or the Ireland is usually not taken as

an appropriate topic. (　)

(11) In the UK, people from Scotland don't mind being referred as English. (　)

(12) Flowers as gifts such as roses or chrysanthemum are universal across all cultures. (　)

2. Pick up one topic in this chapter that you are interested in, for example, taboo topics, or compliments and replies, and make up a questionnaire to find out what your local culture is like to be.

3. List the gift taboos in China in comparison with any other country you are interested in.

Group Work

Choose one of the following tasks to complete.

1. Conduct an interview on the business etiquette of a joint venture in your city or town in comparison with that in China and make a video of the interview.

2. On the basis of this chapter, make up a role-play with cultural conflicts in social or business etiquette.

3. You are with a Chinese petrol company which is to establish business in Saudi Arab lately. What are you going to do in consideration of cultural differences in dealing with the local people in addition to preparation of the business itself?

4. You are with an international corporation in Shanghai, China, and working on the visit of an Indonesian delegation in two months. Make a list of what you have to do in hosting the Indonesians.

Telling China's Stories

One of the international teachers in your university is invited to a wedding ceremony in your city or town, who comes to you for some advice at a Chinese wedding in general and especially the local customs and taboos. You may surf the Internet, talk to your parents or grandparents before you write a script on the etiquette at a Chinese local wedding.

My Learning Reflection

1. What have I learned about Chinese cultures or myself?

2. What have I learned about other cultures?

3. What impressed me most in this chapter?

4. What still confuses me?

Chapter 8 Intercultural Learning and Teaching

> **Learning Objectives**
>
> - To master concepts of classroom culture (i. e. definition, importance, and the impact on classroom teaching), culture shock and learning style preference;
> - To identify the relationships between culture and education to enhance thinking of the similarities and differences of education on diverse cultures;
> - To adapt to learning and teaching patterns across cultures.
>
> **Pre-class Tasks**
>
> - Read the textbook and watch the concerned clips in *xuexitong* (学习通).

Ⅰ. Lead-in Tasks

Activity 1

Read and put numbers in corresponding boxes (Table 8.1) to indicate which of the following situations are more likely to happen in Asian schools and which are more likely to happen in Western schools. And try to explain why there are differences between them.

Table 8.1 Situations in Asian and American Schools

In Asian schools	In American schools

1. Professors encourage students to ask questions in class.
2. Professors pace voice and volume to sound welcoming and friendly.
3. Professors realize some students will chat, use social media, eat, and maybe even nap.
4. Professors believe students learn best from the voice of experience and by working through cases or problems alone.
5. Professors deliver information and students work quietly on their own.
6. Professors are expected to know answers and maintain status.
7. Professors will be gentle if a student gives wrong information saying something like, "Good guess."
8. Professors may not know all the answers and is comfortable with this.
9. Professors rely on homework and tests to see if students are learning.
10. Professors will tell students that they are wrong.
11. Professors are formal in class but quite friendly with students outside of class.
12. Professors organize experiences so students can learn by doing (often in groups).
13. Professors are informal in class but quite formal in meetings outside of class.
14. Professors try to make the material simple enough that almost everyone can get it.
15. Professors share slides, pause for note-taking, and generally try to set a pace that all can follow.
16. Professors may sit on a table, drink coffee, and dress casually.

17. Professors stand to lecture.

18. Professors may be quieter or louder depending on style and materials. Making students comfortable may not be a goal.

19. Professors make the material challenging so everyone must work hard and even the strongest students are challenged.

20. Professors keep students hopping and it is up to them to keep up or not.

21. Professors would like to be seen as the open-minded, easy-going, and knowledgeable facilitator.

22. Professors think students should have strong grasp of basic facts and memorize key items.

23. Professors indicate that education is a luxury to be valued and students had better work hard.

24. Professors expect some students to comment on class procedures and complain about marks.

25. Professors are happy to see students in office hours.

26. Professors think when a student asks for advice they should be non-judgmental and provide resources.

27. Professors would like to be seen as a confident, authoritative expert, lecturer and guide.

28. Professors think when students seek advice they must share their wisdom and experience and guide the student to a good path.

29. Professors think memorization of key data is not as needed as an understanding of problem-solving skills for the area of study.

30. Professors indicate that education is a right for every citizen and he/she will help everyone.

Pre-reading Questions

(1) What is the relationship between culture and education?

(2) Based on your learning of cultures, what does the ancient Chinese proverb "by nature all men are alike, but by education widely different" mean?

Education is a cultural phenomenon and culture and education interact with and affect each other. Different education reflects its cultural connotations while different cultures shape different educational systems and styles. It is worth noting that cultural influence on education, in which students' learning styles have been conditioned, is deeply rooted, strong and persistent, though very often invisible. Moreover, classroom teaching is an integral part of culture and is also the embodiment of a cultural phenomenon. But, it is relatively independent in its process, forming a special cultural context as classroom teaching culture.

According to Tudor, classroom culture refers to "the complex of attitudes and expectations which shape learners' sociocultural personality in the classroom, and thereby their interactions with their language study." That is to say, students' sociocultural personality in the classroom will influence their interaction with various aspects of learning context. The concept of classroom culture encapsulates or contains many of the beliefs and attitudes of the society in question, but they are perceived and experienced by the specific group of learners concerned. Therefore, notions of teachers, behaviors of students, and the class organization form are all the specific activities for the representation of classroom culture. From the definition it can be inferred that classroom culture is a microcosm of the wider society to which it belongs. That is to say, what goes on within the classroom is influenced by factors within the general educational institution, the wider educational environment and the whole society.

There are classrooms where a native teacher instructing some foreign students, or where a foreign professor teaching some native students. There are also courses in which both students and the teachers come from various cultures. These intercultural classrooms display diversities in the cultural experiences of students and teachers, which provide divergence in their frames of references, or the ways in which individuals understand communication in the classroom. As Anderson and Lynch emphasized, when learning a foreign language, learners acquire more than a linguistic system, they also get acquainted with some degree of familiarity with the foreign cultural systems.

Test Your Reading 1

Decide whether the statements are True (T) or False (F).
(1) Classroom teaching is one of cultural phenomenon. (   )
(2) Students' sociocultural personality in the classroom will influence their interaction with various aspects of learning context. (   )

(3) Teaching beliefs and class organization forms of teachers are the specific activities for the representation of classroom culture. (   )

(4) In the foreign or second language learning process, learners need to get familiar with the cultural systems. (   )

II. Culture in Education

There are different educational systems in the world. The primary purpose for education is to increase people's knowledge and skills and to improve the ability of the educated and provide high quality labor force for the society. Meanwhile, education is expected to transmit values, to train the educated for the development of the country and serve the political and economic development of the country. What is taught in a culture is critical to the maintenance and perpetuation of that culture, and much of the responsibility for that instruction stems from the educational systems within the culture. Cultural variations are the result of people being taught different beliefs, values, customs and perspectives. Some factors vary across cultures, such as educational systems, teaching methods, attitudes toward education, academic achievements, classroom departments, and student-teacher relationships.

Given the differences mentioned above, when teachers and students from different cultural backgrounds come into the same classroom, they would face various cultural and educational conflicts due to their rooted concepts in educational philosophy, methods of education, perception of teachers and students, and their relations. Therefore, the influences of culture on education can be presented on two aspects: **how to teach and learn and what to educate**, i.e. teaching and learning styles with the embodiment of a cultural phenomenon on the cultural genial essences through curriculum.

In terms of what to educate, it involves cultural values in the form of educational systems in relation to curriculum settings, teaching contents for individual development and social welfare of workforces. For example, in the US, the main teaching objective is to cultivate personalized abilities, especially to foster their critical thinking ability and creativity, tapping into their learning potentials. Therefore, learning needs, learning styles, and learning motivations of students are taken into consideration, and the concepts of humanism and social constructivism are revealed and students thus are the subjects in the teaching process, which is known as student-centered teaching. For the learning achievement, education sectors and students' parents pay more attention to students' daily performance in addition to exams scores.

However, education in most Asian countries, such as China, Korea and Japan, is mainly characterized with the fact that the teacher decides the curriculum settings and teaching contents, which is usually knowledge-oriented as well. Generally, teachers are responsible for imparting the knowledge points with absolute authority and the role of teachers in the teaching process is the decision-makers and controller, thus is more teacher-centered. Moreover, test scores as learning achievements are emphasized by the society at all levels. However, it has to be noticed that with globalization and development in educational technologies, Asian education is changing from the teacher-centered to the student-centered.

In addition to the educational systems and ways of instruction, attitudes toward education and academic achievements are some of the factors that vary across cultures. The process of school education in a culture is tied directly to its beliefs, values and characteristics. But, how does education reflect the diverse cultures? The cultural attitudes toward education are discussed in comparison of the United States with two Asian nations: China and Japan.

In the United States, education is important but it is not considered an absolutely essential prerequisite for success. Americans believe that one will fulfill his/her dreams if someone has an idea and the determination. American parents take an active role in school activities, who tend to focus on the "nonacademic side of their children's school" and are likely to feel that the best setting for learning is an unstructured environment. But in Asian countries, educational achievements are of the highest values. Students regard education as a serious undertaking centered on "hard work". Parents are involved actively in every phase of education of their children, often functioning as at-home coaches and teachers.

More importantly, attitudes are differently held toward academic achievements of students. In the United States, tests do not assess all of what makes students special and unique, which is not the only criterion for a student. Characters and personal performance of a student are considered even more important than test scores. In most Asian countries, however, high school graduates gained in a single exam largely determines the level of their future life. That is, the exam scores will determine the university that a student attends, which is the most influential factor in his future success i.e. the more prestigious the school, the more successful in life.

Given the different educational systems, teaching and learning methods are also different. For example, in the Western countries, language teaching focuses on language use, aiming for communication, but in most Asian countries, language teaching focuses on language structures, memorizing the grammatical patterns and vocabularies. Therefore, what is taught and how it is taught in school varies across cultures. It is not surprising to discover that there are also differences in how students and teachers participate in the educational process.

The classroom departments display differences as well. Generally in Asian cultures, the normative way of teaching is featured with the teacher lecturing while students sitting quietly and dutifully taking notes, and tests involve iterating the previously received facts. In other cultures, students are more actively engaged in give-and-take verbal discussion and they like to express their own ideas. The exams may involve creative and critical thinking skills. For teachers, being asked questions by students is a sign that they are interested since differences of opinion are often encouraged.

The relationship between teacher and students also varies from culture to culture. The student-teacher relations offer a perspective on the structure of interpersonal relations throughout the culture. In some countries where teachers enjoy considerable social status and power, the teacher-student relationship is very formal and authoritative. But in other nations, the relationship is more relaxed and egalitarian. Even in nonverbal aspects, such as space, distance, time, and dress codes are cultural variables reflected in classroom behaviors. For example, in the American culture, informal attire is acceptable in the classroom, but Chinese and Japanese cultures demand that students attend class in identical uniforms.

In view of the above, the differences in a culturally diverse classroom can be traceable to cultural differences and it is necessary for educators and practitioners to call upon cross-cultural awareness since Hofstede states that "interactions between teachers and learners from different cultures are fundamentally problematic and cross-cultural misunderstandings often occur because classroom interaction is an archetypal human phenomenon that is deeply rooted in the culture of a society".

Test Your Reading 2

Decide whether the statements are True (T) or False (F).

(1) Teaching method and beliefs of a teacher reflects his/her deeply rooted concepts in educational experiences and philosophy. (   )

(2) In most Asian countries, educational systems reflect the main concepts of humanism and social constructivism. (   )

(3) In Korea, teachers have absolutely authority and they tend to impart the knowledge points. (   )

(4) What is taught and how it is taught in schools varies across cultures. (   )

(5) In the United States, education is considered an absolutely essential prerequisite for success. (   )

(6) In most Asian countries, tests do not assess all of what makes students special and unique, and the test score is not the only criterion for a student. (   )

(7) Classroom interactions are deeply rooted in the culture of a society and leads to some fundamentally problematic and cross-cultural misunderstandings often occur. (   )

A. Are There Different Learning Styles Across Cultures?

Case Study 1

What caused the conflict in the following case?

> A group of Chinese students are participating in an exchange program in New York. Mia, one of the language teachers, prepared a variety of classroom activities for the students, trying to build up a good relationship with them. Recently she often feels bad at ease about the silence shown by the Chinese students, who seemed reluctant to speak or to participate in the activities she organized at class or for group works. She complained that the responses to her requirements were "just stare at me or at each other ... I lost my passion for teaching."

The above case illustrates the differences between China and America in terms of teaching and learning cultures, concepts and conduct in education. In other words, it reflects the different beliefs in learning styles. In this case, the American teacher obviously felt quite uncomfortable about the learning atmosphere. In her culture the more questions the students ask, the more communicative between teachers and students, the more interested students are, and therefore more successful the class is. In the West, there is a high emphasis on communication in the classroom to learn a language; and it places a high value on actual use of the language in the classroom. Teachers believe that it will provide students with equal chances to join in class discussions.

In addition, teachers push students to think and imagine by asking questions at class, encouraging students to discuss and raise questions, which is believed that the sharper the better. But in China, it is regarded as good manners for students to listen to the teacher or other speakers without asking any questions, and silence indicates respect for the speaker from the listener. In other words, it is in accordance with the traditional Chinese learning cultures for students to keep silent in class instead of questioning or talking. Moreover, in China, many students are embarrassed to speak English in class because they feel that they are subpart in their language, fearing loss of face by possible mistakes.

A learning style preference may be considered as the manner in which individuals prefer to receive and process information, such as auditory, visual, or kinesthetic learning styles. It is an internal manner of processing information that envelops an individual's cultural elements. There are a variety of culturally influenced learning preferences, and students from diverse backgrounds enter the multicultural classroom with different ideas about learning and education. In other words, students from different cultures have their own preferred ways of gathering and processing information that called learning styles or learning preferences.

Figure 8.1　Learning Style Preferences

　　Previous studies have applied various instruments to explore the role that culture may have in determining students' learning styles, for example, Study Process Questionnaire by Biggs, Perceptual Learning-Style Preference Questionnaire by Reid, Index Learning Style (ILS) by Soloman and Felder, Inventory of Learning Styles (ILS) by Vermunt and Learning Style Inventory (LSI) by Kolb.

　　Based on the previous studies, Chinese and Korean students are found to more preference of visual learning style. In other words, at a lecture or classroom discussion, visual learners prefer to take detailed notes for information. For example, in most of the Chinese and Korean classrooms, students prefer to concentrate on what the teacher says and writes on the blackboard, and teachers in turn will ask students to be attentive and keep quiet. Therefore kinesthetic learning styles may not be encouraged by most teachers in the Chinese and Korean classrooms.

　　Furthermore, Asian students are hesitant to answer questions before they are sure of the exact answer because they are waiting for the teacher to impart knowledge upon them instead of searching for answers on their own by trying with errors. Moreover questions from students in classroom are considered impolite, implying that the teacher is challenged due to an ineligible quality for his/her job.

In addition, the learning style reveals preference of students who tend to work together in a cooperative environment or to work independently in competition with one another. In other words, it also relates to their preference for cooperative or competitive ways of learning, and their perceived value of education and schooling. For example, students from collectivist cultures, such as China, Korea, Japan, expect and accept group work since their culture has taught them to cooperate and work collectively in groups. In fact, they often work harder in a group than they do individually. However, students in individualistic cultures, such as the United States or the Great Britain, usually expect to be graded on individual work because they are taught to work individually to compete with one another.

Moreover, it is also important that students themselves become aware of their own learning style, which is the first and most important step to achieve a degree of self-sufficiency in learning. Meanwhile, effective instructions and guidance should be offered for learners to have a thorough understanding of their learning style preferences. It is possible that a hostile atmosphere in the classroom will occur when students feel that their problems in learning are not to be facilitated by the teachers if teachers are less aware of the learning styles of students or regardless the needs of students. Therefore, differences in learning style are to be discussed openly in tolerant and appropriate attitudes in order to identify any possible sociocultural influences that might have helped to create the variances and students will understand the essence of learning process and be comfortable in learning if they recognize their learning style.

What should language teachers do? Teachers play an important role in making learning happen. For optimal language progress, language teachers need to understand their students' learning style preference and the cultural as cultural influences help shape those styles. That is, teachers will understand what students do with information, how students learn socially, their patterns of motivation, what culture they bring from home to school, and so on. It's worth noting that it is very important for language teachers to know the concept of learning styles. Understanding learning styles will help teachers plan and implement different methods to counter different learning styles in a multicultural classroom that help in the learning process. In other words, to know about the preferred learning styles of the students will help teachers to plan their lessons to match or adapt their teaching and to provide the most appropriate and meaningful activities or tasks to suit a particular learner group at different stages.

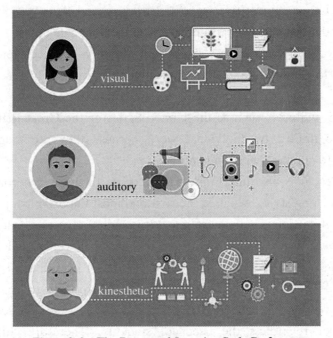

Figure 8.2　The Perceptual Learning Style Preference

For example, problems may take place for Chinese students either in China or in other countries because Chinese "collectivist" culture sometimes causes a mismatch between teaching styles of Western teachers and learning styles of Chinese students in the face of the Western "individualist" approach to teaching and learning. Also, notes on blackboard, maps, or pictures by teachers would improve learning for students of visual preference, such as those from China or Korea. But for most Western students, they should be encouraged to speak and engage in discussions and debates with teachers and their peers.

Therefore, a variety of instructional environments and activities can be created in which teachers and instructors will adjust their own teaching styles and instructional environment for different styles of learners who come from different culture backgrounds. On the one hand, teachers will pay attention to culturally influenced learning styles of students by designing various activities that go with those styles, who can also help students to recognize the power of understanding their language learning styles for making learning quicker, easier and more effective. On the other hand, they will be triggered to be adapted in applying different teaching methods for different learning styles of students. For example, they can "style-match" parts of every lesson to meet the needs of diverse styles through judicious, creative lessons that highlight varieties.

Activity 2

Watch video clips "Learning Styles and the Importance of Critical Self-Reflection" in *xuexitong*. Do you agree with the idea that "learning styles don't exist"? Why or why not? Share your opinions with your classmates.

B. How Do People Learn in Intercultural Classrooms?

Nowadays, multicultural classroom is a distinguishing characteristic of globalized society. There is a very definite possibility that one is teaching or learning in a multicultural classroom, with some of the students or classmates coming from a variety of cultural backgrounds. If students study abroad, a new culture brings them advanced education opportunities, broadening their horizons, and cultivating their independence. However, international students are also confronted with differences in languages, academic works, thinking patterns, social norms, educational systems, teaching methods as well as learning styles, all of which may bring students not only pleasure, but also culture shock.

People to a new culture or new environment will go across cultural boundaries. Oberg regarded culture shock as "an occupational disease of people who have been suddenly transplanted abroad". Adler defined cultural shock as "a set of emotional reactions to the loss of perceptual reinforcements from one's own culture, to new stimuli which have little or no meaning, and to the misunderstanding of new and diverse experiences." Exposure to a new environment and culture for the very first time affects everyone differently. After the initial excitement of being in a new place and discovering a new culture, some people start to have mixed feelings about having left their comfort zone.

Case Study 2

Try to find out what caused the problem in the following case and explain the cultural reasons for it.

> Li Ming, a Chinese student, has been studying Fashion Design in Britain for one month. He gradually overcomes his homesickness and the dietary habit. But the biggest pressure comes from the different learning environment. All the classes are active and student-centered learning atmosphere. Students are active to express their own views freely, debating fiercely, or even questioning professors. Li Ming doesn't know how to participate in classroom activities or group discussions to express his opinions critically. He feels that he doesn't belong to those people or is not involved in the class, which makes him feel very anxious.

Obviously, in this case, Li Ming is experiencing a culture shock in a new educational structure together with different learning and teaching styles. Teachers in such cultures as China, Korea, Japan and some African countries would talk or lecture a great deal of the time whereas in others, for example, America and Britain, students would do most of the talking. In different cultures, silence and minimal vocal participation characterize some classrooms whereas others tend to be noisy and active respectively. Li Ming, who is accustomed to acquiring knowledge by listening and note-taking, expects British teachers to provide explicit instructions, who tend to guide and encourage students to think critically. In other words, when a new teaching pattern does not satisfy students' expectation, students are more likely to be struggling in understanding the classroom contents and may experience cultural shock.

In addition, Li Ming found classroom atmospheres different in interactions between teachers and students which made him alien to the activities. For instance, it is hard for Li Ming to initiate questions at class as Asian students do not talk until they are called to answer questions since they believe that keeping silent in the classroom is a sigh of respect to teachers. Therefore, Li Ming felt uncomfortable with informal relationships between teachers and students, which students contribute to class activities without being called.

What Li Ming needs to do is to clear off the confusion about these differences which have interfered with his adjustment to the new system as soon as possible by shifting his learning styles. For example, he may prepare his lessons by listing questions in reading rather than reading to memorize the facts, or communicating more with his learning peers for more ideas, or training himself by thinking more critically, etc.

Above all, an international student has to learn more about the target culture, and get accustomed to the learning and teaching styles when getting into a new educational context. He/she has to develop an appropriate attitude toward the target culture by recognizing that one's own culturally based perspectives and behaviors may be different from some of his/her learning peers. In addition, he/she needs to improve their understanding of and tolerance to diverse cultures, continually exposing oneself to the target cultures.

Test Your Reading 3

Decide whether the statements are True (T) or False (F).

(1) In most English-speaking countries, modesty is regarded as a disrespectful behavior. (   )

(2) When studying abroad, learners may experience culture shock because of the different educational structures. (   )

(3) When learners get familiar with the teaching method, they don't need to learn the target culture. (   )

(4) In a new culture, it is possible that students are more likely to be struggling in teaching patterns which may lead to cultural shock. (   )

(5) When one recognizes that his own perspectives and behaviors are culturally based and are different from some of his classmates', he/she will refuse to expose himself to the target cultures. (   )

III. Teaching Chinese across Cultures

In the last couple of decades, rapid growth in Chinese economy has coincided with its expanding influence in international business. Simultaneously, influences of China have strengthened appeal of the Chinese language to the outside world. The Chinese language has been commonly acknowledged around the world and has been increasingly taught and learnt as an important second or foreign language (CSL/CFL) both within and outside China. It has been considered as a language of instrumental value which provides jobs or business opportunities, enabling greater international nobilities. Accordingly, a craze for the Chinese language, known as "the Chinese language fever" has been sweeping over the world and bringing with it a sharp rise of Chinese language learners in many countries around the world. By December 2018, 492, 185 foreign students from 196 countries studied in 1,004 universities or colleges in China (Ministry of Education of the People's Republic of China, 2019).

Activity 3

Conduct a survey on learning of the Chinese Language by the international students in your university by filling in Table 8.2. You may ask more questions if you are interested.

Table 8.2 Chinese Language Learning in China

Name	Country	Reasons	Difficulties

As a matter of fact, intensified efforts by China to popularize Chinese (*putonghua*, 普通话) in the last few decades have yielded two Chinese promotion programs: the Chinese Confucius Institutes and the Program of Study in China. By December 2019, 550 Confucius Institutes and 1,172 Confucius Classrooms have been set up in 162 countries; and courses of the Chinese language are offered in more than 30,000 elementary and middle schools and more than 4,000 universities with more than 25 million people learning Chinese. The Chinese government sees the teaching of Chinese as a crucial means to promote Chinese culture and enhance the international understanding of China as a nation, a point explicitly expressed on the webpage of the Chinese Government Scholarships (CSC).

Aimed at promoting "mutual understanding, cooperation and exchanges", the Chinese government has greatly scaled up offers of Chinese Government Scholarships to international students. Along with this policy, universities view international student education as an opportunity for a diverse student population, thus promoting the image of internationalization of Chinese higher education.

The rise of Chinese as an international language arguably plays an important role in "diversifying it as one of the lingua franca in the world and sharing the market of education worldwide". In the last decade, Chinese as a second or foreign language has emerged as an increasingly important one. In 2016, more than 2.1 million people were reportedly learning the Chinese language as a second or foreign language, and six million learners of Chinese as a foreign language took Chinese tests of various kinds around the globe. A total of 442,773 international students are also studying in the mainland China, among whom 38.2% are learning Chinese as a foreign language in higher educational institutions.

A. How to Teach Chinese to Speakers of Other Languages in China?

Teaching Chinese as a foreign or second language, which is now known as Teaching Chinese to Speakers of Other Languages (TCSOL, 国际中文教育) is not only a language teaching but an important carrier of cultures, both of which are the process of social development and bear the characteristics of national, social, systematic and constantly changing culture in a certain environment.

International students are the learners and receivers of Chinese culture, and they are likely to be the main actors in spreading Chinese culture. As a Chinese teacher of the Chinese language or a Chinese teacher of the English language, it is important to recognize the differences in customs, language and culture of international students, and help them to integrate into the school and society as soon as possible.

Case Study 3

Read the following case and try to analyze the cultural reasons.

> Miss Li, a Chinese teacher, is teaching Chinese to a group of international students who come from the University of Virginia. When the students have acquired accurate Chinese pronunciation or expressions, she is extremely proud of their progress and would give non-verbal compliments, such as "en, en" or "nodding" or "a positive look". Sometimes, she provides verbally compliment, such as "very good" or "excellent". But, feedback from her students reads like "Sometimes it seems like I have said something wrong but she just doesn't correct me and I think that is because she gives less positive feedback then other teachers." Miss Li is confused with the feedback from her students.

Why are Miss Li and her students confused? What are the problems about the "feedback"? What cultural differences reflect from this case?

Obviously, this case reflects a different understanding on compliment and feedback. In other words, the differences between high-context and low-context culture are demonstrated in the above case. As discussed in Chapter 2 Chinese culture is considered as the high context culture, in which participants share many common experiences and information, messages or meanings are decided by the gestures, intonation, speed, and other factors together with the statements or contents of the speaker. In other words, information is provided through gestures, the use of space, and even silence. Meanings are also conveyed through status (i.e. ages, the sex, education, titles) and the listeners therefore need to interpret what is said.

For Miss Li, who grows up in a traditional Chinese culture, the non-verbal feedback such as "en, en" or a "nodding" is considered as the proper expression for praise and appreciation. But, her students from the US need more positive verbal feedback, such as "Your pronunciation is good!" or "I'm glad to read a lot more new words or phrases in your writing." The clear and specific feedback on their progress are what these students wanted.

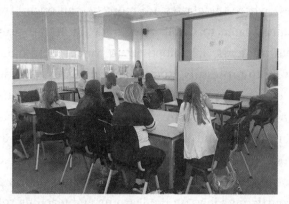

Figure 8.3　Teaching Chinese in a Intercultural Classroom

Case Study 4

Read the following case and try to answer the questions: What is the conflict of the following case? What makes the professor angry? What makes James leave the program?

> James, an American student, is taking part in a graduate program in Shanghai. He had studied Chinese history, international business, Chinese politics and Chinese language in his undergraduate and graduate programs in the US before he started this program in China. He is well versed in content knowledge of Chinese and critical thinking skills. In James's own words, he is "very argumentative and aggressive," and he is confident in articulating in class and in fact he likes to challenge others and argue with others. However, some of his arguments and the way he argues are not well received by one of his Chinese professors, who left the classroom in fury one day when James tried to support one of his classmates against the professor. Finally, James left the program, arguing that: "the level of my classmates and the courses are restrictive".

Different teaching approaches in Chinese and the Western cultures have created difficulties in classroom for international students. As shown in this case, James is fluent in Chinese but he is not aware of the cultural difference in teaching even though he has taken courses on China and the Chinese language in the United States, where the classes are more like an open, free and academic debate. When James came to China as a graduate at this program, he had a strong belief that students are supposed to voice their opinions instead of listening attentively to professors especially in graduate education.

But when it comes to the Chinese professor, it is not like that at all because it is well-known that teachers are authoritative in the classroom and are expected to be respected and obeyed in Chinese culture, and the Chinese professor thus felt insulted by being challenged by his students, who are supposed to take in what is instructed. At this point, James and the Chinese professor have conflicting views on the learning and teaching roles as to the way of learning and teaching. To James, he did not mean to have "more fun" to argue with authorities, proving them wrong in public, but he fails to adjust himself to the environment, ignoring the Chinese ways of teaching with strong affiliation to his culture. On the other hand, the Chinese professor would not have felt humiliated with strong rejection to the "Chinese culture" and himself by James if he had been aware of various ways of learning and teaching across cultures, adapting to cultural diversities in his teaching.

As a matter of fact, in foreign/second language learning contexts, the relationship between language and culture has always been a topic of discussion. Cultural differences in learning are recognized, such as the Eastern Asian holistic thinking and reproductive learning in contrast to the Western analytical thinking and creative learning. Seeing the differences in educational culture, different responses of these students mirrored the power relations nested in language and culture.

There is a link between engagement with the culture and sense of belonging. When one accepts a culture as it is with desires to immerse oneself in it, one is inclined to fit in regardless of his/her language proficiency. International students are from different countries, sharing the same open-mindedness about the host culture. It is equally necessary to have concerns on the living of international students and to better understand how students are engaging in cross-cultural interactions in this context as well even though it is a big challenge to make the programs accommodating to students from different countries with different educational levels. And at the same time, the teaching staff has to be equipped with intercultural repertoire with openness and inclusiveness so that effective teaching will take place on the basis of understanding of the learning styles of the students.

Test Your Reading 4

Decide whether the statements are True (T) or False (F).

(1) In Chinese culture, the information, messages or meanings can be conveyed by non-verbal behaviors, such as gestures, intonation, speed and even silence. (   )

(2) International students are the learners and receivers of Chinese culture, and they are likely to be the main actors in spreading Chinese culture. (   )

(3) For a language learner, when he/she accepts a culture as it is and desires to immerse oneself in it, he/she is inclined to fit in regardless of his/her language proficiency. (   )

(4) When teaching Chinese as a second language in China, language teaching goes before helping the students to adapt to the language learning classroom atmosphere. (   )

B. How to Teach Chinese to Speakers of Other Languages Outside of China?

The growing interest in learning Chinese has led to a growing demand to recruit qualified Chinese teachers. However, teaching a language is not only about teaching the language itself. In a multicultural classroom where teachers and students come from varied backgrounds, both may have the behaviors and actions with different cultural values and expectations about their roles. As products of a different culture and educational system, people who teach Chinese as a foreign language in other countries often find themselves adrift within a system in which they are professionally and culturally isolated.

Case Study 5

Read the following case and try to find out what the cultural differences in classroom management are.

> In a British high school, the Chinese lesson had begun when it was still noisy in the classroom. Some students were talking and some were singing. Miss Yang, the Chinese teacher, said "Excuse me, as you are talking, I'm not going to talk until you stop talking." "You're (pointing to one student) going to swap, please." "Will you listen to me?" "Why are you talking (pointing to another student)? Keep talking? Stand there, please." The British students were shocked at Miss Yang's behaviors.

In this case, Miss Yang encounters cultural conflicts in classroom management and maintaining disciplines, which is out of expectation back at home. Influenced by Chinese cultural practice of valuing the goals, duties and benefits of the whole group more than individual interests, Chinese teachers expect and teach students to behave in accordance with the greater benefit of the whole class. To comply with this expectation, Chinese students following a series of procedures in the classroom. For example, students are required to sit quietly in their seats before class, waiting for the teacher to come; they are called to stand up and bow to the teacher by the class president as soon as the teacher comes in, and quickly move into learning activities when "students should sit in lines and rows straightly, listen to the teacher and should not interrupt the teacher's talk with questions".

However, complexity of teaching and learning increases when teaching is put into a context of cross-cultural practices. Like in this case, Chinese language teachers in the British classrooms felt frustrated and difficult in managing students' misbehaviors and in maintaining an orderly learning environment. Zhou and Li pointed out that Chinese teachers experienced cultural mismatches between their Chinese cultural expectations and behaviors of American students in actual classroom, struggling with challenges of understanding the demands of American classroom management.

Previous studies have found that Chinese language teachers struggled with the cultural differences with tremendous challenges in their teaching process. In other words, they face a wide range of challenges in a context different from the culture and educational system in their country of origin, such as the appropriate language to teach or communicate with students, classroom management and disciplines, communication with parents, colleagues and students with special needs, learner-centered and self-regulated instruction, and teacher-student relationship. Among them, how to manage classroom may be the most demanding issues for the Chinese language teachers.

In addition, styles and strategies of classroom management by Chinese teachers in China are found to be shaped by several different cultural factors such as valuing collective interest over individualism, the hierarchical nature of teacher-student relationships, and the concept of face-saving. Applying these "collective principles", Chinese teachers adopt some instructional routines and approaches to foster student self-disciplines and conformity in the school settings. Given the steady increase in the number of Chinese language teachers recruited to teach in the world, there is a critical need to better understand their classroom management practices in such cross-cultural contexts. Thus, the classroom management is mediated by culture in cross-cultural contexts where teachers do not share the same language or cultural backgrounds with their students.

It seems that the Chinese teachers need to develop cultural competency to interact within and across two distinct cultures directly affected their classroom behavior management because Chinese teachers may not have experiences instructing in countries where the languages and cultures are radically different from their own even though they are of extensive teaching experience. Hence, they are likely to encounter problems with acculturation, induction, and developing competency within the new educational system, environment, and expectations inherent in that setting.

Case Study 6

Read the following case and try to find out the cultural expectations in teaching.

> Mr. Cai has been teaching Chinese in Barcelona for about one month. In his Chinese class, there are 12 students who are from different countries (e.g. Spanish, Netherlands, Korea, the Czech Republic, and Japan). He prepares various activities to stimulate learning motivation and participation of the students, such as role plays and information-gap activities for better teaching effects. He tries to design various activities, dividing the students into three groups, telling them: "The only group that finishes the tasks first will get an award." But, students do not respond enthusiastically, showing no interest in the activity. Finally, it turns out that both the group that have won the first place and the groups that has lost are satisfied with the process of cooperation rather than the award.

What does the case reveals in terms of cultural expectations in teaching? There are some differences between Mr. Cai's presupposition and the actual situation of the students. First of all, Mr. Cai underestimated the psychological status of his students. In a multi-cultural classroom, teachers and students tend to show different responses to the same thing since they come from different cultural backgrounds. In his learning and teaching experiences, appropriate competitive activities will stimulate interests and create active learning atmosphere, and Mr. Cai is accustomed to the fact that Chinese students prefer competitive activities, enjoying prizes and awards. However, he ignores the differences of learning in the intercultural background. In other words, not all students like competitive activities as students in different cultures possess their own features and characteristics. As effective teaching aims to achieve the teaching goals or teaching objectives, it is important for those who teach Chinese as a foreign language in other countries to be aware of the differences of their teaching targets, learning how to adjust and optimize his/her teaching strategies.

Besides, teachers teaching Chinese as a foreign language in other countries are also faced with the challenges of culturally different status of teachers and changing teacher-centered teaching methodologies as well as the language barriers. For example, stress is reported on dealing with students with special needs, and communication with the American parents who did not have the same respect for teachers as Chinese parents. These challenges indicate an urgent need to examine cultural influences on cross-cultural teaching competence of Chinese language teachers when they teach non-Chinese language learners in other countries as well.

Efficient cross-cultural communication is also a significant component in foreign language education. Previous studies have found that teachers practice, convey, and act on beliefs and expectations through their culturally educational experiences. In order to be effective with culturally diverse students, it is crucial for native Chinese teachers to first recognize and understand their own worldviews only when will they be able to understand the worldviews of their students come from other cultures.

Therefore, in order to interact effectively with their students, Chinese language teachers must confront with their own biases, learning about cultures of their students such as different learning styles and perceiving the world through diverse cultural lenses. In addition, it is equally crucial to prepare Chinese teachers to adapt to the target education culture through teacher education programs and appropriate training for successful career in the target classrooms.

Test Your Reading 5

Decide whether the statements are True (T) or False (F).

(1) In Chinese culture, the teaching contents tend to be focused on the needs of a majority of the students as well as individual interests. (   )

(2) Previous studies found that appropriate language use is not a main challenge for the Chinese teachers who teach Chinese language in other cultures. (   )

(3) In cross-cultural contexts, culture can be seen as mediation in the aspect of the classroom management when teachers and students do not share the same language or cultural backgrounds. (   )

(4) Obviously, teachers practice, convey, and act on beliefs and expectations through their culturally educational experiences. (   )

IV. Some Considerations

As discussed above, both in the process of studying abroad and communicating with foreign teachers at home, it is obviously noticed that there are quite a lot of different points in classroom ranging from teaching methodologies to the overall classroom atmosphere. It cannot be denied that increased cultural diversities in classrooms present challenges for education sectors, especially for students and teachers. In other words, communicating effectively in a culturally diverse educational setting will present teachers and students with a variety of challenges which requires an expanded knowledge of the role of culture in the classroom. According to the studies of Samovar and his colleagues, here are some considerations that must be taken into account when learning or teaching in a multicultural classroom.

The first issue that should be addressed is to develop an appropriate attitude toward the differences. A culturally diverse class is likely to be composed of students who have been conditioned to learn differently. For example, students from the United States have been taught to participate actively in the learning process by asking questions and engaging in discussions, and they are therefore familiar with the activities such as debates, argumentation, public speaking skills, discussions, and critical thinking. However, students from Asian countries, such as China, Korea or Japan, tend to listen passively to teachers and take notes since they have learned that the proper classroom deportment is to sit silently, to listen, to watch, to imitate, and to memorize all the key points. Also, students from the US prefer to present information orally while students from China emphasize texts. Therefore, cultural cognition of the students in terms of learning helps educators to understand why their students do and act the way they do.

Then, it is vital to understand that different cultures have varied thinking patterns that influence reasoning, problem solving, and social interactions. Westerners generally use a linear, cause-and-effect thinking process that emphasizes logic and rationality and problems are approached through a systematic, in-depth analysis of each component, progressing individually from the simple to the more difficult. In contrast, people from China, Japan, and Korea rely on a holistic thinking pattern and problems are seen as complex and interrelated, requiring a greater understanding of and emphasis on the collective and contextual thinking. These varied patterns of cognitive processing will influence the ways that students communicate, interact with others and perform problem-solving tasks.

Finally, protocols of student-teacher interactions are another consideration in the multicultural classroom. Students from different cultures will have varied attitudes toward their teachers. For example, students from hierarchical cultures, such as Asian students, will probably see teachers as high-status authoritative figures. Therefore, students and teachers tend to interact formally, and students maintain a proper relationship of distance with teachers. In contrast to students of egalitarian cultures, such as the United States, they frequently call each other or instructors on the first-name basis, and students and teachers will likely address each other informally. Students may openly challenge the instructor, eye and physical contract can also vary.

Being aware of such cultural and individual differences, teachers will be able to interact more profitably with their learners, who are from a different cultural background. A discussion with learners is needed concerning whether they consider they work better at certain times of day, whether they prefer structured or less structured environments, to work alone, in pairs or in groups and what external figures influence their motivation to learn is likely to produce fascinating and helpful information. It should also make it clear that some learner behaviors previously interpreted as rude or disruptive may be no more than a reflection of cultural differences.

It is clear that cultural differences are to be viewed from a tolerant perspective. It is important to understand and appreciate the impact that cultural diversity has on the educational context since not all students can be taught in the same way because they are not the same. In other words, their cultures and experiences influence the way they learn and interact with their teachers and peers. Samovar and his colleague writes:

> Effectiveness in the multicultural classroom requires an understanding of the students' culturally based learning behaviors and

communication styles. In order to extend and enhance the learning experience, the competent educator will have the ability to use the richness of values, worldviews, and lifestyles represented in the students' diversity.

In a multicultural learning and teaching situation, one doesn't need to worry about cultural differences. Diversities will always exist in the classroom where the success of learning and teaching is based on the ability to be aware of differences, facilitating skills to make these differences benefit the students and the class as a whole. As it's always true that there're more similarities than differences, and mutual understanding and respect will pave the way for adjustments and indusiveness between people from different cultures.

V. Extended Reading

Young German Man Studies TCM in China
(China Daily, April 29, 2022)

According to report from *Chinanews. com*, Wu Ming (cultural transplantation name) is a young German born after 1995. Wu is a big fan of Chinese culture, such as the *Shaolin kung fu*, a traditional Chinese martial art. He has been learning traditional Chinese medicine since 2016, almost seven years. Now he is studying for his master degree at Henan University of Chinese Medicine.

As he thought some diseases can't be treated thoroughly with Western medicine, he decided to dig into TCM. Wu came to Central China's Henan province in 2015, where a profound TCM culture can be enjoyed because Henan province it is the hometown of Zhang Zhongjing, the medical sage of ancient China. After one-year of learning the Chinese language, he started to learn Chinese medicine. "TCM is one of the best-preserved aspects of Chinese culture", said Wu. He hopes to solve problems and understand Chinese culture intimately by learning TCM.

In the early stages, Wu always tasted some Chinese herbal medicine by himself, just like Shen Nong, a character in Chinese legend, who tasted most of the herbal medicine himself to know their properties and therapeutic effects. He also conquered the language barrier by learning and practicing Chinese, especially the Henan dialect, as his teachers, schoolmates, and even some patients speak with the Henan dialect in their daily conversations. Although sometimes he still has trouble distinguishing between Mandarin and the dialect, he can use the Henan dialect to communicate with others.

Without a language barrier, Wu read some of the ancient Chinese medical classics, such as *Huangdi Neijing* (*Inner Canon of the Yellow Emperor*). He believes different aspects of traditional Chinese culture interact with each other. Taking *Huangdi Neijing* as an example, it is closely intertwined with culture from *Yi Jing* (*The Book of Changes*) and Taoism, one of the ancient Chinese philosophies.

Post-class Tasks

Self-test Tasks

1. Answer the questions in your own words for key concepts and basic knowledge.

(1) What is your understanding on learning style preferences?

(2) Based on your understanding of culture shock, try to explain how to cope with culture shock.

2. Decide whether the statements are true (T) or false (F).

(1) British students who are accustomed to acquiring knowledge by listening usually expect teachers to provide explicit instructions, while Chinese teachers tend to guide and encourage students to think critically. (   )

(2) Students of egalitarian cultures may openly criticize the instructor, and eye and physical contacts can also vary. (   )

(3) If one, who teach Chinese as a foreign or second language in other

countries, has extensive teaching experience, he/she should not encounter such problems as acculturation or developing competency within the new educational system, environment or expectations inherent in that setting. (　　)

(4) Students will be uncomfortable in their learning process if teachers are less aware of the learning styles of students or regardless the needs of students. (　　)

(5) In a multicultural classroom, different atmospheres and interactive activities may also lead to culture shock among international students. (　　)

Group Work

1. Imagine you are planning to study abroad, what will you do to avoid cultural shock and to develop intercultural competence?

2. Watch the documentary film *Childhood Elsewhere*, analyze the differences in education between Finland, Japan, India, Israel, the United Kingdom and China. You may present your findings in the form of debate, role plays, speeches or talk shows, etc.

3. Share your experience of communication with international teachers at school or other educational institutions either online or off-line.

Telling China's Stories

You have been admitted as a teacher of TCSOL (Teaching Chinese to Speakers of Other Languages) and are going to Argentina in six months. When you prepare your luggage, what are you going to take with you as symbols of the Chinese culture? And how are you going to tell your Argentina students about China of today with innovations and development for the shared community of the mankind?

My Learning Reflection

1. What have I learned about Chinese cultures or myself?

2. What have I learned about other cultures?

3. What impressed me most in this chapter?

4. What still confuses me?

Chapter 9　Working in Multicultural Business Context

> **Learning Objectives**
>
> - To identify factors affecting intercultural communication at workplace;
> - To deal with the general cultural differences at intercultural workplace;
> - To master communication strategies in intercultural business context.
>
> **Pre-class Tasks**
>
> - Read the textbook and watch the concerned clips in *xuexitong* （学习通）.

Ⅰ. Lead-in Tasks

Read the following dialogue to answer the questions thereafter.

> Pablo Diaz, a Spanish executive working for a Chinese textile company in China for fifteen years had the following discussion with a Chinese employee.
>
> Mr. Diaz: It looks that some of us are going to have to be here on Sunday to host the client visit.
>
> Mr. Chen: I see.
>
> Mr. Diaz: Can you join us on Sunday?
>
> Mr. Chen: Yes, I think so.
>
> Mr. Diaz: That would be a great help.

> Mr. Chen: Yes, Sunday is an important day.
> Mr. Diaz: In what way?
> Mr. Chen: It's my daughter's birthday.
> Mr. Diaz: How nice. I hope you all enjoy it.
> Mr. Chen: Thank you. I appreciate your understanding.

Questions for discussion:

(1) Is Mr. Chen going to host the client visit on Sunday? Why do you think so?

(2) Is Mr. Diaz certain that Mr. Chen will come on Sunday? Why do you think so?

(3) If you were Mr. Chen, how would you do in this situation?

(4) What have you learned from this dialogue?

Having worked in China for years, Mr. Diaz realized that in Chinese culture, *pangqiao ceji* (旁敲侧击) i.e. beating around the bush, is a style that nurtures an implicit understanding. As he later remarked, "My Chinese colleagues would drop hints, and I wouldn't pick them up. Later when thinking it over, I would realize I had missed something important."

Therefore, speaking the same working language in the intercultural workplace doesn't necessarily ensure effective communication as there is something more that makes communication more complicated.

II. Communication Factors in Multicultural Workplace

Globalization has brought more organizations to find themselves involved in communication across cultures, between cultures and among cultures as they are doing business in foreign countries, sourcing from another country, seeking financing from another country or having an increasing multicultural workforce. Since the 80's of the 20th century China also has attracted many foreign enterprises in the form of foreign firms and joint ventures, thus becoming more international in workplace. With the turn of the 21st century, increasing Chinese firms have been going abroad for cooperation and development, therefore intercultural communication has appeared crucial in business context.

Intercultural business context refers to culturally diverse workplace environment both at home and abroad. It involves understanding other cultures, establishing relationship, processing information, making decisions, managing conflicts and so forth. Either at home or abroad, intercultural communication competence has gained more attention as people are both culturally based and cultural biased.

In addition to what have been discussed on the relationship between culture and communication in the previous chapters, there are some factors which affect the communication in intercultural workplace context. Question to be asked are as follows.

A. What Is the Corporal Culture Concerned?

Corporal culture determines the general communication modes. Same as national cultures, different cultures create their own business forms. At the heart of each organization are the goals and objectives defined by the organization, which enables the organization to focus on human activities so that everyone works with shared aims. The cultural norms facilitate the organization to manage the flow of information, people, events and energies that feed it. Organization culture is defined by Carbaugh as "a shared system of symbols and meaning, performed in speech that constitute and reveals a sense of work life; it is a particular way of speaking and meaning, a way of sense-making, that recurs in the oral activities surrounding common tasks."

When the chief executive officer (CEO) of a firm identifies its goals in public speeches for customers, shareholders, joint ventures and the government, the organization culture is presented, which generates the image of the organization to the outside.

Varying forms of international cooperation add to the domestic ones with globalization. And the apparent similarities cover up different underlying cultural approaches to do business. The staffs and workers have brought their own corporate culture to the merged one together with production, marketing, rules and norms which present their values, beliefs, attitudes and behaviors. In this way the corporate culture acts as a glue to connect employees from many different cultures as Harris and Uoran noted in 1987 that "Organizations create cultures ... to be renewed and restricted, and alter it. Culture explains the patterns of assumptions and behaviors formulated by human systems in response to their environment, whether it is a nation with its macroculture, a local community with its needs and customs, a market with consumers and supplies, or an industry with its colleagues and competitors".

There are many factors that contribute to the corporate culture. The corporate culture is developed in regard with its particular industry culture, the general business culture and the larger general culture of a country for their norms and behaviors values, attitudes, beliefs and symbols (Figure 9.1).

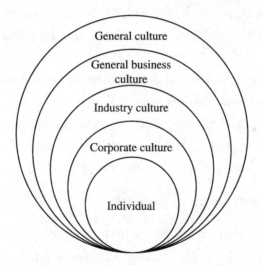

Figure 9.1 The Cultural Environment of Business People (Varner & Beamer, 2008)

On the other hand, with growing diversities of the market, the corporate culture has also to adjust to the culture of the customers in other countries, to different ethnic groups and/or religious groups in language and local cultures as well. For example, the Estee Lauder cosmetic applies several languages in its product instructions and it also launches specific marketing strategies for its individual target markets, such as China, Korea, or Europe. Other examples are France and Germany. With Algerians and Turkish immigrants in respective countries, many firms in French and Germany have developed handbooks and instructions in various languages of the workers. Managers have to adapt work rules to employees with different religious background as well, for example, time for prayers for Muslims and food in company cafeteria to Islamic dietary restrictions.

Test Your Reading 1

Decide whether the statements are True (T) or False (F).

(1) Intercultural working contexts refers to the culturally diverse workplace both at home and abroad.

(2) Corporate culture is what is unique to the individual business which has nothing to do with the local culture or the business culture. (　　)

(3) An international business establishes its corporate culture in relation to the general cultural context together with the business culture in general and the industry culture without the influence from the individual cultures of the managing group.

(4) The corporate culture also has to adjust to the culture of its local, regional and international customers as well.

(5) Intercultural competence in international business context involves understanding other cultures, establishing relationship, processing information, making decisions, managing conflicts and so forth.

B. Are There Any Language Barriers?

Language is another factor that affects intercultural business communication. English has become lingua franca of international business, but the level of fluency of each individual and the meaning of words in each culture may not always be in consistent due to varied cultural background which may lead to miscommunication as well.

Every language has its own speech patterns, idioms and metaphors that is hard to understand by people from other cultures. For example, the "*Lin Daiyu* style" is an expression that is known to Chinese people but hard to interpret for most of the English speakers. Business people from the United States use many words and idioms from sports, which may sound unfamiliar to those who don't know much of baseball or football. Clearly, the more one knows about another culture and language, the easier it will be to communicate. Therefore, when doing business in alien cultures, one has to learn the basic phrases for greeting, asking for directions, making apologies and showing appreciation and sincerity. The same is true in intercultural workplace when there are colleagues with diverse culture background.

Language functions basically in intercultural communication but language alone does necessarily make effective communication. Both management and individuals have to see to it that people from different background get along with each other. Intercultural training should be provided to employees from the top to bottom so as to facilitate the work towards a common goal, and individuals also will gain by trying to adapt to workplace with the mixed cultures.

Activity 1

Read the following case to find out the secret of success by answering the questions.

(1) In what ways does the Chinese saleswoman in the States adapt to the American business culture?

(2) How does she balance the American culture and the culture of her clientele?

> A woman from China who sells insurance in central Illinois has developed the Asian community as her major client. She has been extremely successful with that group and ascribes her success to the cultural and linguistic adaptation of American insurance practice to the values of the Asian clientele. She has business cards and brochures printed in Japanese, Chinese and Korean for her major client groups. She wants to sell insurance; therefore she works very hard at pleasing her clientele. This saleswoman has adapted to the culture of the United States in many ways: she is assertive and outgoing, and she has a good grasp of the concept of profit. She also knows, given her own background, that she must be more indirect and willing to enter into long-term relationships with her clients that in many cases go beyond a typical American business relationship. A number of her clients ask her to give martial advice for their children, act as a go-between in marriage arrangements, and help with other personal matters.

C. What Is the Organizational Structure Concerned?

The structure of firms also affects communication in the intercultural workplace context, and the ways they view organizational patterns influence their communication policies and practice. Varner and Beamer believe that there are three implications for communication based on organizational patterns, i. e. communication based on credentials, context and family orientation.

Communication on credentials is based on personal qualifications and achievements. Professional attributes such as accountants, engineers, lawyers are identifications of education degrees or job qualifications, which are regarded as portable credentials. The emphasis on portable credentials and individual achievements influences communication within a firm. People want a job that best fits their qualifications, but cultures may lead to his/her loyalty to the firm or possible mobility to other firms. In the result-oriented cultures such as the United States, most new graduates would stay with their first job for three to four years before they jump if a better opportunity comes as they would constantly evaluate their employment situation on a regular basis. As portable credentials are related to individual advancement and individual opportunities, communication will restrict on job-specific information with features of low-context communication. Most of American firms belong to this category. On the contrary, people from a culture with emphasis on relationship, commitment and loyalty will stay with the firm as long as possible, even life-long, examples are Japan, Korea and China. Communication therefore tends to be high-context as they share more information which does not need to be communicated.

Communication on context is related to loyalty and shared information. Firms organized on the basis of frame and group belonging result from the concept of household, which emphasizes importance of group over the individual. Credentials are valid within that context but don't mean much outside the context so that job mobility is limited and a certain degree of security provided. In turn the employees support the goals of the firm and put personal consideration after group ones as the system is reciprocity. Harmony in the group is considered most important. Consequently the communication styles tend to avoid open conflicts and direct confrontation which are common in individual cultures. Much more shared information is another feature of this system and communication is more high-contextualized. Seniority matters in promotions, and people would like to reach positions with fairly high status in the firm because titles matter in giving face. Within the frame or context, employees know clearly how to act and behave as they know their place; they know what to say and how to address someone, such as superiors, subordinates or strangers. Examples of this category are common in Eastern Asian cultures.

Communication on family orientation is based on the concept of family. Firms based on family orientation are ruled by the senior male member of the family. This system is more authoritarian and autocratic as it creates clear lines of communication with unique communication codes that are difficult for outsiders to decipher. When the senior manager asks for advice, family members understand that the senior member has the cultural right to make decisions. He may listen but doesn't have to do what the family members prefer to because he is the one in charge and makes final decisions. In this environment, authority is established through appropriate introductions, credentials and connections. Business in the Middle East belongs to this category as they are based on the concept of the family.

Test Your Reading 2

Decide whether the statements are True (T) or False (F).

(1) Corporate culture, language barriers and organizational structures contribute to communication styles at intercultural workplace. (　)

(2) Corporate culture is visible as a combination of the local culture, industry culture and individual culture by observing individuals of a firm in a specific culture. (　)

(3) When people speak the same working language at the intercultural workplace, there would be no problems of communication as the words used mean the same to both the speaker and the listener. (　)

(4) The organization structure of a firm influences communication in terms of credentials, contexts and family orientations. (　)

(5) Communication on credentials is more likely related to individual cultures where communication tends to be in low-context with more specific information. (　　)

(6) Most of the Middle East business is established on family basis where portable qualifications are appreciated and communication is more restricted to job-related topics. (　　)

Group Discussions 1

(1) What is the communication situation in China in general? Are there any changes after the establishment of the New China in 1949? Have there been any other changes since 1980s?

(2) What kind of corporate culture would you prefer?

Ⅲ. Communication Barriers in Multicultural Working Context

Culture is a key factor that affects communication styles in many ways for understanding, tolerance, respect and collaboration in the intercultural business context to build trust, to persuade, to express disagreements, to make decisions and to manage conflicts.

A. How Is Trust Built?

Trust, either within or between organizations is the basis for business cooperation and development, and the ways that trust is built varies across cultures.

Activity 2

Make a list of five to ten people from different areas of your life that you trust, and think about how the trust is built and what particular incidents made you trust them.

The list may include your personal relationships and other professional or business relationships. You may begin your statements with, "I trust him/her because ..."

Trust from Head vs. Trust from Heart

The type of trust one feels for one person is very different from the type of trust for another. According to Ueyer, the differences may be complicated but the major one lies in the distinction between the forms of trust: cognitive trust and affective trust.

"Cognitive trust is based on the confidence you feel in another person's achievements, skills, and reliability. This is trust that come from the head" Trust from head is built from the interactions by working together, i. e. one works well and demonstrates through work that he/she is "reliable, pleasant, consistent, intelligent and transparent".

"Affective trust arises from feelings of emotional closeness, empathy, or friendship, which comes from the heart". Trust from heart is derived from the experiences that "we laugh together, relax together, and see each other at personal level" and feel each other the same affection and empathy to each other. Think about why you trust your parents, friends or spouse, you will know that it is more related to affective trust. But in the business context, it will be more complicated, especially in business across cultures.

Case Study 1

Read the following to answer the questions:
(1) In this case, what kind of trust did Ren Jing and Jeb Bobko expect?
(2) What are the perceptions of the relationship at the beginning?
(3) What are the features of the trust that the relationship has brought about?

> Ren Jing, a thirty-five-year-old Chinese sales manager told a story when he worked in the United States. "In China, if we have lunch together, we can build a relationship that leads us to work together. But here in Houston, it doesn't work like that."
>
> Ren hadn't been looking to develop a friendship when he bumped into Jeb Bobko at the gym.

> "I was working out on the rowing machine when I asked him what time it was. We started talking and I learned that he was preparing for an upcoming month-long trip to China.
>
> We had a great first connection, and he invited me to his house for dinner several times with his wife and children and I invited him back. I got to know him and his family well. We developed a great relationship.
>
> Just by chance, his organization was a potential client for us, and I have to say that initially I thought that was great luck. But when we started discussing how our organizations would work together, I was taken aback to find that Jeb wanted to look at every detail of the contract closely and negotiate the price as if I was a stranger. He was treating me as if we had no relationship at all."

In Case 1 both parties had different expectations from this relationship which turned out hard for Ren Jing to accept. The Chinese salesman expected a trust of "heart" while Jeb Bobko treated it as trust of "head" when there were business potentials. Even though they get to know each on an amicable basis, Jeb Bobko preferred to negotiate the deal by reading the contract carefully as he believed in cognitive trust.

The Trusting Scale by Meyer is helpful in understanding the cultures in which each types of trust is nurtured, i.e. the task-based culture and the relationship-based culture (Figure 9.2).

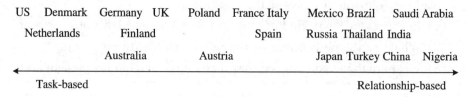

Figure 9.2　The Trusting Scale (Meyer, 2015)

As shown in the Trusting Scale, countries are rated from high task-based to high relationship-based. The further a culture falls towards the task-based end of the scale, the more people from that culture tend to separate affective and cognitive trust, and to rely mainly on cognitive trust for work relationship. The further a culture falls toward the relationship-based end of the scale, the more cognitive and affective trust are woven together in business.

As indicated in Figure 9.2, trust in the task-based culture is built through business-related activities on the practicality of the situation where work relationship are built and dropped easily. This is the trust from head which implies that "You do good work consistently, you are reliable, I enjoy working with you, I trust you."

On the other hand, trust in the relationship-based culture is built through sharing meals, evening drinks, and visits at the coffee machine and work relationships are built up slowly over a long time. This is the trust from heart which implies that "I've seen you who you are at a deep level, I've shared personal time with you, I know others who trust you, I trust you." In the task-based societies like the United States, the United Kingdom and Australia, relationships are defined by functionality and practicality while relationships in relationship-based societies are built slowly and founded not only on professional credibility but also on deeper emotional connections, which is not easily dropped once built.

It has to be noted that the center of gravity in the global business world has fundamentally shifted over the recent decades. For many years in the past, people engaged in international business have felt themselves pulled towards working in more American manners because the US dominated most world markets, and building trust in a task-based way was therefore one of the keys to success. However, the BRIC countries (Brazil, Russia, India and China), together with countries in the southern hemisphere such as Indonesia and Saudi Arabia are growing in weight, which belong to the relationship-based culture and trust from heart together with trust from head are to be combined.

Strategies to Build Trust

As trust can be built either from head or heart depending on task-based and relationship-based cultures, strategies for trust-building vary but there are general rules that can be followed both from head and heart as follows:
- seeking for common interests;
- Adjusting to the context;
- Choosing your communication medium.

Case Study 2

Read the following to answer the questions:
(1) What kind of trust has been built in this case?
(2) With the Trusting Scale find the evidence to support your answers.

> Wolfgang Schwartz, a retired Australian working successfully in Russia for over two decades, was called up by his younger successor for advice as the client seemed dragging his feet for the business. Schwartz met this client face to face after his arrival at Moscow.
>
> "The first thing I noticed when I saw him was that he was about my age — we both have white hair. So I spoke of my family, and we spent the first half hour talking about our grandchildren. Then I noticed he had a model of a fighter plane on his desk. I also flew planes in the military, and I saw this as an incredible opportunity. We spent the next hour talking about the differences between various military planes.
>
> At this point, the Russian client signaled that he had to leave. But he invited me to go with him to the ballet that evening. Now, in truth, I dislike the ballet but I am not stupid. When an opportunity this good comes along, I jump on it. The evening went beautifully and ended in a drink with the client and his wife."
>
> When they met the second day the Russian client promised the contract and Schwartz found the €2 million down payment was already in his account when he arrived at his office next Monday.

The trust in this case was constructed in relationship-based orientation. As an Australian, Wolfgang Schwartz tends to be task-based in the Trust Scale, but he was smart in looking for similarities to build trust with his Russian client who is more inclined to set up trust based on relationship. And the same age, experience as pilots, identities as grandfathers, enjoyable hours at ballet and drinks afterwards contribute to trust from heart, which explains the strategies for this contract.

Test Your Reading 3

Decide whether the statements are True (T) or False (F).

(1) Business trust is built either from head or from heart, which is related to culture specific on the basis of cultural similarities. (　)

(2) Cognitive trust is built from working together with the professional knowledge and skills without much to do with personal relationships. (　)

(3) Affective trust is established on the basis of professional interactions together with personal relationships. (　)

(4) In the Trusting Scale by Meyer, Asians, Latin Americans and Africans are more likely to built trust on relationships in general. (　)

(5) As people tend to build trust in different ways, there are no chances of establishing trust across cultures. (　)

Case Study 3

Discuss in groups to answer the questions:

(1) Referring to the Trusting Scale, what are the problems that Krooner is facing with in terms of cultures and trust-building?

(2) What are the functions of these affective relationships in such countries as Nigeria, India, Argentine, Japan and Korea? What advice will you give to him? Why?

(3) What is the traditional China like? Are there any changes in the recent decades in these respects?

> Ted Krooner, an American businessman who often travels to Latin American, complained:
>
> "I just got so exhausted on those trips to Mexico. After a long day of meetings, we go out to a restaurant and then out for more drinks. I can hang on for an hour or an hour and a half. But the evenings drag on and on and they are drinking and laughing, really having a good time ... but I feel like my head is about to hit the table. I just can't concentrate any longer."

(1) As shown in the Trust Scale, Ted Krooner is from the individualistic culture with the tendency of head-trust while his clients in the Latin American countries are more likely to be relationship-based. The Mexicans would like very much to build trust in relationship with meals, drinks and sightseeing, i.e. spending time together so as to get to know more about each other.

(2) In such countries as Nigeria, India, Argentine, Japan and Korea, people would like to trust those they know of better and more, thus trust will be set up with heart and business will be possible. It's conducive for Ted Krooner to know that being engaged in the social events pave the ways to business, therefore he would be better prepared for it so that there are chances of business.

(3) As shown in the Trust Scale, trust in China is built on the basis of relationship and it has been the tradition for Chinese people to do business with those whom they know well. But with globalization and technology, Chinese people have learned to trust those with reasons and communication has been more on credentials, which means that they are turning from relationship-based to task-based in business connections, but appreciation for relationship and trust still remain as one of the features of the Chinese culture.

When doing business with people from task-based or relationship-based cultures, there are different ways to deal with the relationships. Business people from task-based cultures prefer to be professional and effective and would get to the point right after they meet the client, discussing details one by one with firm decisions. The task-based cultures evaluate the outcome of cooperation by the contract terms and value efficiency of work, thus establishing trust from head. On the other hand, in the relationship-based cultures, business is discussed after relationships are built by socializing in amicable atmospheres, in other word, there would be no business before trust is gained from heart by establishing relationships.

When doing business with people from task-based or relationship-based cultures, trust is developed either from head or heart, attention therefore has to be paid to trust in business which requires varied ways. Being professional or showing your true self is worth of considering in business. For example, meals function differently in different cultures but people rarely resist the temptation of local delicacy, therefore consider meals carefully because lunch may be your tickets to business with relationship-based cultures as they believe trust is thus built for future cooperation. On the contrary, task-based people would regard time and energies invested in meals, drinks or recreations with business partners as waste of time. Relationship-based businesspeople would be prepared for lunch with sandwiches or hotdogs.

After-work activities have varied connotations as well. Activities after work tend to enhance relationships, which in turn ensure the business, as Meyer said, "the relationship is the contract: you can't have one without the other." Relationship-based people would spend hours on dinner or drinks after work to further relationships in relaxation without mentioning business, and they don't mind drinking to fall. But the task-based business people, when they have to be engaged in, they consider it continuation of work and remain "concentrated" as professionals, fearing being judged for doing something wrong or unprofessional.

One of German working in Japan consulted a Japanese culture specialist, "They are so formal and quiet. I wonder if I am not able to build the necessary trust, I won't get the information I need from them." The Japanese culture specialist thought for a moment before he responded with a small trace of humor in his eyes: "(the) best strategy is to drink with them ... and drink until you fall down."

It is popular to build trust by drinking across East Asia, such as China, Thailand and Korea, and a substantial drinking with customers and collaborates is a common step in the trust-building process. Or a round of Karaoke or a trip to the SPA will also do well. But in Arabian cultures where alcohol is forbidden, a cup of tea will do the same. However, in the recent decades, China has experienced changes in the ways of trust-building.

Case Study 4

What is the cultural conflict between Sarah Teebone and her French and Portuguese colleagues?

> Sarah Teebone is one of the most senior women in a company based in New York, who told of her experience as follows:
>
> "Over the past two years it happened several times. On several occasions, managers from the French and Portuguese offices have requested one-to-one meetings with me while they are in New York. But when they arrive in my office, they don't have anything specific they need to talk about. After a minute or two of social talk, I start to wonder why they wanted to meet with me, and on several occasions I have asked, "What can I do for you?" To which they replied, "I just wanted to say hello and get to know you as we will be working together in the future."
>
> Later, when emailing employees in Paris, I have often had the experience that people don't respond to my emails. Later I found it out that it is because I haven't established a relationship with that person."

This case shows how trust and relationship are established in business communication. As shown in the Trust Scale, French people are more likely to be relationship-based, who would like to have personal contacts instead of business-like ones. They would like to meet Sarah Teebone when it is possible so that they know each other better for future communication regardless of phones, emails or face-to-face talks.

Technology has made global communication easier, faster, and more effective which has taken place of some of face-to-face communication. The choice of a phone call, an email or a face-to-face discussion deserves cultural consideration when a lot of trust-building has to take place long distance.

When working with a task-based culture, a phone call, an email or face-to-face talk with "the to-the-point approach" is effective as long as the message is communicated clearly and succinctly. In the past century, business people all over the world have been advised to do international business in this way, especially with Americans.

However, it is another story to do business with those from relationship-based cultures. One has to begin by choosing a communication medium that relationship-based people prefer. People in relationship-based cultures often do not reply on emails from someone with whom they don't have prior relationship. For example, in Japan, China or Korea, it is a practical way to find someone as an intermediate in the social network in relationship with the target person. A quick call of introduction from the intermediate will work wonders in establishing a first step to a personal relationship. Consequently emails are to be answered rapidly, and phone calls will be more natural. Of course, a face-to-face talk will benefit more if time and budge allow. In relationship-based cultures such as many countries in East Asia, Africa and Middle East and some European countries such as France and Portugal, "a just-to-know-you meeting" will make connections to build trust before emails and phone calls.

Furthermore, amount of time devoted to social talks before getting down to business has also to be taken into consideration. With phones, emails or face-to-face meetings are getting popular, it differs from culture to culture in how much time spent before moving to business. In general, relationship-based cultures spend more minutes on personal talks than task-based ones. For example, it is appropriate in Saudi Arabia to call to establish the social connection first before another call a few days later to introduce the business because it would be considered a disrespectful approach in the Saudi culture to initial a call with business purpose.

Test Your Reading 4

Decide whether the statements are True (T) or False (F).

(1) Relationship trust is also referred to as affective trust or the trust from heart. (　)

(2) An intermediate in the social network in relationships with the target person is necessary when doing business in the task-based culture. (　)

(3) It is the preliminary routine to have meals, drinks or sightseeing to establish trust before formal business is discussed in Netherlands and Finland. (　)

(4) "A just-to-know-you meeting" will make connections to build trust in East Asia, Africa and Middle East and some European countries such as France and Portugal before emails and phone calls are exchanged personally. (　)

(5) Some taboos have to be taken into consideration when efforts and time are devoted to build trust with business partners from Arabian cultures. (   )

Group Discussion 2

(1) To your experience, do Chinese share some of the features of relationship-based or task-based cultures in some way? Or both?

(2) What suggestions will you offer to one of your Chinese friends, who is going on a business trip to the UK? What else if someone is going to establish a firm in Spain?

(3) Summarize the major features of trust-building in both task-based and relationship-based cultures based on the Trusting Scale.

B. What Are the Skills of Persuasion?

The art of persuasion is one of the crucial business skills that ensure the support one gets. The ways of persuading and the kinds of arguments one finds persuasive are profoundly culture-based from the philosophical, religious and educational assumptions and attitudes.

Case Study 5

Find out the problems that Karen Williams and Jens Hupert meet with.

> Karen Williams, an American engineer newly working as a research manager for a German automotive firm, was questioned repeatedly in her presentation on her foundations for her conclusion in terms of methodology and data. Jens Hupert, a German director at the same company that Williams worked for had the opposite experience in presentations when he was in the United States, who was instructed to "get to the point" before the audience would lose their attention.

The problems that Williams and Huppert met with demonstrate the cultural differences between German and American styles of persuasion as Huppert explained in the following.

"Germans try to understand the theoretical concept before adapting it to the practical situation. To understand something, we first want to analyze all of the conceptual data before coming to a conclusion. When colleagues from cultures, like the US or the UK, make presentations to us, we don't realize that they were taught to think differently from us. When they begin by presenting conclusions and recommendations without setting up the parameters and how they got to those conclusions, it can actually shock us. We may feel insulted. Do they think we are stupid that we will just swallow anything? Or we may question whether their decision was well thought out. This reaction is based on the deep-seated belief that you cannot come to a conclusion without first defining the parameters."

What Williams and Hupert experience are related to different styles of reasoning known as principles-first and applications-first.

According to Meyer, principles-first reasoning also is referred to as deductive reasoning which derives from conclusions of facts from general principles or concepts while applications-first reasoning is also called inductive reasoning, which general conclusions are reached based on a patterns of factual observations from the real life. Most people are capable of practicing both principles-first and application-first reasoning. But the habitual pattern of reasoning is heavily influenced by the thinking pattern emphasized in the cultural structure of education.

For example, in the principles-first math class students would first prove the general principle and develop a concrete formula before it can be applied to various problems. School systems in Latin Europe, (France, Italy, Spain, Portugal), the Germanic countries (Germany, Austria), and Latin America (Mexico, Brazil, Argentina) tend to emphasize this method of teaching, focusing on "why". On the contrary, in the applications-first math class, students will learn the formula first to apply to practical use of it before understanding the concept and principles. In other words, attention is on "how" to use it. School systems of Anglo-Saxon countries tend to emphasize applications-first methods, so do some Asian cultures. For example, in the math class, the students are instructed with the concept and formula before they are given exercises to apply the formula.

The same is true in the language class. Students of foreign languages in principles-first cultures are instructed with detailed grammar rules and vocabulary before they make sentences based on the rules. On the other hand, in the applications-first cultures, students are thrown with sentences in the foreign language and are encouraged to use them without much knowing about the conceptual grammatical framework.

To summarize, the principles-first style of reasoning is featured with focus on **why** something functions like this or **why** it develops in certain ways while the applications-first style of reasoning is characterized with **how** something is done or **how** the problem is solved. Consequently, as Meyer summarized, in the culture of applications-first, "individuals are trained to begin with a fact, statement, or opinion and later add concepts to back up or explain the conclusions as necessary. The preference is to begin a message or report with an executive summary or bullet points. Discussions are approached in a practical and concrete manner. Theoretical or philosophical discussions are avoided in a business context". In the principles-first cultures, "Individuals have been trained to first develop the theory or complete concept before presenting a fact, statement or opinion. The preference is to begin a message or report by building up a theoretical argument before moving on to a conclusion. The conceptual principles underlying each situation are valued."

The following scale indicates the extent of persuasion in terms of principles-first and applications-first cultures in the Western cultures.

What has to be noted is that cultural relativity is to be taken into consideration when persuasion is conducted in business with multicultural background. For example, an Egyptian would find the United Kingdom is quite applications-first when Egyptian culture is involved, but when the UK is compared with the US, the UK appears strongly principles-first (Figure 9.3).

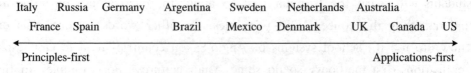

Figure 9.3　Persuading (Meyer, 2015)

In conclusion, when trying to persuade others, cultural background of the audience has to be taken into consideration in choosing the strategy of presentation. As shown in the previous case study, Williams would have explained to her German colleagues more on her foundations and data for her conclusion and recommendations, and she would appreciate the counter arguments in the deductive process as a sign of interest instead of a lack of respect.

When the principles-first and applications-first are the major differences across the Western cultures, Asians tend to have a holistic thinking patterns in contrast with the specific approach by the Western cultures. The tenet of the Western philosophies and religions is that an item can be removed from its environment and analyzed separately. For example, Aristotle would emphasize attention to a salient object, the properties of which could then be assessed and assigned a category with the goal of finding rules governing its behaviors, such as the wood and the rock as if each was a separate and isolate object for the concepts of "levity" and "gravity". Cultural theorists term it as specific thinking.

Chinese culture is characterized with the tradition emphasizing interdependencies and interconnections with a holistic thinking which resembles most of the Asian cultures. The Chinese attend to the field in which an object was located, believing that action always occurs in a field of forces that influence the action. The terms "*yin and yang*" describe how seemingly contrary forces are interconnected and interdependent. With this background, Chinese people think from macro to micro whereas Western people think from micro to macro, which can be seen in the writing of address in the Chinese language and that in English in Chapter 4.

It's easy to understand that the differences of thinking may lead to difficulty or misunderstanding when Asian and Western cultures are involved in communication. Given to the fact that both parties speak English, the Westerners may think that the Chinese are going around to the key points without addressing them deliberately. On the other hand, East Asians may experience Westerners as trying to make a decision by isolating a single factor and ignoring significant interdependencies, sometimes regardless of relationships.

Test Your Reading 5

Decide whether the statements are True (T) or False (F).

(1) The styles of reasoning known as principles-first and applications-first are employed in intercultural business context depending on the corporate culture. (   )

(2) The principles-first approach of persuasion is also known as deductive thinking pattern which focuses on why something functions like this or why it develops in certain ways. (   )

(3) The applications-first style of reasoning is characterized with how something is done or how the problem is solved. (   )

(4) Many Chinese tend to learn a foreign language with the principles-first approach by learning grammar rules in details and remembering as many vocabulary as possible. (   )

(5) In persuasion Chinese tend to think from macro to micro by presenting an overall picture with more detailed information.

Group Discussion 3

(1) Suppose you are a manager of a global team with four cultures such as Japanese, British, French and Danish, and you are going to assign the tasks among them. What are you going to do in the following contexts?

　A. Your goal is to motivate innovation and creativity;

　B. You aim at speed and efficiency.

(2) As a Chinese employee in an international company, you are to report your sales proposal to your Sweden supervisor by means of presentation on the basis of your market researches over the last two months.

　A. What kind of persuasion are you going to apply? What are the persuasive arguments?

　B. How are you going to do if you are to report to a Japanese boss?

C. How Is Disagreement Expressed?

Disagreement is inevitable in the intercultural business context. Among a team of people from varying cultures, dramatically different attitudes towards open disagreements will present, some will feel uncomfortable as loss of face, or problems remaining unsettled.

Case Study 6

Read the following to answer the questions:
(1) What makes Shen realize that she was much more Chinese than she had thought to be?
(2) What makes Shen feel she was attacked and humiliated?

> Shen Li, a Chinese as marketing manager for the French multicultural L'Oréal after earning her MBA at a prestigious European institution. Working at L'Oréal's Shanghai Office, Shen's excellent English and acceptable French gave her confidence working with her European colleagues. She recalls, "I hadn't actually registered the cultural gap between myself and my French colleagues. After all, I studied for several years abroad, and I am much more international than most people in China. I like to feel I am able to easily move from one cultural arena to another."
>
> Shen doubted about it when she was invited to Paris, presenting her ideas on tailoring a market campaign to the Chinese market. To make her points polished and convincing, she spent thirteen hours on the plane rehearsing each slide.
>
> There were twelve people at the meeting and Shen was the only non-European in the group. Her ideas were clear and her presentation has been meticulous. She started with a question about why she had chosen to change a specific color in a print ad but she was taken aback by the challenges thrown at her by her French colleagues when she explained her rationale.
>
> She felt attacked and humiliated, "But mostly I felt upset with myself," she says, "They obviously did not feel that I was the marketing expert that I claimed to be." She did her best to keep her voice steady through the presentation, but she admits, "In truth, I was almost in tears."

> Gathering her things quickly, she made a dash for the door when the meeting finally ended. To her surprise, several participants, the very ones who challenged her went up to congratulate her before she could escape, "They commented on how polished and interesting my presentation was. And at that moment, I realized I was much more Chinese than I had thought."

After Shen returned to China, she told several European colleagues about what had happened at her presentation in Paris and she later learned that students in the French school system are taught to disagree openly. Consequently, French business people intuitively conduct meetings in this fashion, viewing conflict and dissonance as bringing hidden contradictions to light and stimulating fresh thinking. On the contrary, raised in China, Shen was shocked by willingness of her French colleagues to challenge her ideas in a public forum, "In China, protecting another person's face is more important than stating what you believe is correct."

The concept of "face" exists in all societies but with varying levels of importance. In Confucian societies like China, Korea and Japan, preserving harmony by saving face for all members of the team is of utmost importance. Disagreement can be expressed either by avoiding confrontation or presenting confrontational ideas.

In the cultures of avoiding confrontation, Mayer found, "disagreements and debates are negative for the team or organization. Open confrontation is inappropriate and will break group harmony or negatively impact the relationship". For example, disagreement is not expressed openly in China, especially to superiors or the elders so as to show respect and obedience for the purpose of harmony as it's believed that group harmony exist when everyone plays his prescribed role and reinforces the role of others. Other Asian cultures such as Japan, Indonesia and Thailand are even more uncomfortable with direct disagreements than the Chinese. The Japanese Constitution states that "Harmony should be valued and quarrels should be avoided" and it is considered deeply impolite to challenge or refute another person's point of view openly or publicly as the disagreement is considered as a denial of the person himself rather than the opinion.

On the other hand, people in the confrontational cultures view that "Disagreements and debates are positive for the team or organization. Open confrontation is appropriate and will not negatively impact the relationship". People in these cultures are brought up with the idea that everyone is expected to have a different idea from everyone else. For example, French children are taught to disagree openly and French businesspeople would like to view conflict and dissonance as bringing hidden contradictions to light and stimulating fresh thinking for solutions. The following shows the attitudes towards open disagreements.

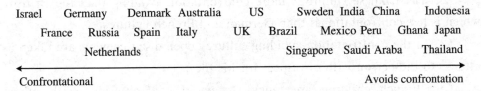

Figure 9.4 Disagreeing Scale (Meyer, 2015)

In more confrontational cultures, it seems quite natural to attack someone's opinion without attacking that person, while in avoid-confrontation societies these two are tightly interconnected as it's believed that disagreements hurt one's "face" thus violating his image, leadership and power (Figure 9.4).

Language is the indicator of confrontational or confrontation-avoiding cultures. Upgrading expressions such as " absolutely" " totally" or "completely" are more often applied to express disagreement by the confrontational cultures which will stun the confrontation-avoiding people, who will use downgrading expressions like " sort of" " kind of" "slightly" or "partially" when expressing their opinions. For example, a Chinese will say, "Maybe we could think about it slightly differently ... perhaps ... what do you think?"

Strategies dealing with disagreements are to focus on whether an open disagreement is likely to have a negative impact on a relationship by asking oneself, "Does the disagreement suggest that they are disapproving of me or just of the idea?"

It has to be noted that people from confrontation-avoiding cultures have to learn to voice their ideas more directly in English than in Chinese when communicating with people from confrontational cultures as the linguistic hints in disagreement are hard to infer for those who are used to open disagreements.

As the Bahamian proverb goes that "To engage in conflict, one doesn't need to bring a knife that cuts, but a needle that sews." With efforts, one will find many ways to encourage and learn from alternative points of view while safeguarding valuable relationships.

Test Your Reading 6

Decide whether the statements are True (T) or False (F).

(1) The Chinese culture is more confrontation-avoiding than the British, which is less confrontational than German and French cultures. (　)

(2) In the confrontation-avoiding culture, open disagreements are taken as attacks to the person with disrespect for his face. (　)

(3) French children are taught to avoid confrontations with others whenever there are disagreements. (　)

(4) "Perhaps" "maybe" or "probably" are the linguistics signs of confrontation-avoiding culture.

(5) When English is applied as the working language, it is better for people of confrontation-avoiding culture to express disagreement more directly and firmly to avoid confusion. (　)

D. How Are Decisions Made?

Decision-making goes through business routine steps, which characterizes cultural traits as well and globalization has increased awareness of the role of culture in the decision-making process. Effective multicultural corporation managers have to understand who makes decisions and how those decisions are made.

Meyer classified cultures into consensual or top-down ones in terms of decision-making. In a consensual culture, the decision making may take quite a long time, since everyone is consulted. But once the decision has been made, the implementation is quite rapid since everyone has been completely brought in and the decision is fixed and inflexible, which can be referred to as a Decision with capital D (Figure 9.5).

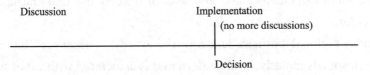

Figure 9.5 Consensual Decision-making (Meyer, 2015)

By contrast, in a top-down culture, the decision-making responsibility is invested in an individual, in which decisions tend to be made quickly, early in the process by one person. But the decision is also flexible, which is a lowercase "d", and may be easily revisited or altered and implementation can take quite a long time (Figure 9.6).

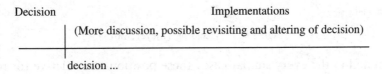

Figure 9.6 Top-down Decision-making (Meyer, 2015)

Consensus is related to decision-making as a result of agreement at different levels in varied ways. General speaking, Northeast Asians apply collectivistic process that attempts to reach an orchestrated consensus that sustain group harmony and preserves the participant's "face". In Chinese organizations, "Leader-mediated compromise" is popular, which includes data collection and analysis, canvassing subordinate for their opinions, distribution of background data, and meetings to discuss the issues. Senior members retain an exercise of personal power by ultimately making a top-down decision crafted to reflect the group's assessments and efforts. The final result is a "harmony-within-hierarchy arrangement" designed to convey a sense of shared responsibility, create cohesion, and lessen loss-of-face opportunities among the work group participants.

In the Western nations, such as Australia, Canada, the United Kingdom, the United States, decision making is more individualistically oriented, with delegated authority usually vested on one person or a small group of personnel who are expected to take full responsibility for the final decision. This type of decision making is a reflection of the strong sense of individualism, egalitarianism, independence and low level of uncertainty that characterizes the Western culture.

In today's global business lexicon, the word, "consensus" has a positive ring, which sounds inclusive and modern and is associated with other universally positive words like "empowerment". In a consensual culture decisions are made in groups through unanimous agreement while in top-down cultures decisions are made by individuals, usually the boss. The following demonstrates how cultures are positioned in terms of these two styles of decision making (Figure 9.7).

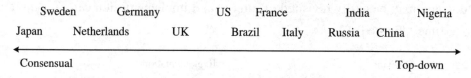

Figure 9.7 Deciding (Meyer, 2015)

As noted in the every similar case, these positions are relative for reference and specific cultures have to be discussed in relation to other factors.

As a matter of fact, both consensual and top-down decision-making processes can be effective. When working in a multicultural team, members are expected to recognize and accommodate to the styles of decision-making, and everyone is encouraged not to take himself or his own style too seriously. To avoid problems, explicit discussions and agreement on the decision making methods are necessary at the early stage of collaboration by defining whether the decision will be made by vote or by the boss so as to keep aware of the decision as a Decision or a decision. When big decisions must be made, revisit the decision-making process to make sure it is generally understood and accepted.

Test Your Reading 7

Decide whether the statements are True (T) or False (F).

(1) The "harmony-within-hierarchy arrangement" is designed to convey a sense of shared responsibility, create cohesion, and lesson loss-of-face opportunities among the work group participants. (   )

(2) Decision making in Australia, Canada, the United Kingdom, the US tend to be more individualistically oriented, i.e. one person or a small group of personnel are expected to take full responsibility for the final decision. (   )

(3) Decisions with capital D are more common in a consensual culture, which takes quite a long time with rapid implementation and decision is flexible. (   )

(4) The decision-making in a top-down culture usually is invested in an individual, which tend to be made quickly and fixed, known as "decision". (   )

(5) "Consensus" has gained a positive meaning which sounds inclusive and modern and is associated with other universally positive words like "empowerment". (   )

E. How Are Conflicts Managed?

Throughout every step of business execution at every level, there exists potential for personal and organizational conflicts. In addition to cultural differences in beliefs and values, it also varies in methods, opinions and attitudes regarding the completion of tasks and achievement of goals. These variations will naturally lead to conflicts either between employees within the team or between clients outside. More often than not, conflicts can even be caused by cultural variances that are beyond participants' awareness.

It's imperative to recognize the conflict as cultural differences or substantive disagreement and deal with them with consideration of cultural traits towards them.

As shown in the table, in the collectivist cultures like China, Japan and Korea, conflicts are regarded as undesirable as it carries the likelihood of harming interpersonal relations and can be threaded with loss of face; therefore, direct and open conflict is usually avoided between in-group members or are managed indirectly. Open disagreements are also taken as conflict because it is closely related to the person concerned thus resulting in loss of face for one or more of the group, consequently, disagreement is resolved either through lengthy discussion of the problem or private informal meetings before the formal one, at which the decision is made with no disagreement. For severe disputes, Northeast Asians prefer to have trusted intermediaries to help reach an amicable solution without face-to-face conflict as shown in Table 9.1 by McDaniel.

Table 9.1 Conflict Management/ Resolution (McDaniel, 2014)

Northeast Asia	Western Nations
(China, Japan, Korea)	(Australia, Canada, the UK, the US)
Detrimental	Beneficial
Conflict and parties connected	Conflict and parties separate
Holistic, logical analysis	Liner, logical analysis
Indirect approach	Direct approach
Confrontation avoided	Confrontation is okay
High face concerns	Low face concerns
Respected mediator	Legal actions expert mediator
More information	Less information

In such individualist cultures as most of the Western nations, to debate conflicting opinions and ideas is seen as a useful tool for airing differences and finding compromise because disagreement or conflicting ideas is not related to the person who owns them, and face concern is individual-based regardless of others or the group. Moreover, professional conflict situation are considered separated and apart from one's relationship with the other party. The severe incidents will go to legal counsel of professional third-party mediation for solution.

In view of the above, there are many aspects that may lead to miscommunication, misunderstanding or conflicts, but the ways of handling conflict is culture-based. When working in multicultural context, it's imperative to be aware of the culture variations in building relationship, making decisions, expressing disagreement and managing conflicts so as to fit into the global engagement in workplace.

Test Your Reading 8

Decide whether the statements are True (T) or False (F).

(1) There are always conflicts in workplace no matter it is monocultural or multicultural. (   )

(2) In collectivist cultures, professional conflicts are separate from personal relationships. (   )

(3) Ways to handle conflicts are culturally based therefore intercultural competence is the key factor to manage conflicts smartly. (   )

(4) People in the individualist culture tend to resolve conflicts face-to-face. (   )

(5) Changing topics and avoiding confrontation are likely to maintain harmony for personal faces in the Eastern cultures. (   )

Ⅳ. Extended Reading

How China, Along with Other BRICS Nations, Turns Aspirations for Common Development into Reality
(Xinhua, June 25, 2022)

Beijing, June 25 (Xinhua) — Traversed by the lower Amazon River flowing into the Atlantic Ocean, the state of Para has one of the busiest port in Brazil and a wealth of mineral and agricultural resources. However, for decades, local people have been struggling to harness the natural abundance to their well-being.

Lack of funds on large projects such as roads and transmission lines delayed the state's integration with markets in the country's rich south. And local residents have limited access to smaller infrastructure that more directly helps them to earn money.

Aline Feitosa, a mother of four who runs a small bar in Brasil Novo in Para state, is upset about muddy roads in the city. "People didn't come to my bar because of the mud in the rainy season and the dust in the drought season."

People-centered Cooperation

In 2018 and 2021, the New Development Bank (NDB) granted loans of over 200 million US dollars to build roads, bridges as well as sanitation and communication facilities in Para.

In the city of Brasil Novo, local authorities managed to pave some 17 km of roads with the NDB funds and construction is expected to finish by August. The renovated roads and a well-designed drainage system will not only renew the community but also improve health condition of the residents as dust in summer used to flow into every single household and cause many to suffer from serious respiratory diseases.

Promoting the welfare of the people has always been a major area of the BRICS cooperation over the past 16 years. Since its inception in 2015, the NDB has become an essential part of the BRICS mechanism tasked with promoting joint development with a people-centered philosophy.

The bank has approved more than 80 projects regarding transportation, energy and other types of infrastructure with a total portfolio of some 30 billion dollars to improve people's well-being.

"We should respond to people's concerns, pursue the larger interests of all countries, and steer global development to a new era to deliver benefit to all," Chinese President Xi Jinping said in his keynote speech at the opening ceremony of the BRICS Business Forum delivered on Wednesday.

His appeal for a people-centered approach resonates with the group's aspirations for shared growth and with his economic philosophy, known as "Xiconomics", which has guided China's own development and promoted its global cooperation programs.

Running a convenience store by an already paved road in Brasil Novo city, 38-year-old Giziany Fernandes Pereira has been enjoying public benefits brought by the project. "It's much more comfortable now as you don't get your feet dirty as soon as you leave the house. Sales increased at my store because of easier accessibility. It is a wonderful program," she said.

The NDB loans have played a significant role in poverty reduction in the state, said Ruy Cabral, secretary of Urban Development and Public Construction of Para. "The NDB has been a spectacular partner for the facilities that it has provided us to date, and we hope to extend this partnership further."

High-quality Partnership

"Standing at the crossroads of history, we should both look back at the journey we have traveled and keep in mind why we established BRICS in the first place, and look forward to a shared future of a more comprehensive, close, practical and inclusive high-quality partnership so as to jointly embark on a new journey of BRICS cooperation," Xi said in his speech at this year's BRICS summit on Thursday.

Twenty-one years ago, when British economist Jim O'Neill coined the term "BRIC" — an acronym for Brazil, Russia, India and China, it read like investment advice, pointing to promising prospects for emerging economies. With South Africa added in 2010 to become the "BRICS," the group, representing a quarter of the global GDP, 18 percent of global trade and 25 percent of the world's foreign investment, has become a vital platform for strengthening cooperation among the five countries and a vital force for improving global governance.

Trade cooperation among the BRICS countries has seen remarkable progress over the years. In 2021, the total volume of trade in goods of BRICS countries reached nearly $8.55 trillion, up by 33.4 percent year on year, official data shows. Meanwhile, China's trade with other BRICS countries totaled 490.42 billion dollars, a yearly jump of 39.2 percent which outpaces the overall growth of China's foreign trade over the same period.

In April, a string of online sales campaigns themed "Buy BRICS" was held in the southeast Chinese coastal city of Xiamen. In a two-week shopping spree, Chinese consumers bought 270 million yuan ($40 million) worth of products from the other four BRICS countries, according to statistics provided by e-commerce platforms.

In 2017, when China hosted the 9th BRICS Summit and other events in Xiamen, Xi suggested that BRICS partners bear in mind their long-term goals rather than narrowly look at growth rates, advance structural reforms and explore new growth drivers and paths to achieve "better quality, more resilient and sustainable growth." His suggestion has proven to be significant to the expansion of BRICS cooperation into more areas. Cooperation in the digital economy has brought tangible benefits to the populations of the BRICS countries, with further digital transformation across various industries expected in the future.

Committed to developing an industrial Internet and digital manufacturing, the five countries seek to build an industrial cooperation network to promote the circulation of capital, goods, talent and technology by facilitating an open and inclusive trade and investment environment. The BRICS members have ample human resources and great economic potential and occupy a pivotal position in the global industrial chain, said Rosalia Varfalovskaya, a leading researcher at the Russian Academy of Sciences.

Amid a complicated international environment, the BRICS cooperation mechanism will play an important role in dealing with external challenges and propelling global economic growth, she said.

BRICS Plus for Sustainable Development

As part of this year's BRICS agenda, the group inaugurated a vaccine research and development center online in March. The five countries vowed to make vaccines accessible and affordable for developing countries as global public goods.

The immunization gap is one of the concerns shared by BRICS countries. To solve such global challenges, the group agreed to promote the expansion of global governance into more developing nations, a move West-dominated organizations are reluctant to take.

Besides vaccines, China and other BRICS countries have been providing other "public goods", such as development experience and technology, particularly to the Global South, to bolster sustainable development. For example, China is helping many African countries, such as Mozambique, to develop modern agriculture with the help of the China-developed BeiDou Navigation Satellite System and unmanned equipment.

In 2017, China steered its involvement of other nations into what has become known as "BRICS Plus" by building a more comprehensive partnership with other developing countries and organizations to turn BRICS into a more influential platform for South-South cooperation.

Gu Qingyang, an associate professor at the Lee Kuan Yew School of Public Policy of the National University of Singapore, said BRICS cooperation has made remarkable progress in green development, science and technology, the digital economy and infrastructure construction.

Expanding BRICS cooperation will be more conducive to rallying developing countries to tackle global challenges, Gu said. Last year, Xi launched the Global Development Initiative (GDI), calling on all countries to forge a united, equal, balanced and inclusive global development partnership. For the Chinese leader, development holds the key to solving various difficult problems facing the world.

In his speech delivered at the 14th BRICS Summit on Thursday, Xi underlined the implementation of the UN's 2030 Agenda for Sustainable Development and the building of a global community of development. He pledged to work with BRICS partners to add more substance to the GDI and contribute to more robust, greener and healthier global growth.

Inclusiveness highlighted in China-proposed initiatives is what the world needs, Gu said, adding that China and other BRICS countries share a broadly similar world view with other developing countries that believe in inclusive development, multilateralism and mutual benefit.

Elaborating on global cooperation for common development, South African Ambassador to China Siyabonga CyprianCwele said, "in order to sustain peace, there must be development."

"What struck me was the message from President Xi Jinping that we should rise to the challenge as leaders, and be able to work together to deal with all these emerging challenges,"Cwele said.

Xi's remarks remind us of "love for our people that they should grow, develop and live a prosperous life,"Cwele added.

Post-class Tasks

Self-test Tasks

1. Answer the questions in your own words.

(1) What are the factors affecting communication in multicultural workplace?

(2) How is trust built for business across cultures?

(3) Where are conflicts likely to take place in intercultural business contexts?

2. Decide whether the statements are True (T) or False (F).

(1) The greatest influence of globalization has been in the education.

(2) Knowledge of cultural differences and competent intercultural communication skills are fundamental to success in the multicultural business community.

(3) Business protocols, such as greetings, personal appearance, communicative behaviors, etc., vary across culture.

(4) Leadership and management styles are not marked by cultural differences.

(5) Culturally instilled individualism or collectivism can influence how employees are motivated and rewarded.

(6) Decision-making has nothing to do with cultures.

(7) The attitude towards conflicts and how they are managed is the function of culture.

(8) Language skill is the only factor that is absolutely critical when working in multicultural organizations.

Group Work

1. Find two or three online articles that discuss globalization of the economy/marketplace, Work with others to identify three positive and negative cultural aspects related to globalization.

2. With the help of your teachers, find out the decision-making styles in one of the foreign venture in your city by interviewing its managing staff.

Telling China's Stories

Draft a report with an example to your class on its corporal culture, company structure, and communication styles, decision-making or conflict-managing approaches by watching the documentary *American Factory* by Barack Obama, the former President of the United States about the Chinese enterprise owned by Cao Dewang in the US.

Or you may also do the same by visiting one of the joint ventures or foreign-invested enterprises in your city on its acculturalization with the Chinese culture and laws together with the relationship with the local people.

My Learning Reflection

1. What have I learned about Chinese cultures or myself?

2. What have I learned about other cultures?

3. What impressed me most in this chapter?

4. What still confuses me?

Chapter 10 Leaning to Become Intercultural Communicators

Learning Objectives

- To recognize barriers and their reasons in intercultural communication;
- To identify efforts to deal with conflicts in intercultural interactions;
- To improve intercultural awareness and skills as intercultural communicators.

Pre-class Tasks

- Read the textbook and watch the concerned clips in *xuexitong* (学习通).

Ⅰ. Lead-in Tasks

Case Study 1

Analyze the quotes by those who have attended intercultural learning or consulting events and present your ideas to your peers by answering the following questions:

(1) What are the problems in each intercultural interaction?
(2) Why has it happened in that way?
(3) How can something be done to solve the problems or to prevent the similar incidents happening?

> **Quote A.** There is really almost nothing in this country that works properly. I know it is wrong, but I can't help comparing everything here with the situation at home. It frustrates me because the people themselves don't seem to understand how much better things could be if they put their minds to it (By a Western European voluntary worker in Africa).
>
> **Quote B.** I just can't believe how lazy the British are. Unmotivated, unenthusiastic and disinterested. Now I just do not employ any at all, full stop. We only have Australians or New Zealanders working in the London office (By a US manager of the London subsidiary of a New York-based architecture firm).
>
> **Quote C.** Since I came to live in Thailand, I have realized just how shallow and meaningless life in Europe is. The stress and anxiety that everybody suffers ... and for what? I'll never go back (By an Irish doctor on assignment in Thailand).
>
> **Quote D.** Working for a music business our people are much the same all over the world. In fact, we look for the same type of people when recruiting. As a result, cultural differences don't come into the equation (By a French HR manager).

Quote A is by one of voluntary workers in an African missionary trip from Western European countries who saw his/her role as educating others in the "right" way to do things and exhibited denial to the local culture. The missionaries did not conceive that others would operate successfully in a completely different value system, or that there are merits and logic in other ways of doing things. When the missionaries saw others doing things differently, they did not see the influence of culture. Instead, they made rush judgments about the individuals concerned, or drew on out-of-date and prescriptive stereotypes. These judgments, based on their own conception about how things "should be done", would classify other people as backward, unsophisticated or uneducated.

Quote B shows that the expats keep contacts with people from other cultures at a minimum. The US manager of the London subsidiary of a New York-based architecture firm was an expat who exhibited defense and denials to the local culture. He recognized that there were, indeed, other ways of doing things, but in general he judged these ways to be vastly inferior to "his ways of doing things" back home. They continued to make faulty attributions or interpretations from his own ethnocentric perceptions with negative judgments attached even though he had recognized the existence of another set of values and behaviors. In the world of these expats, there was limited space for shades of gray, leaving little empathy with other cultures.

Quote C exemplifies stereotyping from neo-natives. The Irish doctor on assignment in Thailand was a neo-native, who, in an opposite response to the expats in Quote B, would begin to assume that everything about the new culture is good and nothing is bad. Moreover, they would stereotype or deride their own cultural background as inferior since they have little time for comprehensive understanding of two cultures and almost everything seems black or white for them.

Quote D talks about what a global citizen is like. The French HR manager is one of global villagers who exhibit minimization. Global villagers admit to a minimal number of differences between cultures, but only at superficial behavioral levels. They consider that "underneath, everyone is the same" and are unsympathetic to the idea of deeper differences in assumptions and values. They believe that what works here will work anywhere else with some simple superficial modifications. In the world of global villagers, differences can be sidelined or ignored, and global villagers see it as their role to identify similarities. They may even disparage those who seek to acknowledge cultural variations as being bigoted or prejudiced.

To sum up, these quotes illustrate that intercultural communication is something more than language communication between people, which actually involves more cultural factors than expected. Intercultural conflicts take place because people are cultural animals with their own perceptions and values, and at the same time, the limited knowledge of other cultures prevents awareness and intention to understand the similarities and differences between one and others. What's more, people are usually unconscious of the fact that they are engaged in communication with someone whose culture is different in some way since they have been accustomed to the ways of thinking and communication, which is taken for granted as the only right way to react to others.

II. Understanding Barriers in Intercultural Communication

In addition to different languages people speak, there are a number of barriers in intercultural communication as they perceive the world and interact with each other in different ways. When English is applied as lingua franca in communication, there are some common barriers due to diverse languages, norms, symbols and values, etc.

A. What Is Ethnocentrism?

Ethnocentrism is defined by William Summer as views in which one's own group is the center of everything and all others are scaled and rated with reference to it. In other words, ethnocentrism is the tendency to think of one's own culture as being the center of the world, or the belief that one's own culture is primary to all explanations of reality.

With ethnocentrism, each group nourishes its own pride and vanity, boasts itself as superior, exalts its own divinities, and looks with contempt on outsiders. Therefore one would compare his own culture to others in such elements as religion, behaviors, language, customs, and norms, ennobling his own culture while degrading those of others. Ethnocentrism, as a result, shapes a social sense of identity which is narrow and defensive, usually involving stereotypes of members in other cultures by judging them exclusively from one's own perspective.

Activity 1

Search online the world maps published by China, Japan, Italy, the United States, Tanzania and Iceland, finding the location of China in terms of the host country with your explanations to your classmates.

As shown in Activity 1, ethnocentrism can be subtle although it is regarded as a natural reaction with a series of negative connotations. But overt ethnocentric lens often end in vanity, pride, contempt of outsiders as well as the belief in one's own inherent superiority, leading to stereotypes, racism or culture shock. For example, in most Asian countries, chopsticks are common for meals while forks, knives and spoons in the United States, thus some people from these cultures may view the use of hands for food in some cultures as unclean, barbaric or improper, such as India and parts of Africa. The attitudes towards food from other countries also indicate whether one is open or ethnocentrism. Some foods are considered as weird and gross, for example, Chinese preserved duck eggs, cheese from Europe, dried squids or fried crickets from Oaxaca of Mexico as the result that they are evaluated with criterion in terms of one's own norms, values or beliefs.

Activity 2

Do you think the lady on the left is ethnocentric (Figure 10.1)? Share your reasons with your classmates.

Figure 10.1 Is It Ethnocentric?

In addition to violence as shown in the above, ethnocentrism is shown subconsciously in many other fields, such as in movies and other sources of entertainment which is often portrayed in a humorous, light-hearted manner. For example, in the movie *The Godfather*, racial slurs, discriminatory opinions about African-Americans, and the male domination was depicted in the Italian community and ethnocentrism befitted the times the story was set in. The same is true in the movie *The Big Fat Greek Wedding*, in which the ethnocentric belief was shown in a positive and acceptable way that being Greek is the one and only acceptable way of living.

Ethnocentrism can be seen on a large scale in business and at the workplace. For instance, a business owner might yell at his foreign employees, calling them "stupid" because of their different races, cultures or values that are different from the owner himself/herself. An entrepreneur based in a developed country may refuse to merge with a company originated in a developing country because he/she believes that the latter is inferior to his/her own in some ways. Consumer ethnocentrism has become much more common with globalization as a result that purchasing foreign goods is criticized to be unpatriotic because it is assumed that it helps foreign economies instead of supporting the domestic ones.

Ethnocentrism can be demonstrated in various degrees. Low ethnocentrism reflects the lack of sensitivity in verbal and nonverbal interactions when dealing with others who are different. Moderate ethnocentrism reflects attempted language or dialect switching in the presence of out-group members with displayed nonverbal inattention to accentuate in-group connection and avoidance of out-group members. High ethnocentrism refers to the use of verbal sarcasms, racist jokes, hate-filled speeches or physical violence to marginalize or obliterate the existence of out-group members.

As nobody is immune from ethnocentrism in one way or the other, it does harm to intercultural communication to some extent. To overcome ethnocentrism, one needs to develop empathy, i.e. to become capable of seeing things from the point of view of others. Briefly speaking, empathy in intercultural communication enables one to transform cultural positions, consciously going beyond their cultural conventions and constraints to comprehend and experience what others feel in their cultural situations, and reacting with proper verbal and nonverbal means so that cultural relativism thus is developed.

Cultural relativism refers to the attitudes that one would try to understand cultural practices of other groups in the cultural context of others instead of judging a culture by one's own standards on what is right or wrong, strange or normal. Figure 10.2 shows responses to fried insects by ethnocentrism and cultural relativism.

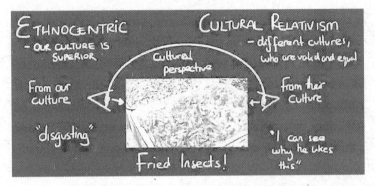

Figure 10.2 Different Comments on Fried Insects

As shown by the remarks in the above figure, the ethnocentric may think that "Fried crickets are disgusting!" refusing to explore further about the dish. However, cultural relativism is demonstrated by asking "Why do some cultures eat fried insects?" In this way one will be informed that fried crickets or grasshoppers is a famous regional cuisine as healthy food for thousands of years in Oaxaca of Mexico because it is full of protein.

Test Your Reading 1

Decide whether the statements are True (T) or False (F).

(1) Everyone is ethnocentrism to some extent as he/she is accustomed to the ways of life based on his/her own cultural values. (   )

(2) Ethnocentrism is same as patriotism in some way therefore it is good for intercultural communication. (   )

(3) It has nothing to do with ethnocentrism when someone switches

language from one to another in the presence of other people (not for the purpose of translation). (   )

(4) Prejudice, racism and wars may result from ethnocentric points of views. (   )

(5) Ethnocentrism can be reduced by developing empathy to cultural relativism. (   )

(6) Intercultural communication is interfered with ethnocentrism because it implies that other cultures are not respected. (   )

B. What Are Stereotypes?

Stereotyping refers to the means of organizing images into fixed and simple categories to represent an entire collection of human beings. It comes from perceptions or beliefs held by some people about other groups or individuals based on previously formed opinions and attitudes.

Stereotyping, defined by Frank Fitzpatrick, is part of a natural cognitive process of categorization, in which people organize and simplify what they experience and relate this to previous knowledge through mental shortcuts in order to structure and make sense of what happens around them. This will lead to fixed attitudes and prejudices, which may reduce others to exaggerated representations and influence how people approach intercultural interaction.

Case Study 2

Who is the surgeon?

> A father and son were hurt in a car accident in which the father was pronounced dead, and the son was taken to the hospital for an operation. Upon seeing the boy on the table, the surgeon said, "I can't operate on him. He is my son".

Yes, the surgeon is the mother of the boy. It may seem embarrassing not to get the answer right away because this riddle is meant to be tricky by playing on the image of surgeons who are stereotyped males. Thus, many women are discouraged from entering the surgical profession due to what a surgeon should look like and what occupations are proper for women.

These unconscious stereotypes include implicit assumptions. For example, white people may be associated with more positive traits or LGBTQs (the acronym for lesbians, gays, bisexuals, transgender and queers) with more negative traits. A stereotype may be the idea that a male is a better leader than a female, or that the overweight is lazy, or the homeless are drug addicts, or that black and Latino males are violent or criminals or that Chinese are good at math and Kungfu, etc.

While all stereotypes are generalizations, not all generalizations are stereotypes. Generalizations are necessary in intercultural communication as they help anticipate, sort and make sense of new information and sensations experienced in intercultural situations. Generalizations become stereotypes when all members of a group are categorized as having the same characteristics, which can be related to any type of cultural membership, such as nationality, religion, gender, race, or age. For example, conservative and gentlemen-like English people, demonstrative and talkative Italians, or music-loving and masculine Latinos are stereotypes.

Stereotypes may sound positive or negative. For example, a positive stereotype would be "Participants from Country Y are good students" or "Host families in Country Z are great hosts to participants." They, however, tend to be more negative stereotype than generalizations, which are typically inflexible and resistant to new information, and often lead to prejudice and intentional or unintentional discrimination, for example, "People from Country A are superficial."

Activity 3

Read the following statements to classify the stereotypes in terms of gender, cultures, or groups of individuals.

> (1) Girls are not good at sports.
> (2) Men are geeks who spend too much time on the computer or reading.
> (3) Italian or French people are the best lovers.
> (4) Asians like to eat rice and drive slowly and they are good at math.
> (5) Americans are generally considered to be friendly, generous, and tolerant, but also arrogant, impatient and domineering.
> (6) All blonds are unintelligent.
> (7) Punks, who wear Mohawks, spikes, chains, are a menace to society and are always getting in trouble.
> (8) The elderly have health issues and behave like children.

Stereotypes would impede intercultural communication in that they repeat and reinforce beliefs until they are taken for "truth", failing to specify individual characteristics which keep people from being successful communicators because they are over-simplified, over-generalized, and/or exaggerated. Even they seem "positive", they are harmful in some way. For example, the myth of the "model minority" in the US has attached itself broadly to people of Asian descendants. However, not every Asian is an ace student or inexhaustible employee. Even framed as "positive," stereotypes of certain groups are of negative effects, ignoring differences between individuals.

Stereotypes seem similar to generalizations which are different. Cultural generalizations are awareness and knowledge of the cultural patterns to which one belongs, such as nations, ages or genders, etc. to provide the basis for understanding other cultures and their subcultures or co-cultures by categorizing members of the same group for similar characteristics, which are flexible for the incorporation of new cultural information. They are a type of hypothesis, or a guess of what people expect to encounter when they interact with people from a certain culture. This flexibility subsequently leads to increased cultural curiosity and awareness for improvement of intercultural relationships.

Cultural generalizations are the base for more information about individuals from other cultures, which, however, are not applied to everyone within a culture group as cultural stereotypes. For example, that "People from Country

X tend to have an indirect style of communication" helps build cultural awareness for individual differences.

Activity 4

Read the following passage and identify the stereotypes about Brazil contained in it.

> Back in 1995, I studied abroad for six weeks in Rio de Janeiro, Brazil on a language and culture immersion program. I was only 19 years old and had hardly spent any time outside of my home country, the United States. While I fell in love with Brazil immediately, there were certain things that shocked me about how my host family lived.
>
> For example, the elder of the two daughters worked in a bikini store and was about my age. As a welcoming gift, she gave me a Brazilian bikini. I couldn't believe how skimpy it was! I felt naked wearing it on Copacabana Beach, and my tan lines showed just how much more conservative my previous bikini had been.
>
> I was also surprised that my host family had a maid who came every day to cook and clean for them, and yet, judging by my own standard of living in the US, they didn't seem to be very wealthy. They didn't have a VCR or cable TV, both of which I viewed as necessities. It's funny to look back now at how I viewed the world back then.
>
> In the years since I have rejected the consumerist culture I grew up in and try to live a minimalist lifestyle. I have also returned to Brazil to explore more about the country, not just Rio de Janeiro but also São Paulo and many other cities. I was afraid that it wouldn't live up to my memories of it, but instead, I loved it even more the second time around.

Test Your Reading 2

Decide whether the statements are True (T) or false (F).

(1) Stereotypes are helpful in building up cultural generalizations in

intercultural communication as long as they are positive. (   )

(2) People tend to generalize as it helps learning and reasoning and cultural generalization serves as basis for more information about individuals. (   )

(3) Positive stereotypes are encouraging in intercultural communication as they state something true. (   )

(4) Stereotypes are over-simplified, over-generalized, and/or exaggerated assumptions about a certain group of people in terms of nationalities, races, genders or regions. (   )

(5) Personal experiences, media and literature are the sources of stereotypes which are held as unbiased beliefs. (   )

C. What Are Prejudices?

Different from stereotypes as beliefs, prejudices are the negative attitudes and feelings toward an individual solely based on one's membership in a particular social group. Prejudices are formed on the basis of a number of factors including the sex, races, ages, sexual orientations, nationalities, socioeconomic status, and religions. Some of the most well-known types of prejudice include: racism, sexism, ageism, classism, homophobia, nationalism, religious prejudice and xenophobia.

Activity 5

Discuss the following questions with your classmates.

> Give an example when you felt that someone prejudiced against you. What caused this attitude? Did he/she display any discrimination behaviors and, if so, how?

Prejudice is based on stereotypes which are of a strong influence on how individuals behave and interact with others, particularly with those who are different from them, even unconsciously or without realizing that they are under the influence of their internalized prejudices. When one hold prejudicial attitudes toward others, he tends to view everyone who fits into a certain group as being "all the same", painting every individual who holds particular characteristics or beliefs with a very broad brush, failing to really look at each person as a unique individual.

Common features of prejudices include negative feelings, stereotyped beliefs, and a tendency to discriminate against members of a group. For instance, prejudice may cause fear of resentments towards someone from a particular group. Gordon W. Allport identified expressions of prejudice in speaking ill of someone from a target group, "You cannot trust people of color" or avoiding interactions with a certain group, "Stay away from people who are not of a certain blood." Prejudice is also illustrated by depriving a member of a particular group of his rights of education, employment or others. A prejudiced person may also resort to physical attacks, such as burning or destroying a group's possessions. Finally, prejudice is demonstrated through extermination or physical violence in attempts to destroy a particular culture, such as Jewish Holocaust or the genocide in Kenya. Some prejudice may come from naming of something, for example, the various names of the virus of 2019 has resulted in some prejudice against Asians or Chinese before COVID-19 is officially designated by the World Health Organization (WHO).

Prejudice often operates out of one's awareness, which one is frequently unwilling to admit. These implicit biases are unexamined and sometimes unconscious but real in their consequences. They are automatic, ambiguous, and ambivalent, but nonetheless biased, unfair, and disrespectful to the belief in equality. There is one indirect measure of prejudice frequently used in intercultural communication research by assessing nonverbal behaviors such as physical closeness. People are observed and measured how far away the person sits when taking a seat on a chair near someone else from a different racial or ethnic group. Those who sit farther away are assumed to be more prejudiced toward the members of the group.

Case Study 3

Read the news extracts below and highlight any evidence of prejudiced attitudes. Then answer the questions following each extract.

> **News Extract 1**
>
> More than 7,600 viewers complained about racism on the reality show *Celebrity Big Brother*. Viewers complained that the contestants of *Big Brother* were racially abusing the Bollywood star Shilpa Shetty. They claimed that Shetty, from India, was being victimized and bullied. Shetty, 31, broke down in tears after allegedly being taunted about her skin color, accent and cooking.
>
> (1) What is the prejudiced attitude?
>
> (2) Who is the prejudice directed towards?
>
> **News Extract 2**
>
> Sky Sports presenters Andy Gray and Richard Keys have been accused of sexism after making several comments about a female referee, called Sian Massey. They commented on her understanding of the offside rule during a Premier League match. The commentators believed their microphones were switched off but were actually recorded making remarks such as:
>
> "Somebody better get down there and explain offside to her."
>
> "Can you believe that? A female linesman. Women don't know the offside rule."
>
> (1) What is the prejudiced attitude?
>
> (2) Who is the prejudice directed towards?

In News Extract 1, racism is the prejudiced attitude on the reality show *Celebrity Big Brother*. The contestants of *Big Brother* were racially abusing the Bollywood star Shilpa Shetty. And the prejudice is directed toward Shilpa Shetty from India, the Bollywood star, since she was being victimized and bullied about her skin color, accent and cooking.

In News Extract 2, sexism is the prejudiced attitude. Andy Gray and Richard Keys, the Sky Sports presenters, made comments on a female referee, showing their prejudice against female linesman. And Sian Massey, the female referee, was doubted about her understanding of the offside rule just because of her gender.

Why is there prejudice? Everyone belongs to a specific gender, race, age, and social economic group which provide a powerful source of their identity and self-esteem. These groups serve as one's in-groups to which one identifies with or belongs. An out-group is one that individuals view as different from themselves or a group that they do not belong to. Perceiving others as members of in-groups or out-groups is one of the most important perceptual distinctions that people make. People often feel strongly connected to their in-groups, especially when they are centrally tied to their identities and culture so that in-group favoritism is developed, i.e. the tendency to respond more positively to the people from their in-groups than they do to the people from out-groups because they often feel a strong sense of belonging and emotional connection to their in-groups.

When prejudice occurs, stereotyping, discrimination, and bullying may also result and in many cases, prejudices are based on stereotypes.

D. What Is Culture Shock?

"Culture Shock" was first mentioned by Kalvero Oberg in 1960, who defined that "Culture shock is precipitated by the anxiety that results from losing all our familiar signs and symbols of social communication. These signs or cues include the thousand and one ways in which we orient ourselves to the situations of daily life." To put it simple, culture shock is an unpleasant reaction to being faced with a foreign culture, i.e., it happens when an individual is away from his/her own home culture.

Culture shock is a phenomenon that one experiences when he/she moves from one place to another with different rituals, ceremonies etc. Anyone who spends some time abroad, such as tourists, exchange students, sojourners, expatriates, migrants and refugees, would have experienced culture shock, which is often the deeper cultural difference in mindset, customs and interpersonal interactions that trigger the phenomenon and turn cultural transition into a struggle.

Culture shock may result from a range of things, both big and small, such as unfamiliar greetings and hand gestures, different food, language barriers, getting lost in a new city or making a cultural faux pas, which lead to symptoms, such as confusion, anxiety, depression, frustration, loneliness, and homesickness. It is found that when one is displaced from his/her home culture in loss of common experiences and familiar surroundings, he/she will experience varying degrees of consequences, for example, the physical reactions as insomnia or headache and pains in body as a result of time zone changes, or colds and stomach bugs due to foods and bacteria, or anger and aggression toward the new culture, or even total withdrawal from the culture.

In general, culture shock is a feeling of disorientation and unease in a new and unfamiliar cultural environment as a result of relocation, which has been widely recognized that there are four different stages, i.e. honeymoon, crisis, recovery and adjustment, as presented in form of the "U-Curve". However, it is noticeable that the four stages cannot be precisely isolated from each other and not everyone passes these stages automatically (Figure 10.3).

The honeymoon stage as the first stage of culture shock often lasts for several weeks or even months. This is an euphoric phase when one is fascinated by the exciting and exotic aspects of the new life, such as sights, smells, paces of life and cultural habits. At this stage everything new is exciting, interesting and different to the familiar situations, thus mannerisms are seen as something good and special and it is exciting to meet new people who behave different in the home country and are found hospitable and friendly. Therefore, one is quick to identify similarities between the new culture and his/her own, and differences in the new culture lead to motivational push or the volition to face new things for more about the country and its culture. As a result, smells or sounds in the new location appear interesting and the same nuisance back home will be found amusing and charming, such as a traffic jam.

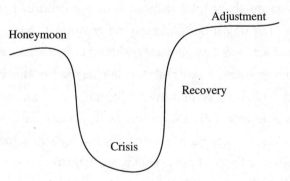

Figure 10.3 The "U-Curve" of Culture Shock

Unfortunately, "honeymoon" will be replaced by **the crisis stage** as the next stage, also known as disenchantment stage, which is characterized by frustration and anxiety, hitting around the three-month mark although it can be earlier for some individuals. It is time of difficulties or offensive and disconnected situations that appear with language problems or other barriers as the excitement gradually disappears.

In the crisis stage, one experiences disappointment, feeling sad about things that do not work at first try with the simple things setting them off. For example, he/she may not remember the way back to the new home because the street signs are confusing, or he/she cannot fathom how and what to order in a restaurant, all of which lead to lack of motivation, making him/her feel that everything seems to be awful. Furthermore, minor differences are handled as catastrophes, leading to massive stress and frustration. For example, he/she may find the local people cold, thus prejudice is developed. At last, he/she starts to miss his/her friends and family back home by idealizing the life there. Some typical symptoms of this stage are disorientation, homesickness, mental and physical illness, and feelings of rejection, sense of misunderstood or even withdrawn from staying aboard.

The crisis stage comes to an end as **the recovery stage** begins around six to twelve months, where life gradually gets better and routine sets in. Then the individual begins to increase understanding for the other culture, getting more familiar with the local ways of life, food and customs. It is time for him/her to know how to behave in order to get along with the culture and natives. He/she has got to know more about the background of the culture, understanding how and why it works the way it does because the emotional stage is over so that he concentrates more on new knowledge. By this point he/she may have made a few friends, having learned some of the languages for the local culture and being motivated with success in return. In spite of some difficulties at this stage, he/she is able to handle the problems in a more rational and measured way, and misunderstandings do not automatically lead to stress or frustration, rather, they often end in funny situations which can be laughed away. Acceptance and adjustment slowly take place with everything being more objective.

Finally, **the adjustment stage** arrives, also known as the adaptation stage or the bi-cultural stage, when one feels no longer isolated and lonely and is accustomed to the new routines and friends, and he/she feels comfortable in the new country and better integrated, i.e. he/she has successfully adapted to the new way of life. Now it is possible to identify oneself with the host culture and exploring new differences do not affect him in a negative way anymore. And he/she solves upcoming problems in a more host culture oriented way and he/she becomes attached to the host country a second time and enjoys living with the current situation. While he/she may never get back to the heightened euphoria he/she felt during the honeymoon stage, he/she has now gained a strong sense of belonging and finally feels at home in the new environment.

Test Your Reading 3

Decide whether the statements are true (T) or false (F).

(1) In the U-Curve model of culture shock, there are four stages, including the crisis stage, the honeymoon stage, and the adjustment stage and the recovery stage. (　)

(2) In the honeymoon stage, everything new is exciting, interesting and different to the own and familiar situations, and mannerisms are seen as something good and special. (　)

(3) In the crisis stage, people experience disappointment, feeling sad about things that do not work at first try. (　)

(4) In the adjustment stage, life gradually gets better and routine sets in. And one begins to increase understanding of the other culture and becomes more familiar with the local ways of life, food and customs. (　)

(5) In the recovery stage, known as the adaptation stage or the bi-cultural stage, people are used to their new daily activities and friends and become attached to the host country a second time and enjoy living with their current situation. (　)

Actually, there are additional phases relating to disappointment at abandoning the familiar new environment to re-entry shock of the home environment when one returns to home culture. A re-entry shock, also called reverse culture shock, happens once again when one goes back home after living abroad for an extended period shown in the "W-Curve" model (Figure 10.4).

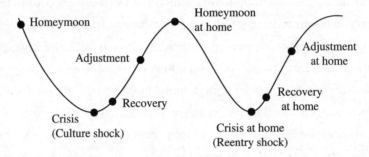

Figure 10.4　The "W-Curve" Model of Culture Shock (Kovaleski Alison, 2013)

At first, one feels excited about returning home, but soon he/she may realize that life back home is no longer what he/she has known about, which he/she feels no longer belong to as his/her family, friends and even the world has changed and moved on without him/her. He/she feels like a stranger at his/her own home, disappointing at that the newly learned customs and tradition are not applicable at home country, which causes discomfort and psychological anguish. Therefore, he/she begins to feel frustrated, lonely, depressed and angry, missing the host culture and friends there and looking for ways to return.

Reverse culture shock may take place for minor changes in life. For example, when one is used to the measurements of time and weight of the host country, he/she takes the same to the home country by stating that "The dental appointment is 15:00 on Monday" instead of "3 o'clock on Monday afternoon." Another example is the opening hours of shops. Some Chinese students returned from European cultures would like to finish grocery shopping on Friday because shops are closed at weekend and holidays in Europe, which is different from China.

Long-term travelers, digital nomads, exchange students or anyone who is going abroad may face these stages of reverse culture shock at some point. In such cases, the main difference is that the cultural environment is familiar, although their experience of it may not be the same as they remembered. In this sense, culture is not in question, but changing circumstances and a contextual approach to this phenomenon would help reveal what features of the environment are different and in what way the individuals have changed in terms of how they view their identities. This would re-iterate the cognitive and affective processes in relocation and culture shock.

Culture shock experience is full of ups and downs like an emotional roller-coaster and it is helpful to note that everyone getting to a new culture will undergo all of these stages. In fact, some will skip stages or rush through them while others may experience certain stages of cultural transition more than once or in a different order. However, an individual will have to go through the whole process of crisis and adjustment all over again, gradually adjusting to life at home, and things seem more normal and routine, even though not the same any more. In this way one incorporates the new experience and knowledge in life and career.

To sum up, culture shock is a rather nerve-wrecking phenomenon, a sense of anxiety, nervousness and alienation caused by being exposed to an alien environment and culture. It is natural that new environment, a different culture or a new language might mix up complicated feelings to trigger emotions, which an individual may not experience at home. However, it is an essential part of the transition process, which is a willingness to work through intercultural communication as the first step towards integration.

Test Your Reading 4

Decide whether the statements are true (T) or false (F).

(1) Culture shock takes place when one is away from the familiar home culture, being exposed to different one. (   )

(2) When one experiences culture shock, there are usually four stages, i.e., the honeymoon, the crisis, the recovery and the adjustment, each of which happens in the same order and for the same period of time. (   )

(3) The reverse cultural shock occurs in the same order as the first culture shock to the same degree. (   )

(4) One is more bi-cultural with experience of culture shock as life in a foreign country enables him/her more comprehensive and inclusive of both the

host and home culture.

(5) More knowledge of other cultures and skills of communication with open mind will help reduce the effect of culture shock so that intercultural communication competence will increase as well. (   )

Activity 6

Classify the stages of culture shock that the couple experienced by filling Table 10.1.

> One of the more prominent times I've experienced culture shock while traveling when my husband and I moved to Korea to teach English. We signed a year contract to teach English in a town called Changwon on the southern coast of Korea. When we moved to Korea, it was my husband's first time outside of the United States and my second time.
>
> We had no idea what we were getting ourselves into but we were ready for an adventure! Upon arriving in Korea, we were met by the director of the school who had hired us and we soon found out how much of a language barrier we were going to be dealing with.
>
> We were thrown into teaching right away and were given 3 days with the previous teachers to learn about the school, how to teach our classes, Korean culture, where and what to eat, and how to get around.
>
> The first couple of weeks were a whirlwind of new, confusing, but exciting things. A situation that sticks out to me the most was that I had a very hard time eating because I couldn't use chopsticks and forks were nowhere to be found! I can now confidently say I am a chopstick pro, and I can even read Hangul (Korean writing.)
>
> Moving to Korea was one of the best choices my husband and I have ever made, and we are so glad we had the experience (and culture shock) of a lifetime!

Table 10.1 Stages of Culture Shock

Phases/Stages	Phenomenon/Statements
The Honeymoon	
The Crisis	
The Recovery	
The Adjustment	

Ⅲ. Developing Intercultural Competence

Intercultural communication is a process of interactions in which people from different backgrounds face with various barriers or difficulties, and there are efforts for people of varied cultures to overcome these barriers for goals of effectively and appropriately intercultural interactions.

A. What Are the Attitudes towards Cultural Differences?

It is accepted that intercultural communication competence is composed of different elements. Deardorff proposed three constituent elements of intercultural competence, i. e. attitudes, knowledge and skills. With globalization, the ultimate goal of cultural learning is to understand more cultural groups by mastering the common rules of intercultural communication to improve intercultural awareness and enhance intercultural communication competence.

Case Study 4

Identify the reasons why this meeting does not attain the expected goals.

> At a meeting of a Japanese firm with a Dutch company, the Dutch company brought about a proposal in which they saw great potentials, expecting a positive reaction or constructive counter-proposals from the Japanese partner. After the proposal was presented, the Japanese party expressed how they deemed it a nice idea and thanked the Dutch partner for their efforts with smiles and nodding, which the Dutch company therefore took as confirmation, looking forward to their further steps for the project. However, the Dutch company waited long enough without any communication from the Japanese firm on the project. As a matter of fact, the Japanese firm was not engaged with the collaboration because the project was not agreed upon which was not verbally expressed to proceed.

This case demonstrates that the business relationship will be improved when both companies are capable of understanding each other culturally to cope with the conflicts in intercultural miscommunication.

In this case, there is confusion and miscommunication between the Dutch and Japanese for the project or possibly deterioration of the business relationship because they come from different context cultures which affect their ways of communication. Generally speaking, Dutch people are direct when communicating, while Japanese people tend to be implicit in expressing their ideas. According to E. T. Hall, Japanese culture is considered as a higher context culture, in which harmony in communication is valued with implicit expression that the listener is responsible to interpret what is said or expressed nonverbally. On the contrary, the Dutch belongs to what Hall ranked as low-context culture where people tend to communicate in direct ways that the speaker is responsible for clear expressions. In this case, when the Dutch had presented their ideas, it seems to both parties that the position is clear. On the part of the Japanese firm, it is more acceptable to express appreciation without mentioning disagreement to the project, which is supposed to be inferred from the verbal statements. However, the Dutch is looking forward to further discussion on or objection of the project in concise and straightforward statements.

In addition to the communication differences, the Japanese firm and the Dutch one may not be aware that their counterpart doesn't share the same nonverbal behaviors, working codes or values. For example, nodding in the Dutch culture indicates agreement while the same in Japan and other Asian cultures simply means "I'm listening." Or they may neither have equivalent intercultural knowledge nor get accustomed to working in a culturally diverse environment. Or they may not obtain the essential skills needed to put the intercultural knowledge into practice.

There are three ways to cultivate intercultural communication competence, i.e. to foster attitudes that motivate people, to discover knowledge that informs people, and to develop skills that enable people.

To foster attitudes those motivate oneself means to develop the intercultural awareness. Intercultural awareness enables to have an understanding of both one's own and other cultures, and particularly the similarities and differences between them, which help transform potentially frustrating experiences into teachable moments, as the following example shown.

In June 2015, Eleanor Hawkins, a British tourist was arrested in Malaysia because she stripped herself naked, along with several others, on the top of a mountain which the locals viewed as sacred. This might have been overlooked had there not been an earthquake a few days later, which the locals put down to the mountain spirit being angry with the group of tourists. In the UK, stripping off is not a big deal, which is more likely to raise a laugh than to offend a few. However, it is quite another thing in Malaysia and Eleanor Hawkins returned home sadder and wiser with her trip cut short.

Activity 7

Study the following information about intercultural awareness in Table 10.2 and identify which level you are at.

Table 10.2 Four Levels of Intercultural Awareness

My way is the only way	People either do not know, or do not care, that there is any other way of doing things. This can be seen in small children, who are often stunned when they hear people talking another language because it has never occurred to them before that anyone might not be the same as them.
My way is the best way	People are aware that other people do things differently, or have different beliefs, but they don't think that's appropriate. Their way is not the only way, but it is unmistakably the best. This worldview could be called the "colonial" approach: one will show other people how to do it his or her way because it is the best thing for other people.
There are several ways, my way and others	People have a clear understanding that there are other world views, and that different people behave and believe differently. They make no judgement about the relative merits of these views as a whole, but recognize that different cultures and views may have different merits. They are willing to bring together the good from several different aspects in a synergistic way.
Our way	People are brought together to create a new, shared culture, which has new meaning for everyone.

The following tips are helpful in develop intercultural awareness:

• Admit that one doesn't know. It is the first step towards learning about other cultures when one acknowledges that he/she is ignorant.

• Develop an awareness of one's own views, assumptions and beliefs, and know well how they are shaped by his/her culture. Questions like "what do I see as 'national' characteristics in this country?" or "Which 'national' characteristic do I like or dislike in myself?"

• Do not make judgments. Ask neutral questions and clarify meaning before assuming what one knows what is going on by collecting information.

• Listen attentively and observe carefully. Pay close attention to what is said and what are the nonverbal cues in the context and try to understand with empathy.

B. What Is Needed as Knowledge?

Discovering knowledge that is informative will help build one's intercultural awareness. That is to say, to find out the cognitive styles and the ways how one learns. Bennett suggested the cognitive style consists of the preferred patterns of "gathering information, constructing meaning, and organizing and applying knowledge". The cognitive style of some cultures focuses more on tasks in analytic and objective thinking with details and precision in the form of inner direction and independence while others focus on relationships over tasks and things in concrete and metaphorical thinking for a group consciousness and harmony.

Learn a new Language. It is by means of language that values, ideas, and thoughts are exchanged between people from different cultures. In order to reduce the communication gap in language differences, one needs to learn the host language or one of the international languages, for example, English. However, that is not to say that one needs to sign up for a language course to communicate with every person around them. They may attend some special training programs, which are organized to improve speech tendency and language frequency. A few key phrases, including greetings and thanks, can go a long way to show that people are paying attention and want to engage with others in a more personal way. Most importantly, one has to learn how to pronounce others' names correctly. It is seen as insensitive to mangle others' names as the language is unfamiliar. When unsure about the proper pronunciation, it is polite to ask the person how to get it right.

Understand one's own culture. Self-awareness is the first step for effective intercultural competence and it is important to realize how culture has programmed to define people. Try to find out answers to the following questions: What kinds of behaviors do people see as appropriate and acceptable? Do they like to communicate directly or let them read between the lines? Do they like obedience or seek arguments from other people? All these factors and many others determine how their interaction style has been shaped by their own culture.

Learn other cultures. The more people try to learn about and understand the culture of the person they wish to communicate with, the better will be their intercultural competence as a skill. Before people give their personal opinion on what is wrong and what is right, it is important that they listen to the ideas and opinions of others, observe the verbal as well as no non-verbal cues as they communicate, and try to find out what it reflects by learning more about their cultural behaviors and practices. This will help people avoid misunderstandings caused by cultural clashes.

C. What Are More Skills to be Developed?

Another part of intercultural communicative competence is to develop skills that enable people, which include the ability to empathize, accumulate cultural information, listen, resolve conflicts, and manage anxiety.

One needs to develop intercultural empathy, which is essential in building a good relationship for a smooth intercultural communication. When one is engaged in intercultural communication, he/she usually exhibits his empathy by applying knowledge about his own and others' cultures and consciously shifting into a third culture. He/she empathizes or takes another person's perspective in order to understand and be understood across cultural boundaries. In addition, he/she goes beyond personal boundaries, trying to learn about the experiences of others who are different so as to know others better with an empathetic eye. Here are some ways to develop one's empathy.

Understand others. This is to sense others' feelings and perspectives, and take an active interest in their concerns. In this way one needs to tune into emotional cues. That is to say, one has to listen well, paying attention to non-verbal communication and picking up subtle cues almost subconsciously to find out what it reflects by learning more about cultural behaviors and practices. And he/she also has to show sensitivity to understand others' perspectives.

Leverage diversity. Leveraging diversity means being able to create and develop opportunities through different kinds of people, recognizing and celebrating that people all have something different. Leveraging diversity does not mean that one treats everyone in exactly the same way, but that he/she tailors the way to fit with those in communication to needs and feelings. With this skill he/she respects and relates well to others, regardless of different backgrounds. As a general rule, one sees diversity as an opportunity, for example, diverse teams work is much better than homogeneous ones. When one is good at leveraging diversity, he/she also challenges intolerance, bias and stereotyping wherever there are, creating a respectful atmosphere.

In general, one needs to know himself/herself, including his/her own culture, attitudes, and even communication styles in order to deal with the barriers in intercultural communication. And he/she also has to consider the physical and human settings of intercultural communication, including different timing, physical setting and customs. As a result, he/she will learn to appreciate similarities and respect differences between cultures and develop empathy and have an open mind and be flexible.

Activity 8

Read the incident to answer the following questions.
(1) Do you find any intercultural barriers in this incident?
(2) How would you explain the reasons for the intercultural barriers?
(3) What tips would you give to Sarah Marshall to overcome cultural barriers?

> Sarah Marshall is the head of the business development group at a US-based law firm. Recently she was assigned the task of winning a contract for a new project with the Colombian government. She felt confident that the company would win the contract even though she was competing with teams from Spain and France because Sarah had quite a lot of background information on the proposed project and on the packages her competitors were offering.
>
> On the basis of the information and her organization's extensive resources Sarah drew up a proposal that was time and cost-effective with a presentation based on convincing data and a persuasive argument. After arriving in Bogota, Sarah personally made the sales pitch in which she detailed all the relevant facts, highlighted the various ways forward and made a clear recommendation of the best solution. However, she eventually lost the project to the Spanish team even though her Columbian counterparts acknowledged the quality of her proposals.

Living in an interconnected world with a growing focus on being more globally-minded, it is positive to pursue a path of global citizenship. Global citizens see themselves as part of an emerging world community, being committed to helping build this community with shared values and goals. In the shared community, they respect and value diversities by working together with efforts to achieve social development goals where global citizens participate at all levels, from local to global, taking responsibilities for their actions and interactions with members of their own community and communities abroad.

To become a global citizen, one needs to be creative, flexible, dedicated and proactive. One needs to be open minded in order to learn more about the world. An international travel is a good way which may not be available for everyone at all times but the Internet provides virtue opportunities where people visit specific countries or cultures, learn and understand their experiences with clicks or taps. People from varied cultures may understand others better by connecting across the world to share and contrast their life experiences. What's more, one has to be open-minded in order to learn more about themselves. As they learn more about the world and themselves, they will see some changes in mindsets, discovering new interests to explore. Global citizenship is developed by knowing what other people care about and what they want to offer to the world in communicating with people from other cultures.

In summary, culture is one of the key factors of one's perception and interpretation of his/her surroundings. It is quite natural to face some barriers when one communicates with people from other cultures, either in one's home country, or studying, working or travailing in another country. In any case, one is to have confidence in the possibility to overcome such barriers as cognitive barriers, stereotyping, ethnocentrism and cultural shock by having information about the given country and culture in advance, joining some cultural adaptation programs as well as having new experiences by living in that culture.

IV. Extended Reading

My Experiences of Culture Shock

I remember when I first came to the US as an exchange student in 2008. I stayed five months in Georgia and the first thing I loved was the muscle cars, skyscrapers in Atlanta, free-refills and the best BBQ.

During my first trip to the US, I realized how bad public transport is built. Teenagers can't be mobile without owning a car. As an exchange student, I could not own the car. My host family was busy most of the time which caused me being dependent on someone with a car. In Europe, this isn't the problem since you can easily move with public transportation to anywhere.

At the end of 2018, I moved to South East Asia to spend the winter here. I traveled to Indonesia, Taiwan, and Vietnam before but now I moved to Thailand and I stayed for several months. Within Thailand, I stayed in different islands. I learned a few words in Thai, joined Muay Thai classes, went to eat local food and rent accommodation with locals. If you know the drill, this stage will take only a few days.

As a kid, I moved with my mum and sister from the Czech Republic to Austria, where I pursued my studies and stayed for another 12 years. I learned the language, went through the school system and adapted to the Austrian culture. Although I don't feel like 100% Austrian I am very comfortable with the Austrian culture and its traditions.

I remember when I came back from my exchange semester in the US. I had difficulties to talk German again as for five months I barely spoke German. Upon arrival, I also realized that nothing has changed, while I changed, which caused a certain disappointment. Eventually, I coped with my feelings and adapted.

Post-class Tasks

Self-test Tasks

1. Answer the questions in your own words.
   (1) What are the barriers to intercultural communication?
   (2) Give examples of ethnocentrism in addition to those mentioned in the text.
   (3) How are stereotypes developed?
   (4) What are the functions of empathy?

2. Fill in the table of the proposed phases of culture shock (Table 10.3).

Table 10.3 Four Phases of Culture Shock

Honeymoon	
	A second phase characterized by frustration and anger with the new environment and feeling of inadequacy in adjusting due to unfamiliarity with contextual factors.
Recovery	
	The final phase which is characterized by full adjustment to the new cultural milieu.

3. Decide whether the statements are True (T) or False (F).
   (1) Barriers of intercultural communication are the problems arising in contacting people with different cultural backgrounds when neither side understands the others' cultural rules. (   )
   (2) Stereotyping is positive since it refers to the means of organizing images into fixed and simple categories that people use to represent an entire collection of people. (   )

(3) Ethnocentrism is necessary to build one's confidence in his culture because it is the tendency to think of one's own culture as being the center of the world, or the belief that one's own culture is primary to all explanations of reality. (   )

(4) Culture shock is not a big issue since everyone will overcome it sooner or later. (   )

(5) In general, intercultural communication competence refers to the comprehensive competence to communicate successfully with people of other cultures. (   )

(6) From the natural connection between culture and language learning, Deardorff defined intercultural communication competence as the ability to develop targeted knowledge, skills and attitudes that lead to visible behaviors and communication which are both effective and appropriate in intercultural interactions. (   )

(7) Intercultural communication competence is not important since people will communicate well naturally in whatever language. (   )

(8) If one wants to have high intercultural communication competence, he/she needs to have such skills as listening, observing and evaluating, analyzing, interpreting and relating, and critical thinking. (   )

(9) The three sides of the ABC Model represent the corresponding aspects of cognition, affection, and behavior of intercultural communication competence. (   )

(10) In order to communicate well with people from different cultures, one needs to learn others' cultures and understand one's own culture at the same time. (   )

4. Analyze Figure 10.5 and write down your suggestions of removing ethnocentrism or encouraging ethnorelativism.

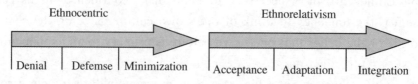

Figure 10.5 Ethnocentric and Ethnorelativism

Group Work

1. Find examples of barriers in intercultural communication in your life. If you do not have the experience of intercultural communication with people from other countries, you may find some examples of communication in movies or literature.

2. Read the following case and consider what suggestions you would offer to Lin and Tom with the help of ABC Model.

Lin, a Chinese oversea student in the U.S. has treated his American friend Tom several times, and at long last Tom invited Lin to his home one day. Tom told Lin to get there at 3 pm. Lin thought they could chat and have a meal together. He gave Tom a Chinese calendar and a bottle of Chinese white wine. Tom only took out a dish of nuts, a plate of bread and a bottle of wine. After two hours' chat, Lin found there was no hint of a meal and said goodbye to Tom. Tom only gave Lin a box of chocolate as a present for the New Year. Lin felt unhappy and Tom felt confused.

Telling China's Stories

Movies are the effective means to learn about cultures of other countries. Introduce some Chinese movies to the international students of your university, or friends from other cultures and try to discuss the intercultural differences shown in these movies and in the movies.

My Learning Reflection

1. What have I learned about Chinese cultures or myself?

2. What have I learned about other cultures?

3. What impressed me most in this chapter?

4. What still confuses me?

References

Chapter 1

[1] ALDER N J, GUNDERSON A. International dimensions of organizational behaviors [M]. 5th ed. Mason: Thomas South-Western, 2008.
[2] ALLPORT G W. The nature of prejudice[M]. Reading: Addison-Wesley, 1954.
[3] BYRAM M. Intercultural competence in foreign languages: the intercultural speaker and the pedagogy of foreign language education [C]//The Sage handbo[4]　ok of intercultural competence. Thousand Oaks: Sage Publications, 2009: 321-332.
[5] CARDINER H W, KOSMITZKI C. Lives across cultures[M]. 4th ed. Boston: Allyn and Bacon, 2008.
[6] COLLIER M J. Researching cultural identity: reconciling interpretive and postcolonial perspective, in communication and identity across cultures[M]. Thousand Oaks: Sage Publications, 1998.
[7] CROSS S E, HARDIN E E, GERCEK-SWING B. The what, how, why and where of self-construal[J]. Personality and Social Psychology Review, 2011,15(2): 142-179.
[8] DAI X D, CHEN G M. Intercultural communication competence: conceptualization and its development in cultural contexts and interactions[M]. Newcastle Upon Tyne: Cambridge Scholars Publishing, 2014.
[9] DEARDORFF D K. Identification and assessment of intercultural competence as a student outcome of internationalization [J]. Journal of International Education, 2006, 10(3): 241-266.
[10] DEARDORFF D K. The Sage handbook of intercultural competence[M]. Thousand Oaks: Sage Publications; 2009.
[11] FERRARO G, ANDREATTA S. Cultural anthology: an applied perspective[M]. 8th ed. Belmont: Wadsworth Cengage Learning, 2010.
[12] FLEXNER S B, HAUCK L C. Random house dictionary of the English dictionary[M]. 2nd ed. New York: Random House, 1987.
[13] GIDDENS A. Ruanaway world: how globalization is reshaping our lives[M]. New

York: Routledge, 1999.
- [14] HALL B J. Among cultures: the challenge of communication[M]. 2nd ed. Belmont: Thomas-Wadsworth, 2005.
- [15] HALL E T. Silent Language[M]. New York: Anchor Books, 1990.
- [16] ONWUMECHILI C, NWOSU P O, JACKSON II R L. Straddling cultural borders: exploring identity in multiple Reacculturation [C]//Intercultural communication: a reader. 14th ed. Boston: Cengage Learning, 2015: 92-104.
- [17] SAMOVAR L A, PORTER R E, MCDANIEL E, et al. Communication between cultures[M]. 9th ed. United States: Cengage Learning, 2017.
- [18] TING-TOOMY S, CHUNG L C. Understanding intercultural communication[M]. Los Angeles: Roxbury, 2005.
- [19] TING-TOOMY S. Identity negotiation theory: Crossing cultural boundaries[C]// Theorizing about intercultural communication. Los Angeles: Sage Publications, 2005: 212.
- [20] WOOD J T. Communication mosaics [M]. 7th ed. Boston: Wadsworth Cengage Learning, 2014.
- [21] 戴晓东. 跨文化能力研究[M]. 北京:外语教学与研究出版社, 2018.
- [22] 高一虹. 跨文化交际能力的"道"与"器"[J]. 外语与外语教学, 1998(10): 27-31.
- [23] 高永晨. 中国大学生跨文化交际能力测评体系的理论框架构建[J]. 外语界, 2014(4): 80-88.
- [24] 孙有中. 外语教育与跨文化能力培养[J]. 中国外语, 2016(3): 17-22.
- [25] 许力生, 孙淑女. 跨文化能力递进:交互培养模式构建[J]. 浙江大学学报(人文社会科学版), 2013(4): 113-121.
- [26] 张红玲. 跨文化视角下的中国:外国专家的中国文化故事[M]. 上海:上海外语教育出版社, 2016.
- [27] 张红玲, 姚春雨. 建构中国学生跨文化能力发展一体化模型[J]. 外语界, 2020(4): 35-44.

Chapter 2

- [1] ANDERSEN K E. Introduction to communication theory and practice[M]. Menlo Park: Cummings, 1972.
- [2] BARLEY G, PEOPLES J. Essentials of cultural anthropology[M]. 3rd ed. Boston: Wadsworth Cengage Learning, 2014.
- [3] FERRARO G, ANDREATTA S. Cultural anthropology: an applied perspective [M].

8th ed. Belmont: Wadsworth Cengage Learning, 2010.
[4] HALL B J. Among cultures: the challenges of communication[M]. Orlando: Harcourt Colleage, 2002.
[5] HALL E T, HALL M R. Understanding cultural differences [M]. Yarmouth: Intercultural Press, 1990.
[6] HALL E T. Beyond culture[M]. Garden City: Doubleday, 1976.
[7] HALL E T. The silent language[M]. New York: Doubleday & CO, 1959.
[8] HUNTERA, SEXTON J. Contemporary China[M]. New York: Martin's Press, 1999.
[9] KLUCKHOHM C. Mirror for man[M]. New York: McGraw-Hill Inc, 1959.
[10] LUSTIG M W, KOESTER J. Intercultural competence: communication across cultures [M]. 5th ed. Shanghai: Shanghai Foreign Language Education Press, 2007.
[11] MATSUMOTO D, FRANK M G, HWANG H S. Nonverbal communication: science and applications[M]. Los Angeles: Sage, 2013.
[12] NEWMAN D M. Sociology: exploring the architecture of everyday life[M]. 3rd ed. Los Angeles: Sage Publication, 2013.
[13] NOLAN R W. Communicating and adapting across cultures: living and working in the global village[M]. Westpoint, CT: Bergin and Garvey, 1999.
[14] SAMOVAR L A, PORTER R E, MCDANIEL E, et al. Communication between cultures[M]. 9th ed. Boston: Cengage Learning, 2017.
[15] TING-TOMME S, CHUNG L C. Understanding intercultural communication[M]. Los Angeles: Roxbury, 2005.
[16] TRIANDIS H. Culture and social behaviors[M]. New York: McGraw-Hill, 1994.
[17] WANG R, ZHANG A L. Bridge between minds: intercultural communication[M]. Chongqing: Chongqing University Press, 2018.
[18] WOOD J T. Communication mosaics [M]. 7th ed. Boston: Wadsworth Cengage Learning, 2014.
[19] WOOD J T. Interpersonal communication: everyday encounters[M]. 7th ed. Boston: Wadworth Cengage Learning, 2013.

Chapter 3

[1] ADLER N J, GUNDERSON A. International dimensions of organizational behaviors [M]. 5th ed. Mason OH: Thomson South-Westerns, 2008.
[2] ADLER N J, JELINEK M. Is "Organization culture" culture bound in culture, communication, and conflict: readings in intercultural relations[M]. 2nd ed. Boston:

Pearson, 2000.

[3] ADLER N J, JELINEK M. Is "Organization culture" culture bound? [J]. Human Resource Management, 2006, 25(1):73-90.

[4] ANDERSON P A, HECHT M L, HOOBLE G D, et al. Nonverbal communication across cultures[C]//Cross-cultural and intercultural communication. Thousand Oaks: Sage Punlications, 2003:73-80.

[5] DRZEWIECKA J A, DRAZNIN N. A polish Jewish American story: collective memories and intergroup relations[C]// Intercultural communication: a reader. 11th ed. Thompson-Wadsworth: Cengage Learning, 2005:73.

[6] GAO G, TING-TOOM S. Communicating effectively with the Chinese[M]. Thousand Oaks:Sage Publications, 1998.

[7] GELFAND M J. Differences between tight and loose cultures: a 33-nations study[J]. Science, 2011, 332(6033):1100-1104.

[8] GUDYKUNST W B. Bridging differences: effective intergroup communication[M]. Thousand Oaks: Sage, 2001.

[9] HALL E T, HALL M R. Understanding cultural differences [M]. Yarmouth: Intercultural Press, 1990.

[10] HAUSMANNN R, TYSON L D, BEKHOUCHE Y, et al. The global gender gap index [M]. Geneva: World Economic Forum, 2013.

[11] HOFSTEDE G, HOFSTED G J, MINKOV M. Cultures and organizations: software of the mind[M]. 3rd ed. New York: Mc Graw-Hill, 2010.

[12] HOFSTEDE G, HOFSTED G J. Culture and organizations: software of mind[M]. New York: Mc-Graw Hill, 2005.

[13] HOFSTEDE G. Culture's consequences: comparing values, behaviors, institutions and organizations across nations[M]. 2nd ed. Beverly Hills: Sage, 2001.

[14] MINKOV M, HOFSTED G. Hofstede's fifth dimension: new evidence from the world values survey[J]. Journal of Cross-Cultural Psychology, 2012, 43(1):3-14.

[15] MINKOV M. Cultural differences in a globalized world [M]. United Kingdom: Emerald, 2011.

[16] OETZEL J, TING-TOOMY S, CHEW-SANCHEZ M I, et al. Face and face work in conflicts with parents and siblings: a cross-cultural comparison of Germans, Japanese, Mexicans, and U.S. Americans[J]. Journal of Family Communication, 2003, 3(2):67-93.

[17] SAMOVAR L A, PORTER R E, MCDANIEL E, et al. Communication between cultures[M]. 9th ed. United States: Cengage Learning, 2017.

[18] SCHNEIDER L, SILVERMAN A. Global sociology: introducing five contemporary societies[M]. 5th ed. Boston: McGraw-Hill, 2010.

[19] 老子. 道德经[M]. 许渊冲,译. 北京:五洲传播出版社, 2012.

Chapter 4

[1] ABRANTES A M. Euphemisms and cooperation in discourse[C]//Power without domination, dialogism and the empowering property of communication. Amsterdam: John Benjamins, 2005: 85-103.

[2] CARROLL J B. Language, thought, and reality: selected writings of Benjamin Lee Whorf[M]. Cambridge: MIT Press, 1956: 212.

[3] HALL E T. The silent language[M]. New York: Anchor Books, 1979.

[4] SAMOVAR L, RICHARD E P, EDWIN R M, et al. Communication between cultures[M]. 9th ed. Boston: Cengage Learning, 2015.

[5] SAPIR E. The status of linguistics as a science[J]. Language, 1929, 5(4): 207-214.

[6] SCHULTZ E A, LAVENDA R H. Cultural anthropology: a perspective on the human condition[M]. 8th ed. New York: Oxford University Press, 2012.

[7] SOLOMON, THEISS J. Interpersonal communication: putting theory into practice[M]. New York: Routledge, 2013.

[8] YULE G. The study of language[M]. 5th ed. Cambridge: Cambridge University Press, 2015.

[9] 王蓉,张爱琳. 跨文化交际[M]. 4版. 重庆:重庆大学出版社, 2018.

Chapter 5

[1] HALL E T. The silent language[M]. New York: Doubleday & Company, 1959.

[2] HARGIE O. Skilled interpersonal interaction: research, theory, and practice[M]. 5th ed. London: Routledge, 2011.

[3] SAMOVAR L A, PORTER R E, MCDANIEL E R, et al. Communication between cultures[M]. 9th ed. Boston: Cengage Learning, 2017.

[4] SINGH N N, MCKAY J D, SINGH A N. Culture and mental health: nonverbal communication[J]. Journal of Child and Family Studies, 1988, 7(4): 403-409.

[5] SINGH R, CHOO W M, POH L L. In-group bias and fair-mindedness as strategies of self-presentation in intergroup perception[J]. Personality and Social Psychology Bulletin, 1998, 24(2): 147-162.

[6] WERTHEIM E G. The importance of effective communication[D]. Boston:

Northeastern University, 2010.

[7] 熊金才, 孙丽霞. 非语言代码的跨文化交际功能[J]. 外语与外语教学, 2001(5): 56-58.

Chapter 6

[1] BACKSCHEIDER R. A companion to the eighteenth-century English novel and culture [M]. Jersey City: Wiley-Blackwell Publishing House, 2009.

[2] GERRARD C. A companion to eighteenth-century poetry[M]. Jersey City: Blackwell Publishing House, 2006.

[3] HUHN P. The narratological analysis of lyric poetry: studies in English poetry from the 16th to the 20th century[M]. Berlin: Walter de Gruyter, 2005.

[4] KEHOE M, KAPLAN R, LI S, et al. Poetry and the creation of a Whig literary culture 1681-1714[M]. Oxford: Oxford University Press, 2009.

[5] LOVETT W. Robinson Crusoe: a bibliographical checklist of English language edition (1719-1979)[M]. New York: Greenwood Press, 1991.

[6] MUTO T. A change of narrative forms in English novels[J]. Otsuma Womens University Annual Report of Humanities & Social Sciences, 1997, 29(3): 1-8.

[7] TAKAHASHI D. In search of Robinson Crusoe[J]. Japanese Journal of Applied Physics, 2002, 42(7): 876-878.

[8] WALLACE M. Revolutionary subjects in the English "Jacobin" novel (1790—1805) [M]. Lewisburg: Bucknell University Press, 2009.

[9] ZEBA S. Crusoe in post-colonial times: an analysis of Foe by Coetzee[J]. International Journal of English Language, Literature and Humanities, 2014, 2(2): 456-460.

[10] 李志红. 历史文化语境下中国文学经典解析24讲[M]. 北京: 九州出版社, 2012.

[11] 陆玉林. 传统诗词的文化解释[M]. 北京: 中国社会科学出版社, 2003.

[12] 顾正阳. 古诗词曲英译文化探幽[M]. 北京: 国防工业出版社, 2012.

[13] 翁再红. 走向经典之路: 以中国古典小说为例[M]. 南京: 南京大学出版社, 2014.

[14] 吴福辉. 地方籍·地域性·文化叙事与经典[J]. 文史哲, 2006, 293(2): 109-113.

[15] 杨仲义, 黄红霞. 诗词大家的文化评论[M]. 北京: 学苑出版社, 2011.

[16] 姚继中. 《源氏物语》与中国传统文化[M]. 北京: 中央编译出版社, 2004.

[17] 赵毅衡. 苦恼的叙述者: 中国小说的叙述形式与中国文化[M]. 北京: 十月文艺出版社, 1994.

[18] 郑日男. 中国古典小说与文化[M]. 延边: 延边大学出版社, 2013.

[19] 埃德加·斯诺. 红星照耀中国[M]. 董乐山, 译. 北京: 外语教学与研究出版社, 2005.

Chapter 7

[1] BIXLER S. The new professional image[M]. 2nd ed. Avon: Adams Media, 2005.
[2] BOSROCK M M. Put your best foot forward: Asia[M]. St. Paul: International Education Systems, 1997.
[3] COTTE J, RANESHWAR S. Typestyle and leisure decisions[J]. Journal of Leisure Research, 2001, 33(4): 396-409.
[4] DAVIS L. Doing culture: cross-cultural communication in action[M]. Beijing: Foreign Language Teaching and Research Press, 2005.
[5] ROSS E. It pays to be well mannered [N]. Business Review Weekly, 2004-8-26.
[6] FONTAINE G. Skills for successful international assignments to, from and with Asian and the Pacific: implications for preparation, support, and training[J]. Management Decisions,1997, 35(8): 640-641.
[7] HALLE T. The hidden dimension[M]. New York: Anchor Books, 1990.
[8] KUILICH S J. Intercultural perspectives on Chinese communication[M]. Shanghai: Shanghai Foreign Language Education Press, 2007.
[9] SAMOVAR L A, PORTE R, E. Communication between cultures [M]. 5th ed. Beijing: Peking University Press, 2004.
[10] LUSTIG M W, KOESTER J. Intercultural competence: interpersonal communication across cultures[M]. Shanghai: Shanghai Foreign Language Education Press, 2007.
[11] MARTIN J S, CHANEY L H. Global business etiquette: a guide to international communication and customs[M]. 2nd ed. Santa Barbara, Californian: Praeger, 2012.
[12] MAYSONAVE S. Casual Power: how to power up your nonverbal communication and dress down for success[M]. Austin: Bright Books, 1999.
[13] POWELL M. Behave Yourself! The essential guide to international etiquette [M]. Guilford: Global Pequot Press, 2005.
[14] SAMOVAR L A, PORTER R E, MCDANIEL E R, et al. Communication between cultures[M]. 9th ed. United States: Cengage Learning, 2017.
[15] SEITZ V. Your executive image[M]. Austin, MA: Adams Media, 2000.
[16] SPENCER-OATEY H. Rapport management: a framework for analysis [C]// Culturally speaking: managing rapport through talk across cultures. London: Continuum, 2000:20.
[17] STEVE J K. Intercultural perspectives on Chinese communication [M]. Shanghai: Shanghai Foreign Language Education Press, 2007.

[18] VARNER I, BEAMER L. Intercultural communication in the global workplace[M]. Shanghai: Shanghai Foreign Language Education Press, 2006.

[19] ZHUANG E P. Intercultural business communication: readings and cases [M]. Shanghai: Shanghai Foreign Language Education Press, 2018.

[20] 杜琳, 李永生. 涉外交际礼仪[M]. 北京: 外语教学与研究出版社, 2020.

Chapter 8

[1] ADLER P S. The transitional experience: an alternative view of culture shock[J]. Journal of Humanistic Psychology, 1975, 15(4): 13-23.

[2] ANDERSON A, LYNCH A J. Listening[M]. Oxford: Oxford University Press, 1988.

[3] BALLARD B, CLANCHY J. Teaching students from overseas: a brief guide for lecturers and supervisors[M]. Melbourne: Longman Cheshire, 1991.

[4] BANKS J. Multiethnic education: theory and practice[M]. 3rd ed. Boston: Allyn and Bacon, 1994.

[5] BIGGS J B. Student approaches to learning and studying[M]. Hawthorn: Australian Council for Educational Research, 1987.

[6] CHEN P. Political, economical and ethnographical perspectives on teaching Chinese as a second language[J]. Chinese Teaching in the World, 2013, 27(3): 400-412.

[7] EVERTSON C M, WEINSTEIN C S. Classroom management as a field of inquiry[C]// Handbook of classroom management: research, practice, and contemporary issues. Mahwah: Lawrence Erlbaum Associates, 2006:3-16.

[8] GOOD T L. Teacher expectations and student perceptions: a decade of research[J]. Educational Leadership, 1981, 38(5): 415-422.

[9] GOOD T L. Two decades of research on teacher expectations: findings and future directions[J]. Journal of Teacher Education, 1987, 38(4):32-47.

[10] GOLLNICK D M, CHINN P C. Multicultural education in a pluralistic society[M]. 9th ed. New York: Pearson, 2013.

[11] HOFSTEDE G. Cultural differences in teaching and learning[J]. International Journal of Intercultural Relations, 1986, 10(3), 301-320.

[12] HUE M, LI W. Classroom management: creating a positive learning environment[M]. Hong Kong: Hong Kong University Press, 2008.

[13] JASON K. Language teaching and skill learning[M]. Cambridge: Blackwell Publishers, 1996.

[14] JIN L, CORTAZZI M. Dimensions of dialogue: large classes in China[J]. International

Journal of Educational Research, 1998, 29(8): 739-761.
[15] KIM T Y. Korean elementary school students' perceptual learning style, ideal L2 self, and motivated behavior[J]. Korean Journal of English Language and Linguistics, 2009, 9(3): 461-486.
[16] KIM Y K, KIM T Y. The effect of Korean secondary school students' perceptual learning styles and ideal L2 self on motivated L2 behavior and English proficiency[J]. Korean Journal of English Language and Linguistic, 2011, 11(1): 21-42.
[17] KINSELLA K. Perceptual learning preferences survey[C]//Learning styles in the ESL/EFL classroom. Boston: Heinle & Heinle,1995: 221-238.
[18] KOLB D A. Learning style inventory: technical manual[M]. Boston: McBer, 1976.
[19] KOLB D A. Experiential learning[M]. Englewood Cliffs: Prentice Hall, 1984.
[20] LIAO W, YUAN R, ZHANG H. Chinese language teachers' challenges in teaching in U. S. public schools: a dynamic portrayal[J]. Asia-Pacific Education Research, 2017, 26(6):369-381.
[21] NISBETT R E, PENG K P, CHOI I, et al. Culture and systems of thought: holistic versus analytic cognition[J]. Psychological Review, 2001, 108(2), 291-310.
[22] OBERG K. Culture shock: adjustment to new cultural environments [J]. Practical Anthropology, 1960, 7(4): 177-182.
[23] QI X D, LAI C. The effects of deductive instruction and inductive instruction on learners' development of pragmatic competence in the teaching of Chinese as a second language[J]. System, 2017, 70(3): 26-37.
[24] REID J M. The learning style preferences of ESL students[J]. TESOL Quarterly, 1987, 21(1): 87-111.
[25] SAMOVAR L A, PORTER R L, MCDANIEL E R, et al. Communication between cultures[M]. 9th ed. Boston: Wadsworth-Cengage, 2016.
[26] SLEETER C E. Keepers of the American dream: a study of staff development and multicultural education[M]. Washington: The Flamer Press, 1992.
[27] TWEED R. G, LEHMAN D. Learning considered within a cultural context: Confucian and socratic approaches[J]. American Psychologist, 2002, 57(2): 89-99.
[28] TUDOR I. Learner-centeredness as language education[M]. New York: Cambridge University Press, 1996.
[29] VALDES J M. Culture bound: bridging the cultural gap in language teaching[M]. Cambridge: Cambridge University Press, 1986.
[30] VERMUNT J D. Metacognitive, cognitive and affective aspects of learning styles and strategies: A phenomenographic analysis[J]. Higher Education, 1996;31, 25-50.
[31] WANG W, Curdt-Christiansen X L. Teaching Chinese to international students in China: political rhetoric and ground realities [J]. The Asia-pacific Education Researcher, 2016, 25(5-6): 723-734.

[32] XU W. Learning styles and their implication in learning and teaching[J]. Theory and Practice in Language Studies, 2011, 1(4): 413-416.

[33] ZHAO H, HUANG J. China's policy of Chinese as a foreign language and the use of overseas Confucius Institutes[J]. Educational Research for Policy and Practice, 2010, 9(2): 127-142.

[34] ZHAO Y. Cultural conflicts in an intercultural classroom discourse and interpretations from a cultural perspective[J]. Intercultural Communication Studies, 2007, 16(1):129-136.

[35] ZHANG Q M. A study on Chinese students' perceptual learning styles, ideal L2 self, and L2 motivated L2 behavior[J]. Chinese Journal of Applied Linguistics, 2015, 38(1): 93-109.

[36] ZHOU W, LI G. Chinese language teachers' expectations and perceptions of American students' behavior: exploring the nexus of cultural differences and classroom management[J]. System, 2015: 49, 17-27.

[37] 高永晨. 跨文化交际与地球村民[M]. 北京:高等教育出版社, 2017.

[38] 朱勇. 跨文化交际案例与分析[M]. 北京:高等教育出版社, 2018.

Chapter 9

[1] CARBOUGH D. Cultural communication and organizing [C]// Communication, culture, and organizational processes, intercultural and intercultural communication annual: Vol 9. Newbury Park: Sage, 1985: 37.

[2] MCDANIEL E R. Nonverbal communication: a reflection of cultural theme[C]// Intercultural communication: a reader. 14th ed. Boston: Wadsworth Cengage, Learning, 2014: 246.

[3] MEYER E. The culture map: decoding how people think, lead, and get things done across cultures[M]. New York: Public affairs, 2015.

[4] HARRIS P H, MORAN R T. Managing culture differences[M]. 2nd ed. Houston: Gulf, 1987.

[5] SAMOVAR L A, PORTER R E, MCDANIEL ER et al. Communication between cultures[M]. 9th ed. United States: Cengage Learning, 2017.

[6] TERPSTRA V, DAVID K. The cultural environment of intercultural business[M]. 2nd ed. Chicago: Southwestern, 1985.

Chapter 10

[1] ALLPORT G W. The nature of prejudice[M]. Massachusetts: Addison-Wesley, 1954.
[2] BENNETT J M. Cultivating intercultural competence: a process perspective[C]// The Sage Handbook of intercultural competence. California: Thousand Oaks, 2009: 121-140.
[3] BROWN R. Prejudice: its social psychology[M]. 2nd ed. Massachusetts: Oxford and Malden, Wiley-Blackwell, 2010.
[4] DEARDORFF D K. The identification and assessment of intercultural competence as a student outcome of internationalization at institutions of higher education in the United States[J]. Studies in International Education, 2006, 10(3): 241-266.
[5] FITZPATRICK F. Understanding intercultural interaction: an analysis of key concepts [M]. Bingley: Emerald Publishing, 2020.
[6] HOWELL W S. The empathic communicator[M]. Illinois: Prospect Heights, Waveland Press, Inc., 1982.
[7] OBERG K. Culture shock: adjustment to new cultural environments[J]. Practical Anthropology, 1960, 7(4): 177-182.
[8] SUMNER W. Folkways: a study of the sociological importance of usages manners customs mores and morals[M]. Boston: Ginn and Co, 1906.
[9] TAJFEL H, TURNER J C. An integrative theory of intergroup conflict[C]//The social psychology of intergroup relations. California: Monterey, 1979: 33-37.